BURNING THE BIG HOUSE

BURNING THE BIG HOUSE

THE STORY OF THE IRISH COUNTRY HOUSE IN A TIME OF WAR AND REVOLUTION

TERENCE DOOLEY

YALE UNIVERSITY PRESS
NEW HAVEN AND LONDON

For information about this and other Yale University Press publications, please contact:
U.S. Office: sales.press@yale.edu yalebooks.com
Europe Office: sales@yaleup.co.uk yalebooks.co.uk

Set in Adobe Garamond Pro by IDSUK (DataConnection) Ltd
Printed in Great Britain by TJ Books, Padstow, Cornwall

Library of Congress Control Number: 2021952546

ISBN 978-0-300-26074-8

A catalogue record for this book is available from the British Library.

10 9 8 7 6 5 4 3 2

CONTENTS

CONTENTS

ILLUSTRATIONS AND MAPS

Illustrations

vii

Maps

ACKNOWLEDGEMENTS

This book was begun at a very exciting time for historians of the revolutionary period in Ireland when a wealth of primary sources, kept under wraps for decades, were being opened in digital format to the research public for the very first time, sources such as IRA pension files, brigade reports and Bureau of Military History Witness Statements. It was finished at a time when access to traditional paper sources in public repositories and private collections were closed because of a global pandemic. I hope any resulting gaps are not too great; if they are, it certainly is not the fault of those who have been so generous with their time and assistance.

For providing access to sources, I would like to thank the keepers and staff in the following repositories and institutions: Cavan County Museum (Savina Donohoe); Clare Co Library (Helen Walsh and Dolores Meaney); Department of Culture, Heritage and the Gaeltacht (Terry Allen and Ronan Whelan); Fingal County Archives (Colm McQuinn); Irish Architectural Archives; Maynooth University Library (Cathal McCauley, Hugh Murphy); Military Archives, Cathal Brugha Barracks; Monaghan County Museum (Liam Bradley); National Archives of Ireland; National Gallery of Ireland; National Library of Ireland (special word of thanks to Berni Metcalfe); OPW-Maynooth Archive and Research Centre (Mary Heffernan, Nicola Kelly); Public Record Office, Northern Ireland (Brett Irwin); Somerset Record Office; The National Archives; Trinity College Dublin, Manuscripts Department; University College Dublin, Archives Department.

When writing a book, one continuously makes demands of colleagues, friends and family, dependent on their generosity to answer queries, testing their patience with follow ups, requesting them to read chapters, looking for information on sources and images, or simply asking to enjoy their convivial company when breaks are required. I am most grateful to the following for one or various combinations of the above: Lord Ashtown, Beaumont-Nesbitt family, Claire Besnyoe, Declan Brady, Laura Servilan Brown, Edward Bujak, Philip Bull, Robin Bury, Fidelma Byrne, Donough Cahill, Adam Coleman, Marie Coleman, Ann Purdon-Coote, Mario Corrigan, Maura Cronin, Emer Crooke, Brian Crowley, Jacqueline Crowley, Ian d'Alton, Sir David Davies, Eugene Dunne, Mel Farrell, the late Desmond FitzGerald (Knight of Glin), Brian Fizell, Ronan Foley, David Gahan, Aidan Gilsenan, George Gossip, the late Hon. Desmond Guinness, Charles Hamilton, Emmeline Henderson, Jack Kavanagh, Sir Charles Keane, Susan Kellett, Sammy Leslie, Cora McDonagh, Conor Mallaghan, Declan Mullen, Catherine Murphy, Sean Neary, Robert O'Byrne (The Irish Aesthete), Dáithí Ó Corráin, Daniel O'Reilly, Ann O'Riordan, Maeve O'Riordan, Eve Power, Lord Roden, Ailbhe Rogers, Brendan Scott, Mattie Shinnors, Den Stubbs (of Stubbs Design), Glascott and Adrienne Symes, Jack Tenison, Robert Towers, Edward Tynan, Lesley Whiteside, Tim Wilson and Jean Young. I am especially indebted to Robert Smith for many of the images used in this book. If I have unintentionally left anyone out who has helped me along the way, I offer my sincere apologies.

I owe a special debt to colleagues in the Centre for the Study of Historic Irish Houses and Estates. I have been privileged to have worked for the best part of two decades with Christopher Ridgway, whose scholarship I greatly admire and whose friendship I greatly cherish. Veronica Barry has helped in numerous ways and always with consummate good humour and patience.

Over the years, I have benefited immensely from the professional support and warm friendship of David Cannadine, Oliver Cox, Shaun Evans, Tony McCarthy, Olwen Purdue, Lowri Rees, Ciarán Reilly, Einion Thomas and Annie Tindley, with whom it has been an absolute pleasure (and very often 'great craic') to work on various country house and landed estate projects. Donal Hall has helped in a multitude of ways; his sharp insights and droll wit brighten every conversation. I cannot possibly finish a book without thanking my great friend and mentor Vincent Comerford, whose company is always stimulating.

For the length of time this book has been in gestation, I have benefited from the warm friendship and collegiality of academic colleagues and administrative staff in the History Department at the National University of Ireland, Maynooth.

ACKNOWLEDGEMENTS

I would like to thank all the undergraduate and postgraduate students I have had the privilege to teach over the years and post-doctoral fellows I have mentored, from whom I have learned so much.

It has been a particular pleasure to work with Yale University Press and I extend my deepest gratitude to Julian Loose for his enthusiasm for this project, Katie Urquhart for keeping it to a tight deadline, and to Eve Leckey for her wonderful copy-editing.

Anyone who has written a book will know how selfish one must be at times, regularly locked away in isolation, if not physical then very often mental. That is when the support of those closest is most important. Annette has always been selfless in her understanding and monumental in her support. Conor and Áine grew to adulthood and to find their own place in life during the research and writing of this book. It is an absolute joy to know them as my dearest friends as well as my children.

Finally, this book is dedicated to the memory of my beautiful niece Elaine Tate (née O'Hart, 1975–2021), a dearly loved and greatly missed friend, taken from this life far too soon, but whose memory will forever be cherished.

ABBREVIATIONS

BCA	Birr Castle Archives
BMH	Bureau of Military History
CDB	Congested Districts Board
CICMR	County Inspector's Confidential Monthly Report
CO	Colonial Office, Dublin Castle Records
GHQ	General Headquarters
IAA	Irish Architectural Archives
IGCMR	Inspector General's Confidential Monthly Report
INV	Irish National Volunteers
IRA	Irish Republican Army
ITGWU	Irish Transport and General Workers Union
IUA	Irish Unionist Alliance
MP	Member of Parliament
NAI	National Archives of Ireland
NLI	National Library of Ireland
NUI	National University of Ireland
OC	Officer in Command
ODNB	Oxford Dictionary of National Biography
OPW	Office of Public Works
PRONI	Public Record Office Northern Ireland
RIC	Royal Irish Constabulary
TNA	The National Archives, London
TD	Teachta Dála (a member of Dáil Éireann)
UCD	University College Dublin
UIL	United Irish League
UUC	Ulster Unionist Council
UVF	Ulster Volunteer Force
WS	Witness Statement

I
'DAYS OF GRANDEUR AND GRAVITY'
The Great War, 1914–18

1

'THE IRISH LANDLORDS HAVE BECOME THE VICTIMS OF A REVOLUTION'
BEFORE THE GREAT WAR, 1879–1914

The time has come when controversies die down and history can be written. The history of the Anglo-Irish will be an astonishing tome. Their achievements were as remarkable as their delinquencies. What they accomplished in Ireland remains in wreckage: huge, blackened houses, endless battered demesne walls, slowly falling timber, derelict mills and festering canals, long deserted avenues – all the marks and symbols that once a powerful race passed this way.

(Shane Leslie, *The Irish Tangle for English Readers*,
London, n.d. [1946], p. 146)

1. 'Particular aristocratic style'

In 1946, Sir Shane Leslie of Glaslough House (now Castle Leslie) in Co Monaghan attempted to explain for an English readership how his class, commonly referred to as the Anglo-Irish gentry or aristocracy (depending on the level of social gradation), had declined in the twenty-six county area of the Irish Free State, which would be declared a republic three years later.[1] Leslie's vast corpus of work is not renowned for historical accuracy or rigid analysis, and he was highly unlikely to let fact get in the way of his literary imagination or a good story. Nevertheless, it was quite true that a quarter of a century after independence much of Georgian Ireland's country house architecture – mansions, grand stables and other outbuildings around courtyards sometimes as large as an Irish village, demesne walls, gate lodges, demesne churches, garden follies, imposing entrances – lay in overgrown ruins, or had completely disappeared from the landscape. Leslie's 'wreckage' was a metaphor for the disappearance of a way of life, his juxtaposition of 'achievements' and 'delinquencies' a summation of the competing narratives that explained the history of the landed elite from different viewpoints.

1

Around the same time, other writers from similar backgrounds to Leslie's were contemplating the consequences of a colonial past. Elizabeth Bowen, whose Cromwellian ancestors settled on confiscated lands in north Cork and later built Bowen's Court in Kildorrery, recalled: 'My family got their position and drew their power from a situation that shows an inherent wrong . . . having gained this position through an injustice, they enjoyed their position through privilege.'[2] And they guarded privilege to an oppressive degree: Bowen's grandmother would receive barristers but not solicitors, wine merchants but not brewers, and the only social ranks lower than her own whose company she would tolerate were Church of Ireland clergymen and officers of the army and the navy (invariably drawn from landed backgrounds). Similarly, in 1880, Isabel Chavasse of Newcourt wrote: 'Such a thing as shaking hands with anyone who was not of our own class was unheard of. I remember my father's indignation once when some farmer tried to shake hands with him. To us the world was divided into two classes, the people to shake hands with and the people not to shake hands with.'[3] In 1880, at the height of the Land War, there would have been plenty of farmers with little inclination to shake Chavasse's hand even if he were amenable, for the Land War proved a major turning point in landlord history: from 1879, their privileged position was challenged at every level – political, economic and social – as Irish life, politics and society underwent revolutionary change over the next half century or so.[4]

The idea for this book was inspired by the Irish Government's decision to initiate a Decade of Centenaries Programme in 2012 to commemorate the historical events of the revolutionary period, dated 1912–22, including the third Home Rule crisis (1912–14), the First World War (1914–18), the Easter Rising (May 1916), the War of Independence 1919–21, the establishment of the Free State (1922) and the partition of Ireland (under the Government of Ireland Act passed into law in December 1920). At first there was no mention of the Civil War period, 1922–23. Commemoration, the Government decided, was to be carried out in a way that was to be 'broad and inclusive, highlighting the economic and social conditions of the period, the shifts in cultural norms and the experience of the Irish abroad'. The programme was intended to encompass 'the different traditions on the island of Ireland . . . to enhance understanding of and respect for events of importance among the population as a whole', as well as to provide 'opportunities to focus on the everyday experience of ordinary people living in extraordinary times'. Finally, it was hoped 'to offer fresh insights and constructive dialogue, and to foster deeper mutual understanding among people from the different traditions'.[5] These were worthy aspirations and the inclusive and sensitive way key events such as the Great War and the 1916 Rising were subsequently remembered was both commendable and commended. However, there appeared certain gaps in the commemorative narrative, most notably the experience of the Irish landed gentry and aristocracy, and the fate of their Big Houses, during war and revolution.

By the late nineteenth century, landlords were by no means a socially homogenous group. K.T. Hoppen used a 500-acre threshold for admission to the landlord class – which this author also used in *The Decline of the Big House in Ireland* – and drawing on a return of Irish landowners for the 1870s he enumerated and categorised landlords in Ireland as follows: those who owned between 500 and 1,000 acres (of whom there were 2,683 persons); 1,000 to 2,000 acres (1,788); 2,000 to 5,000 acres (1,225); 5,000 to 10,000 acres (438); and more than 10,000 acres (303).[6] At the top of the social hierarchy were the aristocracy, those landlords who comprised the upper echelon of landownership, wealth and power (social and political), up to the late nineteenth century, incorporating the nobility (dukes, marquesses, earls, viscounts, barons) and the greater commoners, those with similar levels of wealth and power but no titles. In the Irish context, over 2,000 acres is a reasonable estate size to qualify as aristocratic as over 75 per cent of peers in Britain and Ireland owned at least this acreage c.1880.[7] In Ireland, 1,966 landowners fell into this category, with 741 owning estates over 5,000 acres. Those who owned estates under 2,000 acres are more generally referred to as the landed gentry. It is important to point out that it is with the aristocracy that this book is primarily, though not exclusively concerned. This is in very large part because they both generated and bequeathed the most comprehensive estate records and personal papers (as is clear in the bibliography), and also because the vast majority of Big Houses burned, the principal theme of this book, belonged to that social cohort.

Other than landownership, the aristocracy and gentry had certain other common characteristics that gave them definition.[8] The vast majority belonged to the Church of Ireland – with notable exceptions including the Earls of Fingall and the Barons Carbery and Bellingham, who were Roman Catholic. Unlike in Britain, this meant they did not share the religion of the majority population. This is important because for centuries national identities determined by politico-religious divides, accentuated by matters of origin – native versus coloniser – and further complicated by issues related to land ownership, defined Irish politics and society. In the second half of the nineteenth century, at least in appearance, the aristocracy were the wealthy elite whether in their own parish, their county of residence or the country. W.E. Vaughan has estimated that between 1850 and 1879 Irish landlords as a whole 'continued to extract a large surplus from agriculture', in the region of £340 million, 'a sum far greater', he says, 'than that collected by any other agency in Ireland'.[9] But appearances can be deceptive: by the late 1870s, and the onset of agricultural depression, the majority were already burdened with massive debts, mainly inherited over generations, and this was crucial going forward.[10]

For the uninitiated reader, a brief historical introduction is necessary. The early antecedents of some of the more powerful nineteenth-century aristocratic families, such as the FitzGeralds, Dukes of Leinster (c.1766), Ireland's pre-eminent aristocratic family, can be traced all the way back to the Anglo-Norman invasion of Ireland in the late twelfth century. While largely confined to a geographical area in the east of the country, generally referred to as the English Pale, the Anglo-Normans began the process of replacing the existing tenurial arrangements determined by Gaelic kinship with a feudal system that would eventually evolve into an estate system. They also built great castles as the focal and defensive centres of their estates – some of which survived as private residences into the twentieth century, including Malahide and Kilkenny.

For over three centuries their descendants regarded themselves and were accepted as the upholders of English rule in Ireland.[11] But in the 1540s, their hegemony was threatened by the ambitious plans of the Tudor regime to exert its control over Ireland and to expedite religious conversion of the mainly Catholic population. This resulted in a series of plantation schemes that encouraged the settlement of English and Scots Protestants on lands confiscated from Gaelic as well as Anglo-Norman families, beginning with King's County (now Offaly) and Queen's County (Laois) in 1556, then the more ambitious Munster plantation in the 1580s and culminating in the most successful plantation of all in the northern province of Ulster following the end of the Nine Years War in 1607. Some accommodations were made with the Old English ruling elite (largely descendants of the Anglo-Norman settlers), and English titles of nobility and landownership were offered to any Gaelic lord prepared to renounce his Gaelic title, surrender his lands, recognise the king and promise to promote English law and custom (an instrument of policy usually referred to as 'surrender and regrant').[12] From that point, Catholics were progressively deprived of land ownership and religion became inextricably entangled with the land question.

Other significant phases of social engineering were to follow. The Cromwellian Wars of 1649–53 gave nationalist Ireland one of its primary hate-figures, Oliver Cromwell, whose name became synonymous with the further expropriation of Catholic lands. Officers and administrators who served the defeated Confederate Catholic cause were forced to forfeit their estates and were banished to Connaught by Cromwell where they received much smaller allocations. Around 7,500 of Cromwell's men and officers, in lieu of wages, and another 1,000 so-called Adventurers, who had invested almost £360,000 in the military campaign, were the beneficiaries of the confiscated Catholic lands, totalling 1.6 million acres.[13] Finally, at the end of the seventeenth century, the defeat of the Catholic King James in 1690–91 by William III prompted the introduction of the Penal (or anti-popery) Laws. In summary, these were a series of discriminatory measures which represented the culmination of all previous attempts to exclude Catholics from landownership and positions of political and administrative influence and to repress Catholic worship. Allied to the accelerating subdivision or sale of Catholic estates during the depressed 1720s and 1730s (when they could legally be bought only by Protestants) this resulted in the almost total erosion of Catholic ownership.[14] By the early eighteenth century, Catholics owned only around 5 per cent of land, mainly in Connaught and to a lesser extent in counties such as Meath, Dublin, Louth and Kerry.

The period from roughly the beginning of the Georgian era in 1714 to the Act of Union in 1801 represented the heyday of the emergent aristocracy. The most obvious manifestation of their landed power and wealth was the construction of hundreds of Big Houses of varying architectural sizes, shapes and styles that for generations to come would dominate the physical landscape, and which were to be found in numbers in every county of Ireland. The grander houses of the aristocracy were generally located amidst hundreds of acres of demesne parkland, woodland and gardens, and most were surrounded by high demesne walls.[15] Some had their origins in the tower houses and medieval fortified castles of the Anglo-Norman era (Kilkenny, Malahide and Leixlip

Castles for example), or the semi-fortified structure of the seventeenth-century (such as Portumna in Galway), but the architectural preference became the more ubiquitous defenceless Classical and Palladian mansions, which characterised the apogee of Big House construction in Ireland c.1720–40. These symbolised not just the aristocracy's wealth but also their confidence in the future stability and economic prosperity of the country, now that the Catholic threat had been disabled, and they were also a deliberately powerful and symbolic signifier of their specific social and political ambitions and agendas of future colonial control and power.

Mainly designed by the leading architects of their day, the most magnificent of these houses – such as Carton, Castletown, Kilboy, Powerscourt, Russborough and Summerhill – had their interiors embellished by foreign and native craftsmen, and they became repositories of fine arts collected over many generations.[16]

1.1 Carton House, Maynooth, Co Kildare, ancestral home of the FitzGerald family, Dukes of Leinster. Construction began in the late 1730s and over the following decades both house and demesne were developed to become amongst the grandest in Ireland. It passed out of family ownership in the 1920s, ending the 700-year link of the FitzGeralds with Maynooth, Co Kildare.

Take, for example, Carton House in Maynooth, Co Kildare. In the early 1880s it was owned by Charles FitzGerald, 4th Duke of Leinster. This impressive Palladian mansion had been built 150 years before to the design of Richard Castle, the pre-eminent architect working in Ireland at the time, and was the focal point of a 72,000-acre estate, drawing agricultural rents of around £40,000 per annum. (Fergus Campbell puts this level of income into perspective by pointing out that the Lord Chancellor in the nineteenth century earned £6,000 per annum while a high court judge earned £3,500.[17]) Carton sat amidst a magnificent eighteenth-century designed landscape, encompassing around 1,200 acres of undulating parkland, woodland, a winding river, ornamental gardens and pleasure grounds, all enclosed within a seven-kilometre-long demesne wall, interspersed with elegant gate lodges.

Inside the house, the Gold Salon was amongst the finest rooms in all of Britain and Ireland, the magnificent stuccowork having been carried out by the Lafranchini brothers in the late 1730s.[18] The Duke of Leinster and his family were surrounded by a rich material culture collected over many generations. Around 200 paintings hung on the walls, with attributions to many famous artists including Gainsborough, Lawrence, Breughel, Cuyp and Holbein.[19] Carton epitomised Shane Leslie's observation that 'country life was entirely organised to give nobility and gentry and demi-gentry a good time', and Elizabeth Bowen's contention that country houses 'were planned for spacious living – for hospitality above all . . . The idea that begot them was a purely social one.'[20] Its multitude of bedrooms was intended to accommodate numerous guests staying for the shooting and hunting, their enfilades to facilitate balls, dinner parties, recitals, theatricals and so on. In the 1880s, despite the economic downturn, there were still at least forty-four indoor servants to cater for family and guests, and around 60 to 100 estate employees including skilled artisans, craftsmen, gardeners, gamekeepers, bailiffs, grooms and labourers to maintain house, gardens, estate farm and parkland.[21]

The aristocracy – whether Protestant or Catholic – also shared common cultural characteristics. They kept their estates intact by bequeathing them through primogeniture; they closely guarded their social status through intermarriage; they shared public schools, sporting fields and exclusive clubs; they entertained on a lavish scale and offered hospitality to their social equals. Importantly, they were also the political elite at both national and local levels. Almost without exception, aristocratic families, and landlords in general, were loyal subjects of the British crown and the empire, determined to maintain Ireland's place in the United Kingdom as established by statute under the Act of Union in 1801. Until the 1880s, the majority of Irish members of parliament (MPs) were drawn from landed backgrounds, while they and their representatives also controlled local government, dominating the grand juries responsible for the county infrastructure and the officerships on the boards of Poor Law Guardians, and monopolising titles such as High Sheriff, Lieutenant of the County and Custos Rotulorum.[22] They connected to the empire by participating widely in its administration: their sons officered the army and the navy and administered the colonies (failing that or by choice they joined the church and professions). As Annie Tindley points out, 'Their will to rule and particular aristocratic style' was very much British in character and 'included gentlemanly codes and behaviours, hierarchy and form, pomp and ceremony, which were not just ornamental froth: they had their hands firmly on the levers of power, were embedded in that power and part of its operation'.[23]

However, in the changing political and social circumstances of the late nineteenth century, particularly with the rise of Irish nationalism and the growing significance of the land question, the Anglo-Irish landed elite's ambivalent identity – suggested in the hyphenated monicker ascribed to them – did not serve them well in Ireland, nor arguably in Britain. As the land and national questions coalesced in Ireland, the perpetual legacies of enmity, related to the confiscation of land over the centuries, religious divides, aristocratic imperialism and social exclusivity, provided rising Catholic nationalists with the potential for significant political capital as they could malign landlords as symbols of 'spoliation and conquest, as well as religious distance and tyranny'.[24] There was one very notable exception – Charles Stewart Parnell (1846–91), Wicklow landlord, leader of the Irish Parliamentary Party and President of the Irish National Land League. Ironically, it was his political duty to undermine the very bedrock – land and political power – upon which the ascendancy of his own class had been built, and he managed to do so with considerable success during the 1880s.[25]

2. 'The age of the masses'

This book is about the aristocracy in war and revolution, as principally seen through the prism of their Big Houses. The war is straightforward, referring to the First World War, 1914–18, regarded as a major watershed in the history of aristocracies across Europe. Revolution is more nuanced. As R.F. Foster points out: 'the idea of the Irish revolution is still in the process of definition, and not just its duration'.[26] Foster's *Vivid Faces* (2014) rightly points to the fact that the 1916–23 period has 'been closely excavated' and to the need to examine more closely the 'pre-revolution' period, suggesting the death of Parnell in 1891 as a starting point.[27] But the Parnell era itself was one of revolutionary change. From the aristocracy perspective, Lord Dufferin wrote to Brinsley Sheridan as early as 1881 that 'The Irish landlords have become the victims of a revolution.'[28] This brusque summation was based on the dramatic impact of global agricultural recession from the late 1870s – which also gave rise to agrarian revolts and nationalist movements across Europe in Germany, Austro-Hungary and Russia – which had led in Ireland to the establishment of a mass movement, the Irish National Land League, in 1879, drawing its leadership from a rural alliance of large farmers, predominantly Roman Catholic, backed by their clergy and townsmen.[29] The Land League's initial aim was to protect beleaguered tenants from the consequences of the agricultural depression by ensuring that rent levels remained affordable.

Landlords were caught between a rock and a hard place. The vast majority carried heavy debt burdens accumulated over generations, and more recently compounded by the easy access to money during the post-Famine economic upturn, raised on the collateral strength of their landed estates.[30] As a class, they argued that they could not afford to grant rent abatements. Procrastination or the downright refusal to grant rent reductions resulted in a land war from 1879 to 1881, characterised by tenant rent strikes, increased agrarian agitation and violence, the invention of boycotting against those who transgressed Land League law, and a dramatic increase in evictions carried out by landlords against striking tenants. Mutual antagonisms between landlords and tenants played themselves out in a variety of different spaces: political platforms, Land League platforms, pamphlets of landlord-dominated organisations (for example the Irish Landowners Convention or the Irish Unionist Alliance), open letters to the newspapers, even sermons from church pulpits.[31] As the development of nationalism and nationality became increasingly bound up with the struggle for land, landlords were characterised by popular nationalist writers as 'cruel oppressors and heartless exterminators', by Roman Catholic priests as 'territorial monsters', by the founder and leader of the Land League, Michael Davitt, as 'absentee, rack-renting, depopulating' oppressors who made 'laws in a foreign parliament for their miserable serfs at home'.[32]

It was not all fabrication, and neither was it all fact, but the long-term significance of the emergence of this type of anti-landlord vitriol should not be underestimated. For one thing, as R.V. Comerford puts it, Big Houses were made into symbols 'of oppression and decadence' in order to justify the Land War.[33] Land League rhetoric reminded the masses of the provenance of Big Houses, that the high point of their construction had coincided with the emergence of the Protestant Ascendancy to social and political dominance on the back of the repression of Catholic civil and religious liberties under the Penal Laws, and that the descendants of Cromwellian officers still inhabited many of them. One of these was Bowen's Court in Cork. Years after Irish independence, Elizabeth Bowen contemplated the equivocacy of her ancestral home, captured in the very infrastructure itself: while it had been built of native Irish stone, it had been 'imposed on seized land [and] built in the ruler's ruling tradition' so that it was 'isolated by something very much more lasting than the physical fact of space: the isolation is innate; it is an affair of origin.'[34] Nationalists were even more forthright. For instance, on 30 August 1879, shortly before the formation of the Land League, the editor of the *Connaught Telegraph* protested:

> Our magnates revel in luxury, unknown to the kings of other countries. Their mansions, widespread pleasure grounds, and ornamental gardens are truly magnificent, while their tenants whose wretched huts are the only blemishes on the beautiful view, which lies open from the site of each lordly residence, pine away in all but utter destitution.[35]

As Comerford suggests, this representation of Big Houses as symbols of the aristocracy's opulence and decadence practised amidst poverty and destitution served a political purpose and had a damaging long-term impact. As we shall see in later chapters, it bequeathed generations of ancestral resentment which, along with other more tangible motives, was used as a form of justification for the destruction of Big Houses during the War of Independence (1919–21) and the Civil War (1922–23). Tom Barry, Cork leader of the Irish Republican Army (IRA), for example, delighted in celebrating the destruction of the 4th Earl of

Bandon's Castle Bernard in June 1921, one of the county's finest houses, knowing that he was 'witnessing another symbol of the Conquest being destroyed'.[36]

Simultaneously, from the 1880s, the rise of the nationalist Home Rule movement demanding Irish independence severely compromised the aristocracy's sphere of political influence (except for parts of Ulster). This rise was accommodated by British political reform acts which introduced the secret ballot in 1872, dramatically expanded the electorate and redrew political constituencies in the mid-1880s.[37] The result, as David Cannadine put it, 'was a political revolution of the greatest magnitude, well displayed in the fact that, at the 1885 election, not one of the 53 candidates put up in the south by the newly established and landlord-controlled Irish Loyal and Patriotic union was elected'.[38] This was the trend thereafter as national representation was taken over by middle-class nationalists. At local government level, following the introduction of the Local Government (Ireland) Act in 1898, the pattern was precisely the same. At the first elections held in 1899, there was another bloodless revolution as Catholic nationalists took control of county councils (and other local government bodies) established to replace the landlord-dominated grand juries (having already, at Parnell's instigation, taken control of the Boards of Poor Law Guardians).[39]

The Irish aristocracy's plight was not helped by the attitude of their British counterparts; as Cannadine points out, they were much disparaged within the upper echelons of British political circles (in part explaining why they were so poorly represented at cabinet level): 'The Tory hierarchy', he contends, 'thought no more of the Irish landlords themselves than did the Liberals or the Land League' and he quotes Arthur Balfour, who arrived as Chief Secretary to a very turbulent Ireland in 1887: 'What fools the Irish landowners are, some stupid, some criminal, many injudicious.'[40] The Irish aristocracy were well aware of these damaging attitudes: Lord Dufferin, Tindley tells us, 'was dismayed by the declining influence of the Irish landed classes over the late nineteenth century as they were denigrated, not just by Irish nationalists and radicals, but also by their landed and titled brethren in Britain, whose disapproval hardened and sympathy evaporated by the late 1880s.'[41]

In many respects what typified this was the Liberal government response to the Land War. In August 1881, to defuse the politically and socially volatile situation, W.E. Gladstone introduced a milestone Land Act that had far-reaching repercussions for all indebted landlords. It legislated for the establishment of the Irish Land Commission, a body with statutory power to adjudicate on fair rents. From 1882, its land courts did what was politically expedient and reduced rent levels by an average of 21 per cent across the country, a reduction that was to last for fifteen years. In response to this government interference, financial institutions, wary of the plummeting value of agricultural land, closed all avenues of borrowing. In fact, panicky lenders (banks and assurance companies) began to call in their mortgages.[42] Shane Leslie's fictitious Henry Deluce, a poorly camouflaged version of his father, Sir John Leslie of Glaslough, epitomised the aristocracy's growing predicament:

> All through the fifties and the sixties he had totted up the great roll of twenty thousand pounds a year, quarter by quarter through the depreciating seventies, and, as one generation died, he lifted the rent off their sons, so that Sir Edward [Henry's son] might continue living the life of the fine old Irish gentleman on a fine estate, until the eighties came and the rents tumbled by a third and a half, and the nineties brought arrears and debt and a strict entrenchment . . . Sir Edward must always have enough to keep up ancient state and pay full wage to his pensioners, and keep white ducks and fantails and swans, and pay parsons to pray for his good estate and a full cellar to warm his hospitality, and fifty odd gardeners and bailiffs and keepers and servants and retainers and a coachman and foresters.[43]

From the 1880s, such aspirations were merely that; even the most prestigious families could not aspire to the continuation of a traditional aristocratic lifestyle. In the mid-1880s, the 4th Duke of Leinster was informed by his agent that rents were hard to get in, and it was impossible to get access to money on the collateral strength of his estate.[44] By 1887, he had reduced his household establishment by over 50 per cent. In April of the same year, Lord Clonbrock's agent wrote: 'His lordship has reduced his establishment considerably . . . unless times change, he cannot uphold his present one.'[45] Expenditure at Clonbrock House fell by 30 per cent during the period 1882–89 compared to that of 1880.[46]

The traditionally precarious position of Irish landlords had now become critical. In 1887, Sir Henry Gore-Booth of Lissadell told the Cowper

1.2 Clonbrock House, Co Galway, in ruins, ancestral home of
the Dillon family, Barons Clonbrock.

Commission, appointed to enquire into the 1881 and 1885 Land Acts, 'I would be willing to sell every acre, it would be a great saving to me if I could get twenty-three years' purchase on the Ordnance Valuation, one fourth added.'[47] Lord Cloncurry of Lyons said he had conversations with 'nearly all the large landed proprietors' and that they were willing to sell 'all the outlying portion of their estates'. He himself 'would gladly sell all outlying properties and retain only that part of estate within a day's drive or journey of residence'.[48] Both their comments were revealing; landlords, they said, were prepared to sell their 'outlying properties' to their tenants, but only at a price, with a bonus added, that was guaranteed to yield a return on investments that was at least equivalent to their nett rental incomes. Cloncurry also pointed out that landlords wanted to retain demesne and untenanted lands adjacent to their homes. The demesne (the private lands surrounding the country house generally made up of gardens, parkland, woodland and farmland) would continue to offer privacy, and might remain a hub of sport and leisure, but it could also be profitably farmed to supplement invested income. The retention of large tracts of untenanted lands to be let on the eleven-month system (or conacre) to graziers (extensive farmers involved in dry cattle and sheep rearing) would also provide profitable revenue. Significant swathes of countryside had been untenanted since the early evictions of the Land War era and by letting them only for eleven months each year landlords circumvented the fair rent fixing terms of the 1881 Land Act. The annual auction prices were determined by market demand, and were therefore potentially more profitable. But the eleven-month system was problematic on two levels: firstly, evicted holdings were an emotive subject in rural Ireland and would generate powerful political capital for Nationalists in the future, and, secondly, extensive grazing tracts were anathema to the small uneconomic holders who craved access to more lands simply to make their farms viable.[49]

3. 'To fulfil the true functions of an aristocracy'

The Land Acts of 1881 and 1885, which Gore-Booth and Cloncurry commented upon, were largely unsuccessful in terms of land transfer. It was the 1903 Land Act, commonly referred to as the Wyndham Act after its principal architect, George Wyndham, then Chief Secretary of Ireland, that dramatically expedited the process, resulting in another non-violent, but this time social, revolution, that culminated in the transfer of roughly 75 per cent of Irish land from landlords to tenant occupiers by 1914. Wyndham succeeded where others had previously failed because he put in place the incentives that landlords had demanded (and were agreed to by tenant representatives): they received generous prices of up to twenty-five years' purchase on their annual rental incomes, plus a 12 per cent cash bonus, tantamount to a government bailout. The unprecedented prices meant, for example, that the 6th Duke of Leinster received an impressive £786,000 for roughly 41,000 acres; the Kingston/King-Harmans of Mitchelstown Castle (and several other houses) eventually sold 70,000 acres for £625,000; Lord Crofton of Mote Park in Roscommon, who sold 5,300 acres under the 1891 Act for £43,500, received £67,500 for the same acreage under the 1903 Act; the Earl of Mayo who lived in Palmerstown House in Kildare received £103,000 for only 3,600 acres.[50]

All these aristocrats had one thing in common: they remained resident in Ireland after 1903. To be sure, there were very many more landlords who simply took the money and left, thereby selling or even abandoning their houses. As of yet, no definitive inventory has been compiled of who these were, but that migration was prevalent after the passing of the Wyndham Act is suggested in the writings of several contemporaries: for example, in 1906, George Moore of Moore Hall in Mayo wrote to Lady Evelyn de Vesci at Abbey Leix (Queen's County) lamenting: 'One feels so sorry for Ireland in the loss of some of her noblest inhabitants by the 1903 Land Purchase Act.'[51] Five years later, Moore did a tour of his native Mayo and found that Athy Valley was empty, Browne Hall had disappeared from the landscape, Ballinafad was a monastery, Cornfield was empty and about to be demolished, the Knoxes were gone from Creagher and Newbrook was sold and demolished and the salvage distributed for recycling.[52]

Around 1911, Lord Ashtown told Andrew Bonar Law that he knew of sixteen abandoned mansions in Galway: 'It is simply lamentable', he wrote, 'to see their empty demesnes, with their houses falling down.'[53] Shane Leslie recalled that 'A great number [of landlords] had departed after the Wyndham purchase, while the going was good.'[54] Sir Henry Lynch Blosse's uncle was one of these: after selling his Mayo estate, 'Uncle Henry . . . betook himself to Canada . . . and spent the lot in a few months living like a millionaire, after which he returned home and settled down in Worthing where he soon afterwards died.'[55] In 1913, Shane Leslie's brother, Seymour, wrote of Co Monaghan: 'The diminishing population, the end of the landlord system, the disappearance of old county families, are now part of the past.'[56] That same year, the London dealer Burgess Hill reported in *Connoisseur*: 'From a variety of contributory causes, chiefly owing to the various land acts, the large landowners in Ireland have, during the past decade or so, been disposing of their land to the tenants, and consequently many lovely collections have been brought onto the market.'[57] Thus, the great age of dispersal began long before 'the Troubles', a euphemism popular with the Anglo-Irish to describe the more violent revolutionary period of 1920–23, which has traditionally been seen as the catalyst for this process.[58]

However, this book is about those who had remained in Ireland by 1914. Some indication of how many can be gleaned from a British government-produced 400-page return of untenanted lands in the rural districts of Ireland in 1906 which distinguished 1,629 demesnes on which there was 'a mansion' and calculated that their owners – the vast majority of whom were aristocrats as defined here, with a respectable smattering of gentry, clergymen, merchants and professionals – continued to hold approximately 2.6 million acres of demesne and untenanted lands (across the thirty-two counties).[59] Big Houses did not look out of place as long as they continued to be surrounded by hundreds of acres of demesne and parkland. And in very many parishes, towns and villages (those built by aristocratic landlords included Maynooth, Abbeyleix, Westport, Mitchelstown, Rockcorry, Strokestown, Birr) the bonds between aristocratic families and the wider local community were far from sundered or irretrievably dissolved by either the Land War or the break-up of estates. (There were even a few aristocrats – notably Lady Gregory of Coole Park and Edward Martyn of Tulira – who embraced Irish cultural nationalism.)

Primarily, a resident aristocracy continued to be important to the local economy. When the Duke of Leinster came in for criticism for retaining the sporting rights on his estates after their sale in 1903, John Rice, a shopkeeper in Castledermot, responded: 'It is better to have these men in the country than have no one. We want the landlords to stop in the country and spend their money in it.'[60] As far as the business community and middle-class farmers around Maynooth were concerned, Carton House remained an important economic cornerstone. The only ducal family in Ireland brought prestige – there were the royal visits to Maynooth of King Edward VII and King George V in 1903 and 1911 – and prosperity. Carton House and its demesne continued to provide large-scale employment, and the employees, many of whom were housed in town cottages with regular wages to spend, were important to the local business community. Even after the sale of the estate, Lord Frederick FitzGerald, chief trustee during the minority of his nephew Maurice, later 6th Duke, campaigned vigorously to promote good agricultural practice in the region: he established the North Kildare Farming Society Ltd in November 1904; he farmed the Carton demesne intensively and became a renowned and prize-winning breeder of Kerry Blues; in 1908, he introduced the Leinster Cup as a perpetual trophy to stimulate competition amongst local farmers by rewarding them for excellence in livestock breeding and market gardening.[61] Lord Frederick was also vice-president of the North Kildare Horticultural Society and served as chairman on the Co Kildare Committee of Agriculture and the Co Kildare Technical Committee. In 1908, when his nephew came of age the event was celebrated in the traditional way: in Maynooth, bonfires blazed, barrels of beer 'flowed freely' and a torchlight procession led by two marching bands processed through the streets to Carton. The event had been planned for months by a local committee headed by farmers of substance such as Robert Mooney, town merchants such as James Kavanagh (he and Mooney had organised the Maynooth tenants during the 1903 sale negotiations), professionals such as Dr Stanley Moore, as well as the Catholic clergy, Canon James Hunt (elected committee chairman) and his curate, Father Patrick McDonnell. In time-honoured fashion, the committee presented an address to Maurice telling him that 'The people of Maynooth rejoice and heartily congratulate you on this propitious occasion of your coming of age', and reminding him that he had to be mindful of 'the close and felicitous association which has at all times existed between your noble family and our town'.[62] However, he was also subtly reminded that much had changed: now 'it was legitimate for the Nationalists of Ireland to honour the Geraldine name', which by extension meant he was expected to recognise the new force which had superseded the old order.

Finally, the address emphasised 'the magnanimous interest' that former dukes and duchesses took in local affairs, the 'whole-hearted co-operation in all that tended to our material progress' and 'their great munificence to our poor'. Lord Frederick, on behalf of the Duke, reciprocated the gift of the address by announcing a donation of £25 to the board of guardians for the relief of destitution in the area, while Canon Joseph O'Keefe, the local parish priest, was given a cheque for £160, the Church Auxiliary Fund received £100 and the Sisters of Mercy £30.[63] The final paragraph of the address made it clear what the 200 or so signatories expected to gain: 'We trust your Grace's advent to the duties appertaining to your exalted position at a time of intellectual and industrial awakening will presage a future of much happiness and prosperity for our motherland.'[64] It was public knowledge how much the Leinsters had received from the sale of their estate; the address suggested that the local community expected investment in the industrial and intellectual life of the county.

In the long term, the Duke of Leinster's former tenants and the townspeople were to be disappointed. The 1902–03 Land Conference had hoped that: 'For the benefit of the whole community, it is of the greatest importance that income derived from sale of property in Ireland should continue to be expended in Ireland.'[65] It was not to be the case in Maynooth or, it seems, anywhere else. Tony McCarthy's seminal work on landlord investment behaviour post-1903 has located the reasons for lack of investment in Ireland in the unparalleled growth in overseas investments as Britain led the world in global stock exchange business. 'In 1850', he writes, 'overseas investment grew from 7 per cent in 1850, to 14 per cent in 1870 to 32 per cent by 1913. By the start of the First World War almost one third of all British wealth was invested overseas. No country before or since has ever invested so much of its wealth in overseas projects.'[66] Rather than generating economic growth in Ireland, the aristocracy looked to the global markets. In 1907, Lord Ashtown made it clear to the Royal Commission on Congestion in Ireland that: 'As matters are going on now, the money they invest will leave the country. It will not be invested here.'[67] Alvin Jackson found that the owner of the Castlesaunderson estate in Cavan converted the proceeds 'into an extensive colonial share portfolio' and that 'only in Ireland did Somerset [Saunderson] resist investment'.[68] The Leinster estate made the extraordinary financial decision to invest £603,000 of the capital received in just five mortgages to English aristocrats, and a miniscule 5 per cent in Ireland.

By failing to embrace the spirit of the 1903 Land Act, the aristocracy lost an opportunity to create a more meaningful role for themselves in Irish rural society. It was not the first time: W.E. Vaughan has argued of their ancestors during the Victorian era that if 'they had spent generously on the improvement of their estates, they might have had enough influence, through wages, orders for slates, timber, and fertilizers, to keep some shopkeepers at least in a deferential state.'[69] They failed to do so and, therefore, Vaughan contends, during the Land War: 'The past was captured by their opponents . . . and used against them.'[70] The 1903 Land Act provided them with another, possibly better, opportunity to act as an aristocracy. The Earl of Dunraven, who had played an influential role in the formulation of the 1903 Land Act, made clear his intention to remain resident in Ireland and anticipated that the aristocracy would continue 'farming their own land, retaining the amenities of their position and finding . . . a larger scope for usefulness than they have hitherto enjoyed'.[71] Similarly, in 1908, Horace Plunket in his oft-quoted *Noblesse Oblige* (1908) believed he spoke for landlords who had much to give to Ireland after the sale of their estates:

> The abolition of landlordism, so far from destroying the usefulness of the Irish gentry, really gives them their first opportunity, within the memory of living men, to fulfil the true functions of an aristocracy. They have ceased

to be the masters; they are no longer dealing with dependants. My appeal to them is that they should recognise this fact, and take their new position as men who, working among others in a rural community, have by their wealth and education special advantages which they desire to use for the common good; and I assure them that for men who are willing and qualified to take that position it will open.[72]

When judged by the way they invested their capital, the aristocracy once again failed to deliver. Their investment behaviour said much about their imperialism but also their lack of confidence or interest in the future prosperity of Ireland (which was partially influenced by the fall-out from the Devolution Crisis of 1904–05 which forced Wyndham's resignation), and so their past would continue to be used against them.

Of course, not all landlords benefited from the level of windfall received by the Leinsters. There were those who received no more than enough to pay off their inherited debts, mortgages to insurance companies, loans to individuals, or family obligations, and so were left with very little to invest.[73] Some of these could not afford to leave Ireland; as Sir John Keane of Cappoquin in Waterford later put it in 1924: 'Those people who live in these Big Houses are sometimes almost prisoners in them; they have got no capital; they cannot get away, and they cannot sell their houses.'[74] But, in comparative terms, they were still wealthy and remained 'at the apex of rural society'.[75] In 1907, Lord Ashtown of Woodlawn House in Galway made around £1,330 from letting untenanted land on the conacre system.[76] A labourer would have to work 133 years to earn that amount.

There were many like Ashtown who were happy to transition to being farmers. On his 1911 census household schedule return, John Ribton Garstin of Braganstown in Louth said he was 'deriving income chiefly from land rents, dividends, in fact what the French call "rentier" and retired farmer'. Charles Mervyn Doyne of Wells in Wexford described himself as a farmer, John Lenigan of Castleffogarty in Tipperary stated he was 'a retired lieutenant-colonel in the British army and a farmer'. Emmet O'Connor makes the point that in Waterford, 'Those landowners who joined the I[rish] F[armers'] U[nion] were precisely those who wished to remain in Ireland and retain their estates.'[77] These included Sir John Keane who in Glascott Symes' study emerges as a progressive farmer and supporter of the co-operative movement (in 1914 he was secretary of the Blackwater Valley Co-Operative Agricultural Society Limited).[78] Sir John also developed new income streams on his demesne by investing in arbori-culture, sporting and fishing licensing and forestry, building a sawmill and developing a tree-nursery business that provided extensive local employment.[79] At the opposite end of Munster, in Clare, the first meeting of the Co Clare Ratepayers and Farmers' Association took place in April 1918. Founded by Colonel Tottenham, he was joined by another former landlord, R.J. Stacpoole, who was elected chairman, as well as the enigmatic Colonel O'Callaghan Westropp. In Monaghan, Edward Lucas Scudamore, J.C.W. Madden, E.J. Richardson and Sir John Leslie were all aristocrats appointed to the county's agricultural committee.

However, while the traditional class of wealthy farmers may have been happy to work alongside the aristocracy, their monopolisation of untenanted lands at the expense of the land-hungry smallholders, created agrarian tensions that came to the fore once again in 1908–12.[80] The so-called Ranch War was driven by the United Irish League (UIL), founded in the late nineteenth century, which Philip Bull points out was 'the most highly developed expression of the integration of the land and national questions'.[81] The UIL's main aim was the redistribution of untenanted lands but many of those in the front ranks of the organisation were graziers; as Maura Cronin has put it: 'The very organisation established in 1898 for the express purpose of challenging the grazier system, reminds us that the complexities of local life and relationships defy any simple class or economic explanation.'[82] Naturally, landowners objected strenuously to the call for the redistribution of their untenanted lands; for many these were now their only livelihood. In June 1904, Lord Oranmore and Browne told the House of Lords that he was opposed to such calls coming from all directions – 'county councils, district councils, local newspapers, village agitators':

And what are these grazing ranches? Grass lands on which the landlords have spent large sums of money in drainage and in various improvements. These are the lands on which cattle are fed – those cattle which are one of the most valuable assets we have in the west of Ireland. Everybody is agreed that it is desirable that landlords should remain in Ireland ... But you cannot expect men to live in a country if they have no inducement to live here, and if you take away all their grasslands you take away from the landlords every inducement to live there.[83]

Untenanted estates were by no means geographically confined: by the early 1920s, the Persse family in Galway still retained 5,714 acres of demesne and untenanted lands, the Hibberts in Clare 2,717 acres, Chichester-Constable in Roscommon 2,101 acres, Wilson in Longford and Westmeath 1,993 acres, Lord Castlemaine in Westmeath 1,142 acres, Dames in Offaly, 987 acres, Lucas-Scudamore in Monaghan, 626 acres.[84] These families all had one thing in common: their Big Houses were burned in 1920–23. By then, there were those who believed that the most effective way to take the grasslands from their owners was to force them away and to coerce them into giving them up (chapter five).

4. 'There was no longer a viable landlord system'

This brings us to the central theme of this book, the burning of Big Houses. It is twenty years since this author dedicated a chapter in *The Decline of the Big House in Ireland* (2001) to this phenomenon. Based on limited sources, it was very tentative in its conclusions.[85] It soon became obvious that a much more substantial study was required. In the meantime, a considerable body of archival sources have become available, and because of these and an expanding historiography on the subject, it is now possible to put ample more flesh on the bones of the arguments previously advanced, and to be more definitive in relation to the number of Big Houses burned.[86] But even so, the generally biased nature of the sources does not make the task a simple one. For example, in their compensation claims the Irish Grants Committee (IGC) asked country house owners the very leading question: 'Do you claim that the loss or injury described was occasioned in respect or on account of your allegiance to the Government of the United Kingdom?' Those filling in the forms, or their legal representatives, deduced very quickly that the IGC payment was going to be firmly based on their ability to prove their loyalism, which unfortunately for the historian means that the often formulaic answers skewed the facts: 'I was always loyal to the British government' was considered a better response than

'I knew the raiders belonged to local families who wanted my demesne land divided.' Similarly, on the other side, IRA members invariably reported burning houses for patriotic reasons, however loosely defined, rather than for agrarian reasons.

Thus far it has been established that the Irish aristocracy experienced both political and social revolution during the tumultuous quarter century from 1879 to 1903. They were stripped of virtually all political power at national and local levels and the majority, but crucially not all, of their lands. Both political and social change was initiated by legislation introduced by the British Government for Ireland, instigated by the mass actions of the Home Rule and land movements. Historians have tended to separate this revolutionary phase from the second stage, the start date of which is assigned various years – 1912, 1916, 1919, 1920 – and the end date generally agreed upon as 1923.[87] There was one common denominator in both phases: the sustained campaign to strip the aristocracy of *all* their lands. Thus, in 1920–23 they continued to be victims of revolution, not only because they were Loyalists opposed to the establishment of an independent Irish republic, or any form of Home Rule – the more traditionally accepted reasons – but also because there were still land-related issues to be dealt with – the completion of the transfer of tenanted holdings that had been stalled by the Great War and the redistribution of demesne and untenanted lands. Thus, the aristocracy's revolutionary experience lasted from 1879 to well beyond 1923, but this rarely features in the historiography.

The reason for this is not difficult to find: it is related to the misconception that the Irish land question ended before the Great War and, therefore, could hardly have played a role in the burning of Big Houses. In his pioneering *Politics and Irish Life 1913–21* (1977), David Fitzpatrick did touch on Big House burnings in Co Clare during the War of Independence noting: 'It is true that six Big Houses in Clare were burnt down just before the Truce as a regular Volunteer operation, of which the Chief of Staff "fully approved". But the houses were unoccupied, and the Volunteers appeared to have feared that the military or police would commandeer them for barracks.'[88] As we shall see (chapter 4), this was a commonly cited reason both in contemporary reports and in subsequent remembrances. Fitzpatrick did point out in his endnotes that a local landlord claimed that one house was burned by persons 'land grabbing, not Sinn Féin'.[89] He further mentioned there were still landlords who had not sold by c.1917, and that by keeping their stake in the country they provoked 'more open hostility than at any time since 1903', and subsequently 'the frustrations of land-hungry men began to assume more organised form'.[90] He was on the verge of a more nuanced interpretation of the connection between land-hunger and Big House burnings but historians of the revolutionary period who followed in the path of Fitzpatrick were not generally interested in pursuing research on this particular phenomenon. For instance, Peter Hart's study of the IRA and its enemies in Cork avoided Big House burnings, even though that county had by far the highest incidence and possibly the most famous memoir of the period, Tom Barry's *Guerilla Days in Ireland* (1949), was screaming at him of the IRA's role in their destruction. Burning Big Houses was such an obvious case of the IRA 'taking it out on its enemies' that its exclusion might be difficult to explain, except that Hart also avoided any rigorous discussion of the social dimension to the revolution, contending in another work that 'not only did the Irish Revolution not bring social transformation, there was no socially revolutionary situation in Ireland even in prospect' because 'most farmers owned their farms by 1922'.[91]

Professor Hart was not the first scholar to come to this conclusion. Many of his predecessors had been influenced by a paper delivered in 1966 by Patrick Lynch (1917–2001) entitled 'The Social Revolution That Never Was' and subsequently published in a volume of essays edited by T. Desmond Williams, then Professor of Modern History at University College Dublin (UCD). Lynch was a highly esteemed lecturer in Economics (later Professor of Political Economy) in UCD, a former senior civil servant, who, after his death, would rightly be praised as 'one of the most respected and influential social and economic thinkers during the critical period of the Sixties'.[92] Lynch asked: 'Why did the Rising of 1916 fail to produce also a social revolution of corresponding significance and consequence? What happened to avert it? Was it betrayed?'[93] He answered his own questions by asserting that 'by 1916 most agricultural holdings had been purchased by their occupiers, subject to land annuities, which were not then a matter of contention. The tenant had become a proprietor, the owner of his land; and little land remained, to which the system of voluntary purchase could be applied.'[94]

Lynch's argument displayed an inadequate understanding of the land question, which seems extraordinary for a number of reasons: as an economist he would have been well versed in the significance of the 1923 Land Act (and the reasons for the introduction of the other dozen or so that followed, up to the 1960s); he would have known that the British government funded the 1923 Land Act to the tune of £30 million, without which the Irish Free State would not have stabilised as quickly as it did (chapter 9); and he lived through decades in which Irish rural life after independence remained animated by the politics of land redistribution (even if no agrarian political party came to dominance).[95] Of course, Lynch's pronouncements promoted a viewpoint that suited the agenda of the day: 1966 was the golden anniversary of the Easter Rising, which had become the iconic site of memory marking the beginning of the Irish struggle for independence, and Lynch's argument did not detract from the political revolution that had resulted in Irish independence. Stories of agrarian tensions in 1920–23, land grabs and the burning of country houses would have provided an unwelcome subtext to the nationalist narrative of the foundation of the Irish Republic. It is notable that in the same year, Kevin O'Shiel (1891–1970) serialised his memoir 'The Last Land War' in the *Irish Times* (November 1966), and that it received very little traction. O'Shiel, a Tyrone-born Nationalist, had not just witnessed the Land War, he had played an important role in repressing it: he had acted as a Republican judge in the Dáil land courts specially convened in 1920 to deal with the rising agitation, and he claimed to have adjudicated on at least 150 court cases in fourteen different counties.[96] O'Shiel countered Lynch's hypothesis with rather dramatic statements such as: 'In the spring of 1920 . . . the fever [of agrarian agitation] swept with the fury of a prairie fire over Connacht and portions of the other provinces, sparing neither great ranch nor medium farm and inflicting in its headlong course, sad havoc on man, beast and property.'[97] If O'Shiel pointed to a need for a much more thorough investigation of the social dimension of the revolutionary period, the notion failed to gather much momentum.

It might be expected that Brian O'Neill's *The War for the Land in Ireland* (1933), with an introduction by Peadar O'Donnell, the leading Republican socialist of the revolutionary era, would hold little appeal for Lynch and other academics. At the time, this short book was disparagingly dismissed by one reviewer as the nonsensical ramblings of 'a young communist' with an absurd theory.[98] It was certainly a propagandist piece but O'Neill's statistical appendices, transcribed from official sources such as agricultural statistical reports, were illuminating. They showed clearly that the issue was not the transfer of landownership from landlords to tenants but rather farm viability (chapter 3). O'Donnell's introduction was fiercely reflective of his disenchantment with what independence had delivered and his bitterness with the lack of social radicalism shown by the IRA leadership of the War of Independence, with the exception of Liam Mellows.[99] The tone also reflected the frustration of living in an Ireland subjugated to a Catholic Church that was ferociously anti-socialist, exemplified in 1933, the year of publication, in its role in the deportation of former IRA leader and agrarian agitator Jimmy Gralton, the only Irishman to be deported from independent Ireland.[100] O'Donnell pointed out that when the potential for social revolution raised its head in 1919–20, the IRA 'middle-class leadership exerted itself frantically to keep the movement "clean"', and that 'in many areas Volunteers were actually used to control the rural masses who would identify the national struggle with their own struggle for free land'.[101] No more than O'Shiel, his argument did not fit in with the prevailing narrative of what happened in the 'four glorious years'. And, yet, in 1932 Fianna Fáil had come to power in large part because it had embraced O'Donnell's successful organisation of the small farmer community campaign against the payment of land annuities.[102] Had land transfer alone satiated the small farmers, the 1923 Land Act would not have been necessary, and the land annuities campaign would never have taken off. And many more Big Houses might have continued in existence.

Most historians stuck with Lynch's viewpoint but in 1983 Charles Townshend argued that 'The real dynamism which underlay the national movement remained the pressure of population on the land. Land hunger, exacerbated by the cessation of emigration, seems to have remained the only force which generated large-scale popular action.'[103] Paul Bew followed: he argued that Sinn Féin emerged as the dominant force in Irish nationalist politics between 1916 and 1918, outflanking 'the Irish Party both on the left and on the right in agrarian matters according to convenience. In short, by 1918 Irish agrarian radicalism was, from the nationalist point of view, a profoundly ambiguous force.'[104] Bew recognised that it was 'something of an overstatement to claim that the 1903 Act virtually solved the Irish land question. Significant agrarian grievances remained and played their part in generating tensions which Nationalists attempted to exploit.'[105] But most historians remained unconvinced.

Even Fergus Campbell, who edited Kevin O'Shiel's memoir for publication, had some doubts. In his *Land and Revolution: Nationalist Politics in the West of Ireland 1891–1921* (2005), Campbell argued that Ireland experienced two revolutions between 1879 and 1923, the first a social revolution which resulted in the transfer of landownership from landlords to tenants (over an extended period beyond independence) and the second a political revolution between 1916 and 1923 that resulted in independence.[106] He contended that 'Land played a critical role in both revolutions; and in the absence of the first, the second would undoubtedly have been accompanied by an extensive (and probably violent) redistribution of property.'[107] But the second was accompanied, or more accurately followed, by an extensive non-violent redistribution of property (chapter 9). It was through the legislative process, but it was revolutionary in intent. Like Lynch and others before him, Campbell had decided that there was no real potential for a social dimension because British land acts created 'a class of sturdy smallholders who would dominate Irish society for most of the twentieth century'.[108] 'Sturdy smallholder' is an oxymoron as anyone familiar with the drudgery of small farm life from the 1920s would testify to; moreover, even the sturdiest smallholder had very little political clout.[109]

Responding to Patrick Cosgrove's criticism that his *Land and Revolution* had not engaged with the history of local landed estates in east Galway, Campbell countered: 'One of the aims of my book was to turn the historical gaze away from its obsession with the House of Commons and the Big House, and towards the cabins and forges where the tenant farmers, labourers and artisans lived and thought about their lives, and worked out political and agrarian strategies for improving them.'[110] In fact, it was very possible that the men gathered in the cabins and forges realised that one of the ways to improve their social condition was to burn a local Big House, leaving hundreds of acres available for redistribution, just as Ann O'Riordan revealed in her study of the burning of Ballydugan House, which was located in Campbell's case study area.[111] In summation, the transfer of landownership from landlords to tenants was not the final solution to the Irish land question, nor the answer to rural inequality. Contemporaries sought it in the redistribution of lands and this objective became central to the Irish revolution.[112]

There had been several socialist commentators in the post-Famine period, including James Fintan Lalor, one of the founding fathers of Irish agrarianism,

1.3 Col. O'Callaghan Westropp, centre in back row, and family outside the family home, Lismehane House, Co Clare, 1912. Even at that stage O'Callaghan Westropp feared revolution that would result in the burning of country houses and wrote a pamphlet around this time setting out how to defend them.

and of course Karl Marx, who believed that land hunger, the drive for the equal redistribution of lands, would be the stimulus to an Irish revolution.[113] There were also landlords in the post-Wyndham years who believed this as well. In 1912, Colonel O'Callaghan Westropp of Clare published and widely circulated a short pamphlet entitled *Notes on the Defence of Irish Country Houses* (1912) in response to the growing political crisis in Ireland.

John Redmond's Irish Parliamentary Party held the balance of power in the House of Commons and the price he demanded to maintain the Liberal government was the introduction of a third Home Rule Bill. The previous year, following a major row over the budget, the Parliament Act 1911 removed the House of Lords' right to veto money bills completely and to veto other bills for only two years. This meant a Home Rule Bill introduced in 1912 would become law two years later. The Ulster Unionist movement prepared to oppose the implementation of Home Rule by force, if necessary. The southern aristocracy and gentry mobilised along more constitutional lines. As O'Callaghan Westropp's pamphlet suggested, opposition to Home Rule put them in an invidious position. If tensions were to develop, Westropp advised that 'precautions of a purely defensive nature' should be 'undertaken without offence to or distrust of respectable neighbours'.[114] 'Respectable' suggested class distinction, in other words the threat would not come from 'respectable Nationalists' but rather from 'organised secret societies' or 'the rowdy or criminal elements of the population', a typical aristocratic stereotyping of the lower classes.[115] Westropp was convinced that, 'Quite apart from any religious or political antagonism, the greed for land ... will inevitably cause trouble' and the country house would become the main focus because 'unexhausted and well-cared for land is attached to mansion houses in the shape of house farms and demesnes'.[116] In the decade ahead it was to prove prophetic, but neither O'Callaghan Westropp nor anyone else could have envisaged everything that was to happen in those ten tumultuous years.

2

'THE UN-MARTIALLED LOYALISTS OF THE SOUTH'

THE GREAT WAR, PART I

[The] gods he [Colonel Head] worshipped were not gods of Ireland, patriotism meant love of England, duty meant duty to England, loyalty to the King of England.

(Peter Somerville-Large, *The Irish Country House: A Social History*, London, 1995, p. 355)

1. 'Their last great gesture of political leadership'

From the late nineteenth century with the growth of Irish nationalism, the advent of the Home Rule movement, mass democratisation and the loss of political power, the aristocracy viewed retention of their place in the British Empire as a prerequisite to their future survival. As Annie Tindley points out: 'The empire represented a context in which aristocrats were able to escape the challenges of democracy in the metropole, and to perform their traditional functions and identities for longer.'[1] As the colonies expanded they provided the natural career outlet for aristocratic sons and the means by which they could continue to justify, at least to themselves, their social privileges. In Ireland, protecting the Union became their political priority. Beginning with the pioneering work of Patrick Buckland, the southern aristocracy's plight as Unionists has attracted a good deal of scholarly attention and needs only to be summarised here.[2] In their campaign against the first two Home Rule Bills of 1886 and 1893, their close, if fraught, connections with the British upper classes, their impressive pamphlet and propaganda campaign in England and their alliance, if loose, with the Unionists of the industrial north-eastern corner of Ulster, helped them fight and win the first two battles. The loss of the protection of the House of Lords' veto in 1911, making the passing of Home Rule inevitable, raised the opposition stakes considerably. On 10 October that year, the 'Great Demonstration' of Unionists, held in the Rotunda in Dublin, and organised by the Irish Unionist Alliance (IUA), attracted a crowd of over 6,000. Most of the Irish nobility were there. The Duke of Abercorn (c.1868), who resided at Baronscourt in Co Tyrone, could not attend and, while he sent his assurances of support to his southern brethren, they hinted of a superior Ulster Unionist attitude and a split that was imminent: 'The Ulster people', he declared, 'will never forsake their co-religionists in the South and West of Ireland – those loyal men who have suffered and are now suffering under the cruel domination of the Land League.'³

The southern Unionists were in a much more isolated and precarious position than those of the north: they lacked the demographic strength, the financial backing of a wealthy industrial class, and ultimately the resolve to fight to the bitter end. Their long-time leader and chairman of the IUA, Lord Midleton, later reflected in his 1930s memoirs: 'With rare exceptions they [southern Unionists] lacked the political insight and cohesion. Contented to air their feelings at intervals, they restricted themselves to the easy tasks of attending meetings in Dublin and voting strong resolutions which they expected the British Government to respect.'⁴ However, as Buckland has suggested, Midleton was being somewhat disingenuous, and credit needs to be given to their efforts to defeat the first two Home Rule Bills, but the hopelessness of their position became evident during the third Home Rule crisis and was compounded by the many consequences of the First World War.⁵

When the third Home Rule Bill was introduced in April 1912, Ulster Unionists made clear their intention to fight it by force, a stance which their more isolated southern counterparts could ill-afford to take. At that stage, the aristocracy of Monaghan, Cavan and Donegal were very much part of the Ulster movement. In the lead up to the signing of the Ulster Solemn League and Covenant in September, which pledged the signatories 'to stand by one another in defending, for ourselves and our children, our cherished position of equal citizenship in the United Kingdom, and in using all means which may be found necessary to defeat the present conspiracy to set up a Home Rule Parliament in Ireland', they joined leading aristocrats across Ulster including Abercorn (in failing health), the Marquess of Londonderry, the Earl of Clanwilliam and Viscounts Templetown and Castlereagh, in taking charge.

Olwen Purdue points out that, 'While the main ceremony in Belfast was dominated by the city's politicians and leading businessmen, the signing of the covenant across the north took place against the backdrop of the Big House' in what was 'their last great gesture of political leadership'.[6] Purdue emphasises the significance of the event and its symbolism:

> For many heads of old landed families this was their political swansong, the last great occasion in which they could truly feel that they occupied their rightful place as the leaders of their people. Their estates were in the process of being broken up, their social connections with England's and Scotland's landed class were rapidly being devalued with the democratisation of British politics and, as leaders of unionism, they had been largely replaced by the middle-class elite that were gathering at Belfast's City Hall. Yet, at this moment, as each of them presided over the enactment of this historic event in the demesnes and villages and towns where generations of their families had held sway, their old family names continued to lend weight and authority to the proceedings as they had done in the past.[7]

In the three counties, the likes of Lords Leitrim, Farnham, and Dartrey, Sir John Leslie and J.C.W. Madden moved to the next stage by taking leadership of the Ulster Volunteer Force (UVF). Major General Lord Edward Gleichen captured their contribution across the province:

> The large landowners, almost to a man Unionists, and many of them ex-officers of the Regulars or late Militia, peers and commoners, rich men, and well-to-do farmers, held local meetings and enrolled nearly all their men in the Volunteer Force. They went round their properties night after night, superintending the organisation and attending at the drill halls to see that all was going well.[8]

In Cavan, Lord Farnham, Somerset Saunderson and Capt. Mervyn Pratt were amongst those who put their past military experience to use. Shane Leslie recalled an occasion when Colonel Saunderson passed through the predominantly Protestant village of Glaslough 'on his way to fight Home Rule'. 'Generals have gone to war', he wrote, 'and not received such a delirious reception.'[9] In

September 1913, speaking at Randalstown, Farnham told those gathered: 'Their womenfolk would cheerfully say to them, "Go and do your duty, and if necessary sacrifice your lives in order that you may hand down to your children these civil and religious rights which our forefathers have handed down to us".'[10] The irony was not lost on Catholics in whose folklore long memories of the Penal Laws existed. Thus, in the borderlands – and they had always been the borderlands – political rhetoric became sour with ancestral bitterness.[11] When, in July 1912, Lord Roden came to Dundalk, in the other border county of Louth, to speak against Home Rule, the Redmondite editor of the local newspaper objected strenuously: 'They [landlords] are not forgotten; and such ill-advised action as his lordship's appearance at this gathering . . . inevitably revives their hateful memories.' He advised Roden: 'Do not speak of intolerance to Irishmen who know the history that was written in the blood and tears of a persecuted people by those who went before you.'[12]

All the posturing and rhetoric on both sides increased political tensions, and heavily tainted them with sectarianism. On 18 June 1914, almost seven acres of game plantation on Lord Leitrim's demesne near Mulroy in Donegal were burned, according to the police, 'maliciously because Lord Leitrim is unpopular with a certain section owing to his extreme activity in the Unionist movement'.[13] When Gerald Madden of Hilton Park, commander of the North Monaghan UVF, heard that his brother had 'some bother' with local Nationalists around Clones, he wrote to him: 'I am sorry you had difficulty with the Roman Catholics about the presentation of colours, it just shows how they would treat Protestants or British troops if they got their way . . . They shan't get the upper hand if we can prevent it.'[14] This was politico-religious scission with an obvious class and sectarian dimension.

In Louth, the case of Roger Bellingham of Castle Bellingham was atypical. A member of an old Catholic family, he was a rare example of an aristocrat who wholeheartedly supported the Irish National Volunteers, formed in 1913 to counter the UVF. In his account of the Bellingham family during the First World War, Donal Hall explained how Lieutenant Bellingham, then aide-de-camp (ADC) to the Lord Lieutenant of Ireland, Lord Aberdeen, was severely rebuked in the House of Lords for comments he made during an inspection of a parade of Irish National Volunteers in his native Co Louth: 'the immediate and manifest duty of the Volunteers', he told his audience, 'was to secure the triumph of the Home Rule movement, and to defend [a Home Rule parliament] which had been so shamefully lost and nobly won.'[15] The Marquess of Crewe maintained that Bellingham could only have said such things because 'He was under the influence of being at home, forgot the obligation of reticence that rested upon him as aide-de-camp to the Lord Lieutenant, and regretted any offence.'[16] Bellingham was forced to retract his statement. In response, Joseph Devlin, the Irish Parliamentary Party MP for west Belfast, addressing the Commons, informed Prime Minister Asquith that the Marquess of Londonderry, ADC to the king, had appeared at UVF rallies in opposition to Home Rule on at least six occasions, and yet he had not been admonished. Asquith's inadequate reply claimed that in contrast to an ADC to the Lord Lieutenant, an ADC to the king 'does not normally carry with it any active duties or responsibilities . . . I have not thought it worthwhile to take any notice of the matter.' It was grist to the mill to Irish Nationalists; the Redmondite editor of the *Dundalk Democrat*, James Gahan, raged: 'Let us have the same sauce for the most noble Marquis as for the Lord Lieutenant's ADC. These Ulster notables have played with treason. They should be taught that the law exacts from them the same obedience that it exacts from the most humble servant.'[17]

The blind eye turned by the authorities to all that was going on behind demesne walls was equally objectionable to Nationalists such as Gahan. In March 1912 the UVF were drilling in Castlesaunderson demesne on the Cavan–Fermanagh border, 'a written authority having been obtained from two magistrates'.[18] In June 1913, the police were aware that 300 rifles and bayonets consigned as 'furniture' manufactured by Ferguson and Co. in London had arrived at the North Wall destined for Lord Farnham in Cavan.[19] In March 1914 a week long instruction camp was held on the Farnham demesne attended by an estimated 230 men.[20] In Donegal, in March 1914, the Earl of Leitrim organised local UVF units.[21] A couple of months previously, he had been in Monaghan transporting a submachine gun from Orange hall to Orange hall for instructional purposes.[22] On 24 April 1914, a huge shipment of arms destined for the UVF was landed at Larne, Bangor and Donaghadee. The motor car corps conveyed the arms to secret dumps. The inspector general of the Royal Irish Constabulary (RIC) knew that 'as a rule' these weapons were 'stored in quantities at the houses of the country gentry'.[23] It was certainly the case in Monaghan, where on 8 May 'large quantities' of arms and ammunition – including around 1,700 rifles – were brought for safe keeping to Glaslough (where Shane Leslie recalled 'stores of rifles had been concealed' in the stables), Dartrey Castle, Poplar Vale, Hilton Park and Beech Hill. There was no interference from the police; County Inspector Tyacke claimed that as the cars arrived in the county between midnight and 6 a.m. it was too dark to identify the registration plates of the vehicles involved. Furthermore, he could not be certain if arms were taken to Dartrey because 'there [were] so many gates to the demesne that the police could not watch them all'.[24] His lame excuses drew upon him the wrath of James Gahan, incensed by the fact that the Royal Proclamation of 4 December 1913 had been flaunted.[25] Under a banner headline pronouncing 'Treason', he wrote:

Any person even slightly acquainted with the history of Ireland during the latter half of the nineteenth century, must be struck by the remarkable contrast between the inaction and apparent cowardice – if not treasonable participation in outrage – of the authorities in Ulster last week and the whole-heartedness with which the forces of the law were brought to bear on Nationalists in the past.[26]

In the early summer of 1914, the air was thick with the Unionist rhetoric of threat and militarism and revolt. At the 12 July celebrations in Monaghan, for example, the Grand Master told his fellow Orangemen that they were rapidly approaching a time 'when it might become necessary for them to translate their words into deeds' and when that time came, in Monaghan they 'would not be found wanting when called upon'. Reverend William Armstrong asserted that 'County Monaghan will never submit to a Dublin parliament. Ulster Protestants will never be slaves,' while John Madden of Hilton Park declared: 'We seek no quarrel with the United Irish League or Hibernians but if we have to fight, we will do so.'[27] As summer progressed, Dartrey and Glaslough demesnes were used for skirmishing and manoeuvres.[28] In April 1914 the *Belfast Newsletter* reported on an instruction camp at Glaslough House:

A large crowd of spectators witnessed the operations, amongst those present being Mrs Guthrie, Lord and Lady Kerry, Lady Caledon, Mrs Crowsley,

2.1 Sir John Leslie of Glaslough House inspecting the Ulster Volunteer Force in Co Monaghan in 1913. He is looking directly at his son, Lionel, in the light-coloured uniform.

the venerable archdeacon Abbott and Miss Abbott . . . At the conclusion tea was supplied to the men by Col. and Mrs Leslie who along with the members of the house party present were indefatigable in attending to their wants.[29]

It was as if military manoeuvring had become a recreational pastime, but there was a much more serious side to it and the women of the Big House were heavily involved: in Donegal, the UVF had 'a good staff of nurses ready to act; a supply of hospital requirements; and in some places provisions have been stored in considerable quantities'.[30] Chatelaines prepared several Big Houses as hospitals including Newbliss and Glaslough in Monaghan and Drumbarness House, near Manorcunningham in Leitrim, which had five tons of hospital provisions stored there.[31]

The aristocracy and gentry further south were not so flagrant, adopting a more constitutional route. In 1913, the IUA had a nucleus of only 683 members, and this organisational failure merely 'reflected the limited social basis of southern Unionism, which tended to be protestant, anglicised, propertied, and aristocratic'.[32] By the early summer of 1914, southern Unionists were both jealous of their northern counterparts and apprehensive of their own future position, knowing that the Ulster Unionists were independently marshalling. On Friday 15 May, Lord Oranmore recorded in his diary that the UVF gun-running 'was a marvellous feat to bring off successfully and everyone agrees that the organisation of the whole business was splendid. Even the government have been struck dumb with astonishment and have wisely decided to take no steps against those concerned.'[33] Nevertheless, he was more concerned that Ireland was on the brink of civil war and, he feared, 'we in the west and south are to be forsaken if an agreement is come to'.[34]

Civil war was brought a stage closer on 26 July 1914 when three civilians were shot dead, and several others injured on Bachelor's Walk in Dublin by soldiers of the King's Own Scottish Borderers. The soldiers had been shepherding a group of Irish National Volunteers who had collected guns and ammunition landed at Howth earlier that day; it was a very modest consignment compared to the Larne landing, where there had been no similar police or army interference. Taunted by the Dublin crowds, the Borderers lost their discipline and opened fire. Nationalist Ireland was incensed by the murders. At that stage, the British cabinet believed that the Irish crisis was 'a much nearer and graver risk than war in Europe'.[35] However, events on the continent ultimately averted civil war in Ireland but plunged the southern aristocracy deeper into crisis; as Countess Fingall saw it: 'Those three deaths in Ireland [at Bachelor's Walk], and the assassination of the Austrian Archduke, lit a torch that set fire to Europe. Our eyes had been turned west to Ireland those last days of that incredible Season of 1914 when we were all riding madly towards the gulf and had nearly reached it. From another quarter, as a thunderbolt, came the war.'[36]

2. 'That incredible Season of 1914'

On Tuesday 4 August 1914, the resident aristocracy of north Cork and the surrounding counties of Munster gathered for a garden party at Mitchelstown Castle, the magnificent Gothic Revival extravaganza built c.1823–25 for the

Earl of Kingston, to the design of James and George Richard Pain.[37] Up to that point, despite the threat of Home Rule, Irish aristocratic families had revelled as usual in the whirl of the summer season, participating in balls and banquets, race meetings and yachting outings, shooting and garden parties that characterised the tail end of the Edwardian belle époque.[38] Elizabeth Bowen was a fifteen-year-old guest at the Mitchelstown party. She would remember the event not for its gaiety and frivolity – no doubt anticipated when the first invitations were sent out – but rather as a defining day in the life of the southern aristocracy:

> Almost everyone said they wondered if they really ought to have come, but they *had* come – rightly: this was a time to gather. For miles round, each isolated Big House had disgorged its talker, this first day of the war. The tension of months, of years – outlying tensions of Europe, inner tensions of Ireland – broke in a spate of words. These were the un-martialled Loyalists of the south. Not a family had not put out its generation of military brothers – tablets in Protestant churches recorded deaths in remote battles; swords hung in halls. If the Anglo-Irish live on and for a myth, for that myth they constantly shed their blood. So, on this August, 1914, day of grandeur and gravity, the Ascendancy rallied, renewed itself.[39]

Written almost thirty years after the event, and amidst another global conflict, Bowen's was a personal eulogy to those aristocratic families who once governed Ireland because they believed they had the right and were the best qualified to do so. Characteristically of her class, she believed that when the declaration of war on 4 August 1914 provided Irish Loyalists with a final opportunity to rally, they were not found wanting. They forgot the local bother of Home Rule as they answered the call of the empire or, as Ian d'Alton has written: 'To this class, and to that generation, military service in time of war was axiomatic, requiring an almost unthinking sense of duty and unity.'[40] D'Alton has estimated that almost half the Irish landed elite 'born between 1830 and 1929 who survived to adulthood were commissioned into the armed forces' at one time or other.[41] In 1914, they comprised 33 per cent of the army's officer corps.[42] Duty and unity were also tightly bound to the fact that the British army had for generations provided career outlets to their younger sons who, denied access to family estates by primogeniture, looked for alternative careers to perpetuate their social position, and that allowed them continued access to Big House society. The financial benefits of a professional career had been especially important from the 1880s as Irish landlords' economic circumstances diminished, and even eldest sons were glad of a supplementary income. In 1892, Hugh Montgomery, a Co Tyrone landlord, explained in a letter to his cousin in New Zealand:

> I have no doubt that within the next twenty or thirty years we shall be directly or indirectly compelled to agree to the conversion of our agricultural tenants into owners of their farms, on terms which will involve a serious diminution of our (already substantially reduced) incomes . . . I should have liked to give my eldest boy a thorough scientific farming education and make him farmer and manager of my property . . . But I had to decide on his profession at a moment when the question of Home Rule being [sic] in the balance and I thought it fairer to him to let him enter a profession where he could always be sure of his day's pay and educated comrades.[43]

This was impressively perceptive of Montgomery and, indeed, it became a trend in the years ahead.

Duty to the empire was ingrained in the aristocratic mindset from an early age in public schools such as Eton and Harrow. Forty per cent of the 270 British and Irish peers or their sons who would die in the war attended Eton.[44] There, young men began to experience the ambivalence of their identity. Sir Hubert Gough, born at Gurteen in Co Waterford, who famously led the 'Curragh Mutiny' in 1914 (see below), wrote in his memoirs:

> I am Irish by blood and upbringing, though I was born in London on 12th August 1870 . . . In upbringing I am an example of so many other people, brought up in one country and taught to love it and be proud of it but educated in another country and taught there to love that also and to be proud of it as well.[45]

Lord Desmond FitzGerald, younger brother of the 6th Duke of Leinster, came from a family that supplied both arch supporters of the crown and rebels (most particularly 'Silken' Thomas FitzGerald, who rebelled against Tudor rule in the 1530s, and Lord Edward FitzGerald, United Irishman, who was a son of the 1st Duke). Shortly after being posted to the Western Front, FitzGerald wrote to his aunt: 'To a great extent I am a futurist but if I am granted to die for my country, it is the one death above all others that I should wish for and gladly accept.'[46] His country was Ireland but an Ireland that was an integral part of the United Kingdom. At the outbreak of war it was, therefore, no surprise that the executive committee of the Irish Unionist Alliance, dominated by the southern aristocracy, passed a resolution declaring that it was 'the duty of Irishmen to undertake their full share of Imperial responsibility in the present national emergency' and called upon its members 'in the three Southern provinces of Ireland to continue their efforts to secure an adequate number of recruits for His Majesty's Army.'[47]

However, what did surprise southern aristocrats was the speech delivered by John Redmond, the leader of the Irish Parliamentary Party, in the House of Commons on 3 August (most likely a topic of conversation at the Mitchelstown Castle party the following day):

I say to the Government that they may tomorrow withdraw every one of their troops from Ireland. I say that the coast of Ireland will be defended from foreign invasion by her armed sons, and for this purpose armed Nationalist Catholics in the South will be only too glad to join arms with the armed Protestant Ulstermen in the North. Is it too much to hope that out of this situation there may spring a result which will be good not merely for the Empire, but good for the future welfare and integrity of the Irish nation? . . . If the dire necessity is forced upon this country we offer to the Government of the day that they may take their troops away, and that if it is allowed to us, in comradeship with our brethren in the North, we will ourselves defend the coasts of our country.[48]

A few weeks later, on 21 September 1914, Redmond, perhaps exhilarated by the reception of his first offer, made another historic speech at Woodenbridge in Co Wicklow where he offered the Irish National Volunteers to go 'wherever the firing line extends in defence of right, of freedom, and religion in this war.'[49] It immediately drew a negative reaction from a separatist minority within the Irish National Volunteers: it was one thing to be asked to defend Ireland's shores, it was quite another to be asked to wear a British army uniform and go wherever the Empire demanded to fight on its behalf. A minority broke away to form the Irish Volunteers; these would be in the vanguard of the 1916 Rising.

As Paul Bew points out, Redmond's reasons for supporting the British war effort were complex, but he concludes that the parliamentary leader genuinely 'hoped that common sacrifice by Irish Nationalists and Unionists would bring them closer together'.[50] At first there were tentative signs that Redmond's optimism was not misplaced as his speeches elicited very positive responses from the southern aristocracy. A buoyed Bryan Cooper of Markree House in Sligo telegrammed Redmond immediately: 'Your speech has united Ireland. I join National Volunteers today and will urge every Unionist to do same.'[51] A significant number of Irish nobles offered to join Redmond's National Volunteers, to drill them or to provide demesne land for skirmishing purposes. In Bray, Viscount Powerscourt addressed 400 National Volunteers: '[he] expressed approval of Mr Redmond's speech, and said that he had tendered his services to lead a Wicklow corps should occasion arise'.[52] Lord Headfort wrote to the *Irish Times*: 'I gladly welcome Mr Redmond's declaration . . . I proposed forthwith to join the local corps of the Irish Volunteers, and thus contribute my part towards the defence of a united Ireland against the common enemy.'[53] Also in Meath, Lord Fingall was appointed chief inspecting officer of the Volunteers, while Marquess Conyngham of Slane expressed a desire to work with them in 'the defence of our country'.[54] Amongst the others who expressed similar sentiments were Lords Gormanston, Monteagle and Sir Mallaby Crofton.[55] In mid-August at a meeting of the Kingstown Corps of the Volunteers, a letter was read from Lord Longford offering land as a drill ground and rifle range, while the Duke of Leinster and Sir Algernon Coote allowed the Volunteers to drill in their demesnes at Carton and Ballyfin.[56]

In this first flush of war excitement, there were even calls for unity between the Ulster Volunteer Force and the Irish National Volunteers: Lord Dunraven wanted to see the two paramilitary organisations 'march together and unite'. Francis Spring Rice, 4th Baron Monteagle, suggested the terms 'Ulster' and 'Nationalist' be dropped in favour of 'the comprehensive title of Irish Volunteers'.[57] George Taafe of Smarmore Castle in Louth was premature in thanking God 'from the bottom of my heart that today we stand a united Ireland, and that the realisation of my dreams has come true, and that Nationalist and Unionist will forever work hand in hand for their country'.[58] Others were much more guarded. W.H. Mahon of Castlegar was happy to support any territorial force for Ireland but on the condition that it would embody 'loyalty to the king and participation in the defence of the Empire'.[59] Lady Inchiquin's remarks to her husband were more pointed: 'What do you think of Redmond's manifesto? I suppose he <u>means</u> it! – (as they have got Home Rule) – Will they all enlist now? And are we to be friendly with them & try and make them enlist? I suppose so!'[60] The 'we' and 'them' and use of exclamation marks suggested that old prejudices were hard to extinguish, further exemplified in the case of Sir Lawrence Parsons, recalled from retirement in 1914 as General Officer Commanding 16th (Irish) Division, who was reluctant to commission Irish Nationalist MPs (and, yet, his relationship with Willie Redmond, brother of the Irish Parliamentary Party leader, seems to have been a warm one).[61] In the end, Redmond was denied a specifically Irish army corps, whereas the 36th (Ulster) Division retained the structures of the UVF with an undeniable Unionist and Orange influence.[62]

On the day before the battle of the Somme commenced, the 36th's commander Sir Oliver Nugent, from a Cavan gentry background, wrote home to Colonel Sir George Richardson, the commander of the UVF: 'We could hardly have a date better calculated to inspire national traditions amongst our men of the North.'[63] It was 1 July 1916, the anniversary of the Battle of the Boyne: the 'national traditions' of the 'men of the North' were Unionist traditions of Ulster men and the slaughter of the Ulster Division on that first day of the Somme would consolidate the myth of Ulster loyalism. Thus, the Ulster aristocracy did not respond to Redmond's speeches with any alacrity; supported by a wider and much more vibrant unionist demography they were never likely to support unity as it would have been an admission that Home Rule was irreversible. Instead, they made much of the fact that on 4 August, the very day that war broke out, the Earl of Leitrim was physically assaulted by Nationalists in Milford, Co Donegal because he had come to *their* town to inspect a company of the local UVF.[64] In the middle of September, Lord Erne called upon his fellow Orangemen 'to avail themselves of this opportunity of showing the loyalty of Ulster Protestants', as if they comprised a distinctive and separate nation.[65] At the end of that month, instead of embracing unity, the Ulster Unionist Council called for an annual commemoration of Ulster Day, 28 September 1912, and the signing of the Ulster Solemn League and Covenant.[66] With Ulster Unionists determined to go their own way, southern aristocratic interest in the Irish National Volunteers cooled rapidly but it did not diminish their overall contribution to the war effort.[67]

3. 'We live our little lives and die'

By the end of the war almost 82 per cent of Irish families listed in *Burke's Peerage, Baronetage and Knightage* were represented at the Front.[68] Lord Dunsany 'made no secret of his dislike for war but still joined up promptly and expected to fight'.[69] Arthur Maxwell, 11th Baron Farnham, an ardent opponent of Home Rule and a UVF instructor before the war, came out of army retirement and rejoined as a lieutenant colonel of the North Irish Horse, impatient to see action. When stationed at Woolwich barracks waiting to be sent to the Front, he wrote to his wife, Aileen: 'They don't seem to be in a bit of a hurry to send me out, bad luck to them.'[70] Those less experienced than Farnham also felt a rush of excitement: Thomas Henn of Paradise House in Clare remembered his brother and cousins enlisting immediately 'for the unreasoning adventure of it'.[71] Matthew Fortescue's excitement got too much for him: a retired major with the Royal Irish Rifles, he volunteered for active service but died of a heart attack when his call-up telegram arrived at Stephenstown House in Louth on 24 August 1914.[72]

Beyond the universal sense of duty and obligation, there were undoubtedly personal motivations.[73] Norman Leslie's desires to share in the past glories of ancestors, to chivalrously defend the Empire and to die in glory rather than survive in shame were set out to a lady friend, Zoe Farquharson (possibly embellished to impress her; he was, after all, 'an aristocratic rogue with a raffish eye for several ladies'[74]):

> Try not to worry too much about the war anyhow. Units, individuals cannot count. Remember we are writing a new page of history. Future generations cannot be allowed to read the decline of the British empire and attribute it to us. We live our little lives and die. To some are given chances of proving

2.2 Norman Leslie of Glaslough House with his mother, Lady Leonie Leslie, taken in September 1914, shortly before he left for the Front, where he would be an early casualty of the Great War.

themselves men, and to others no chance comes. Whatever our individual faults, virtues or qualities may be, it matters not, for when we are up against big things, let us forget individuals and let us act as one great British unit, mixed and fearless. Some will live and many will die but count the loss not. It is better by far to go out with honour than survive with shame.[75]

Indeed, one had to be braver to face the certainty of social shame and ostracisation for not enlisting than the fear of the unknown in Flanders fields.[76]

Just before he left for the Front, Norman wrote to his father, Sir John, assuring him that his 'affairs are all in order & my debts will be easily outbalanced by my insurance money of £1,000.'[77] But not all were so well circumstanced. On 8 October 1914, Captain Charles Monck, heir to the Charleville estate in Wicklow, wrote to his solicitor, J.E. McDermott:

I fear after reading this letter, that any regard you may have had for me before will disappear and you will only think of me as a coward and a hypocrite . . . I am about to acquaint you with the grave state of my finances, but I want you to understand that it is not the present life that I am living that has prompted me to do so but, since I have been away, certain of my debts, though a small part only of them, have become known to my wife who has heretofore been ignorant of them . . . When I started out here, I fully realised that the odds were very long against my ever returning, and if I die today my difficulties and those of my family would to a great extent disappear with me. But although I have seen two thirds of our original number of officers struck off the roll and there is still more work to be done, I realise that the 100 to 1 chance may yet come off . . . At present I cannot myself see anything but disaster [at home], which is far worse to face than what is at present going on here.[78]

Monck was only a few weeks at the Front when he wrote this. The war had taken him away from the secrets he had hidden at home, the financial responsibilities he did not want to face up to. Between 1887 and the war, the bulk of his family estate in Co Wicklow had been sold under the land purchase acts. However, because of the levels of family indebtedness there was little left to sustain Charleville. Charles's self-admitted 'sheer carelessness' had led him to drift from one financial crisis to another and, without the courage to go to either his solicitor or his father for help, he instead borrowed 'trusting to luck in the matter all coming right'.[79] Charles asked his solicitor to find 'a way out without letting the burden fall too heavily on those dependent on me and on my father', but McDermott replied that he could do nothing in a financial climate characterised by an 'ever-increasing disinclination among lenders to advance on estates which are subject to heavy paramount charges'.[80] In any case, McDermott's letter of 19 October 1914 would not have reached Charles, who was killed in action at Ypres on 21 October. Perhaps Monck epitomises Patrick Buckland's contention that 'Some of the young and not so young men of Anglo-Ireland may have thrown themselves into Flanders and Gallipoli impelled by a kind of despair, because the habits of Ireland no longer fitted the country gentry, and their position and great houses had become straitjackets.'[81] There was undoubtedly an element of truth in this, and the death of this young heir certainly had future implications for the family estate, as we will see below.

4. 'A tale of horror and destruction'

Shane Leslie's war journal of his first few weeks at the Front reveal the dying embers of an aristocratic army lifestyle; in October 1914, he recorded the officers had 'honey for breakfast and the most gorgeous lunch of apple tart and goose cooked by our soldier servants.'[82] Similarly, in April 1915, Sir John Keane of Cappoquin in Waterford reported that the officers had champagne which they had rescued from a burning house, but his 'current servant, who was the leader in the rescue of the wine, celebrated the occasion yesterday and was quite unfit for duty when I wanted him in the afternoon'.[83] In the early days of September 1914, Dick Hely-Hutchinson of Lissen Hall in Dublin wrote to his mother about his billet: 'We are in a farm house & very comfortable, they have most beautiful farm buildings here, enormous barns and stables & acres & acres of corn . . .'[84]

And to his sister, Cissy: 'We really live most extraordinarily well & there is never any lack of food . . . It is a nice village & they have not shelled us so far; & the enemy don't seem very active at present.'[85] In those early days, the likes

2.3 Coote Robert Hely-Hutchinson of Lissen Hall, Dublin. He was one of two sons who went to war with the Royal Fusiliers and survived. His surviving war correspondence describes vividly the horrors of life at the Front for both officers and men.

of Leslie, Keane and Hely-Hutchinson may have been writing to comfort loved ones, but it was not long before veterans and war virgins alike encountered terrors and horrors they could never have envisaged.[86] By December 1914, the stoicism that Hely-Hutchinson had displayed in his letters to his mother and sister was absent in the truths he told his father: 'You would not believe the state of the trenches, it's worse than any mud you can imagine . . . It is beastly country.'[87] By 1915, conditions had radically altered and his living quarters made him 'positively sick, those blasted huts are roofed with ordinary sacking and there is at least a foot of mud all round and the water pours into them'.[88] In March 1915, he no longer held back in his description of the horrors to his parents:

> The trenches were in an awful state, one trench we had to abandon and dig a new one, we filled in the old one with 26 dead bodies in it, some of them all swollen up and so churned into the mud and slush that we could not pull them out even with a rope. In another they had to take the bodies out in bits and bury them, as the arms etc. came away if you pulled them. I should think we buried at least 120 bodies, all under heavy fire at night.[89]

In the same month, John Keane wrote to his wife, Eleanor: 'We buried poor Griffiths in the churchyard on the square. No coffin, just tied up in a blanket and I do not know that men even have this.' It was impossible, he told her, to float a barge on the Yser canal in Ypres, 'as the water is so choked with corpses'.[90] In November 1916, he described the dreaded 'malady of trench foot', for which 'oils and anti-frostbite grease are only a very imperfect antidote'. Changing seasons simply brought different problems. In March 1915, Dick Hely-Hutchinson told Cissy: 'There is a beastly NE wind blowing and some snow, very cold, but it has really begun to dry up a little at last; if you could see the mud, you would say Thank God, but I suppose as soon as the dust begins to fly about, we shall have all sorts of stinking microbes coming along to go into the men's food, and further complications will arise.'[91] And in the summer of 1916: 'The heat here is real bad, and there are nothing but flies and mosquitos everywhere about and things that eat one.'[92] Thus, the harsh realities soon swept away any romantic notions attached to the type of cavalier lifestyle previously enjoyed by young officers such as Norman Leslie. Already by the end of September 1914, he was coming to terms with the savagery of total warfare. On 22 September, Leslie's regiment relieved another one that had lost 25 per cent of its men. At 7.30 a.m., he wrote, 'Hell broke loose above us and shrapnel fairly tore around us'. An hour later:

> A man ran from A round to me and said he'd got about 7 men badly hit in their trenches, so I dashed round with him [soldier] and found a proper charnel house – all shrapnel wounds, one arm hanging by a shred, another pierced through the lungs, another neck, back and thigh, 2 broken legs . . . I was trying to tie up one fellow's leg when crash came another shrapnel and wiped out another man 20 yards off. At the end of the job I was drenched with their blood, the unpleasant part being that we have no water to drink at present, far less to wash with.[93]

Later in the night came earth-quaking shells – there was 'something peculiarly terrifying about their noise and the disturbance they cause to earth and air' – followed by the roar of rifle fire and artillery, and the incessant sound of Germans digging trenches close by. In the morning came the Taube monoplane aircrafts circling, and, all the while, men dropped dead beside him shot through the head by snipers.[94] Psychological stress took a huge toll on officers and men; as early as December 1914, John Keane wrote to his wife: 'The casualties are heavy but the nerve strain is incessant.' The futility of war was beginning to dawn on Keane, who wished that 'a party of representative men, Irish as well as English, could be sent here to see the devastation of war'.[95] Personality change was inevitable. Men became emotionally hardened. Dick Hely-Hutchinson's mother died in March 1915 and he was unable to get leave to go home to the funeral. He wrote to his sister: 'But now we must only realize that it has to be and we must carry on; so you both of you must catch hold, say to yourselves – well everybody else in the world had to go through this and we must too.'[96]

On 17 November 1914, in only the fourth month of war, Lord Desmond FitzGerald wrote an open letter (later found amongst his belongings after he was killed on 3 March 1916), which suggested how much he had been imagining death: 'This is just to say that except for the sorrow it may cause to my dear relations, I have no reason to fear death and I hope this will be a comfort to anybody who sorrows over it.' In the event of his death, he wanted no memorial service, but to be commemorated in a small tablet in the Guards Chapel in Eton.[97] The total carnage Desmond witnessed at the first battle of Ypres had left an obvious psychological scar; the initial enthusiasm to be involved in the war had dissipated and was replaced by the foreboding of his own death. When he was killed, the human tragedy was poignantly revealed in a letter from Edward, Prince of Wales to Desmond's aunt, Lady Cynthia Graham:

> It is one of the greatest blows or shocks I have ever had for in Desmond's death I have lost my greatest friend. I can't yet realise what has happened or bring myself to think I shall never see him again . . . It is too terribly tragic for me to be able to express myself better . . . He was my greatest friend and that is really why I write.[98]

In September 1914, after he had been wounded for the first time, Edward Woulfe Flanagan prayed to God 'that this insane and senseless slaughter may before long be brought to an end'.[99] Like John Keane, he began to despair at the futility of the war, and questioned 'what was running through the minds of the high commanders' who ordered 'futile attacks . . . again and again in broad daylight in [?face] of strongly held machine gun position'.[100] He was blistering in his condemnation: 'What the total slaughter during the last few days has been I have no conception . . . No army could stand this ceaseless sacrifice and the men who are responsible for it should be hung.'[101] He had recently lost 800 men of his battalion: 'Never', he wrote home, 'was there such a scene of carnage. Nothing that anyone has ever witnessed would equal in horror the truth. The wounded of all regiments could not be got away and lay there for days shouting and yelling for water which could not be got and under an intense bombardment were wounded again and again.'[102] There were other experienced aristocratic officers equally angered by military tactics and blundering. Lord Granard fumed from Suvla in July 1915 that 'The way the campaign is being run is an absolute disgrace.'[103] Lord Castletown saw the campaign there as 'a wicked and cruel scheme', its failure he put down to the complete incompetency of those who orchestrated and led it.[104] The longer war dragged on the more it degenerated into what Castletown described as 'a tale of horror and destruction'.[105]

5. 'Whatever small luxuries are possible'

By the end of the first winter of war, national and local newspapers teemed with lists of dead, injured and missing, as well as reports of the dreadful conditions which men endured. In December 1914, the editor of the *Irish Times* urged that 'It remains for us at home to see that the men in the trenches are provided also with whatever small luxuries are possible in the circumstances.'[106] Typical of the steps taken by the aristocracy in most counties is Donal Hall's description of Louth: shortly after the war broke out, the Dundalk War Relief Committee was established to look after the long-term needs of returning wounded soldiers; a branch of the National War Relief Fund 'for the relief of women and children who are faced with privation as a consequence of the war' was also set up the same year by Sir Henry Bellingham, whose wife established a branch of the Red Cross and raised over £400 in subscriptions before the end of July 1915. Through numerous fundraisers, Lady Bellingham raised £12,000 over the course of the war, which funded ambulances for the Front and a Red Cross hospital for the wounded set up in Dundalk in 1917. Meanwhile, her husband Sir Henry was president of the county recruiting committee.[107]

Couples such as the Bellinghams very often worked in tandem. In north Tipperary, Henry O'Callaghan Prittie (1851–1927) 4th Baron Dunalley of Kilboy House, organised recruitment drives, while his wife Mary's efforts at fundraising and providing for the soldiers and prisoners of war were rewarded with an MBE in 1920.[108] From Doneraile Court in Cork, Lord Castletown spearheaded recruitment campaigns, while his wife 'took up with keen interest all the work that was to be done for the wounded' of the 16th (Irish) Division.[109] In June 1916, the Marquess of Sligo, who had founded the Co Mayo Branch of the Aid Fund for the Connaught Rangers, worked with the Irish Women's Association of which his wife and daughter were committee members. Every fortnight, they organised parcels for prisoners of war made up of provisions such as biscuits, tins of beef, vegetables, milk, fish, jam, fruit, coffee, cheese, tea and sugar, cocoa and fifty cigarettes or a plug of tobacco. They also sent socks, toothbrushes and, once a year, a great coat, vests, pants, cardigans and shirts.[110]

As Maeve O'Riordan's important study of women in the country house elucidates, the home front was a parallel universe connected to the soldiers in the trenches where aristocratic women used their full range of social skills as committee members and volunteers in various organisations to develop philanthropic endeavours.[111] They had traditionally acted in rural and urban areas as dispensers of charity and so war work was merely an extension of past voluntary activities.[112] Lady Powerscourt worked for the Serbian Red Cross Hospitals (using Powerscourt House as the central depot for donations). She raised over £500 in October 1915 alone.[113] Many young aristocratic women worked in the nursing profession with the British Red Cross or as part of the Voluntary Aid Detachment, trained to provide medical and other assistance. The De Robeck sisters of Gowran Grange, Naas, Co Kildare volunteered as ambulance drivers with the Red Cross. Edith Anne Stoney of Rosturk Castle in Mayo was a rare example of a woman with a professional qualification who served at the Front; educated in Newham College Cambridge, she qualified as a radiologist and received a Croix de Guerre for her service in the war. Lady Waterford set up the first Red Cross War Hospital Supply Depot, and then fifty more across the country, with the central depot at 40 Merrion Square in Dublin. Over 1,500 people were employed in the Dublin depot alone. Lady Ormonde of Kilkenny worked for the Irish Distressed Ladies Fund. Lady Talbot de Malahide, president of the Dublin Branch of the British Red Cross, was awarded an OBE for services after the war and Dame Commander of the Order in the 1920 civilian war honours.[114] Augusta, Lady Clonbrock, was in her seventies when the war broke out, but she worked tirelessly on behalf of prisoners of war in raising funds and organising parcels or 'comforts' for the men of the Connaught Rangers. In the first three months of the war, from 14 August to 18 November 1914, she collected 18,106 items in Galway, including 5,407 pairs of socks and 1,994 shirts.[115] Under her stewardship, £14,000 was raised in Galway between 1914 and 1918, through various fundraising events including bazaars, raffles and a concert by the renowned singer-songwriter Percy French.[116] Needless to say, this level of funding could only have been raised with wider public participation beyond aristocratic circles.

In the absence of many of their husbands, wives became the public faces on platforms. Lady Fingall tutored the less experienced in how to speak in public and to chair meetings (she served as chair of the Central Committee for Women's Employment).[117] Some were, of course, long experienced in the public sphere; none more so than Edith Lady Londonderry, who made her

2.4 Lady Augusta Clonbrock (1840–1928) and her husband Luke Gerald
Dillon, 4th Baron Clonbrock. Their activities during the war years epitomised
the commitment of the aristocracy at home to supporting the British war effort.

strong independent opinions clear when she asked 'are women merely to be a
burden to others, which in this case means their menfolk, and helpless as
regards themselves?'[118] Brett Irwin has noted that 'The influence and commitment of Lady Londonderry and the Women's Legion made a significant contribution to the lives of thousands of women in Ireland and Britain and arguably
paved the way for the Representation of the People Act of 1918, whereby
8.4 million people gained the right to vote.'[119] She and her husband gave over
two of their English mansions – Londonderry House in London and Wynard
in Durham – for use as military hospitals.[120] This use of country houses was
not as prevalent in Ireland as in England, but there were examples: in March
1916, in Kildare, the Countess of Mayo offered Moorefield House for free
(though it was in poor condition) as a convalescent home for soldiers, while
Major Henry offered Firmount as a home for officers only and at a rent of
£150 per annum.[121] Corrig Castle, a disused house in Kingstown, was set up
as a hospital (with the financial support of Lords Longford and De Vesci),

while Arthur Kinahan made Roebuck House in Dundrum available to the local St John's Ambulance unit.[122] In something of a variation, in November 1914 Lord Longford offered Pakenham Hall in Westmeath to the War Office for the accommodation and training of recruits.[123]

The adaptation of country houses as hospitals or convalescent homes brought changes to the architectural integrity of houses as large reception rooms were transformed into hospital wards and operating theatres, while a clear demarcation of space was necessary to separate officers from the rank and file (a continuation of the traditional upstairs-downstairs hierarchies within country houses). Ronan Foley's pioneering study of the temporary transformations of wartime care carried out in Mount Stuart on the Isle of Bute highlights the role of Augusta Bellingham, marchioness of Bute, born in 1880 and reared in Castle Bellingham in Co Louth.[124] Foley explains that 'the specific interior and exterior spaces of the house functioned as examples of therapeutic land-scapes, where recovery and restoration in soothing locations contrasted sharply with the traumatizing surrounds of front-line combat'. Outdoors, in the extensive grounds men could draw curative value from gardening, using the estate workshops for arts and crafts or simply strolling the wider demesne landscape with its extensive woods and walkways.[125]

Most of the male aristocrats' time and energies were taken up with recruitment drives. In December 1914, in Queen's County, the Earl of Portarlington used the relatively new medium of cinematograph to show pictures from the Front, to bring home the realities of the war and to try to stimulate local recruitment.[126] In Britain, some landlords acted feudally and gave their employees an ultimatum to enlist or be sacked. Lord Derby, for example, warned his tenants and workers: 'When the war is over, I intend, as far as I possibly can, to employ nobody except men who have taken their duty at the front. I go further than that, and say that, all things being equal, if two men come to me for a farm and one has been at the front there is no doubt which is going to get the farm.'[127] Similarly, Lord Edward FitzGerald's biological father, the 11th Earl of Wemyss – Edward's mother, Hermione, Duchess of Leinster, had an affair with him in the 1880s – issued an 'abrupt ultimatum to all his employees, servants etc. to join the Army or leave his service'.[128] It is difficult to determine how widespread this strategy was in Ireland, but there is some evidence of variations of it: R.H. Prior-Wandesforde of Castlecomer in

Kilkenny undertook to pay one shilling per day during their term of service to the first squad of men who would recruit from his collieries and estate.[129] (His eldest son, Christopher, was killed in action in 1917.) In early September 1914, the Earl of Meath provided a bounty of £5 to the family of every recruit amongst his employees who enlisted, and promised to keep their positions open until the war was ended.[130] That same month, Bryan Cooper of Markree Castle in Sligo issued the following guarantee: 'that the families of all reservists called up for service, who are tenants on his property, and pay less than £10 a year rent, shall be excused all rent until the end of the war, while those who pay more than that sum will be allowed to deduct £10 from their present rent.'[131] Lord Donoughmore offered to continue to pay the wages of his men who recruited but only two volunteered and they failed the subsequent medical examination.[132] It was said that Lady de Vesci of Abbey Leix (then living in Surrey) put her chauffeur at the disposal of the Red Cross, but the unfortunate man was enlisted by the army and sent to East Africa where he died shortly after from dysentery.[133] If the aristocracy coerced their employees on a wider scale than is being suggested here it had the potential to leave a legacy of local bitterness not easily forgotten. It may be worth noting, for example, that when Moydrum Castle in Westmeath was burned in July 1921, one of the IRA officers involved later recalled that Lord Castlemaine 'was a member of the British House of Lords who always opposed anything which was patriotic or Irish national and was really an enemy of Ireland. He had dismissed men from his employment because they would not join the British army.'[134]

Likewise, the aristocracy's universal support for conscription in 1917–18 pitted them against a rainbow coalition of Irish Nationalists, supported by the Catholic Church, at a time when, in the wake of the 1916 Rebellion, Irish nationalism was moving towards a more radical phase and Sinn Féin was stealing the march on the moribund Irish Parliamentary Party (see below). In 1918, Limerick Corporation called to have Lord Dunraven struck from the list of the city's freemen, councillor Griffin stating that he 'never thought his lordship would turn on his fellow countrymen and try to enforce a blood tax'.[135] James Ormsby Lawder of Leitrim, a staunch Unionist and former Conservative candidate for the county in 1885, contended later that: 'The whole trouble came from cowardice in not having conscription the same as in

England', his argument being that it would have taken the radicals out of Ireland.[136] In December 1921, J.M. Wilson, brother of Field Marshal Sir Henry, reflected:

> When it was proposed to conscribe Ireland, the Revolutionary Party [Sinn Féin] made this the chief plank in their platform. They were instantly supported by the Roman Catholic Church, which in Ireland, as in Melbourne and Ottawa, had adopted a very hostile attitude towards the Allies. All that vast multitude which desired to profit out of the war and not to fight in it, became very friendly to their saviours. Men with small businesses, farmers with one son [sic] or one labourer, clerks in snug positions, timid young men with pacifist views in time of war and bloody aims in time of peace, turned with relief to this doctrine that Ireland was 'an independent nation whom aliens had no right to conscribe'.[137]

There were reasons why both their houses – Lawderdale and Currygrane – were burned in 1920–23 other than their political stance on issues such as conscription, but, as will be argued in a later chapter, nothing should be overlooked in trying to elucidate those reasons. A simple search of witness statements in the Bureau of Military History (BMH) using the term 'conscription' turns up over 700 hits, suggesting the impact it had on young men who would go on to fight in the Irish Republican Army during the War of Independence and whose revolutionary mindsets were formed during imposed martial law after the 1916 Rising, the conscription crisis of 1917–18, the internment of 'German Plot' suspects (May 1918), the banning of organised Gaelic Athletic Association events (July 1918) and so on.

While most of the landed elite were disappointed at the British government's failure to impose conscription, they were also disillusioned with rural recruitment numbers as the war progressed, even amongst the Protestant population in the three Ulster counties. Granted, Irishmen made a very significant voluntary contribution to recruitment between 1914 and 1918; over 206,000 Irishmen served in the British forces, but the majority joined early in the war and were predominantly drawn from urban areas.[138] Very soon recruitment from rural areas diminished to a trickle. Several reasons have been put forward. In the first place, most young Irish Nationalists had no ambition to fight and die for the British Empire. There was gradual dissatisfaction with the British government's procrastination over the implementation of Home Rule. Early on, Lord Donoughmore's land agent, R.B. Seigne, gauged the temper of nationalist Ireland, advising that attempts at recruitment from its ranks would fail 'unless something is decided soon about the Home Rule Bill satisfactory to those who influence public opinion in the South and West of Ireland.'[139]

Secondly, the war generated a greater incentive for young men in rural Ireland to stay at home. This was the first generation of Irish farm owners, as opposed to tenant farmers, with no obligations, however they might be defined, to their landlords. They were now making money for themselves and their families to purchase their farms, as opposed to making it to pay the rent.[140] In the decades from the beginning of the Land War to the First World War the prices of Irish agricultural produce had stagnated, but there was an explosion from 1914 to 1920, and every type of farming system benefited: tillage, livestock and mixed.[141] Wheat rose from 8.8 shillings a ton in 1914 to 21.6 shillings in 1920; oats from 7.1 to 17.3; barley from 7.3 to 22.5; potatoes from 3.4 to 10.2; butter from 108.6 to 320.6 (in all cases, prices had almost trebled).[142] Pork rose from 59.9 shillings per ton to 187; beef from just over 60 per ton to almost 160; mutton from 70 shillings to 183; eggs from 10 shillings for 6 dozen to 31 shillings. Lambs made 30 shillings per head in 1914 but 77 shillings in 1920.[143] That the livestock farmer profited from the war is further suggested in the increased quantity of all cattle exported (fat, store, calves and others) from 814,000 head in 1905–09 to 935,000 in 1913–17.[144] Kevin O'Shiel (1891–1970), a judge in the land courts of 1920, later remembered how he was 'amazed at the prices people were getting for their land'. In some areas, conacre was making £20 per acre in 1916–17, almost seven times what might have been expected in pre-war days. By the end of the war, he recalled, 'it seemed that land had become almost literally as valuable as gold'.[145]

In Cavan, Lord Farnham was disappointed to enlist only three men from a recruitment meeting in September 1914, while 'hundreds of strapping young farmers' stayed at home, but the reason should have been obvious to him on a number of levels, not least the natural inclination to take advantage of the new-found prosperity rather than dying in the muddied fields of Flanders.[146] In Donegal, in November 1914, an impressive recruiting party of 200 under

Lord Leitrim visited several towns in Donegal but 'got only a few recruits'; the County Inspector contended that higher agricultural prices were the incentive to stay at home.[147] Similarly, in May 1915 the County Inspector of Clare reported: 'Farmers and others from the agricultural districts have contributed scarcely anyone to the army'; from Cork, 'Farmers' sons and shop assistants are not coming forward'; from Queen's, 'Shop assistants and farmers' sons still hang back'. More ominous from the aristocracy's perspective was the fact that younger sons of farmers (denied access to landownership by accident of birth), agricultural labourers and landless men began to turn their attention to radical Sinn Féin as it moved to exploit once again the land question in rural Ireland (chapter three).

6. 'Hard at work plugging the rebels'

In August 1914, shortly after the breakdown of the Buckingham Palace Conference (21–24 July) called by King George V to address the Irish Home Rule question, Sir William Hutcheson Poe, formerly High Sheriff of Queen's County and Tyrone, publicly appealed to Redmond and Carson:

> I refuse to believe that, in this golden hour of Ireland's opportunity, either Sir Edward Carson or Mr Redmond is so blind to his country's interests, so deaf to her longing cry for peace, that they will not, each of them, be prepared to forego an immediate party triumph for the more glorious prospect of a united Ireland . . . when under Ireland's providence, the dangers which now threaten the empire shall have passed away.[148]

Back in January 1913, Carson had proposed to the British Prime Minister, H.H. Asquith, the exclusion of the nine counties of Ulster from the operation of the third Home Rule Bill. At the Buckingham Palace Conference, he modified his proposal by arguing for the permanent exclusion of six counties, thus preparing to sacrifice the unionist minorities in Cavan, Donegal and Monaghan for a safer Protestant majority. As the war lingered, Carson, who had a seat in the cabinet as first Lord of the Admiralty, showed no signs of compromising on Ulster unionist gains.[149] Redmond refused a place at the cabinet table, but he was unwavering in his continued support for the British war effort even though the War Office refused his requests to form an 'Irish brigade' or division.[150] In

September 1916, he wrote passionately: 'Would that all those who still may harbour bitterness and rancour against any of their countrymen in Ireland might stand for even one moment and read the cross inscriptions in the cemeteries of France! Those inscriptions which tell of the glorious and eternal union of brave Protestant and Catholic and Northern and Southern Irish hearts.'[151] But the 'glorious and eternal union' was never a realistic aspiration. By then, Redmond's own party members had become disillusioned with his weak attempts to deal with partition, wider nationalist Ireland was frustrated by Britain's failure to deliver on Home Rule, and those who had split away from the Irish National Volunteers after his Woodenbridge speech had orchestrated a rebellion just four months previously, in Easter week of 1916.

In the very many academic studies of the 1916 Rising, it is rare to encounter reference to the Irish landed elite's experience of the event or their reaction to it.[152] As to be expected, the aristocracy and gentry regarded the Rising as the greatest of treasonable acts (while conveniently disregarding the arming of the UVF). At first, they bought into wild exaggerations, often fuelled by unionist propaganda, that overstated the extent of disorder in Ireland. Lord Oranmore heard that '25,000 Sinn Féiners seized the Post Office, Stephen's Green, the Law Courts and large portions of the City of Dublin' and had set all of the capital on fire.[153] Letitia Overend of Airfield House, near Dundrum, on the outskirts of the city, became fearful that 'things had wound back to [17]98 again' and that all Loyalists would be murdered in their beds.[154] Charles Hamilton of Hamwood House, Dunboyne, Co Meath, agent to the Duke of Leinster, was at Fairyhouse races on Easter Monday when rumours of the rebellion began to circulate. He had been told that '3,000 Germans were in Cork and 10,000 rebels were on the route to Dublin from Athlone'. On Friday night, 28 April, he was awakened by an explosion in Dublin (about twelve miles away) that 'shook the house and brought the soot out of the chimney'. With news that the rebels were reputedly approaching Ashbourne, Dunshaughlin and Dunboyne, there were growing apprehensions that Hamwood would be attacked. Hamilton recorded in his diary how he lay awake and listened 'half the night to hear if people were creeping up to the house'.[155]

The rebellion fully illustrated on which side of the hyphenated 'Anglo-Irish' designation the aristocracy's loyalties lay. When Captain Anketell Moutray learned he would not get a chance to suppress the rebels in Enniscorthy, he wrote: 'I was, I admit, much distressed that we were not able to pull off a scrap with the rebels – I would [have] loved to have been able to swot them – dirty dogs.'[156] Hubert Preston, Lord Gormanston's brother, was an officer in the 3rd Royal Irish Regiment and, like Charles Hamilton, was at Fairyhouse races on Easter Monday when he was summoned back to Dublin, where, according to Reverend Richard Butler, he ended up in the 'thick of the fray and was lucky to have escaped' the 'organised hooliganism'.[157] Gormanston gleefully told their sister that Hubert and his men were 'hard at work plugging the rebels'.[158] William Upton Tyrell of Ballindoolin House in Kildare wrote home to his mother from the Western Front: 'If I could only get at those fellows now . . . if only I had been another month at home. All the Irishmen here are frightfully mad with the scoundrels and want to get back to get a shot at them.'[159] Edward Bellingham of Castle Bellingham in Louth was commanding the 8th Battalion of the Royal Dublin Fusiliers when they suffered 500 casualties on the western Front during the week of the rebellion. He wrote to his father: 'Our men are furious with the Sinn Féiners, and asked to be allowed to go and finish them up. We were defending the empire with serious losses the very day these people were trying to help the Germans that we were fighting. It is all too sad.'[160]

His cousin, Vera, got caught up in Dublin that week. She made a telling comment when, on 3 May, she eventually got to leave Kingstown for London: 'It is odd to think I have been through an exciting episode of history, sometimes during the last week I felt it must have been a queer dream. What effect it will have on our unhappy country goodness knows, it is heart rending for <u>anyone</u> who really loves their country.'[161] Her sense of patriotism and the Irish nation was very different to that of the rebels and, like many of her class, she scorned the fact that one of their own, 'that wretched Countess Marhievits (recte Markievicz)', was rumoured 'to be at the head of it'.[162] Constance Gore-Booth (1868–1927), who married the Polish Count Markievicz, was the sister of Sir Josslyn Gore-Booth of Lissadell House in Sligo, who, so untypical of her class, became an advocate of Irish separatism. Sir John Leslie of Glaslough derided 'my friend the Countess Markovitch [sic]' who 'massacred the Dublin police with her own fair hands' and regretted that after her imprisonment she was 'doing nothing for her sins beyond a little fancy sewing in detention'.[163] Jenico Preston, 15th Viscount Gormanston, was equally disgusted by

Markievicz: '[she] deserves shooting . . . When she was taken near the Castle and disarmed, I am told she kissed her revolver before handing it over – a dangerous and clever woman. If only her energies had been directed in a good cause.'[164]

Peter Martin shows in his study of the Irish nobility and revolution that Markievicz was a rare though not exceptional example of an aristocrat who sympathised with the Republican cause.[165] There was also Albinia Brodrick, the sister of Lord Midleton, the leading southern Unionist, and Mary Spring-Rice, sister of Lord Monteagle, who in the years after 1916 funded republicanism, ran missions for the IRA's headquarters in Dublin, provided shelter to men on the run at Mount Trenchard and was outspoken in her condemnation of British reprisal policy.[166] The most prominent was Robert Barton of Glendalough House in Wicklow, who was born into a staunchly Church of Ireland and unionist background.[167] He began life as most aristocratic sons, educated at Rugby and Oxford, before moving to Agricultural College in Cirencester. He was intent on being a progressive farmer. In 1908, his interest in the co-operative movement brought him into contact with the Home Rule movement and he became converted. In 1913, he joined the Irish National Volunteers, rising to the rank of commandant. However, in 1915 he considered it his duty to join the British army to fight in the war but, rather ironically, after he was given a commission in the Royal Dublin Fusiliers on 26 April 1916, instead of being sent to the Front he was sent to Dublin to suppress the Rising. His biographer writes that 'he was horrified at the treatment meted out to the defeated rebels' and resigned his commission.[168] He joined Sinn Féin and in the general election of 1918 won a seat in West Wicklow. He became Director of Agriculture in the First Dáil Éireann, comprised of MPs who refused to take their seats at Westminster. He spent most of the War of Independence in prison for sedition but was released in time to sign the Anglo-Irish truce with General Sir Neville Macready on 11 July 1921. Three months later, Barton was one of the plenipotentiaries who travelled to London to negotiate the terms of a treaty. It was a very different path to that travelled by most of his class.

While the rebellion was a complete military failure, the British government's brutal execution of the rebel leaders and the internment of thousands who had no role in the insurrection, while simultaneously toying with the idea of introducing conscription, altered completely the Irish political landscape. Sinn Féin connected with people and local leaders across urban, rural, religious, labour and business communities to build a sufficiently powerful nationalist opposition to challenge Britain's right to introduce conscription. The Representation of the People Act 1918 introduced tens of thousands of young Irishmen and women who were more amenable to Sinn Féin to the vote for the first time, with the result that the Irish Parliamentary Party was virtually obliterated in the general election of December 1918.

All the while, the war was diluting the future strength of southern Unionism as its potential leaders were being slaughtered at the Somme, Verdun, Passchendaele and dozens of other battle sites on different fronts. For those who remained in Ireland or who returned after the war, 1916 represented a major watershed; Frederick Beaumont-Nesbitt of Tubberdaly House in King's County, for instance, wrote in his memoirs: 'I do not recall a single incident during my boyhood when hostility was shown either to myself or a member of my family, at least not until the outbreak of Easter week 1916.'[169] While the war confirmed the Irish landed elite's loyalty to king and empire, it accentuated their deracination from mainstream Irish life as Irish nationalist politics entered a new and more radical phase. This was part of a much wider European phenomenon where in the years ahead aristocracies would crumble with empires and suffer a diverse range of experiences from economic collapse to social and cultural alienation to personal humiliation and degradation, to say nothing of the destruction and expropriation of their property.

3

'ALL THE GENTRY HAVE SUFFERED'
THE GREAT WAR, PART II

[The Great War] was to be the last chapter in the history of many families. Behind the high stone walls at the end of the long avenue, in that Georgian house or sham Gothic castle, there remained now only an old father and mother and a couple of ageing daughters.

(Lennox Robinson, *Bryan Cooper*, London, 1931, p. 131)

1. 'They have behaved magnificently'

Lennox Robinson in his biography of Major Bryan Cooper (1884–1930) of Markree Castle in Sligo, published thirteen years after the war ended, may very well have begun the myth that so closely associated the decline of the Irish aristocracy with their contribution to the First World War.[1] His comments were certainly echoed by later writers. For example, in his introduction to the 1958 edition of *Burke's Landed Gentry of Ireland*, Mark Bence-Jones described 4 August 1914 as 'the last day of Ireland's ancient regime' and claimed that 'this was not just the beginning of a war but the end of a nation'. Later, in his seminal *Twilight of the Ascendancy* (1987), he reiterated that 'In all too many houses in 1919 the young master was no more than a memory and a photograph in uniform on a side table.'[2] It is not difficult to understand how or why the myth originated and was advanced. By the end of 1914, after less than five months of fighting, the British and Irish peerage and baronetage had suffered the deaths of 6 peers and 16 baronets, while the sons of 95 peers and 82 baronets had been killed.[3] The point has earlier been made that of over 500 families listed in Burke's *Landed Gentry of Ireland* and *Baronetage & Peerage*, 82 per cent were represented at the Front by at least one member – confined to father, son, grandson – and of these around 25 per cent were killed in action or later died of wounds.[4]

Peter Martin in his more specific study of the Irish nobility found that 27 per cent of his sample group of 109 nobles who were mobilised were killed; significantly, his sample revealed a 39 per cent loss of heirs.[5] Therefore, statistics show that the Irish (and wider British) aristocracy suffered proportionately more casualties than any other class.[6] That was inevitable given the early 'over-the-top' military strategy adopted by the ground forces that catapulted aristocratic officers into the gale of unprecedented carnage produced by weapons of mass destruction. On 16 November 1914, as the battle of Ypres drew to a close, Lord Desmond FitzGerald wrote to his Aunt Dolly: 'The casualties have been so awful that I shall not find more than two officers out of the 30 that started with me and not so many as 100 men out of the original lot.'[7] There were twelve peers or sons of peers in the Irish Guards regiment who sailed with him for France in August 1914.[8] Fergus Forbes, son of the Earl of Granard, was the first to die, killed at Mons on 24 August.[9] Norman Leslie was killed in October 1914.[10] Sir Richard Levinge of Knockdrin Castle had been in France less than three weeks when he was shot in the neck and died at Ypres. By 1917, the heirs to the titles of Westmeath, Clifden, Monck, Templetown, Valentia, Ashtown and Killanin had all been killed.

The losses suffered by individual aristocratic families were great. Of the eight sons of the fourth Baron De Freyne of Frenchpark (by his two marriages), six served, three were killed in action and one died a prisoner of war.[11] Of the five sons of Duc de Stacpoole, two were killed and one returned so severely wounded that his father later claimed: 'I fear he will never be his former self again.'[12] Three sons of the Earl of Bessborough served. Vere, the eldest survived, and succeeded his father in 1920, but Cyril died of wounds received on the opening day of the battle of Loos on 25 September 1915, riddled by machine gun fire, while Bertie was severely wounded by shell fire on 5 May 1915 and played no further role in the war.

Even these few examples provide some sense of why grief and loss would permeate such an isolated self-contained community (not denying that grief pervaded all classes). As early as 1915, Douglas Hyde lamented:

Nearly everyone I know in the army has been killed. Poor Lord de Freyne and his brother were shot the same day and buried in one grave ... MacDermott of Coolavin, my nearest neighbour, has lost his eldest son shot dead in the Dardanelles. All the gentry have suffered. *Nobless oblige.* They have behaved magnificently.[13]

Hyde's letter typified the early stoicism towards heroic death that the landed class portrayed. When Lieutenant Frederick Trench of Woodlawn in Galway died from wounds on 16 November 1916, his mother received the standard letter from his commanding officer telling her of Frederick's 'noble' death, reassuring her that he had every comfort in his last hours, that he had been attended by 'a most able surgeon', given 'rest and warmth', hot drinks and hot water bottles and placed near a fire, and he concluded by assuring her that: 'He never grumbled, and I have seen few who bore pain so bravely, or with such cheerful patience. I thought you might like to know that he had friends near him at the last, and people who were fond of him and would have done anything to save him.'[14] His mother praised her son's fortitude and, by extension, showed her own when she replied to a message of sympathy from Sir Hubert Warren: 'Though he loved every minute of his life, he never feared death and was pleased to do what he could for his God, King and country.'[15] But public stoicism undoubtedly gave way to great private sadness behind closed doors, where the emotional pain suffered by those loved ones left behind was most acutely felt.[16] Baroness De Freyne died in 1923 aged sixty-six; a family friend, Father Edward Pereira, writing in sympathy to her daughter, Lily, could not help suggesting that her death was hastened by the burden of the war:

First Reggie, who had more than made good the slips of the past, and George, a life of singular promise – so straight, so unselfish, so strong. But there was much still to bear. Dear little Ernest, one of the most winning characters I have ever met; and then the long drawn out agony when old Thomas [also known as Fulke] was missing, with no word of news; the short-lived joy when it was known that he was alive and well, the expectation of his speedy return, all making the blow greater when the news came of his death.[17]

Connections in grief reached across the Irish Sea. Lord Desmond FitzGerald's social circle included his first cousin Lt Col Charles Duncombe, 2nd Earl of Feversham, killed in 1916 when commanding the 21st Batallion of the King's Royal Rifles. (Because his grandfather had died only the year before, the family were now left with two sets of death duties and a ten-year old heir and so the great house – Duncombe Park – that they could no longer afford to maintain became a girls' boarding school.) The FitzGerald's chief financial adviser to the Leinster estate, Baron Kinnaird, suffered the death of his eldest son, Douglas, killed in only the third month of fighting, and another son killed in 1917. Yvo Charteris, son of the Earl of Wemyss, who, as noted previously, was father of Desmond's brother Edward, was killed in October 1915, just six weeks after leaving Eton; his older brother, Ego, was killed in Egypt in April 1916. Wemyss, who before the war would have been described as a heartless cad, was deeply affected; his daughter wrote: 'Poor Papa is most piteous – heartbroken and just like a child – tears pouring down his cheeks and so naively astonished. I think he really loved Evo the most of his children and was so proud and hopeful about him.'[18] Percy, the only child of George Wyndham, the Irish Chief Secretary who had revolutionised the transfer of landownership, and distant cousin of Lord Desmond, was killed in the first year of fighting. In total, Madeline Wyndham, George's mother, lost five grandsons. Lady Cynthia Asquith summed up the feelings of an aristocratic generation: 'Oh why was I born for this time? Before one is thirty to have known more dead than living people.'[19] And later in 1918: 'I am beginning to rub my eyes at the prospect of peace. I think it will require more courage than anything that has gone before . . . One will have to look at long vistas again, instead of short ones, and one will at last fully recognise that the dead are not only dead for the duration of the war.'[20]

It was no different in Ireland. After the war Lady Fingall of Killeen Castle lamented: 'I used to think and say, during the war, that if ever that list of dead and wounded would cease, I would never mind anything or grumble at anything again. But when the Armistice came at last, we seemed drained of all feeling. And one felt nothing.'[21] Various members of the Leslie family later told how neither Sir John nor his wife, Leonie, ever got over the death of Norman. On Armistice Day, Sir John wrote poignantly to his wife: 'I wish I was with you to embrace you . . . I feel excited almost to insomnia. The news is the most wonderful since the world began,' to which he added a few days later: 'I should like to go to Armentières in the Spring, not in cold dreary winter, and lay spring flowers on our boy's grave, both of us together. His spirit knows what is going on, and that his life was not lost in vain.'[22] When Anita Leslie and her brother arrived at Glaslough House for the first time in 1919, she found that 'One room frightened us. It had been that of our Uncle Norman, who had been killed five years previously and it was kept just as he had left it . . . a bunch of withered flowers lay on the pillow.'[23] All too often public faces had to hide grieving hearts. Sir John's desire to lay spring flowers on his son's grave reflected the emotional needs of families to bring closure to the death of their sons.[24]

At least the Leslies could take some comfort from the fact that Norman's body was recovered and buried in a marked grave. It was a comfort denied so many. After the Armistice in November 1918, the Imperial War Graves Commission was charged with examining the battle-scarred landscape for the remains of men killed in battle. Almost one quarter, 71 out of the total of 270 British and Irish nobles or their sons killed, had no known grave. Lord De Freyne's body was never found. Neither was that of Edward Stafford-King-Harman of Rockingham. Family lore had it that his widow, Olive, made a comment to a friend in 1981 that she did not know what had happened to Edward's body, to which her friend replied: 'Oh my goodness, I could have

3.1 Olive Pakenham Mahon with baby daughter, Lettice, born shortly after Olive's husband, Edward Stafford-King-Harman, was killed on 6 November 1914. Edward's body was one of the very many never recovered.

told you, my brother was at the other end of the trench. He was blown to bits by a shell and there wasn't anything to find.'[25] It was apocryphal but in 1914 the young and pregnant Olive's loss was very real. Even tangible memorials were not always easy to face. In May 1919, Lady Kenmare visited her son Dermot's grave and later described to Lady Desborough how it was 'all so beyond comprehension, the wide battlefields, so awful, so terrible; the strange hush over all that devastation, the grim ruins, the piteous little crosses standing here and there in utter loneliness; one's mind and soul seemed to break.'[26]

A great deal has been written about nationalist Ireland's antipathy to returning war veterans, especially during the revolutionary years of 1920–23 but it should not be exaggerated.[27] It is not difficult to find evidence of communities outside the Big House – (former) tenants, local businessmen, clergymen, professionals and so on – sharing in the grief of the local aristocratic family. Sir Richard Levinge, 10th Baronet, whose ancestral home was Knockdrin in Co Westmeath, was one of five brothers to go to war. On 23 October 1914, the 1st Life Guards were sent to relieve the 10th Hussars in the Zandvoorde trenches. The following morning, he was shot dead by a sniper.[28] He left behind a wife and a three-year-old heir. Lord Dunsany heard from a local: 'Sure, when Sir Richard was killed, the old people round Knockdrin all cried themselves sick.'[29] The anecdote is unauthenticated and it may be significant that emphasis was put on 'the old people' but as historian Eugene Dunne concludes: 'It probably fairly reflected the esteem in which he was held locally.'[30] While there were some minor agrarian offences reported on the Knockdrin estate at the height of the Civil War, the castle was not attacked.[31] When the young heir, the 11th Baronet, returned in August 1923, after the Civil War, the *Irish Times* reported that triumphal arches were erected on the demesne entrance and the whole estate community – tenants, servants and demesne employees – all turned out with other local residents to welcome him.[32] The key to understanding this is that Knockdrin continued as a major employment centre in the locality.

Similarly, when news reached Co Kildare of the death of Lord Desmond FitzGerald in 1916, the Kildare Committee of Agriculture, the Kildare Distress Committee and most notably the nationalist-dominated Kildare County Council all passed resolutions of sympathy; the latter read: 'We are confident that the sympathetic knowledge which is shared by an appreciative and grateful people, that he gave his life for his country after a brief but glorious period of service will tend to mitigate in some degree the great sorrow which they feel for the early ending of a promising and brilliant career.'[33] The very next resolution passed by the county council unequivocally condemned the leaders of the 1916 Rising: 'We ... strongly deprecate the recent deplorable action of a section of our countrymen in resorting to force of arms.' Afterwards, in the town of Maynooth the British legion erected a hut in honour of Desmond, the secretary assuring his uncle Lord Frederick that 'The people residing in the vicinity of the square have not the least objection to the proposed building and wish it every success.'[34] It was a very long time afterwards that a memorial in the square was dedicated to the Maynooth rebels of 1916.

War memorials to another generation of aristocrats were not only erected in Protestant churches, but they were also installed in public areas. Donal Hall has shown that 'The death of Roger Bellingham [in Louth] triggered a remarkable outpouring of sympathy for the family with obituaries emphasising both his religiosity and nationalism.'[35] In 1920, his father, Sir Henry Bellingham, met only public and cross-confessional sympathy when he erected a memorial in Castlebellingham village. It was at the very time that the War of Independence was moving into a violent phase, but years later even Louth IRA veteran James McGuill made the point in his Bureau of Military History witness statement that Bellingham's popularity 'deserved' to be commemorated.[36] The memorial was in the shape of a Celtic cross, the same as the Great War memorial unveiled in Bray, Co Wicklow, in 1920; it was a symbol that could be used by all traditions.[37]

There were, of course, many families for whom the war was a major turning point. Take for example the case of Lt Robert Heard, heir to the Pallastown estate near Belgooly in Co Cork, who in March 1916 returned home to recover from injury, coinciding with his coming-of-age. There were still tenants on the estate who had not purchased their holdings because of wartime restrictions on sales. In time honoured fashion they presented Heard with a silver salver and an illuminated address offering congratulations 'on your pluck and courage in entering the Army and fighting for your country in the trenches in Flanders before reaching your majority and [we] are thankful to providence that you have recovered from the serious wounds you received'.[38] The rest of the tenants' address was more traditional; it focused firmly on the everyday nuts and bolts of estate management and the expectation of continued paternalism, reflecting the traditional dialectic that had existed on Irish estates for generations:

Your family has been long and favourably known as indulgent landlords, large employers of labour, and liberal supporters of every movement for improving the position of your tenants. They have always been foremost in promoting and encouraging shows and sports and every charitable and benevolent undertaking in this town and district.

According to Fergal Browne, Heard had managed the estate in a progressive manner: he increased employment (no doubt aided by the agricultural demands of the war), and presented prizes for the local agricultural shows in Kinsale. At the Front, he displayed 'splendid courage and fearlessness in face of danger' and 'the greatest bravery and initiative' at Passchendaele in October 1917.[39] He was awarded the Military Cross, injured several times more, acquired bronchitis from the conditions he lived in and suffered significant lung damage during a gas attack, which eventually contributed to his death from septic pneumonia in March 1919 in the military hospital in Purfleet, Essex. He had no heir. In December 1920, Pallastown House and estate were sold, purchased by John Jagoe, owner of Jagoe Mills in Kinsale.[40] (This was part of a growing post-war trend where several country houses were bought by timber merchants who had prospered during the war and who saw the potential in demesne woodlands.) Browne contends: 'The only certainty is that his death contributed significantly to the breaking of a family connection with Kinsale and the surrounding district which had lasted over 300 years.'[41] But had Heard lived, the result might not have been any different. It was not his death but his debts that eventually suffocated Pallastown.

As we have seen, powerful economic forces were already undermining the aristocracy before 1914 and they were compounded by developments during the war years. It is no exaggeration to state that David Lloyd George detested the British aristocracy and what they stood for. On 11 October 1913, at Bedford, he had asserted his determination to break the land monopoly: 'to free British land from landlordism and get the people back on it'. 'Oh! these Dukes', he proclaimed, 'how they oppress us!' To strengthen his argument about the evils of landlordism he turned to Ireland, where he exaggeratedly claimed: 'Millions have been driven away from the land by legal process.'[42] Lloyd George had begun his crusade some years before; David Cannadine considers his People's Budget of 1909 a major turning point in the aristocracy's history of decline: 'This was not just a budget designed to raise money from the rich,' Cannadine argues, 'it was the landed rich who were its principal target and victim.'[43] During the course of the war, they became more susceptible as various forms of taxation rose at unprecedented levels, income tax from 4 per cent in 1914 to almost 25 per cent by 1919, death duties which had been introduced in 1894 at rates of 8 per cent, stood at 15 per cent by 1914, and 40 per cent by 1919.[44] Some relief was offered for the loss of sons and heirs but not enough for some families to avoid catastrophe. For example, in July 1915, Charles Annesley Acton of Kilmacurragh House in Wicklow died from his wounds received at Loos. His brother, Reginald, inherited the estate. In May 1916, Reginald was killed in action at Ypres. His young wife of three years, Isabel, was now widowed with a two-year-old son and a heavily incumbered estate. Fidelma Byrne estimated that 'the cumulative death duties equated to 120 per cent of the value of the estate' and soberly concluded: 'The estate never fully recovered from the Great War.'[45] The financial pressure became too much for Isabel and after 200 years of residence the Acton family left Kilmacurragh.[46]

Charleville, also in Wicklow, had a similar end. By the 1920s, following the death of Charles Monck at the Front, death duties and other incumbrances on the family estate had accumulated to almost £30,000. In 1925, Viscount Monck, then 'in delicate health', and now heirless, appointed J.E. McDermott, the estate solicitor, to oversee estate management. In 1926, the estate income was £4,500 while expenditure on estate and house maintenance, taxes and other expenses amounted to £3,600. In 1932, the contents of Charleville were sold by private auction realising in the region of £11,000, and the following year Viscount Monck was forced to sell off Dublin property to pay another charge of £10,000 that had been created under a settlement of 1874. Eventually, in 1939 Viscount Monck had no choice but to sell Charleville and its demesne. The death of Charles Monck at the Front did not make the decline of his family estate inevitable; that had already been precipitated by the wider economic crisis that faced most landlord families, but it certainly was the last straw.[47]

Similarly, when Norman Leslie was killed it was after his older brother, Shane, had converted to Catholicism and nationalism, and consequently was disinherited by his father. That had been at tremendous financial cost: the leases of hundreds of tenants in several counties including Monaghan, Donegal

3.2 and 3.3 Kilmacurragh House, Co Wicklow, shortly before the war and in ruins c.2010. The cumulative death duties incurred during the war equated to 120 per cent of the value of the estate from which it never recovered.

and Leitrim had to be reconveyanced because the Leslies had still not sold all of their estates.[48] With Norman's death, his brother wrote that 'Taxes had to be met for thousands of pounds, levied on what he had only legally "enjoyed" as a prospect.'[49] The Leslie London house at 10 Great Cumberland Place in London was too great a burden to carry.[50] After the estates had been sold, Sir John, like many more Irish aristocrats, invested all of the capital in a fanciful

3.4 Leslie family photograph, taken to mark the golden wedding anniversary of Sir John and Lady Constance Leslie, 1905. Sir John II and his wife, Leonie, sister of Lady Jennie Churchill, are second and third from left.

share portfolio designed by Ernest Cassels (with little investment in Ireland), which lost them a considerable fortune in the post-war economic collapse. In 1919, when Anita Leslie visited, she could already see signs of encroaching neglect everywhere in Glaslough: 'We found bedrooms that had not been used for years, and a cobwebby box-room lined with enormous hanging cupboards designed to hold dresses of the last century.'[51]

Declining finances, long periods of abandonment during the war years when the family resided in London, and quite possibly lethargy due to financial and emotional strain meant Glaslough House had not been cared for as it had once been.

2. 'A domestic controversy'

At a political level, the war drained the southern unionist movement.[52] The IUA quickly disintegrated; in 1918 *Notes from Ireland* recognised that 'Since the war broke out the political work of the Alliance has ceased, and only the slenderest official threads maintain the life and continuity of the organisation.'[53] By May 1915, twenty-nine members of the executive committee had been mobilised.[54] On 15 July 1916, a fortnight into the battle of the Somme, the list of twenty-one absentees from an IUA executive meeting included Lords Arran, Oranmore, and Wicklow, as well as William Mahon of Castlegar, E.J. Beaumont-Nesbitt of Tubberdaly, H.V. MacNamara of Ennistymon, C.E. Vandeleur of Kilrush, J.M. Wilson of Currygrane and Colonel O'Callaghan Westropp of Kiltanon. The only nobles present were Lords Cloncurry, Langford, Monck and Rathdonnell. The organisation boasted that very many of its members had 'experienced the mingled pride and sorrow which is the heritage of the thousands that have loyally and devotedly borne a share in the great struggle for king and country,' but in the same breath they appealed 'to their fellow Loyalists of Great Britain for sympathy and support and for the protection not only of Imperial interests but also of the liberties and rights of the loyal minority of the south and west of Ireland' against the rise of Sinn Féin, which espoused a more radical and separatist Irish nationalism.[55]

The leading southern Unionist, Lord Midleton, concentrated his attention on the war effort and his old world chivalry convinced him that 'It would be indecent for us to enter upon a domestic controversy when our whole energy should be devoted to the furtherance of the war.'[56] His reminiscences spoke for very many others of his class: 'Practically every civilian of experience found himself called upon to assist the government in some capacity, and I was no exception. Those four years of war were, consequently, as fully occupied as any period in my life.'[57] But not with the unionist cause in southern Ireland, where the movement went into irreversible political retreat.[58]

Political withdrawal was also in part due to the aristocracy's dismay and disillusionment with British government muddling, Asquith's weakness and what Sir Henry Bellingham angrily described as 'Carson's sedition'.[59] When, in May 1916, Lloyd George offered Carson the 1914 Home Rule Act with a proposal for the exclusion of the six north-eastern counties, they more or less closed the deal on partition, without a great deal of opposition from Redmond (and, it should be added, without official sanction of the British cabinet.) On 6 June, Carson brought the proposal to the Ulster Unionist Council (UUC), where it was accepted by the delegates, including those of Cavan, Donegal and Monaghan, the three counties to be excluded, but they had been deceived into believing that they were working in the interest of the empire and that after the war there would be a return to the *status quo ante*.[60] Carson, rather disingenuously, proclaimed 'this sacrifice' as 'the greatest piece of lasting evidence of their devoted, unselfish loyalty to the King, Constitution and Empire' that he had encountered in his political life.[61] By the time that Somerset Saunderson, the Cavan representative, found out in London that Lloyd George had acted without cabinet approval, it was too late.[62] According to Lord Oranmore, a meeting of Irish peers, including Hercules Rowley, 4th Baron Langford, and Valentine Browne, 5th Earl of Kenmare, was held towards the end of June 1916 to counter the proposal to introduce Home Rule with exclusion. On 26 June, a deputation of the IUA was received by five cabinet ministers: Bonar Law, Lord Lansdowne (president of the IUA who had corroborated Lloyd George's deceit for Saunderson), Edgar Gascoyne-Cecil, George Curzon and Joseph Chamberlain. They listened 'sympathetically'. The following day the deputation met with Asquith and Lloyd George. They based 'their whole case on the objections from an Imperial point of view', handing over Ireland to a government that could not control Sinn Féin, they contended, would be disastrous to the long-term prospects of the empire. Their reception was, however, less sympathetic than the day before. Oranmore was resentful of Lloyd George's deviousness: '[he] evidently had tried to promise the Ulstermen that their exclusion was permanent, and the Nationalists that it was provisional.'[63]

Even though Lloyd George's proposals were not implemented, their acceptance by the UUC led to that body's continued adherence to the principle of exclusion, chiefly espoused at the 1917–18 Irish Convention called by Lloyd George in another attempt to settle the Irish question.[64] Chaired by Sir Horace Plunkett, and comprised of Nationalists, southern Unionists, Ulster Unionists, Labour representatives and church hierarchies, the Convention was boycotted by Sinn Féin, and its proceedings would solidly reveal the fractious nature of Unionism. On 21 July, a week before the Convention opened, Lord Oranmore met with the Ulster Unionists and recorded afterwards in his journal: 'I don't much like them. They are a very dour lot and seemed to have sent for us more for the purpose of informing us of their decisions, than of consulting with us.'[65] And on 20 April 1918: 'We southern Unionists have done our best to secure a settlement on terms which would give the Unionists some share in the future government of the country. If Ulster had been reasonable, we might have succeeded.'[66] Having achieved their goal, Ulster Unionists had no intention of being reasonable. When Midleton called for an all-Ireland parliament, he was derided by them and by July 1918 he realised there was no way back, so he wrote to Lord Courtown: 'It is therefore clear that the Ulster leaders, believing that Home Rule is inevitable, are prepared to minimise it by accepting the best terms they can, which terms unfortunately will leave southern Unionists at the mercy of the Nationalists and Sinn Féiners.'[67] Midleton was so disillusioned with Lloyd George's Irish policy that he refused the lord lieutenancy in 1918. The IUA split with a dozen or so Irish peers resigning office, including Barrymore, Arran, Donoughmore, Wicklow, Desart, Sligo, Courtown, Rathdonnell and Oranmore, and establishing the Unionist Anti-Partition League. Thus, by the time the War of Independence broke out in 1919–20, the southern unionist movement was in disarray and the Unionists of Monaghan, Cavan and Donegal were left to regret their decision of June 1916. On 10 March 1920, a month after the Government of Ireland Bill was introduced to parliament, proposing to set up two parliaments, Lord Farnham, not long home in Cavan after a period as a prisoner of war, introduced the following resolution to the UUC:

> That this council abiding by its covenant refuses to accept any form of government which does not include the whole provincial province of Ulster and calls upon its parliamentary leaders to take such steps as may be necessary to see that the term Northern Ireland in the permanent Bill is altered to include the whole province of Ulster.[68]

The resolution was rejected; the three county delegates resigned 'protesting against the breach of the Ulster covenant by the UUC in deserting their fellow covenanters'.[69] In April 1920, Frederick Crawford, the organiser of the Larne gun-running, published a pamphlet entitled *Why I Voted for the Six Counties* in which he argued:

> There are 890,800 Protestants in the whole of the nine counties of Ulster. There are 70,510 Protestants and 260,655 Roman Catholics in the three counties. I cannot believe the Protestants in the three counties are willing to swamp 820,370 Protestants merely for the satisfaction of knowing they are all going down to disaster in the same boat.[70]

It must have been galling to Lord Farnham when Crawford wrote to him to 'think impersonally' as he read the pamphlet: 'You know that there is no personal sacrifice including my own life that I would not make to save you people from being left out, if it were possible to do so and safeguard Ulster as a whole for the Protestant Faith and against being out under a Dublin parliament.'[71] Farnham was not impressed and told Hugh Montgomery that 'Our people look upon themselves as betrayed and deserted.'[72] His fellow Cavan aristocrat Somerset Saunderson left Castlesaunderson and emigrated to England; his descendant later wrote: 'Being himself the most punctilious of men, Somerset's feelings may be imagined when he saw his ancestral home and family estates handed over to his bitterest enemies by the country which he and his forebears had served so loyally and so long. "Now", he said, "I have no country."'[73] Jonathan Cherry points out that Farnham was later a solitary voice in the House of Lords in his opposition to the Government of Ireland Bill in 1920 that would make provision for the new state of Northern Ireland, mockingly dismissed by Lord Curzon, the Foreign Secretary, as a relic of the past, clinging to past glories that were obsolete.[74] By then, the southern Irish aristocracy had clearly lost credibility as well as any semblance of power.

3.5 Arthur Maxwell, 11th Baron Farnham, of Farnham House in Co Cavan, third from left in back row, as a POW at Karlsruhe in Germany, 1918.

3. 'A lop-sided community at home'

During the darkest days of the war, young Aline Henry, granddaughter of Francis Henry of Richardstown Castle in Co Louth, spent four years in the German-occupied town of Saint-Mihiel. When she thought of home, 'She looked forward to music, dances, and all kinds of sport in Ireland after the war.'[75] But by 1919, when she returned home, who had Aline to dance with? As her neighbour Vera Bellingham, from Bellingham Castle, confided to her diary: 'I never seem to meet a man to speak to these times.'[76] At the far end of Ireland, in Clare, Colonel O'Callaghan-Westropp proclaimed that the war had resulted in 'a lop-sided community at home over-stocked with women, the very young and the very old.'[77] Long widowhoods and spinsterhood became the lot of so many aristocratic women. Amongst these was Cecily Catherine Clements of Killadoon in Kildare. Because of the war, Cecily's debutante season was postponed until 1920 and when she was eventually presented at Buckingham Palace there was a noticeable absence of young eligible male partners. Cecily never married and lived out the rest of her life in the family home.[78] She encapsulated J.M. Winter's conclusion: 'The most severely depleted social groups were the most privileged, whose marriage patterns were inevitably distorted by the absence of so many marriageable young men.'[79]

After the war, the remnants of the Irish aristocracy and gentry, no different to their peers in Britain, found themselves marooned in a new, more democratic social world that some resented as plutocratic and vulgar, brought on by the emergence of parvenu wealth. In 1922, Lord Dunraven, for example, despaired that 'The war killed society. The old order passes.' He lamented that the London season from then on included those who 'before the war, would not have formed part of what the press is pleased to term society' and thus the end of 'the refining influence that alone can counteract the crude, ostentatious vulgarity of mere wealth'.[80] Dunraven's observations may have been a stark reminder of the narrow aristocratic mindset and inherent snobbery, but it should not be misconstrued that the aristocracy withdrew completely from society – far from it: the Dublin summer season with the Royal Dublin Society Horse Show as its highlight continued – but even if the aristocracy had the inclination to return to the *belle époque* of the Edwardian era, most did not have the wealth to partake in London society as they had done in the past, while at home, lavish dinners, balls and hunting parties became a rarity (further inhibited by the conflicts of 1919–23.) It was not until 28 May 1921 that Lord Oranmore confided: 'We had our first dinner party since the War on Thursday.'[81] Some years later, Elizabeth Bowen admitted: 'We all eat and drink a good deal less and would not find it any shame in a host not to offer what he has not got.'[82] They were by no means destitute, they were just more impoverished.

Back in December 1914, Dick Hely-Hutchinson was at the Front only a couple of months when, in a letter to his mother, he remarked: 'I suppose the ponds are alive with ducks and pheasants, although at present I feel as if I never want to hear another gun of any sort go off.'[83] It might make for an interesting study to determine what, if any, connection there was between the experience of war and a decline in the popularity of shooting as a sport amongst the aristocratic men who survived the trenches.[84] Even if they were interested, the outbreak of the War of Independence made hunting impossible; the carrying of firearms, for example, became illegal. In 1921, only two guests signed the visitors' book at Dromoland Castle in Clare, compared to twenty-four in 1913; the explanation: 'No shoot, no guns allowed!'[85] In 1923, Lord Castletown bemoaned the passing of shooting parties: 'We used in those days to have the most cheery shooting parties at home . . . [and at] Glenart with its two kind hosts, great woodcock shooting and high pheasants . . . and sometimes my dear old friend Ormonde used to ask me to lodge on Slievenamon, where we had all to get up an hour before the usual time, for the days were short and the woods extensive.'[86] 'Alas!', he declared, 'those jolly days are over, and many of those kind hosts have gone west, never to be replaced, and the lovely old houses are sold, or shut up or burnt.'[87] Similarly, Lady Fingall recollected that amongst the aristocracy in Meath: 'The old pattern struggled to re-emerge. House parties and cricket matches and hunting could be arranged, some of the old verve regained, but the political situation which was bad and growing worse, intruded, and the carelessness of pre-war gaiety would not return.'[88]

Foxhunting, probably the pre-eminent aristocratic sport, was similarly affected during the nine-year period from 1914 to 1923.[89] As the war progressed, there were fewer participants to take to the field; in 1916, an article in *Country Life* described the situation in Britain which was just as relevant to Ireland: 'Distinguished officers who followed the chase have returned to the

Service, and practically all the hunting families are now represented in the field of action or are performing important war work in this country.'[90] When hunting in Ireland was resurrected after the war, it came under threat from political revolutionaries and agrarianists as the dangerous cocktail of land and politics once again came to the fore. This was not new in Ireland. During the Land War era of the 1880s, 'stopping the hunt' had been a favoured tactic, or, indeed, a sport of sorts, popular with Land Leaguers who wanted to threaten landlords.[91] Thus, in January 1919, the month when the first Dáil Éireann was established by Sinn Féin Teachtaí Dála (TDs - deputies), the Kildare Master of Foxhounds received a letter from the secretary of the Kilcock Sinn Féin club to warn him, 'He would not be permitted to hunt until the interned prisoners were released.'[92]

That same month, at Ballykilcavan in Queen's County, a hunt was abandoned because an 'order of the Sinn Féin executive' had been 'published on the previous day at various chapel gates in the county'. On 5 March, the Muskerry Foxhounds in east Cork were set upon by a gang of fifty to sixty Sinn Féin supporters wielding hurleys and sticks and they were forced to retreat to shouts of 'Now you will obey Sinn Féin and the orders of our executive.'[93] Also in March, the *Irish Field* reported that the Sinn Féin campaign had 'stopped every hunt of consequence in Ireland outside of Ulster'.[94] It was certainly the case in the main hunting counties of Kildare, Kilkenny, Meath, Westmeath and Galway.[95] The last meet of the West Carbery hounds was held on St Patrick's Day 1919 and Patrick Buckland tells us that 'For Miss [Edith] Somerville life did not return to normal until 1924.'[96] The close association of hunting with those loyal to the British administration in Ireland motivated young IRA members such as Michael O'Kelly in Kildare; in his BMH witness statement he recalled that he and his comrades had stopped the hunt to warn 'this class in the county that they could not indulge their hostility to Irish ideals . . . with impunity.'[97] An IRA volunteer in Meath associated the local hunt with 'the so-called aristocrats, idlers, who have no occupation, and who have never done a day's work in their lives' – ironically much the same perception the aristocracy had of the IRA – and who were 'almost without exception, bitterly anti-Irish'.[98]

Not everyone wanted to stop the hunt, no more than everyone wanted to take up arms, or burn Big Houses. There were those whose livelihoods were at stake. In February 1918, a correspondent to the *Tuam Herald* argued: 'The stopping of hunting because of the detention of the political prisoners is one of the most stupid acts of suicidal folly on the part of the Irish people that can be conceived. It is cutting our own throats.'[99] In Kildare, where the hunt club comprised Catholic farmers and shopkeepers and professionals as well as the local aristocracy, the attitude was very much the same amongst the townsmen of Naas, Athy, Maynooth and Newbridge. For example, farmers gathered in Naas in February 1919 to request the hunt club to continue hunting and not to abandon the annual Punchestown race meeting as that would be detrimental, they argued, to 'a sport which is the first economic interest to all farmers in Co Kildare'.[100] However, Sinn Féin radicalism won out after Tom Harris's emotive speech drew on memories embedded in ancestral grievances of evicted farmers during the Land War who had, he pronounced, to beg local landlords to leave them with a roof over their heads.[101] Hunting in Kildare was stopped for the season, and the Punchestown annual race festival had to be abandoned in both 1919 and 1920. However, when both were reinvigorated in the years after independence, they were still led by the old landed elite, as was the horse racing industry at national level.[102] An important point in all of this is that in the complex matrix of social relations that made up rural Ireland the aristocracy were certainly not despised by all, nor, as we shall see, by the pragmatic and conservative revolutionaries in government who made the connection between a resident aristocracy and local economic prosperity and employment.

4. 'Reparation for the past'

From the Big House perspective, there was another very significant development during the war years: the re-emergence of the land question (if it had ever gone away).[103] There were several factors in the resurgence. Almost immediately upon the outbreak of war the British Treasury stopped land purchase, its priority now being to finance the war effort. As it was, there had been huge delays in processing purchases under the 1903 and 1909 Land Acts because of inevitable logistical difficulties – there was such a vast number of holdings to be transferred that it was impossible for civil servants to cope with the scale. In 1918, the *Report of the Proceedings of the Irish Convention*, basing its findings on Irish Land Commission statistics, estimated that there were just short of 101,000 pending cases covering an area of 3.3 million acres valued at £23.9 million.[104] During the war, these tenant farmers became aggrieved at having to pay rents when they felt they should be farm proprietors, and during the 1920–23 period many paid no rents at all, using the social chaos as a pretext, and there were undoubtedly others who anticipated an independent Republican government doing away with annuities altogether.[105] In January 1918, the sale of the Leconfield estate in Clare to 276 farmers was the only case of land purchase that month, and the Inspector General of the RIC reported: 'There are . . . signs of growing irritation at the prolonged suspension of land purchase, particularly in counties where grazing farms abound,' further noting that Sinn Féin had become associated with demands for the redistribution of such lands especially in the western counties of Galway, Roscommon, Sligo and Clare.[106]

When land purchase was resumed from 1 April 1919 to 31 March 1920, roughly the first year of the War of Independence, the Irish Land Commission only compounded rural frustrations by refusing advances to 3,568 potential purchasers on grounds that their holdings were too poor to sustain annuity repayments. In another 13,196 cases, the Commission refused to advance the full purchase price because of insufficient collateral.[107] These two categories were made up of people with land who obviously required more to make their farms viable. Moreover, by 31 March 1919, while 3,591 evicted tenants – or their representatives – from the Land War era (post-1879) had been reinstated as purchasing tenants, there were still thousands waiting a settlement,[108] perhaps up to 3,000 families 'scattered from end to end of Ireland' according to agrarian activist and politician Laurence Ginnell.[109] From 1919, evicted tenants' associations became more active in agitating for the redistribution of lands, sometimes taking local initiative, repossessing evicted lands, or to use the more opprobrious term 'grabbing' them.[110]

An even greater social problem related to congestion was the prevalence of uneconomic holdings. In the early 1920s, the Land Commission would decide that 23 acres of mixed land should be the standard size of a farm required to support a family in a degree of comfort. It is very difficult to estimate with certainty the number of farms below that size in Ireland after the war because returns of agricultural statistics divided them into brackets of between 10 and 15 acres, between 15 and 30 acres, or more. Equally, a 15-acre farmer in pasture-rich Meath was much better off than a 50-acre farmer in the boglands of Connemara;

everything depended on the quality of the land as opposed to the quantity. But, to provide some context, if one takes farm size alone as an indicator there were 226,468 farms below 15 acres in 1917, which was almost 40 per cent of the total number of farms in the country; and 112,787 were less than 5 acres. At the same time, there were 57,476 farmers with between 100 and 200 acres (10 per cent), 23,159 with 200 to 500 acres (4 per cent) and 1,967 with 500 or more acres (0.3 per cent), and it may be no coincidence that this latter figure roughly corresponds to the number of houses and demesnes that were recorded in 1906.[111] Put another way: in 1917, 65 per cent of the total number of holdings in Ireland were between 1 and 30 acres in size, but they accounted for only 24 per cent of Irish land, 38.5 per cent of land was held in holdings of between 30 and 100 acres and 37.4 per cent in holdings over 100 acres.[112]

Uneconomic holdings were most prevalent in the geographic area that came under the jurisdiction of the Congested Districts Board (CDB) – the

Table 1.1 Number and size of holdings in Ireland in 1917

	Leinster	Munster	Ulster	Connaught	Ireland
Less than 1 acre	39,131	33,261	32,022	8,373	112,787
More than 1 and less than 5 acres	13,085	9,678	16,387	8,469	47,619
More than 5 and less than 10 acres	10,645	8,076	27,920	19,421	66,062
More than 10 and less than 15 acres	8,211	7,062	25,072	19,411	59,756
More than 15 and less than 30 acres	18,009	20,221	48,593	36,306	123,129
More than 30 and less than 50 acres	13,268	20,494	24,555	14,071	72,388
More than 50 and less than 100 acres	13,055	22,406	15,427	6,588	57,476
More than 100 and less than 200 acres	6,889	9,789	4,112	2,369	23,159
More than 200 and less than 500 acres	2,966	2,901	1,153	1,211	8,231
More than 500 acres	666	481	310	510	1,967
Totals	*125,925*	*134,369*	*195,551*	*116,729*	*572,574*

Source: *Agricultural statistics for Ireland with detailed report for the year 1917* [cmd. 1316], HC 1921, lxi. 135, p. xiv.

3.6 View of the village of Graigue in Co Galway, a typically congested area in the west of Ireland that required a land redistribution scheme to alleviate the poverty of a dense population of farmers eking a living on small parcels of land.

counties along the western seaboard – which had been established under the 1891 Land Act to devise schemes to alleviate poverty in a region exceptionally impoverished by western European standards.[113]

Economic stagnation had not been helped by the British Treasury freezing the acquisition of estates by the CDB from 1915, which meant that the acquisition and redistribution of lands for the relief of congestion was halted. The Treasury also withdrew the offers previously made for ninety estates comprising almost 112,000 acres of tenanted lands and 32,500 of untenanted lands, and suspended negotiations for another 69 estates it had earmarked that comprised 123,000 acres.[114] During the war years, the western smallholders who supplemented their meagre incomes as migrant labourers in Britain could not leave home because the war closed emigration outlets. As they had no alternative employment in Ireland, the inspector general of the RIC feared in September 1916 that 'they must be already in straightened circumstances' and noted they 'were full of resentment towards the [British] government'.[115] Therefore, and not for the first time, agrarian grievance, political resentment and land hunger became enmeshed. In 1921, as he retrospectively surveyed the war years, Art

Map 1 The area of the Congested Districts, Ireland.

O'Connor, Director of Agriculture, reminded his Dáil colleagues that 'thousands of young men had been forced to remain in Ireland during the European War, who in ordinary circumstances would have gone to enrich other countries because there was no living for them in their own, and if in their dire need they swarmed on to the land as their only hope, we may condemn but we can at least understand them.'[116]

And this did not just happen along the western seaboard: throughout Ireland the wider agricultural labourer class had traditional grievances that land grabbing would certainly go some way towards alleviating. Traditionally, they had been treated badly by the wealthier farmers, not merely in terms of working conditions, but also in the way they were manipulated with empty promises to provide mass support to the Land League and other later agrarian movements, but then abandoned without compunction when, for instance, the large farmers benefited from the fair rent fixing terms of the 1881 Land Act. The later land purchase acts of 1903 and 1909 and the Labourers' (Ireland) Act 1906 helped to provide much-needed housing improvements, but the purchase acts, by breaking up estates, had another consequence: they resulted in labourer redundancies.[117] For example, under the 1885 Land Act the Duke of Leinster sold one quarter of his estate which, it was reported, had deprived him 'of a large share of his patrimony'; he had to face his labourers and inform them that 'Under the new conditions . . . his power of giving immense employment was crippled and curtailed and that his labour bills must be contracted accordingly.'[118] In February 1904, after the passing of the Wyndham Act, Lord Muskerry told the Lords that labourers had been 'condemned to impoverishment and banishment . . . the operation of the Land Act must inevitably diminish the demand for labour, must diminish the demand for the products of trade and industry, must diminish every kind of employment which is given in a country by the higher classes of the community.'[119]

During the economic boom, farmers, including aristocratic demesne farmers, benefitted from unprecedented prices, but as the Inspector General reported in March 1916, 'greedy farmers' were not disposed 'to share increased profits with their labourers'.[120] As labourers began to organise, rural tensions were exacerbated. In relation to Big House demesne farms: in July 1916, in Galway, sixty labourers on Lord Iveagh's estate looked for an increase of six shillings per week, while on Lord Gough's property they sought four shillings extra per week.[121] In Donegal, in September 1918, twenty-one labourers on the Steward estate got a wage increase of five shillings per week.[122] In January 1919, the Wages Board increased the minimum wage from twenty to twenty-six shillings per week; Lord Oranmore complained that 'less than two years ago the men were happy' with thirteen shillings.[123] In early 1919, there were labourers' strikes in at least fourteen counties. In March, on the Farnham estate in Cavan forty-five workmen went on strike for higher wages and shorter working hours.[124] In December and through the early months of 1920, William Mahon of Castlegar was visited on several occasions by representatives of agricultural labourers demanding wage increases. However, in this case, there was a portentous development when he was shortly afterwards visited by 'landgrabbers', who he could identify, demanding to be sold parcels of land.[125] At this stage, it seems they were willing to pay. In April 1920, an interesting newspaper report on land agitation in the midlands claimed that labourers, well organised by the Land and Labour League and the Irish Transport and General Workers Union (ITGWU), had 'considerable sums of money – from two to three hundred pounds – which they made within the last few years by taking conacre land and rearing pigs and small cattle, which have brought them very remunerative prices. With the money as a nucleus, they insist upon changing their condition from labourers to farmers.'[126] A progressive Land Commission policy might have been able to facilitate this, but instead labourers and smallholders who required additional lands to bring their farms up to a viable level continued to be ignored.

Sinn Féin quickly realised the political capital there was to be gained from preaching land redistribution in a climate edgy with agrarian grievance. Its policy (loosely termed) was popularly articulated by peripatetic organisers such as Laurence Ginnell. Elected MP for Westmeath North in 1906, Ginnell's extreme left-wing agrarian radicalism made him unpopular within his own Irish Parliamentary Party and he was expelled in 1909.[127] After the 1916 Rising he was the only Nationalist MP to swing to Sinn Féin and the following year was elected treasurer of the executive alongside W.T. Cosgrave. In the 1918 general election, he retained his Westmeath seat as a Sinn Féiner and in the year that followed he continued his radical land agitation campaign. He appealed to the disaffected: the evicted tenants; the 'rackrented tenants' who had not been able to purchase their farms because of wartime restrictions or because their landlords preferred 'high rents to prices'; those who loathed the existence of vast grazing ranches; and he decried the working conditions faced by agricultural labourers.[128] He conflated historical grievances with contemporary ones: the landless men wanted 'the distribution of these [untenanted] lands as reparation for the past, for the general good of the country, for historical and other reasons transcending the cash value of the land'.[129] The emotive plight of the evicted tenants was further grist to Ginnell's propaganda wheel: 'The claim of the evicted and their descendants has been, and must until satisfied continue to be, beyond all question the strongest and most urgent of all the victims of the English garrison. The failure to satisfy those claims is the greatest blot on land legislation.'[130]

Given that the land acts had failed both to complete the transfer of land-ownership and to deal with rural inequalities, it was inevitable that a rising popular political movement such as Sinn Féin would move to exploit land hunger, but it was something of an historical irony that it was the introduction of a British government measure – the Compulsory Tillage Order in 1917 – that provided opportunity. The new tillage regulations required all occupiers of over 10 acres of arable land to cultivate 10 per cent more of it than they had done in 1916. In Britain, the Order was viewed as a patriotic necessity, but, in Ireland, as the Inspector General noted in February 1918, 'Landless men and others saw in the movement for increased food production an opportunity to satisfy their greed for land.'[131] Conacre auctions failed because people abstained in the expectation that the lands would be compulsorily acquired from their owners and let in tillage plots at a nominal rent.[132] In Roscommon, IRA veteran Thomas Lavin later remembered how Sinn Féin 'was interested in the securing of land for the people to cultivate. The Great War was at this time at its height and the production of food was all important.' But, he concluded, 'No land was available for the purpose except that which belonged to the large estates owned by the aristocracy and they were not willing to give it up.'[133] In some places where this happened the Irish Volunteers stepped in; in Kerry, for example, the local Volunteers took over 35 acres from Lord Listowel which they let as tillage plots.[134] In Clare, Andrew O'Donohoe recalled that the Sinn Féin clubs became 'involved in the seizure of farms used for grazing by owners who were never friendly towards any popular movements'.[135]

Sinn Féin exploited the land question for political gain in the same way as the constitutional Irish Parliamentary Party had done from the 1880s to the passing of the Wyndham Land Act in 1903. It appealed to labourers and small-holders by linking the potential fruits of revolutionary intent with land redistribution that could only be achieved through compulsory acquisition of lands. Thus, by the end of 1917, the Inspector General of the RIC reported 'the steady growth of Sinn Féin from a small body to . . . [one of] vast dimension', and, while rightly acknowledging the role that the anti-conscription campaign had played, he also put it down to 'the republican programme' that held 'a

3.7 A grazier farm in Graigueachuillaire, Co Galway, c.1906. This type of
large livestock farm was targeted by agrarian agitators during the Ranch
War of c.1904–10 and later during the revolutionary years 1920–23 for
redistribution amongst smallholders.

powerful attraction' for the youth, while the 'persons of stake' viewed 'this
popular movement with apprehension'.[136] (Perhaps he was unwittingly
suggesting the potential for both social and generational divides that became a
characteristic of the War of Independence.) One of the first to link Sinn Féin's
political intent with agrarian activism before the war's end was the County
Inspector for Galway East Riding, who contended in February 1918 that 'Sinn
Féin is now being worked in this Riding as an agrarian movement for the for-
cible possession of lands . . . This new phase of Sinn Féin will bring many
young men into the movement which had no attraction for them heretofore.'[137]

In its First World War recruitment campaign the British government had
set something of a precedent in June 1918 when, after all thoughts of conscription for Ireland had been abandoned, Lord Lieutenant French issued a proclamation aimed at replenishing the Irish divisions at the Front by 50,000 men
before 1 October. One inducement had potent appeal – the promise of land to
those who would recruit and survive fit enough to farm it. The incentive
was aimed 'almost entirely' at young men in urban areas – shop assistants,

publicans' assistants and so on – who were 'mostly transplanted countrymen, the sons of small farmers'.[138] According to the editor of the *Irish Times*: 'The instinct of the land is strong in them and they are told now that its gratification will be the reward of honourable service in their country's cause.'[139] In December 1919, as Sinn Féin was invigorating its land policy, the British government introduced an act to facilitate the provision of land for those who had recruited and returned home to Ireland. By March 1921, the Irish Land Commission had purchased 5,046 acres of untenanted land for £125,000 (mainly from sympathetic aristocrats wanting to support the process) and were in negotiations to purchase a further 10,600 acres. By then, 2,700 acres had been redistributed amongst 134 ex-servicemen (a respectable average of just over 20 acres each).[140] Could young IRA volunteers expect the same?

Analyses by historians of the socioeconomic backgrounds of IRA volunteers in rural areas have found that it was the small farmers, the landless and the labourers who offered most support. For instance, Peter Hart's examination of Cork IRA membership portrays a movement dominated by young men in their twenties, unmarried and propertyless, 'with no stake in the country'.[141] If the Bureau of Military History had been more probing in the information it sought from IRA veterans, one might now know a great deal more about why they joined and whether they associated revolution with social change and the betterment of their own personal circumstances. There were certainly IRA leaders who knew the appeal that access to land would have.[142] As noted previously, Tom Barry hinted that the burning of country houses in Cork was not all about revolutionary politics, for when country house owners fled, the IRA officers 'encouraged local landless men to settle on the lands and to use them'.[143] A Clare IRA leader, Michael Brennan, later claimed that he 'hadn't the slightest interest in the land agitation, but I had every interest in it as a means to an end . . . to get these fellows into the Volunteers.'[144] This, of course, is not to suggest that all IRA men were agrarian agitators, no more than all agrarian agitators were IRA volunteers. But there is a strong case to be made that land redistribution became a central issue in the Irish revolution, that in its aftermath there was a belief that those who had served Ireland's cause deserved reward and that one of the avenues to reward was through the division of estates which, by extension, had ramifications for the Big House. One of Michael Brennan's IRA comrades in Clare, Joseph Barratt, later admitted:

We took an active part in the local agitation for the acquisition of ranches by the Land Commission and, in the division of such lands, we tried to ensure that our members would get preferences. These large estates had been in the hands of landlords against whom there was a traditional hostility; they were mostly of planter stock and invariably were opposed to every Irish national movement.[145]

Also evident in this quotation was the ideology, popularised in the nineteenth century, that promoted land as the basis of the nation, and the nation had been redefined to exclude those of 'planter stock'. In a similar vein, IRA organiser Ernie O'Malley, more a cosmopolite than a countryman, described his strategy for ridding his men of any residue of servility during the early days of the War of Independence:

The Big House might be spruce, or gaunt in decay; weeds on the avenue and families without issue. Virtue and strength was going from the leeches who had sucked life from the people. The arid brittleness or the harsh brilliance of the ascendancy mind remained. I made the men manoeuvre in demesne land to rid them of their inherent respect for the owners. Even yet their fathers touched their hats to the gentry and to the sergeant of the police.[146]

As he travelled the country organising the IRA, O'Malley also came to appreciate that there was 'a hunger for the soil, an elemental feeling that even the stranger or the foreigner can sense'.[147] What he witnessed throughout Ireland – from 'a hunger' for the land in Donegal to vivid 'memories of the bitter land war' in Clare – suggested to him that the countryman 'was sympathetic enough where a land revolution was concerned'.[148]

In conclusion: by the end of the Great War, Irish rural malcontents from Ventry to Inishowen were much more concerned with what was happening in relation to land division than they were with peace talks in Versailles, and this had ramifications for the country house. Before the war, rural Ireland was still a very safe place for the aristocracy to live but from 1919, coinciding with the beginning of the War of Independence, those traditionally kept outside demesne walls were beginning to break them down. From that point forward, land redistribution became central to the Irish revolution and the 2.6 million acres or so of demesne and untenanted lands recorded in 1906 as still belonging to the aristocracy became green jewels to the land hungry, who included young members of the IRA. There are those who are easily offended by any claims that young men joined the IRA for any other reason than to fight for Irish independence. But it is foolish to consider that they did not anticipate reward because, in all revolutions, patriotism – here defined simply as fighting for the independence of one's country from alien rule – and the desire to improve one's position in life are understandably compatible, and, in an agriculturally dominated society like Ireland, the latter could best be achieved through access to land. That, of course, is not to say that the IRA set out with an agrarian agenda, but there were those, as we have seen, who used an agrarian agenda to get young propertyless men into the IRA with the result that after 1922 they felt that Ireland owed them something for their sacrifices, which could, in large degree, be brought about by ending a social revolution that had begun in 1879.

II
'A BONFIRE FOR A GENERATION'
Burning the Big House, 1920–23

4

'CASTLES, MANSIONS AND RESIDENCES WERE SENT UP IN FLAMES'

The Irish Republican Army came out by night and by day we did the opposite: we went about our affairs in daylight and during the hours of darkness we locked ourselves (as securely as we could) into our houses . . . The castle then seemed extra vast and lonely. Every night . . . in tweed skirt and thick shoes, with valuables packed in suitcases ready to throw out of the window, I lay awake . . . When dawn came and the birds twittered, I slept.

(Mabel M. Annesley, *As the Sight is Bent:*
An Unfinished Autobiography, London, 1964, p. 29)

1. 'Receding imperialism'

The last two chapters have described the great changes on multiple levels which the Irish aristocracy experienced in 1914–18: great changes in a rapidly changing world. Five years before the war, the Church of Ireland rector and novelist Reverend J.O. Hannay [aka George Birmingham] had scorned the aristocracy for continuing to look beyond Ireland's shores to Britain as their spiritual home, and their continued loyalism through the Home Rule crises, Hannay concluded, had compounded their isolation:

The Irish gentleman has not understood that an empire is a quickly passing thing, nailed together by force, varnished by diplomacy, waiting the inevitable dissolution of all such structures. In taking Imperialism to his heart and scorning patriotism he has mistaken the transitory for the permanent . . . Men do not make their homes in empires but in countries . . . Here is the last great mistake of the Irish gentry. They have taken the empire for their country, which is the same as if a man should set himself down in some great *caravanserai* and say that he has found a home.[1]

There was a certain prescience in this. The Irish aristocracy had taken the British Empire to heart at the beginning of the Great War, but at its end empires were crumbling in the face of rising nationalism, and the Ireland that the survivors returned to was very different to the one they had left, not least because the rise of separatist nationalism and the intransigence of Ulster Unionism had swept away any notions that a pre-Home Rule type settlement was now acceptable to either side. After 1918, like the Loyalists in America in the 1770s or, more contemporaneously, like the Greeks in Asia Minor, the Muslims in the Balkans or the Swedes in Finland, the Irish aristocracy became victims in Ireland of what R.B. McDowell has called 'receding imperialism'.[2] And successive British governments did little to alleviate their plight. Reflecting on this period, David Cannadine has concluded: 'For the essence of their tragedy was that the Irish patricians had stood by the empire in its greatest time of mortal danger and had profligately spilled their blood and selflessly given their lives in its defence. Yet in the darkest crisis of their own lives and their own order, the same empire had not lifted a finger to save them.'[3]

2. 'Honest, decent citizens have no protection'

The beginning of the War of Independence in Ireland is traditionally dated to 21 January 1919 when an attack by Irish Volunteers on a police patrol at Soloheadbeg in Tipperary, which resulted in the deaths of two RIC men, coincided with the first sitting of Dáil Éireann in the Mansion House in Dublin. (There was no connection between the two events.) During that year, one of the main priorities of the Volunteers, who would gradually become known as the Irish Republican Army (IRA), was to acquire arms and ammunition. Volunteers believed that country houses had excellent potential in this respect, given that shooting was one of the aristocracy's favourite leisure pursuits, that they had a tradition of service in the military and that further north they had stored UVF arms and ammunition in their houses and on their demesnes. However, in 1918 many of the aristocracy had already chosen to hand in their arms to the local RIC barracks under a government proclamation that had warned of 'uneasiness . . . caused in the minds of law-abiding people in many parts of Ireland by the raiding of houses for arms by gangs of ill-disposed persons'.[4] Some later regretted they had done so. On 24 February 1922, Major

Arthur Blennerhassett of Ballyseedy, for instance, complained that 'the Imperial forces including the Royal Irish Constabulary were removed from Kerry and my arms having been surrendered previously to the British government, my family and I were left at Ballyseedy utterly unprotected'.[5]

By extension, this meant that IRA raids were not as successful as Volunteers might have hoped. In February 1919, only two rifles, two shotguns and a collection of swords and daggers were secured from Ravensdale Park in Louth.[6] On 25 September 1919, Woodbrook, the Roscommon home of Colonel Kirkwood, yielded only a revolver, a blunderbuss, 400 cartridges, a sword and a number of daggers.[7] Volunteer Michael Reilly of Ballyturin in Galway recalled raiding a number of Big Houses for arms but getting only two shotguns from Major Persse's gamekeeper, a haul of mixed ammunition from Bagot's of Ballyturin and facing stiff opposition at Lough Cutra from the well-armed Scots gamekeeper.[8] In January 1920, armed raiders got off with a rifle, a double-barrelled shotgun, a rook rifle and two revolvers from Colonel O'Callaghan Westropp's home in Clare.[9] In February 1920, raiders came to Sir Vincent Nash's Shannon View House in Limerick and demanded guns. He showed them a receipt for those he had handed in to the RIC and told them he only had a service rifle belonging to his son, who had been killed at the Front. In their sympathy for Nash, 'The raiders intimated that they would not take the gun and apologised to Sir Vincent over the matter.'[10] As at Lough Cutra, the IRA did not always have it their own way: in September 1920, Colonel Collis successfully defended his Cork home, Barrymore, from an upstairs window from where 'he kept about thirty men at bay for two hours', but his actions and such examples were rare.[11]

Until the spring of 1920, country houses continued to be well protected by the local RIC, as traditionally had been the case, especially during the more violent period of the Land War, but beginning in February the IRA launched a large-scale offensive on barracks in isolated rural areas, forcing the closure of approximately 500, most of which were destroyed to prevent their future reoccupation.[12] Large swathes of the countryside were, therefore, left without police protection or, at best, occasional patrols, allowing the IRA more freedom of movement. Typical of what this meant can be gauged from Thomas Costello's BMH statement (he was one of the leaders who burned Moydrum Castle, which is described below):

In our area, Creggan and Brawny barracks were evacuated, and we burned both of these on Easter Saturday night, 1920, in conformation with the rest of the country. . . . This evacuation, though only a limited withdrawal, was the beginning of the end, and was a great blessing to us as it allowed us greater freedom of movement.[13]

After the spring offensive, IRA raids on houses for arms became a matter of course: from July to September 1920 alone (and these were only the cases reported in the *Irish Times*), Ballymakee, Knock and Mount Congreve in Waterford, Glenveagh and Brown Hall in Donegal, Castlesaunderson and Crossdowney in Cavan, Adare in Limerick, Ballymore in Cork, Moydrum in Westmeath, Dromoland in Clare, Powerscourt in Wicklow, Lissadell in Sligo (where arms were found stashed on the demesne), Castle Forbes in Longford, Kilkea Castle in Kildare and Mount Juliet in Kilkenny were all raided.

The destruction of RIC barracks was hugely disconcerting for the aristocracy. Nora Robinson described her anxieties following the collapse of rural policing: 'English people in their law-abiding country had no conception of the horror and dread and all-pervading misery of a war fought round one's own home, in one's own countryside: a war which meant daily and hourly suspicion and discomfort as well as fear of maiming and death.'[14] In June 1921, Lord Dunraven complained in the House of Lords: 'There is in Ireland today absolutely no protection whatever for life or property. Honest, decent citizens have no protection, and can get no protection from the police and are not allowed to protect themselves.'[15] Police patrols were not the answer to the problem. In March 1920, Mountifort Longfield thought that 'the chance of their being in the right place at the right time' was 'very remote' and that the small police barracks in rural Ireland should have been '*strengthened* and not vacated'.[16] His home, Castlemary in Cork, was burned six months later.

This is all remindful of the fact that at the most fundamental level Ireland fought a War of Independence between January 1919 and July 1921 (although it was late 1920 before it became violent). Such a war is calculated to win political freedom from an alien power and is fought against occupying forces and those who support the same. From the IRA's perspective, country houses were regarded as highly politicised targets because of the loyalism of their owners, who openly proclaimed the same. When, for example, James Ormsby Lawder of

Leitrim was asked by the Irish Grants Committee if he was a Loyalist, his reply was very typical: 'Most certainly so. I was a JP and DL for 43 years, always an upholder of law and order, actively engaged in recruiting and chairman of the United Services Fund in Co Leitrim. High Sheriff for Leitrim in 1909 and 1919.'[17] The primary objective of the IRA was to cast off the administrative yoke of the British government. Thus, IRA veterans often recalled the destruction of Big Houses as a stage in this process; the physical destruction of the footprint of the coloniser not only rid a locality of an alien presence but did much to address ancestral grievances related to the servility and deference traditionally demanded by their owners. Former IRA leader Tom Barry's *Guerilla Days in Ireland* (1946) frequently stressed his disdain for the Big Houses of Cork and those who resided in them. Barry, whose father was an RIC policeman, claimed to have grown up resenting the Big Houses in which 'lived the leading British Loyalist, secure and affluent in his many acres, enclosed by high demesne walls'; these were 'the conquerors', who demanded subservience from employees and tenants alike.[18]

Volunteers claimed to have imbibed in their youth teachings that challenged aristocratic culture and alien oppression. Another Cork IRA leader, Liam Deasy, fondly remembered his teacher who 'strove constantly to rid us of the attitude of servility and subservience towards the landed gentry which was encouraged by this class, and in its place he endeavoured to plant a sense of self-respect and independence'.[19] Tipperary IRA leader, Dan Breen, recalled the influence of another teacher, Charlie Walshe, who taught a generation of revolutionaries including himself, Dinny Lacey, Seán Treacy and Seán Hogan 'the naked facts about the English conquest of Ireland and the manner in which our country was held in bondage'.[20] Breen wrote:

Many a time I walked for three or four hours without meeting even one human being. Here and there a stately mansion, around it the gate lodge of the serf, the winding avenue, the spreading oaks, and the green fields in which no man was visible. Landlordism, the willing instrument of British rule, had wrought this desolation. I renewed my resolve to do my share in bringing about the change that must come sooner or later.[21]

Breen also gave the impression that Big Houses were resented because they accentuated the difference between aristocrat and peasant, those who had and those who had not. While Breen may not fit into the category of socialist republican, what he hinted at had historic parallels in all modern revolutions: for example, during the French revolution, Lyon's Place de Bellecour was erased because its grand mansions were 'an insult to the poverty of the people and the simplicity of republican morals'.[22] In some BMH witness statements, one can read that certain historical grievances, born out of social class strictures created by the landlord–tenant system, demanded retribution. Thomas Ryan's remembrance of the burning of the Perry home at Newcastle in Limerick noted that while the attack was ostensibly a counter-reprisal for local Black and Tan atrocities, Perry's 'forefathers before him had been tyrannical landlords in the country'.[23] When Lorcan Park House was burned in Tipperary in late June 1921, the local nationalist newspaper made a point of recalling that 200 families had been evicted from the estate 60 years before.[24] Patrick Duffy, one of the IRA volunteers who participated in the burning of Summerhill in Meath, later claimed his personal motive was revenge for an ancestor who had been evicted from the estate.[25] Derrycastle in Co Tipperary was one of the very first houses burned in January 1920.[26] Back in 1844, on the eve of the Famine, Francis Spaight, a Limerick corn merchant, had bought Derrycastle. He found the estate burdened with a 'deadweight' of paupers and, in 1849, he had no hesitation in migrating 1,400 persons, telling another landlord: 'His estate was not to be formed . . . into an electoral division to itself, and that he then anticipated that the poor rates would be within his control [sic] and that his property would be a valuable and improving one.'[27] Spaight told a government enquiry that he had emigrated these people for about seventy shillings per head, that they 'had gone gladly' and he 'had practically wiped out crime and distress on his estate'.[28] The O'Connellite press saw it differently and there were later reports in the *Tipperary Vindicator* and *Freeman's Journal* of men 'who escaped from America' and made their way back to their hovels in Derrycastle.[29] Spaight's actions undoubtedly lived long in the local memory; it was claimed that the burning of Derrycastle was because of local agrarian agitation and the struggle to have its demesne divided.

It was also the case that the desire for revenge, particularly in the spiral of violence that characterised the War of Independence where IRA ambushes led to reprisals from the British armed forces, served to spotlight country houses as legitimate targets for retaliatory counter-reprisals. Once again, this is typical in independence struggles. Pashman tells us that when the rebels in the American Revolution 'saw an occupying army burn towns and turn families out of their homes, New Yorkers came to share a desire to strike back at those responsible for such calamities'.[30] In 1914–18, architectural destruction on an industrial scale had become an everyday occurrence across Europe, familiar to people in Ireland from newspaper photographs, cinema footage and even post-cards sent by soldiers from the Western Front. Irish people had also witnessed the centre of their own capital city razed by British artillery in 1916. When, during the War of Independence, the Black and Tans burned villages and towns such as Balbriggan, Trim, Knockcroghery and Cork, it reminded people of the worst excesses in Europe. Retaliation in the form of dismantling symbols of imperialism in Ireland was inevitable. Thus, Ireland in the 1920s was no different to New York in the 1770s where, in both cases, the lust for recrimi-nation was enough to regularly unleash an orgy of arson.

For instance, Tom Barry led the most successful IRA ambush of the War of Independence at Kilmichael in Cork on 28 November 1920, in which eigh-teen Auxiliaries were killed. This gave rise to retribution by the crown forces in the south-western counties, including the introduction of an official reprisal policy that allowed for the burning of houses of suspected Sinn Féin or IRA sympathisers. Barry later reflected that when the British authorities agreed this policy, they 'forgot to take into consideration [that] Ireland was studded with the castles, mansions and residences of the British ascendancy who had made their homes here'.[31] He triumphantly recalled the burning of several mansions, including Cor Castle, Mayfield, Bandon, Dunboy and the Earl of Bandon's Castle Bernard that 'blazed half a day before it crumbled in ruins'.[32] He went on to boast in a passage that unveiled several possible motivations:

Castles, mansions and residences were sent up in flames by the IRA imme-diately after the British fire gangs had razed the homes of Irish Republicans. Our people were suffering in this competition of terror, but the British Loyalists were paying dearly, the demesne walls were tumbling and the British ascendancy was being destroyed. Our only fear was that, as time went on, there would be no more Loyalist's homes to destroy, for we intended to go on to the bitter end. If the Republicans of West Cork were to be homeless and without shelter, then so too would be the British supporters. West Cork might become a barren land of desolation and misery, but at least the Britishers would have more than their full share of the sufferings.[33]

This destruction of country houses was active rather than collateral damage. Furthermore, when 'the Britishers' fled, Barry claimed, as already noted, that fellow IRA officers 'encouraged local landless men to settle on the lands and to use them'.[34] Whether intentional or not, he signalled that the destruction of a Big House could have the added advantage of expediting more equitable land redistribution (chapter 5).

Big House owners themselves sensed that one reason alone might not be enough to explain the assault on their properties. W.J.H. Tyrell of Ballindoolin House in Kildare contemplated the reasons for an unsuccessful attack on his home: he wondered if it was because he allowed the British military to stay in another vacant house belonging to him at Edenderry in neighbouring King's County (Offaly); was it because he had been a Justice of the Peace for forty-eight years, and a Deputy Lieutenant 'always ready to help the government'; or because he had a son in the British army; or because he had 'tried to get rid of a herd and caretakers' for allowing local people to graze their cattle on his lands.[35] While Tyrell may have focused primarily on his loyalism, it is notable that he added the possibility of an agrarian dimension. Both attacker (Barry) and victim (Tyrell) in separate cases made suggestive rather than overt claims of this largely ignored dimension of the revolutionary period, which will be examined in more detail in the next chapter. What is most illuminating in Tyrell's reflections is that he could not make up his mind as to whether any single motive predominated, and the task is no easier for the historian. Tyrell might have considered that much depended upon the makeup of the anonymous crowd who, individually and collectively, may themselves have had mixed motives: those who resented his loyalism may have been joined by others who had been expelled from his grazing lands.

3. 'In the usual efficient manner'

The burning of Big Houses did not begin until the spring of 1920. It is easy, therefore, to infer a correlation with the breakdown in rural law and order as the RIC withdrew to the large urban areas. But this also needs to take into consideration the consequences of the arrival of RIC reinforcements – the Black and Tans and Auxiliaries. Firstly, the thousands of extra police who arrived had no rural barracks to use as bases and so Big Houses were commandeered as billets; secondly, because of the changing nature of the conflict, an endless cycle of reprisal and counter-reprisal, those same Big Houses were then regarded as legitimate military targets by the IRA. James S. Donnelly Jr in his study of Cork concluded: 'The ceaseless search for suitable quarters for this hugely inflated number of British soldiers and police and their officers – quarters that would put them in close striking distance of their quarry – was to become one of the main reasons for Big House burnings in Cork.'[36]

The same trend was discernible throughout the country. Before moving the discussion on, it is important to note, however, that many of the houses commandeered were described as temporarily vacant or long-time abandoned. The difficulty is that it is not always possible to establish exactly how long: was it since the breakup of their estates under the land acts, which means they had been effectively abandoned and therefore emptied of their contents which would mean a diminished loss of material culture? Was it since the beginning of the Great War when many families temporarily vacated to spend more time in London, or was it much more recent as fears of attack grew?

At any rate, the occupation or threatened occupation of Big Houses by the crown forces provided the IRA with a legitimacy to destroy them. In May 1920, W.P. Hanly informed the *Irish Times* that his home, Anagrove House in Tipperary, had 'recently [been] inspected by the military for occupation without his knowledge'. He had not been resident for a while, but the house was occupied by a caretaker. A few nights later, after it had become rumoured the house was to be commandeered, an estimated one hundred men evicted the caretaker and his family and burned it.[37] That same month, Moorock in King's County was burned for the same reason: six months previously it had been sold by Colonel Cribbon to Thomas Moylett and had remained unoccupied.[38] In December 1920, Timoleague House, owned by Robert Travers, was burned.[39] James S. Donnelly explains that on 10 May three policemen had been killed nearby at Ahawadda Cross; four days later the castle was commandeered 'as a security measure in response to the killings'; they remained for six months and during their stay 'The soldiers conducted frequent patrols and raids and apparently committed or were associated with the commission of a gross sacrilege – the desecration of famed Timoleague Abbey.'[40] When they vacated Timoleague, the IRA ensured they could not return. In June 1921, The Abbey in Templemore, Tipperary, 'considered amongst the finest mansions in the south', was burned but it seems to have been abandoned almost twenty years previously by the owner Sir J. Craven, Carden who had long since migrated to Scotland.[41]

Generally, houses were burned as soon as intelligence was received by the IRA that they were to be taken over, for example both Southpark House and Roundmount House in Roscommon in May 1920.[42] When, in June 1921, three Big Houses were burned in Galway, the County Inspector reported to Dublin Castle: 'The military were warned not to send men out to stay at these kind of houses. The CO disregarded the warning with the above results.'[43] Others were destroyed after the Black and Tans or Auxiliaries left to prevent future reoccupation or perhaps even to get rid of that local contamination. In May 1920, Kilbrittain Castle in Cork, 'a large and ancient mansion', was destroyed after it had been occupied. So were Massey House in the same county, Ballagh Hall in Tipperary, Portloman House in Westmeath and the unoccupied and unfurnished Hermitage in Limerick.[44]

The most outstanding architectural casualty in this category was Summerhill in Co Meath, ancestral home of Barons Langford. It was undoubtedly one of Ireland's grandest houses, 300 feet in length, built 'in the manner of the Renaissance Palaces in Rome – a treatment unusual in Ireland'.[45] Constructed in the early 1730s for Hercules Langford Rowley, the identity of its architect is less certain, with attributions to Richard Castle and Edward Lovett Pearce, and acknowledged influences of Sir John Vanbrugh (1664– 1726), whose most notable construction was Castle Howard in Yorkshire.[46] C.R. Cockerell (1788–1863), English architect, archaeologist and writer, described the entrance front to the house as 'a massive two-storey, seven-bay block the central feature of which were four towering Corinthian columns, the whole executed in crisply cut limestone. On either side two-storey quadrants swept away from the house towards equally vast pavilions topped by towers and shallow domes.'[47]

There was a large and lofty entrance hall which in 1913 contained a group of statuary to the memory of Mary Pakenham, daughter of the 1st Lord Longford of Tullynally Castle, executed by Thomas Banks, the eminent English sculptor, and many family portraits by artists including Battoni. The rest of the rooms had

4.1 Summerhill House, Co Meath, home of Lord Langford. This magnificent Palladian mansion was one of the largest and grandest houses burned during the early stages of the War of Independence because of rumours it was to be occupied by the British forces, although there may also have been an agrarian dimension.

Adam mantels or sienna and white marble and were hung with landscapes and pastels by Guardi and Hamilton. The ceilings were of the most intricate and delicate plasterwork in the rococo style.[48] According to Cockerell, there were 'few sites more magnificently chosen – the close of a long incline so that the gradual approach along a tree-lined avenue created the impression of impending drama'.[49] The magnificent location was to prove its dramatic undoing.

In October 1919, the title of 5th Baron Langford and the Summerhill estate was inherited by John Hercules William Rowley. His younger brother, George, an officer in the King's Royal Rifle Corps, had been killed in action in 1917. John Hercules spent most of his time in London. The house was, therefore, empty for considerable periods of each year, maintained by a modest household staff (the 1911 census returned nine residential servants). Prior to its burning on 4 February 1921, Lady Fingall, whose home at Killeen Castle was about 10 miles away, claimed 'Langford had been corresponding with the military authorities, who proposed to quarter soldiers in the house' and one of his letters had been intercepted by the IRA.[50] Local IRA leader Seán Boylan substantiated this; he recalled that Michael Collins had received information from one of his men in Dublin Castle that the house was to be occupied and ordered it burned immediately.[51] According to Seamus Finn, 'There had been some intensive enemy activity around Summerhill . . . the forerunner to the occupation by a strong force of Auxiliaries', but the destruction 'forced them away from Summerhill and averted a very serious threat to one of our most important lines of communication'.[52] Boylan corroborated this, adding that the burning was imperative because of the house's strategic position, located as it was 'on high ground which commanded one of the routes to the west. The Auxiliaries with field glasses could have swept the country.'[53] On 7 February 1921, an official report from Dublin Castle also confirmed that Summerhill had been burned to prevent military occupation by British forces.[54]

On the night, Colonel Rowley was not in residence, and the house was occupied by only a small number of servants. At around 10 p.m., the butler heard a loud knocking on the door. He saw thirty to forty men outside. Having consulted with the maids, they decided to barricade themselves in. The raiders then proceeded to break down the door, but they also entered 'in a number of different places', presumably meaning windows and other doors, back and basement. They had with them about thirty to fifty gallons of paraffin which they poured over the furniture and floors. The terrified servants escaped through the basement passage and made their way to the woods where they hid until the raiders had left. The butler managed to contact Trim police station but, by the time they arrived, 'The fire had gained such a hold that there were no hopes of saving the building.'[55] The house was 'reduced to a mass of blackened ruins'.[56] Desmond FitzGerald, Knight of Glin, later lamented its burning as 'probably the greatest tragedy in the history of Irish domestic architecture'.[57]

4. 'The Black and Tans should come to the district'

There also may have been ulterior motives for the burning of Summerhill and these will be discussed in the next chapter, but Summerhill's chances of survival were certainly imperilled by a rumour of military occupation, and the owner's suspected collusion with the crown forces. But one person's collusion could be defined as another's co-operation; it depended on perspective. After all,

4.2 Westport House, Co Mayo, home of the Marquess of Sligo, one of the largest houses to have survived in the west of Ireland. Designed by Richard Castle in the 1730s for the Browne family, Marquesses of Sligo, it remained in family ownership until 2017.

working with the colonial administration had been a way of life for the aristocracy and gentry. They had been Deputy Lieutenants of the county, responsible for reporting crimes to Dublin Castle, and they had sat as magistrates at the petty sessions for generations. There is little doubt that the former landed elite provided information to the authorities; reporting and adjudicating crime was what they did. At the end of March 1919, for example, the Marquess of Sligo of Westport House wrote to the Chief Secretary to acquaint him 'with certain circumstances' connected with the murder of a local resident magistrate, J.C. Milling, and called on the government 'to proclaim this part of the Co[unty], to place it under Martial Law, to replace the Garrison here, accompanied by machine automatic guns, and one or more armoured cars'.[58] He would not have considered himself a spy in the traditional sense, but rather an upholder of law and order.

James V. Greated's Lydican Castle in Galway was burned in October 1922; he claimed that it was primarily on account of him being 'very friendly' with the military during the War of Independence. He had W.H.F. Sidley, a former District Inspector of the RIC, provide a reference to that effect:

[Greated] was a personal friend of mine and during the period 1919 to 1922 was constantly in and out of Barracks, and gave me a considerable amount of valuable help and information as to matters that were happening in the country. Mr Greated rendered valuable assistance both to the police and military. He was one of the few cases of consistent and unswerving loyalty to the British connection during the period of the Sinn Féin terror in Ireland.[59]

The IRA saw it differently. During the revolutionary period those who collaborated with 'a foreign people and government', the terminology of the 1916 Proclamation, were adjudged hostile enemies of the republic.[60] After one Big House was burned in Tipperary in April 1921, an official report from Dublin Castle claimed that it was because there had been a rumour the owner 'had suggested that the Black and Tans should come to the district'.[61] When Captain Beresford Molony's house in Tulla, Co Clare, was burned in September 1920, a letter found in the ruins read: 'You have harboured in your house British officers and their wives. You have harboured a Black and Tan family. Now you can look for a house yourself.'[62]

There were two high-profile cases of country house owners being executed and their houses burned because their actions went beyond collusion and they were accused of spying, where the latter involved deliberately gathering information and passing it on to the crown forces which, in turn, led to the deaths or capture of IRA volunteers. On 14 April 1921, members of the Knockanure and Duagh companies of the IRA arrived at Kilmorna House, Listowel, Co Kerry, the home of Sir Arthur Vicars, most famous for having overseen the Irish crown jewels before they were stolen from Dublin Castle in 1907. According to the BMH statement of Matthew Finucane, Vicars had been sentenced to death as a spy and orders given to execute him and burn his home. Finucane described Vicars as an 'ex-British officer' who lived in what was 'known locally as the Great House' and who had a short time previously entertained British officers to a fishing holiday in Kilmorna.[63] Patrick McElligott similarly pointed out that 'Military parties were frequent visitors there and were entertained by Vickers on many occasions.'[64] McElligott was in no doubt Vicars was a spy whose informing was responsible for the death of a young Volunteer, Michael Galvin, on 7 April 1921 in a failed IRA ambush near Kilmorna. McElligott also noted that the IRA had feared Kilmorna was to be commandeered by the military: 'If this happened', McElligott recalled, 'Abbeyfeale and the surrounding areas of Duagh, Knockanure and Newtownsandes would have been in danger.'[65] Michael Murphy, Vicar's valet, who later became an officer in the National Army, and whose statement was also recorded by the BMH, claimed the IRA were mistaken that British officers had been entertained in Kilmorna before Galvin was killed.[66] The statements are also conflicting on what actually happened on the day – did Vicars run from room to room defying and shooting at the IRA raiders or not? Regardless, the outcome was that he was shot dead outside the house, a note pinned to his body telling spies to beware, and Kilmorna destroyed.

The second case of the execution of an alleged spy was that of Maria Lindsay of Leemount House in Coachford, Co Cork, the widow of a senior British army officer. Donnelly contends that her 'loyalism was above all a matter of family tradition and cultural background', equally applicable to most Big House families.[67] At the end of January 1921, she learned locally of a planned IRA ambush at Godfrey's Cross, and she travelled to Ballincollig barracks to inform the officers of the Manchester Regiment. The crown forces soon surrounded the ambush site, eight IRA men were captured, quickly tried and five sentenced to death. On 17 February, Mrs Lindsay and her chauffeur were abducted from Leemount to be held as hostages for the release of the IRA prisoners. General Sir Edward Peter Strickland, on receiving communication from the IRA that unless their comrades were released Lindsay and Clarke would be executed as spies, communicated the information to General Sir Neville Macready, Commander-in-Chief of the British army in Ireland. The execution of the prisoners was carried out on 28 February.

Two weeks later, Leemount was attacked by forty or so IRA men and burned to the ground. On 21 March Lindsay and Clarke were executed by the IRA as spies.[68] Macready later wrote in his memoirs: 'While I would have gone to great lengths to save the gallant lady's life, I could not listen to such a proposal, which would have resulted in the kidnapping of loyal or influential persons every time a death sentence was passed on a rebel.'[69] His calculated comment was redolent of Cannadine's point made at the beginning of this chapter: 'In the darkest crisis of their own lives and their own order, the same empire had not lifted a finger to save them.'[70] Not all Big House owners were as prepared as Mrs Lindsay to openly defy the local IRA. District Inspector Sidley, quoted above, talked of James Greated's 'consistent and unswerving loyalty', but those who upheld the British connection not only put themselves in danger, they also cast suspicion on all their peers and further spotlighted their Big Houses as targets for IRA counter-reprisals.

5. 'You being an aggressively anti-Irish person'

The War of Independence entered a more violent phase from November 1920. On the morning of 21 November – Bloody Sunday – fourteen British intelligence operatives were killed in Dublin by Michael Collins's squad, leading to the reprisal killing of fourteen civilians that afternoon in Croke Park (and three other men that evening in Dublin Castle, two of whom were IRA officers and the third a civilian). A week later, seventeen Auxiliaries were killed in an IRA ambush led by Tom Barry at Kilmichael in Cork. That also gave rise to the spiral of reprisals recounted above. On 10 December, martial law was proclaimed in Munster, which reflected the fact that by then it was the most violent region in the country as defined by IRA activity.[71] A study by Erhard Rumpf and A.C. Hepburn has also shown that British reprisals were mainly located in Cork, Tipperary, Limerick, Kerry and Clare.[72] Taking both the geographic distribution of IRA violence and the geography of reprisal into consideration, one could, therefore, argue that the most obvious factor in the distribution of Big House burnings was location: 72 of the 125 Big Houses burned (almost 58 per cent) were located in these counties.[73] Cork, where forty-two were burned, had by far the highest incidence of IRA violence and the highest number of towns and villages affected by British reprisals (not to mention the razing of the centre of Cork city by rampaging crown forces on 11 December 1920).[74]

As the War of Independence drew to a close and violence escalated, so did Big House burnings. Sixty-four of all the houses destroyed (51 per cent) were burned in the last fourteen weeks of the conflict. In May 1921, the Inspector General of the RIC reported: 'There seemed to be an intention to burn out all Loyalists who owned property.'[75] The County Inspector of Cork had previously reported to him that 'counter reprisals in the form of burning loyalist houses is a more or less new feature'.[76] In June, he repeated that 'Loyalists are being persecuted, their mansions and houses are being burned, and a huge number of them have cleared out of the county.'[77] Similarly in Tipperary, in June 1921 the County Inspector informed his superior: 'It is thought that the campaign of burning country gentlemen's houses is only just starting and that we may expect to see a lot more of it done in the near future.'[78] James S. Donnelly attributed the escalation in Cork to 'the collective determination of the commanders of the southern brigades to devise an effective means of stopping, or at least reducing, the seemingly endless series of official British military reprisals against the property of republicans or their sympathizers'.[79] The burning of Castle Bernard, home of the 4th Earl of Bandon, on 21 June 1921 typified this policy; Tom Barry, who had nothing but disdain for Bandon – 'on whose authority', he declared, 'the

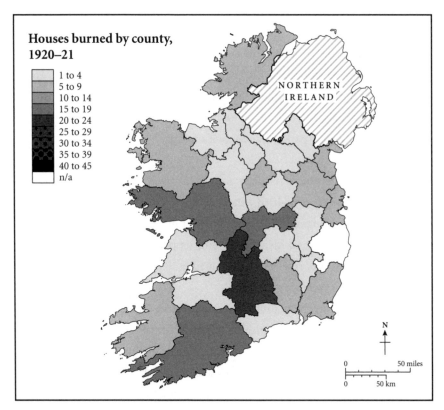

Map 2 County distribution of houses burned during the War of Independence 1920–21. Drafted by Dr Jack Kavanagh.

British armed forces purported to rule, coerce, kill and terrorise the Irish people'
– later recalled his decision to move beyond the Inishannon region: 'As there
were no other active Loyalist homes in that area, we went further afield to teach
the British a lesson, and once and for all end their fire terror.'[80]

Later that month, the *Irish Times* headlined the 'House Burning Mania'
that was sweeping the country as mansions from Cork to Cavan went up in
flames.[81] Several of the finest country houses on the western shore of Lough
Derg were destroyed, including Dewsborough House near Tomgraney, Wood
Park House near Mountshannon and Rinshea House in Whitegate. By this
point, IRA attention had moved from abandoned or vacant country houses
used as billets to inhabited ones such as Convamore, Lord Listowel's magnificent classical mansion overlooking the River Blackwater. Prior to its destruction, Listowel's niece was handed the following note, intended for her uncle,
which clearly illustrated the local IRA's intent to gain retribution for the
destruction of their supporters' properties by the crown forces:

> On Wednesday the 13th inst., the enemy bombed and destroyed six houses
> of Republicans as reprisals for IRA activities on the 10th inst. You being an
> aggressively anti-Irish person, and your residence being in the battalion area
> of enemy reprisals, I [Cmdt. Cork no. 2 brigade] have hereby ordered that
> same be destroyed as part of our counter reprisals.[82]

As Donnelly points out, it is debatable if Listowel would have considered
himself 'an aggressively anti-Irish person'. An admittedly less than biased *Irish
Times* argued in his defence: 'The truth is that Lord Listowel has always shown
a passionate attachment to his country and its people and took little part in
politics.'[83] But that was irrelevant: the burning of such mansions set down a
marker of the IRA's intent.

Moving away from the main theatre of violence, the burning of Moydrum
Castle in Co Westmeath was typical of a reprisal attack.

This early nineteenth-century castellated mansion built to the design of
Richard Morrison was the home of Lord Castlemaine, the pre-eminent aristocrat
of south Westmeath. His ancestors had been granted over 5,000 acres in 1680
under the Act of Settlement, and by the early 1880s the estate had grown to over
12,000 acres.[84] Castlemaine sold the bulk of his estate under the 1903 Land Act,

4.3 Moydrum Castle, Co Westmeath, home of Lord Castlemaine, burned as a counter-reprisal by the IRA during the War of Independence, although there was also a very significant local agrarian dimension to the motive.

but he and his family remained resident in Moydrum surrounded by a demesne of over 500 acres and retaining almost treble that in untenanted lands.[85]

The attack on the castle had its origins in events that had taken place over the previous fortnight. On 20 June 1921, at around 7.30 p.m., Colonel Thomas Lambert, commanding officer of the 13th Brigade Athlone, a decorated veteran of the First World War, and Lieutenant Colonel E.L. Challoner, along with their wives and Challoner's niece Katherine Arthur, were returning to Athlone from a tennis party, probably at Killinure House. Driving towards Glasson, they found their way blocked by an IRA party estimated at between six and twelve men. The IRA were aware of Lambert's movements and it was their intention to kidnap him and hold him hostage for the release of Longford IRA leader Seán MacEoin, who was in Mountjoy prison awaiting execution.[86] But, as there was no actual blockade, the driver of the car, Mrs Lambert, accelerated and attempted to drive on. The IRA opened fire hitting Colonel Lambert, who died from his wounds later that night, and injuring Mrs Challoner.[87] That night, four lorry loads of Black and Tans went on a rampage of revenge in Knockcroghery village, across the county border in Roscommon, and, without warning, burned fifteen houses in reprisal, forcing the terrified occupants to flee across the neighbouring fields. The *Irish Times* reported afterwards: 'The village presents a shocking appearance, being a mass of smouldering ruins, with the occupants of the houses homeless and destitute, all their belongings being consumed in the general conflagration.'[88] A few days later, General H.S. Jeudwine, commanding officer of the 5th Division at the Curragh, issued the following statement:

> His [Lambert's] brigade will best avenge his death, as he himself would have wished, by the strict adherence to duty which he did his best to inculcate, and by a determination to maintain, by regular methods, at all risks and through all difficulties, the sovereignty and authority in Ireland of the King and his government, whose servants we are.[89]

Jeudwine's statement was too late for Knockcroghery and did not put an end to the Black and Tan backlash. On 1–2 July between five and seven farmhouses were burned at Coosan.[90] The 'terror' began at 2 a.m. when masked men called at the home of Thomas Duffy, who, along with his wife, four children and ninety-year-old aunt, was told to 'clear out'. Petrol was poured on the beds and furniture and set alight. The Black and Tans then moved on to the homes of the Wansboro, Farrell, Coghlan and Moore families. All were prevented from saving any of their possessions. Next, the Black and Tans moved on to nearby Mount Temple, where they burned the home of Anne Hanevy, one of whose sons was interned as an IRA prisoner at Ballykinlar.[91] There is no question but that this type of brutality by the Black and Tans led directly to revenge attacks on Big Houses.[92] The wonder is that it was not even more widespread.

In the days after the Black and Tan reprisals, the officers of the Westmeath IRA met to decide what action they would take. Thomas Costello, Commanding Officer (OC) of the Athlone Brigade, later recalled: 'There were a number of small places owned by Protestants in the area, but I did not consider it would be fair to burn these peoples' houses for something which was not their fault.'[93] Their attention turned to Moydrum Castle. Both Frank O'Connor and Henry O'Brien highlighted Lord Castlemaine's loyalism.[94] O'Connor's record states:

[Castlemaine] was a member of the British House of Lords and who always opposed anything which was patriotic or Irish national and was really an enemy of Ireland. He had dismissed men from his employment because they would not join the British army. The destruction of his castle would hit in the spot where it would be most felt, whereas the destruction of a few small Loyalists' houses would not be felt.[95]

In the tit-for-tat reprisals it was inevitable that there would be a sectarian dimension: in this case, it was Protestant homes the Westmeath IRA were allegedly ordered to burn, in the same way that it was Catholic nationalist homes the crown forces destroyed. In the vein of such reminiscences, Costello clearly wanted to give the impression that the IRA behaved in a much fairer way than the Black and Tans. Moydrum was chosen because of Castlemaine's past actions: he was a representative peer in the Lords, a staunch Unionist who had been vice-president of the IUA, 'an enemy of Ireland' who had sacked men for not joining the British army. No mention was made of the fact that before the war he had also served on the nationalist-dominated Westmeath County Council and had been returned unopposed in several local government elections.[96]

The three IRA witness statements that describe events on the night are fairly congruous with each other.[97] When the IRA arrived around 3 a.m., they had with them cans of petrol that had been taken from an oil depot in Athlone, and a few large hammers and sledges 'borrowed' from a nearby forge to break in the front door if necessary.[98] Raids such as this were not spur-of-the-moment decisions: they had to be planned to ensure minimum resistance. O'Connor and his comrades knew British officers from the Athlone garrison often stayed at Moydrum, so, unless properly planned, the IRA 'might meet with a hostile reception'.[99] On the night, Lord Castlemaine was absent, fishing in Scotland, and the IRA knew this from information provided by another officer's cousin who worked on the estate.[100] With Castlemaine away, it was unlikely army officers would be there and so the house would be defended only by Lady Castlemaine, her daughter and a few servants.[101] Moreover, there had been a raid for arms on the house in September 1920, and the IRA got away with 'a large number of shotguns, rifles, revolvers and ammunition'.[102] It might, therefore, have been seen as a safe house to attack.

Having forced their entrance, Costello informed Lady Castlemaine that the house was being burned as a reprisal for the recent burnings at Coosan and Mount Temple.[103] Lady Castlemaine pleaded for time to remove valuables and Costello granted this and allocated ten men to help her. In their BMH statements, both Costello and Frank O'Connor agree that they told her: 'The Tans did not grant the privilege to the people whom they had burned out.'[104] The raiders spent around half an hour going into each of the thirty or so principal rooms in the castle, gathering all the furniture in piles before saturating each pile with petrol as well as some paraffin commandeered from Lady Castlemaine's stores. Holes were made in the ceilings to provide ventilation to fan the flames, and on the roof by stripping the slates.[105] The raiders then escorted the servants to a place of safety. Lady Castlemaine and her daughter were provided with armchairs from the house on which to sit; whether it was to suffer the ignominy of watching their home razed and the memories of generations obliterated is unclear. The raiders left only when the house was a raging inferno with no prospect of being saved. Moydrum was one of the last Big Houses to be burned before the Anglo-Irish truce was called on 11 July 1921. However, as we shall see in the next chapter, the revolution had not quite finished with Moydrum or the Castlemaines.

6. 'And now England has cast us off and given us to the murderers'

On 21 August 1921, John Garvey of Tulley House in Mayo wrote to Frederick Crawford, organiser of the Larne gun running:

> I would have preferred to see the Union cemented rather than dismembered but the Union is now a thing of the past. We have 'our all' in the west and our only chance of saving anything we have is by silence in the midst of this great revolutionary change . . . Any aggressive word or act w[oul]d be fatal to us now and our chances of security and safety are not very hopeful.[106]

The predicament of the southern aristocracy, as articulated by Garvey, was accentuated in the contrasting history of their peers in the new state of

Northern Ireland, established under the Government of Ireland Act of December 1920. There, as Olwen Purdue has chronicled, the much different politico-religious demography meant the aristocracy found 'a political and a social role which ensured that they would retain a degree of relevance in the society in which they lived'.[107] Most importantly from their perspective, the northern aristocracy retained their position within the United Kingdom; it might be said that their role in the Ulster Unionist rebellion of 1912–14 had paid off.

While the thinning of aristocratic society further south had been ongoing since the beginning of the Land War in 1879, revolution proved to be a catalyst. In early 1920, Lady Gregory recorded in her journal: 'An exodus from the county [Galway]. The Goughs leave the weekend and Lough Cutra is to be shut up till they see how things are . . . Lord Killanin has had trouble at Spiddal and has dismissed all his men and gone to London. The Lodells . . . are going to live in England. Amy has left Castle Taylor and lives in England.'[108] After the Anglo-Irish truce (11 July 1921), as Peter Martin has pointed out, the southern aristocracy had 'to choose to be Irish or British and it is not surprising that many of them found the new Ireland insufficiently attractive to keep them'.[109] This was reflected in a report in the *Munster Express* in early January 1922 claiming that thirty country houses had been sold in just five months since August 1921.[110] On the last day of December, just weeks after the Irish plenipotentiaries and representatives of the British government signed the Anglo-Irish treaty, Lady Alice Howard of Shelton Abbey in Wicklow confided in her diary: 'Such a dreadful year of rebellion and murder – and now England has cast us off and given us to the murderers.'[111] Lord Oranmore shared her opinion, recording in his journal: 'It is heartbreaking to see the condition to which Ireland has been reduced by the supineness of this country [England]. When shall I be able to live in my dear home again?'[112]

Lord Bandon left for England in March 1922 to recover from his kidnapping ordeal and destruction of his house and reflected on why others of his class had done likewise: 'In areas where these outrages were most frequent and most cruel no protection was afforded to human life, and many of the exiles would not dare run the risk of placing themselves again in the power of criminals who desire to injure them.'[113] From the beginning of 1922, following the establishment of the Irish Free State, the British army officer class departed and with them the 'dashing and sentimental intercourse' that had long characterised the sociability 'between officers and country house families' (and also another layer of security the Big House had depended upon in the recent Troubles).[114] For many aristocrats, loneliness became their only companion. In 1921, the Duc de Stacpoole noted: 'I saw little or nothing of my neighbours, having no near ones, and English friends were afraid to come to Ireland, so that, mostly alone in my County Galway home, I had little to do but sit before the fire, reading my books or newspapers and ponder.'[115]

A few southern aristocrats had retained enough influence to be involved at different levels in attempts to settle the Anglo-Irish conflict. Lord Midleton was particularly prominent, but when the treaty was framed it omitted the safeguards for the minority position that had been proposed under the 1920 Government of Ireland Bill, which led him to censure it.[116] He became so embittered as to conclude it was 'one of the most deplorable desertions of their supporters of which any ministry has ever been guilty.'[117] Others hoped for some semblance of participation in public affairs in the future. Lord Dunraven was more conciliatory than Midleton; he contended the treaty 'gave to Ireland all I had long laboured for'.[118] The divisions of opinion were reflected in the split of the IUA with hardliners such as Lord Farnham, Lord Dunalley, E.J. Beaumont-Nesbitt and J.M. Wilson remaining, while the likes of Lords Desart, Donoughmore, Courtown, Headfort, Mayo, Sligo and Wicklow joined the new Anti-Partition League, but that organisation was also to have a short lifespan.[119] Before the War of Independence ended, some moderates tried to make peace with the new order. For example, in August 1920, a meeting of the deputy lieutenants and magistrates of Queen's County called for dominion Home Rule. Colonel Cosby of Stradbally Hall told those present: 'I am an old Unionist – as you know a life-long Unionist – and now I have to pocket my feelings and to do what I can for the good and benefit of my beloved country.'[120] After independence, John Bagwell of Marlfield accepted nomination to the Free State Senate to represent the minority interest, and said: 'The southern landlords have ceased to be the backbone of the British garrison in Ireland . . . they have ceased even to be Unionists, they have not ceased, however, and do not want to cease, to enrich their country with inherited gifts of loyalty and leadership and their capacity for public service.'[121] He was joined in the Senate by Lords Mayo, Headfort, Lansdowne, Longford and Wicklow, Sir John Keane, Sir Horace Plunkett, Maurice Moore, Sir Thomas Esmonde, General Bryan Mahon of Mullaboden and Ellen Cuffe, Countess of Desart. Ironically for them, the anti-Treatyites would reframe their loyalism in terms of aristocratic support for the new regime and consequently, as we shall see below, their houses (or in the case of Moore and Cuffe those of their family members) were once again endangered.

John Garvey was a staunch Loyalist who decided to stay on in Mayo while many of his neighbours migrated; on 10 November 1922, he wrote to Major Charles O'Hara of Annaghmore in Sligo: 'Most of the people who can afford to go are leaving. Miss Pery Knox Gore left Ballina House for good this week, and Miss Gore of Killala is leaving next week, and many others have abandoned their homes. We are determined to stay on to the end and my wife says she will only leave when she is carried out.'[122] In his August 1921 letter to Crawford (above), he had written: 'Your position in the north is a very difficult one chiefly on account of the religious atmosphere but with us there has been a tolerant spirit evidenced at all times. Indeed, were it not for that spirit we, a few people swimming in a great ocean, could not survive.'[123]

But, just six months later, he and his wife discovered that the Civil War greatly changed the local dynamic. He wrote again to Charles O'Hara in February 1923 that he and his wife 'had the shock of our lives' when their home was looted and burned: 'My wife had only a coat thrown over her and I had not even a pair of boots or stockings. We had to look on in the rain while they set fire to our beautiful home and it and all its contents that were not looted are now reduced to cinders.'[124] They were later left in no doubt about their future prospects in the area when they received an anonymous letter (poorly composed): 'You will never live heare to see a home built at this communitys expense so take this as a warning to clear out or to suffer the consequence. So to Belfast or to hell with you.'[125] The tone of bitter resentment and ancestral grievance encapsulated how civil wars can bring malice, revenge, spite, hatred, bitterness, jealousy, grievance and all such negatives to the fore. He was no longer welcome to stay, he could migrate to 'his own' in Belfast, the local nationalist community was not going to be burdened with the cost of rebuilding Tulley and, although not expressed, locals undoubtedly had their eye on his demesne lands.

7. 'Undamaged except for a badly needed wash'

Following a bitter and acrimonious debate between mid-December 1921 and early January 1922, Dáil Éireann ratified the Anglo-Irish treaty by sixty-four votes to fifty-seven; unable to support the ratification, Éamon de Valera and his followers withdrew. For the next few months attempts were made to heal the rift but to no avail; the IRA split along the lines of those who supported the treaty (generally referred to as Treatyites or Free Staters) and those who opposed it (anti-Treatyites, more disparagingly referred to as Irregulars). On 14 April 1922, anti-Treaty forces occupied the Four Courts in Dublin; its bombardment from 28 June by the National Army signalled the beginning of civil war. In the months that followed, as Mel Farrell puts it, 'a general state of lawlessness, masquerading as republicanism', became 'the new government's chief concern'.[126]

With the disbandment of the RIC and the withdrawal of the crown forces in the early months of 1922, country houses were even more vulnerable to attack. Co Kildare offers a very good example. During the War of Independence, it had a very high military presence: around 10,000 troops were stationed there in 1920–21. IRA activity in the county was restricted to 'small jobs' and effective intelligence work, rather than the type of largescale IRA ambushes carried out in the Munster counties.[127] Seamus Cullen has concluded: 'Until 1922, loyalists in Kildare enjoyed the security experienced by no other county outside Ulster owing to the presence of British army garrisons who were considered integral members of their community.'[128] No houses were burned in Kildare during the War of Independence, but there were four casualties in the Civil War. A later propagandist publication from the Irish Claims Compensation Association was at pains to emphasise that the destruction of country houses in the Free State as a whole had 'greatly . . . increased since the evacuation by British forces took place and the Free State Government assumed office'.[129] In a similar vein, but also highlighting the rise in ordinary criminality, a disillusioned Lord Midleton wrote to King George V: 'The hasty withdrawal of British troops, against which Your Majesty's Government were repeatedly warned, has left the South of Ireland without any force to preserve order and even if individuals were made amenable, there are no courts sitting effectively to deal with them . . . The mutiny of the IRA is probably the least serious element in crime.'[130]

On 21 February 1922, the government established an unarmed police force, An Garda Siochána, but given the circumstances it took the Gardaí considerable time to assert their authority, especially in strong anti-Treaty areas such as the southern counties.[131] And with so much to cope with, the burning of country houses was never going to be a Garda priority. For example, in August 1922 one of the most high-profile cases was the destruction of Currygrane in Co Longford, the ancestral home of Field Marshal Sir Henry Wilson. He had been assassinated by two IRA members – Reginald Dunne and Joseph Sullivan – on his doorstep in London on 22 June. The burning came just a day after their execution. This was possibly no coincidence, as suggested by Tom Brady, captain of D Company Longford Brigade, when reporting to his superiors: 'Sir H[enry] Wilson's house was burned on the day after the two men were hanged in London.'[132] However, the most prominent IRA leader in the county, Seán MacEoin, 'later speculated that this was a pretext for an underlying agrarian motive'.[133] (This, as shall be argued in the next chapter, was very common.) When asked by the Minister for Home Affairs to enquire into the burning of Currygrane, the Garda Commissioner, Eoin O'Duffy, replied that he did not want to convey 'an impression of impotence concerning the Civic Guard', but there were 'many cases of this kind now engaging the attention of the Guard' so that they could not 'move in these matters so energetically as might be wished and must perforce hasten slowly'.[134] Even if they could, it is doubtful if O'Duffy and his men would have had any great desire to locate the perpetrators in this case; the politics of Sir Henry and his brother, James Mackay, one of Longford's most prominent Unionists, had made them arch enemies of Irish republicanism.

O'Duffy, formerly IRA leader in Co Monaghan during the War of Independence, had been Chief of Staff of the National Army at the beginning of the Civil War and, therefore, familiar with the fact that in that uncertain period between the calling of the truce in July 1921 and the establishment of the Provisional Government in January 1922, the IRA had commandeered vacated country houses in which to drill in the event of another outbreak of hostilities. They were merely continuing the precedent set by the crown forces. Country houses were ideal: they had defensive architectural features comparable to barracks, extensive yards and out-buildings to accommodate men and demesnes where skirmishing could be practised. And they did not belong to the 'Irish people'; in that sense, the revolution against the landed elite continued. (Later, during the Civil War period, in a variation of the same, Dan Breen received orders from anti-Treaty headquarters for columns on active service to billet in mansions 'which were owned by persons hostile to the republic'.[135])

One of the first IRA leaders to commandeer a Big House was O'Duffy's replacement in Monaghan, Major General Dan Hogan, who in September 1921, with about fifty of his men, commandeered Lough Bawn House, home of the Tenison family, who had temporarily departed for England. Hogan had been born into a modest farming background in Tipperary. In 1917, he began his working career as a clerk with the Great Northern Railway in Clones and ended the War of Independence as a major general in command of the 5th Northern Brigade of the IRA. During the occupation of Lough Bawn, Hogan posed for a well-choreographed portrait at the front of the Big House that left no doubt that a new order had taken over and the *ancien régime* was no more. He was splendidly dressed in full military regalia, with all the trappings of his rise clearly visible – his impeccable uniform, silver watch and chain and a Thompson submachine gun on his lap. Then he posed with his men, again deliberately at the front of the house.

Hogan would not have been aware of it but the owner of Lough Bawn, William Tenison, had written to a friend during the War of Independence following an IRA raid: 'It was rather comic, they were such a seedy lot for representatives of the Irish Republic; I could hardly help laughing, it was so very like comic opera! But I did not want them to ransack the house, so I had to give up some guns and old swords and old revolver for which I have never been able to get any ammunition!'[136] Had he read it, Hogan might not have left the house intact when he and his men left.

At least thirty Big Houses were commandeered by the IRA in the second half of 1921. The IRA training camp at Lough Bawn was relatively modest in scale. In September 1921, an estimated 200 IRA men set up in Huntington Castle in Carlow, and 150 more used the demesne of Captain Trench at Ashfield in Queen's County. That same month, Carlow police reported that 'Duckett's Grove is now a large armed camp reported to be full of arms and ammunition' and that it had 'a large republican flag flying outside the front door of the house'.[137] Across the country, there were camps in houses such

4.4 During the Truce period from 11 July 1921, several country houses throughout the country were commandeered by the IRA as billets. This photograph shows the Monaghan IRA under Major General Dan Hogan, second from right in front row with a Thompson machine gun, outside Lough Bawn House.

as Highpark in Wicklow, Aghadoe House in Kerry, Stonehouse in Louth, Ballymacoll in Meath, Mantua in Roscommon, Carrigmore in Mayo, Clooncarrig in Leitrim and Kilfine in Westmeath. At Huntington Castle, a notice was fastened to the demesne gates 'intimating that there was no admission except on business and signed IRA'.[138] Ironically, those previously kept outside demesne walls were now deliberately keeping all others out.

In September 1921, the County Inspector of Kildare mockingly reported to Dublin Castle that training camps were 'run on comfortable lines . . . only the largest houses are fit be commandeered'. These included Harristown (unoccupied since the death of Percy La Touche earlier that year) and Dowdenstown, where the IRA were planning 'to overawe the non-combatant and neutral section of the population'.[139] After both houses were vacated, the Inspector was happy to report that: 'The rebels have, in each case, left the house perfectly tidy and undamaged except for a badly needed wash.'[140] The social class jibe in the comment was not quite as barbed as D.H. Doyne's whose Wicklow residence was occupied on 13 July 1922 by fifteen anti-Treatyites who demanded to be fed and accommodated: 'The damage to the house was mostly caused by dirt.

All bedding, mattresses, carpets, sofas etc. will have to go to Dublin to be thoroughly disinfected.'[141] In October 1921, forty IRA men took over Henry Bourke Jordan's Thornhill House in Mayo for about ten days; they left it 'seriously injured from a decorative point of view', and contents such as bed clothes, pots and pans and cutlery were looted.[142] But, in this case, there was also reported agrarian activity on his demesne and an element of Luddism in the destruction of farm machinery. Jordan's fear that his stock would be injured or rustled made him sell off his thoroughbred cattle and sheep. Without machinery and stock to farm, his only option was to then sell his lands, precisely what the agitators demanded. Were the IRA and local agrarian agitators one and the same? Who benefited from the redistribution of his demesne? These are very important questions of the revolutionary period neglected to date, which will be elucidated in the next chapter.

8. 'We have our orders my lord'

The most intense period of destruction during the Civil War was from the beginning of August to the end of October 1922 when thirty-six houses were burned. Newspapers and compensation files attributed a politico-military reason to most of these. For example, it was reported in July 1922 that anti-Treatyites attempted to blow up Mount Talbot House in Roscommon as it was occupied by Free Staters.[143] On 17 August 1922, the anti-Treatyites occupying Macroom Castle expecting an attack fled to the mountains, burning the castle before they left.[144] A few days before, Mitchelstown Castle, probably the largest house destroyed in the revolutionary period, was burned by evacuating anti-Treatyites (chapter six).[145] In October 1922, Tullamaine Castle in Tipperary was also burned as the National Army approached.

There was a dramatic escalation in burnings between the beginning of January and the end of April 1923 when ninety-four houses were burned. On 21 January 1923, an admittedly biased Free State military report claimed that 'With depleted numbers, lack of resources and unified control, and almost complete ineffectiveness from a military standpoint their [anti-Treaty] policy of military action is slowly changing to one of sheer destruction and obstruction of the Civil Government.'[146] Destruction of all types of property was widespread but more specifically regarding Big Houses there were discernible patterns similar to

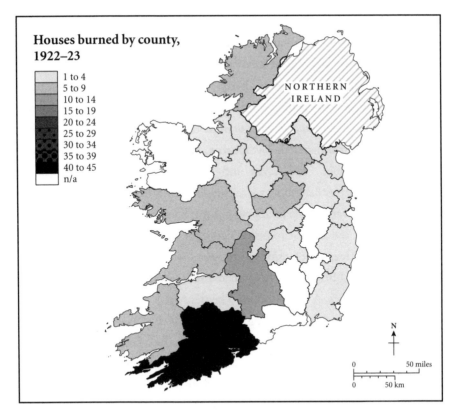

Map 3 County distribution of houses burned, 1922–23.
Drafted by Dr Jack Kavanagh.

the previous months.[147] Thus, when Castle Hackett was burned in January, the *Irish Times* reported: 'The reason given was that they [anti-Treatyites] expected the National Army to occupy it.'[148] After Colonel Bryan's Upton House in Wexford was burned the same month, his solicitors told him: 'The reason why your place was burned was because the Irregulars, knowing you were a Loyalist, feared that Upton would be used as a military barracks.'[149] But what did being a Loyalist mean in this case? Was it a supporter of the new Free State regime? Or was it in the traditional sense, suggesting that the destruction of Big Houses during the Civil War remained a priority of republicans wanting to reshape the landscape?

Those aristocratic senators who had chosen to support the new regime once again put their houses in the invidious position of being the most visible symbolic targets for anti-Treatyite reprisals in reaction to severe public safety legislation. On 28 September 1922, a Public Safety Resolution was sanctioned by the Provisional

Government, which established military courts of enquiry authorised to impose death sentences on captured anti-Treatyites found guilty of attacks against the National Army, or offences related to 'Looting, arson destruction, seizure, unlawful possession or removal of or damage to any public or private property. Having possession without proper authority of any bomb or article in the nature of a bomb or any dynamite, gelignite or other explosive substance or any revolver, rifle gun or other firearm or lethal weapon or any ammunition for such firearm.'[150]

On 19 December 1922, seven anti-Treatyites were executed in Kildare, which Breen Murphy has shown was 'the largest individual set of executions during the Civil War'.[151] The following month, January 1923, thirty-four executions took place, the highest recorded figure for any month.[152] On 26 January, all OCs of anti-Treatyite Divisions were issued with 'Operation Order No. 16: Senators' by GHQ in Dublin. It stipulated those houses of Free State senators identified in two lists, A and B, were to be destroyed as reprisals for executions of anti-Treatyite prisoners, including Sir John Bagwell at Marlfield in Tipperary; the Earl of Granard at Castleforbes in Longford; the Marquess of Headfort at Headfort in Meath; the Marquess of Lansdowne at Derreen in Kerry; Sir Bryan Mahon at Mullaboden in Kildare; the Earl of Mayo at Palmerstown, also in Kildare; the Earl of Wicklow at Shelton Abbey in Wicklow; Sir William Hutcheson-Poe at Heywood in Laois; the Earl of Dunraven at Adare in Limerick; Sir Walter Nugent Everard at Randlestown in Meath; Sir John Keane at Cappoquin in Waterford; Sir Horace Plunkett at Kilteragh in Dublin; and Sir Thomas Esmonde at Ballynastragh in Wexford.[153] In early February, the Chief of Staff of the anti-Treaty IRA, Liam Lynch, was reported in the newspapers as having declared that the IRA would 'hold every member of the so-called Parliament, Senate and other House, and all other Executives responsible [for the executions], and shall certainly visit them with the punishment they deserve'.[154] Eight of the above named senators' homes were burned and an abortive attempt made on Lord Granard's at Castle Forbes. The only exceptions were the homes of Headfort, Hutcheson-Poe, Dunraven and Everard.

On 29 January 1923, a party of armed men arrived at the Earl of Mayo's Palmerstown House in Kildare.

This was one of the few Irish country houses built in the last quarter of the nineteenth century and was very unusual, if not unique, in that it was constructed using funds raised by public subscription in commemoration of Richard

4.5 and 4.6 Palmerstown House, Co Kildare, before and after its burning during the Civil War. The anti-Treatyites told Lord Mayo they were burning the house as a reprisal for the execution of several of their comrades by the National Army. Mayo was also a senator in the Free State government, which made the house a target.

Southwell Bourke, 6th Earl of Mayo, who in 1872, at the age of fifty, was assassinated on a tour of a penal colony on the Andaman Islands when Viceroy of India. Built in the Queen Anne style to the design of T.H. Wyatt, it cost an estimated £21,300.[155] In 1923, its owner was Dermot Bourke, 7th Earl of Mayo. He had been prominent in the founding of the Kildare Archaeological Society, and along with his wife had founded the Irish Arts and Crafts Society. He had been disillusioned by the ousting of the aristocracy from national and local politics, declaring after his failure to win a seat in the 1899 county council election that it was 'a great misfortune that the country gentlemen who have for many years administered and been identified with country government should have been so completely ousted from their position . . . they had spent years on Grand Juries and Boards of Guardians, and worked well with the most violent nationalists'.[156] Nevertheless, he remained a prominent and conciliatory leader of southern Unionism, and was nominated to the Senate by W.T. Cosgrave. When the anti-Treatyites came to the front door of Palmerstown, the butler, suspecting their intentions, refused them entry. Another party knocked on the servants' entrance door at the back of the house; this time, Patrick Behan, the hall-boy, let the raiders in. When they met Lord Mayo, they told him that they were burning his house in reprisal for the execution of their seven comrades in the Curragh, and that his house had been chosen because he was a senator. Mayo supposedly said to them, 'Surely you are not going to burn this house full of beautiful things', to which the reply was, 'We have our orders, my lord.'[157] The deferential tone may have been wishful remembering, or else it pointed to Mayo's claim: 'I know perfectly well who was engaged locally in burning my house.'[158] The Curragh military fire brigade arrived around midnight but 'could do nothing, the whole house being then in the grip of the fire, and the hose lines insufficiently long to secure any considerable quantity of water'. The fire raged all through the night, ceiling after ceiling collapsed with 'deafening noise', cut-stone window facings and turrets split with the heat and 'flew in splinters and crashed to the ground'.[159]

A few weeks later, a group of armed men made their way to Senator Bryan Mahon's home at Mullaboden also in Kildare. Neither he nor his wife were in residence at the time. The raiders had with them seventy tins of petrol stolen from the Anglo-Mexican Petroleum Company in Blessington, across the Wicklow border. The house servants were rounded up and ordered to pile the furniture into the middle of the rooms. The raiders broke the windows with the butts of their rifles to fan the flames. Then came the comedic part. One of the raiders, who had discovered Mahon's British army general's uniform, put it on in an act of mockery, and marched around the house, while a comrade, who had found a gramophone, placed it on the front steps and played a marching tune as an accompaniment to the cacophony of splintering furniture and crackling glass in the background.[160] When the raiders left, the estate firefighting equipment was useless to combat the massive conflagration; so too was the Curragh military fire brigade, despite its 40 horsepower Denny engine capable of drawing water from a pond 130 yards down the avenue.[161] When a reporter arrived from the *Kildare Observer*, he found articles of furniture scattered around the front lawn, and members of the fire brigade passing the family silver out through windows.[162] The more valuable artefacts had already been removed to Dublin as a precaution following the earlier destruction of Palmerstown.

When the raiders came to Marlfield in January 1923, they told the Bagwell family (Bagwell himself was absent) that 'They had orders to burn the house,

4.7 Moore Hall, Co Mayo, one of the grandest country house ruins in the west of Ireland. Burned by anti-Treatyites during the Civil War, its owner was a brother of Senator Maurice Moore, which may have contributed to its destruction.

as Mr Bagwell was a member of the Free State Senate.'[163] A week before, according to the *Clonmel Chronicle*, 100 estate employees and their families had gathered for a party to celebrate Senator John Bagwell's son's coming of age and in time honoured fashion presented a gift signifying their 'good feeling and loyalty'.[164] If the number is accurate, and if many of these subsequently lost their jobs, the burning of Marlfield must have been extremely damaging to the local community and economy. Other houses belonging to senators' relatives were burned too: Desart Court, home of the Earl of Desart, whose sister-in-law was a senator, and Moore Hall, home of George Moore, whose brother, Maurice, was a senator.

But there were also many more houses burned in reprisal – or at least where reprisal was part of the mix – that did not belong to senators. When Greenhills was burned in Offaly in February 1923: 'The leader announced they were Republicans who had come to burn the house as a reprisal for the execution of Patrick Geraghty', who had been tried and executed on 27 January for possession of an automatic pistol at Croghan.[165]

4.8 Macroom Castle, August 1922. This is a rare photograph of a country house as it was burning. Note the crowds of curious people passing by.

In her study of everyday violence in the Irish Civil War, Gemma Clark has argued that 'House burnings, assaults, boycotts and so on did not serve an obviously military plan.'[166] In a like vein, while reflecting on the destruction of Mitchelstown by retreating anti-Treatyites, historian Bill Power has noted: 'They [the IRA] also claimed pathetically, that by destroying the castle they were denying a base to their Free State enemies before whom they intended to retreat anyway.'[167] Not long after the burning of Macroom Castle in the same county, state solicitor Thomas Healy pointed out that 'It was considered by the people as a wanton act, unnecessary for the purpose of military operations or otherwise.'[168]

If there was no military logic to anti-Treatyite strategy, and they were not used as reprisal targets, there is an argument to be made that civil war conditions continued to provide further opportunity to dismantle the architecture of the Big House and to rid the countryside of the physical reminders of the coloniser, and to some this may have been at least as important as political or military struggle.[169] As Robert Bevan argues, 'The erasure of the memories, history and identity attached to architecture and place – enforced forgetting' is very often an objective of the destroyers.

The sectarian dimension has not been comprehensively pursued in this work; would it serve any purpose given that the vast majority of Big Houses were Protestant owned? Big Houses were burned because they were owned by Protestant Loyalists, Protestant spies, Protestant senators or Protestant landlords; the evidence does not suggest they were burned simply because they were owned by Protestants. James Donnelly Jr at the beginning of his study of Big House burnings in Cork stated: 'This is a worthwhile exercise partly because it sheds much new light on the strikingly wide extent of IRA attacks on the heavily Protestant gentry of Cork during the guerrilla war against Britain, especially in its last few months', but concluded: 'This examination of Big House burnings in 1920–21 does not offer any significant support to the view that members of the embattled Protestant landed elite of Cork were victimized because of their religion.'[170]

In this wider study, the same conclusion can be drawn. Knockabbey in Co Louth was Catholic owned. Local lore claims that the IRA burned it so that they would not be accused of sectarianism. In January 1923, when Ballygassan in the same county was attacked, its owner thought that it was for sectarian reasons but, when he put this to the leader of the raiders, he was told that it was 'a protest against executions . . . We care nothing for religion.'[171] In Irish rural society religion mattered a lot: in border counties such as Monaghan during the revolutionary period politico-religious divides gave rise to heightened sectarian tensions, but in the case of Big House burnings, while there is no doubt that religion may at times have been the incendiary, it did not cause the inferno.[172] In the case of Ballygassan and most houses, other factors have to be considered including loyalism, social inequality, local jealousies, the desire for ancestral revenge and agrarian grievances, and these were very often all entwined.[173] This is not, however, to entirely deny, as Clark reminds us, that 'the deep-seated, almost subconscious nature of inter-denominational resentments' remained 'the lived reality for Protestants in the new country', including the aristocracy, and she quotes Sir John Bagwell's mother, who recalled Co Tipperary around the time of the burning of Marlfield: 'Every man went in fear of his neighbour and the plight of Protestants living in lonely farms and cottages . . . was pitiable.'[174] Harriet Bagwell's juxtaposition of Protestants and farms brings us to the central theme of the next chapter, the role of agrarianism in Big House burnings, which will again emphasise that 'anti-Protestantism was far too entangled with issues of landownership to explain on its own the violence against the planters'.[175]

9. 'The corpses buried in the old laundry drying ground'

There were other houses fortunate to have survived occupation by either side in the Civil War and Birr Castle in King's County (Offaly), home of the Parsons family, Earls of Rosse, one of the most significant houses in the midlands, is worth mentioning in this respect.

In July 1922, Crinkle Barracks in Birr was burned by anti-Treatyites and immediately the National Army commandeered Birr Castle as a substitute barracks. At first, Toler Garvey, the estate agent, was relieved as he had feared the worst for the castle after the burning of Crinkle. He explained to Geoffrey Parsons: 'The place is now occupied by Gov[ernmen]t troops & I can feel easy once again as to its safety. There will possibly be fighting in the district but not in here now as it is held in force.'[176] Garvey kept up almost daily correspondence with the family, advising, for example, the removal of furniture but equally assuring the family that 'So far, no damage whatever is being done beyond dirt, which will, no doubt, entail the rooms being done up again when

4.9 Birr Castle, Co Offaly, home of Lord Rosse. Occupied by the National
Army during the Civil War, it was for a while the burial ground of three young
anti-Treatyites executed on the demesne. It remains in the ownership of Brendan
Parsons, 7th Earl of Rosse.

evacuated.'[177] He kept an inventory of the furniture and utensils handed over
by the housekeeper for use by the army; expressed his concerns to army GHQ
about the amount of electricity being consumed, the use of the family boats on
the river and the shooting of game. Eventually, he began to look for compensation for the occupancy of the Castle.[178] On 5 June 1923, he wrote to the
Board of Works explaining that as Lord Rosse's mother could not return to the
castle, she had to take a lease on No 1 Hyde Park Street, London, at a rent of
£322 plus rates which came to £600 per annum. She also had to spend £1,500
'in putting it into order and redecorating it, which was essential'.[179] The reply
was favourable: the government was prepared to pay rent 'at the rate of £1,000
per annum, £500 down for removal of furniture . . . and that the question of
wear and tear, inside and out, is to be dealt with at the end of the occupation'.[180] This sheds a different light on the occupation of houses by the National
Army: they were not commandeered without payment.

There was a disturbing aspect to the occupation of Birr Castle which could
have given the anti-Treatyites strong motivation to burn it. On 26 January

1923, three youths from Tullamore – William Conroy, Patrick Cunningham and Colum Kelly – were court-martialled for armed raids on houses in Ballycowan.[181] The executions were carried out in the grounds of the castle and the young men were buried there. On 26 January 1923, Garvey, realising the dangers inherent in this, wrote to the OC of the National Army: 'Acting on behalf of the Earl of Rosse's Trustees I wish to enter a formal protest against executions taking place at Birr Castle and the burial of executed persons within the grounds. If such unfortunately had to be carried out, I do not think it should be on privately owned premises.'[182] On the same day, he wrote to the Chief of Staff at Portobello Barracks: 'I need hardly point out the stigma which will attach to the place in consequence, especially if the executed persons are buried there and I have to request on behalf of the Earl of Rosse's Trustees that you will make other arrangements.'[183] And, on the following day, he wrote to Geoffrey Parsons:

I am sorry to say that three executions were carried out in the Castle Grounds yesterday morning and the corpses buried in the old laundry drying ground close to the gravel tennis court. I wrote at once on behalf of the Trustees protesting against this having been done in private grounds and requesting that the bodies be re-interred elsewhere.[184]

A year later, on 3 January 1924, Garvey again wrote to the Chief of Staff:

I am directed by Lord Rosse's trustees to inquire whether the time has not now arrived when the remains of the men executed last year and buried in the private grounds of Birr Castle could be safely removed and re-interred elsewhere. It is obvious that for many reasons they cannot be left indefinitely in the private grounds and though of course Lord Rosse's trustees understand that the military authorities would in any case have the removal carried out before the premises are evacuated, there seems to be no good reason why it should not now be done.[185]

The three young men were later re-interred in an unmarked grave in Clonminch cemetery. Had the National Army evacuated before the end of the Civil War, Birr would have been very lucky to survive.

10. 'It's very strange to see a sentry by night in the gallery'

Finally, although outside the area of study, it is worth briefly comparing the Big House situation in the six counties of Ulster that became Northern Ireland following partition. In her study of this region, Olwen Purdue records no houses burned there during the War of Independence. She points to the fact that, given the very different politico-religious demographic, prominent aristocrats had the advantage over their southern counterparts of being better able to protect their homes. Sir Basil Brooke, for example, one of the founders of the Ulster Special Constabulary, had the comfort of four constables permanently guarding his estate, while fourteen policemen also guarded Caledon House in south Tyrone.[186] In June 1921, as burnings in the south intensified, Lord Dufferin and Ava, one of the most prominent political aristocrats in Ulster, wrote to his mother:

I have ten men and 2 officers of the regiment sleeping in the house [Clandeboye]. They were sent here without any suggestion on my part. It's very strange to see a sentry by night in the gallery with rifle and tin hat. . . . The officers stay in the billiard room and the men in the old steward's hall. They have their beds there and it makes a splendid barrack room.[187]

It was not until May 1922 that the attacks on northern houses began, coinciding with the IRA's campaign against Northern Ireland.[188] On 5 May, Eoin O'Duffy, IRA Chief of Staff, decided to launch an IRA offensive in Ulster; according to his biographer this was with the knowledge of Michael Collins but not the rest of the Cabinet.[189] The offensive began two weeks later, according to captured documents with the aim 'to render impotent the so-called Government of Northern Ireland'.[190] This goes some way to explaining the motives for the initial blitz in which eight houses were burned within a very short space of time.[191] For example, Shane's Castle in Randalstown, Co Antrim, which was the home of Lord O'Neill, father of Hugh O'Neill, Speaker of the Northern Ireland parliament. A week later, Culdaff House on the Innishowen peninsula, the home of Lord O'Neill's agent, George Young, was burned.[192] Young's son was private secretary to Speaker O'Neill and his brother was Crown Solicitor for Derry. Crebilly Castle near Ballymena was the home of Ronald McNeill, later 1st Lord Cushendun, who was a Conservative MP and Parliamentary Under Secretary of

State for Foreign Affairs.[193] Political motives might not explain the burning of Garron Tower on 22 May 1922 which, at the time, was being leased as a hotel. According to a report in the *Belfast News Letter* the fifty or so raiders 'appeared to have come over the mountain from the Parkmore district. They were led by men who spoke with southern accents, officers from some of the South of Ireland IRA headquarters, presumably.'[194]

The Northern Ireland government responded to the IRA offensive by proclaiming them as illegal (along with Sinn Féin and Cumann na mBan) and hundreds of suspects were arrested across the jurisdiction in a massive roundup by the Ulster Special Constabulary and the military.[195] Coincident with these arrests came the burning of Oldcourt Castle in Co Down, the home of Lady de Ros, and Crebilly House in Antrim, which 'was reduced to a pile of ruins, nothing standing but gaunt and blackened walls'.[196] The Carnlough, Cushendall and Cushendun areas of Antrim subsequently witnessed pitched battles between the IRA and police (an estimated 150 IRA volunteers overran Cushendall village, where 'for four hours a terrific battle raged between the invaders and the police'.[197]) On their way to Carnlough, the IRA burned Drumnasole House, home of the Turnley family. Thus, in most cases in Northern Ireland, political motives would seem obvious, though not certain, for Purdue also points out that one cannot dismiss the fact that 'the continuing sense of insecurity provided ample opportunity for disaffected individuals to avenge their own personal grudges against landlords'.[198]

This common characteristic of civil wars – retribution for past grievances – also fed into the agrarianism to be dealt with in the next chapter; as Stathis Kalyvas has argued, internecine conflict often 'provides a mere pretext, a costume in which to clothe the pursuit of private conflicts; it just disguises private and local motivations as political ones'.[199] When, for instance, Castleffogarty in Tipperary was burned in April 1922, the *Irish Times* reported that it had been occupied by the Black and Tans until February.[200] Its destruction meant that particular contamination, as local Nationalists might have perceived it, was eradicated. But in 1924, questions were being asked in the Dáil about the redistribution of part of the Castleffogarty demesne.[201] Therefore, another purpose had been served by forcing the family away from the area permanently, which suggests why the role of agrarianism needs to be addressed separately. Land redistribution provides a motive powerful enough to be isolated from the others discussed in this chapter, arguably one which should be looked for in every individual case until it can be definitively excluded from the mix.

5

'I THINK THE GREED OF LAND IS AT THE ROOT OF THIS CLASS OF CRIME'

'Who does that demesne belong to, Colonel Buckley?' 'It belongs to me,' Buckley replied. 'Well, now, take a good luck at me while you can!' the young man retorted, 'That demesne belonged to me before you came over with Cromwell. My name's MacFerris.'

(H.V. Morton, *In Search of Ireland*, London, 1930, p. 118)

When the mansion house is destroyed, the park and adjoining lands are more easily commandeered for distribution among the "soldiers of the republic".

(Irish Claims Compensation Association, *The Irish Free State: The Campaign of Fire*, London, 1923, p. 8)

1. 'Our day has come'

In his paper 'Big House Burnings in County Cork', James S. Donnelly argued:

Though agrarian motives played a relatively modest role in Volunteer decisions to burn particular Big Houses [during the War of Independence], what happened in the wake of these burnings before and especially after the Truce of 11 July 1921 provides strong evidence that agrarian considerations exercised considerable influence over the actions of the Cork IRA brigades and their leaders.[1]

Similarly, in *The Decline of the Big House in Ireland* (2001), this author had earlier made the point that 'Of at least equal importance in the rise of burnings during the Civil War was the continued growth in agrarian agitation.'[2] It was at the time a tentative enough conclusion but now with the benefit of hind-sight, further research and the work of other historians it seems rather an understatement. In his 2011 study of house burnings in Offaly, Ciarán Reilly, for instance, concluded that at least seven of the twelve houses destroyed there 'were targeted because of agrarian issues (and there is no discounting agrari-anism as an ulterior motive in the others)'.[3] Gemma Clark in her 2014 study argued that 'Land hunger was a powerful motivator in Civil War burnings' in the three Munster counties of Limerick, Tipperary and Waterford. But, going back to Donnelly's argument, did agrarian motives only play a modest role during the War of Independence? What follows contends that his argument requires some modification.

Some context is required. Coincident with the ending of the Great War, a proliferation of organisations such as The Evicted Tenants Association, The Unpurchased Tenants Association and The Back to the Land Movement emerged, and these, as well as local committees, or even random gangs, began demanding in political and public arenas, or often in face-to-face confronta-tions with individual owners, that the remnants of the aristocracy and gentry (and, indeed, large farmers, who fall outside the scope of this study) should break up their demesnes and untenanted lands. Most of these worked with impunity. Galway was a very good example: in February 1920 at least seven landlords were approached to sell some of their lands, and it seems there was very little the authorities could do to prevent demands or intimidation.[4] At the most extreme level, in March, Frank Shawe-Taylor was shot dead in the same county because he refused to negotiate the division of his estate. Kevin O'Shiel, a judge in the Dáil land courts, contended that his murder opened the flood-gates to agrarian agitation: 'The fever swept like a prairie fire over Connacht and portions of the other provinces, sparing neither great ranch nor little farm . . . inflicting, in its headlong course, sad havoc on man, beast and property.'[5] In April and May, agitation on Lord Ashtown's Woodlawn estate was aimed at 'making a determined effort to secure land for distribution among the evicted tenants and landless men'.[6] Mrs Palmer of Glenloe Abbey was ordered under threat of death to sell eighty acres of demesne land in front of the mansion to local uneconomic holders. It was reported that she offered to take £4,000, 'but finally sold for £1,600, much below the value of the land'.[7] Galway became such a hotbed of agrarianism that Padraic Fallon, born in 1905 and the son of a Galway cattle dealer, later contentiously recalled that 'The War of Independence [in Galway was] . . . a land war and a class struggle, fought primarily against the Anglo-Irish ruling and landowning class rather than against England.'[8] In total, twenty-four houses were burned there in 1920–23 (eight during the War of Independence and sixteen during the Civil War), by far the highest county total outside Munster. Agrarianism was a leading factor.

One of the more telling episodes occurred on the Ballydugan estate in the east of the county. There had been a generation or more of tension between the landlord, Michael Henry Burke, his tenants and uneconomic holders in the area because of his refusal to sell his estate under the Wyndham Land Act.[9] In 1915, his precarious financial position eventually forced him to sell 300 acres to the Irish Land Commission for redistribution, but this was not enough to satisfy the land hungry. During and after the war, Burke was boycotted, locals grazed their cattle on his demesne and refused to take his lands on conacre, and this activity was intensified during the revolutionary period. The ringleader, Michael Dempsey, was a shepherd on the estate who resided in one of the estate lodges. In 1925, Burke recalled the intimidation to a friend:

> Dempsey had given men to threaten my life on three different occasions and on the last occasion after they rushed into my bedroom [1921] and firing a shot close to my head, and then pointing the rifle towards my stomach made me sign a paper while Dempsey dictated his terms . . . He forcibly broke up my best meadow paddock and put as many stock on my land as he chose.[10]

Burke was determined, he said, not to reward Dempsey and his co-conspirators 'with fine fat holdings and houses in the cream of the demesne'.[11] On the night of 15 June 1922, when Burke was in Dublin seeking protection from the Provisional Government, three armed men broke down the front door, forced Mrs Burke and two servants into the outbuildings and set the house on fire, completely destroying it and its contents.[12] Burke believed that Dempsey was 'backed up by all the Irish Republican Army', but Ann O'Riordan, who forensically investigated this case, found no evidence of IRA involvement, and concluded that: 'The ongoing agrarian intimidation and the history of unrest in this region combined to form the primary motive for the burning of Ballydugan House – the desire for land.'[13] Burke rebuilt

5.1 Ballydugan House, Co Galway, burned in June 1922, the motivation firmly grounded in local agrarian agitation and the demand for the breakup of the estate. The house was subsequently rebuilt in 1930.

Ballydugan in 1930 but he continued to be boycotted, intimidated and his house raided, while those who took his lands on conacre were attacked for years after. Land hunger did not abate after the Civil War, nor did the revolutionary experience of the Big House.

When Art O'Connor, the Director of Agriculture, reported to the Dáil on the rise of agrarian crime that took place from the spring of 1920, he closely echoed O'Shiel's reminiscence, stating that 'The land war broke out with a virulence and a presage of danger which made the worst of previous years seem positively tame.'[14] It is worth recalling that this was the very same time that the IRA were destroying hundreds of rural RIC barracks. It is difficult to quantitatively prove O'Connor's statement because the data does not exist; the RIC could not gather crime statistics as reliably as in the past. However, the qualitative evidence goes some way to supporting both his and O'Shiel's claims – and while agitation impacted all levels of agricultural society, it was certainly the case that the aristocracy came under more widespread attack than at any time in living memory.

In May 1920 alone, in Waterford 600 cattle belonging to C. Nugent Humble were driven off the land and outbuildings on his demesne were burned.[15] In Leitrim, the military were forced to offer protection to Sir Gilbert King of Charlestown House to stop cattle raids.[16] W.R. Hickey of Galtee Castle in Tipperary was threatened with death if he did not give up his grazing lands.[17] The estate herdsman on the J.F. Kenny estate of Ballyglass House in Mayo was battered to death for failing to quit the employment of its owner.[18] In Westmeath, 200 cattle belonging to Colonel J.D. Fetherstonhaugh of Rockview House were driven off the land.[19] In Clare, death threats were made to the labourers on H.V. MacNamara's estate around Ennistymon House because, it was reported, 'Small landowners are endeavouring to compel the owner to surrender land for division.'[20] In Roscommon, all farmhands and servants were forced out of employment on the Walpole estate and the military were called in to protect the land.[21]

The county of Roscommon was particularly affected. On 5 May 1920, buildings (though not yet the Big House) on Major Chichester-Constable's Runnamoat estate were burned.[22] On 29 May 1920, R.A. Corr wrote to the *Roscommon Journal* citing a letter he had in his possession that had been sent by Chichester-Constable to his herdsman in which he threatened he would be fired by 8 June unless he did his duty to 'prevent the trespass of all stock on the lands under your charge, and to only allow such stock on the land as belong to the tenant'. Very publicly, Corr reminded Chichester-Constable that 8 June 1879 was the date on which Parnell and Davitt 'stood side by side at the great Westport Demonstration, and made their first appeal to the Irish people to defend their homesteads and hold the harvest'. Corr concluded: 'Some of us were only boys then, but we are seasoned soldiers today.'[23] The threat was deep-rooted and clearly inherited from the Land War era.

In places where the landowner proved obstinate, O'Shiel recalled that there was often 'a mute, significant and generally effective gesture, in the shape of a grave neatly opened on his lawn, or at his front door'.[24] One landowner who experienced this was Charles Phibbs of Doobeg in Sligo. His ancestors had been landlords in the baronies of Corran and Tiretagh since the mid-seventeenth century. During the extended Land War from 1879 onwards, Phibbs was constantly in conflict with tenants over rents, turbary rights and after 1900 his purchase of a boycotted farm from Lord Harlech.[25] He had long-term protection from the RIC, who were stationed in a hut on his demesne until the spring of 1920 when they were forced to evacuate by the IRA. According to Einion Thomas, Phibbs was at that stage a detested figure locally: firstly, because of his history of arrogant estate management, and, secondly, because of the perception that he was 'the chief British sympathiser in the area'.[26] By 1922, he was the target of both the IRA and local agrarianists. The former kidnapped and threatened to shoot him and the latter (but potentially both one and the same) daubed the walls of his home, Doobeg, with threatening graffiti and dug a grave outside his front door, at the head of which was planted a cross with the following epitaph: 'Here lies the remains of Charles Phibbs/who died with a ball of lead in his ribs/His tenants are all aggrieved at as quick he went/for he went of a sudden without lifting the rent.'[27] Phibbs heeded the warning and emigrated to Wales, where he settled on a 100-acre farm in Plas Gwynfryn, while the IRA took over Doobeg.[28] Ten years later, the Irish Land Commission redistributed his demesne and untenanted lands for the relief of local congestion.[29] It took a while, but the enforced exile of Phibbs had achieved its purpose.

As labour historian Emmet O'Connor has argued 'radicalism was far more widespread' in the post-war period than was once appreciated, and Bolshevism was a powerful inspiration to rural agitators.[30] From the spring of 1920, Bolshevism was certainly a term growing in popularity amongst the aristocracy to describe what was unfamiliar to them, but which they generally equated with expropriation of their lands.[31] In April 1920, Lord Oranmore recorded in his journal that he, Lord Midleton and Lord Desart had met the Lord Lieutenant and 'represented to him the terrible state of the country more particularly with reference to Land Agitation which is starting once more in the West, which is virtually a form of Bolshevism'.[32] Similarly, newspaper clippings kept by Sybil Lucas-Scudamore, who left Ireland after her Monaghan home, Castleshane, was burned in 1920, dealt with sensational accounts of 'Rampant Bolshevism in the south', and a published threatening letter of the type 'received daily by Loyalists in Southern Ireland':

> If you don't give back the money to the grabbers of the farms you sold and also give up the other farms . . . we are a few men who fought for Ireland and who burned your house, who are looking on and are determined to see justice done . . . no protection, official or unofficial, will save you from our

5.2 Charles Phibbs standing in a grave dug for him outside his home, Doobeg, in Co Sligo. The walls of the house were also daubed with graffiti, reflecting political beliefs of the day. After decades of agrarian agitation, the Phibbs family were eventually forced to leave the house for Wales.

vengeance. We might also say we hate Protestants as they would grind us and did when they had power. Our day has come.[33]

Large landowners were perhaps fortunate that, in the early summer of 1920, the Irish Catholic hierarchy stringently denounced Bolshevism in Ireland.[34] This was at precisely the same time that the conservative elements within the revolutionary Dáil began to tackle deep-rooted agrarianism; the coincidence of the two is inferred. The cause that incitement to land agitation had served in the popularisation of Sinn Féin had become problematic with the escalation in agrarianism, and TDs and ministers who came from propertied backgrounds suddenly recoiled. In June the Dáil decreed:[35]

That the present time when the Irish people are locked in a life and death struggle with their traditional enemy, is ill-chosen for the stirring up of strife amongst our fellow-countrymen; and that all our energies must be directed towards the clearing out – not the occupier of this or that piece of land – but the foreign invader of our country.[36]

The Dáil adopted a calculated dual approach of establishing arbitration courts to deal with land disputes and ordering that 'the forces of the Republic be used to protect the citizens against the adoption of high-handed methods by any such person or persons' engaged in agrarianism.[37] Both went some way to quelling the agitation, especially in the west, but the threats to aristocratic land and property were far from over.[38] And in a climate where there was a prevailing hunger for land it was inevitable that Big Houses would be targeted; it was the surest way to drive out landowners and hope that their demesnes, which they had held on to after the 1903 Land Act, would be redistributed. Therefore, agrarianism became a key factor in the burning of Big Houses, though not always the most obvious.

One of the ways to illustrate this is to revisit case studies presented in the previous chapter where the motives seemed clear cut. For instance, in the burning of Moydrum Castle on 3 July 1921 counter-reprisal was the most obvious motive and the one that has been widely accepted since. But might there have been an ulterior motive? Did some of the local IRA have another agenda in mind? What IRA leader Thomas Costello did not mention in his Bureau of Military History witness statement was that he and his two brothers had been actively involved in agrarian agitation in the lead-up to the burning. A year before, he, along with eight others, described as 'sons of small farmers in the Kilgarvan district', had been arrested for cattle driving from a farm belonging to a Protestant farmer from Mount Temple, George Johnston.[39] Johnston had recently purchased a farm for £1,500 that the small farmers of the area had pursued. On the night before the cattle drive, a deputation had visited Johnston and offered him £2,000 for the seventy-acre farm but he refused the offer.

At the trial, Head Constable Feeney described the nine suspects as: 'All small farming people, a lot of them are living on the edge of the bog. I know them all for a number of years. They are well-conducted, hard-working lads.'[40] (Feeney was later described by Costello as 'a moderate type of man', perhaps suggesting that he held some degree of sympathy for republicanism.[41]) At that stage Costello was actually working as a shop assistant. He was, therefore, of the type – shop assistant from a farming background – that Lord Lieutenant French's proclamation was intended to appeal to, except in his case he had already been an avowed Volunteer since 1917 and would become a member of the Irish Republican Brotherhood in early 1919.[42] On 11 April 1921, a few weeks before the burning of Moydrum, Johnston was executed as a spy by the IRA.[43] Costello, by then a local IRA leader, had no doubt that Johnston 'was the principal Intelligence agent for the county', and justified his execution on those grounds.[44] However, one of Costello's comrades, Henry O'Brien, captain of the Coosan company of the IRA admitted: 'I have no knowledge of Johnston's guilt and was just one of a party who were ordered to execute him.'[45] This obviously begs some questions about motive, particularly in light of the prior agitation.

Agitation on the Moydrum estate began very shortly after its burning. Between August 1921 and October 1922, a long series of crimes was committed: they began with the burning of the gatekeeper's cottage on the demesne. On 22 November 1921, the estate office was also destroyed; Eugene Dunne contends this was deliberate as all records such as rentals and accounts were lost, thus none survived of defaulting tenants on the unsold parts of the estate.[46] During the Civil War, in May 1922, when Lord Castlemaine refused to take £2 10 shillings per acre rent for 125 acres of demesne land, locals responded by putting more than fifty head of cattle on the land to graze freely. In April 1923, the steward's house was burned as well as several outbuildings, garages and stables, almost the entire demesne infrastructure. In December 1923, nine bullocks on the demesne had their tails cut, a cruel way of preventing them from swatting at flies, causing the cattle to become irritated and unable to thrive.[47]

Dunne has concluded: 'While the desire for revenge was strong following the burning of houses in the Athlone area by crown forces, it was also a convenient pretext for the destruction of Moydrum Castle and Creggan House.'[48] His point that 'There appears to have been an orchestrated and systematic campaign of vandalism and intimidation to force him to leave the Athlone area' has validity.[49] By that time, Costello had grabbed part of the demesne lands and was grazing his own cattle there. They were seized by the Free State government under the Public Safety (Emergency Powers) Act, 1923, but what happened thereafter has not been ascertained, except that by the time Costello gave his BMH witness statement he was living at Shop Street in Drogheda.[50] It may be the case that he was debarred from a land divide under the terms of the 1923 Land Act (see chapter 9). Nevertheless, in 1924, Lord Castlemaine, now permanently resident in England, had no option but to sell the Moydrum demesne and his other extensive untenanted lands to the Irish Land Commission, which then divided them amongst the small uneconomic holders in the locality.

Paul Bew has made the valid point that, 'It is certainly not difficult to see how incidents which appear to be agrarian in origin, were transformed into significant episodes of the national struggle.'[51] The corollary is equally worth considering: it is not difficult to see that actions that appeared to be driven by the national struggle were, in fact, motivated by local agrarian issues. Like Moydrum, the burning of Summerhill was not the end of its revolutionary experience. Peter Dolan, an IRA volunteer involved, was also a member of the local Garadice Back to the Land Movement. In 1922–23 this movement came together with the ITGWU and occupied a 400-acre holding of Langford's at Laracor on the outskirts of Summerhill village. The intention was to force him to sell it to labourers who had lost their jobs because of the destruction of the house, and to redistribute what was left amongst the landless.

Langford's agents, Thomas Crozier & Sons, defended his decision to dismiss his employees in a letter to the secretary of the ITGWU: 'The wages bill was very heavy and as the house was burnt the present Lord Langford could not reside there, as he always intended to do. It cannot reasonably be expected that he should continue to pay some thousands of pounds per year in labour, which was almost entirely utilised in the upkeep of large gardens, pleasure grounds, avenues etc.'[52] The ITGWU response was to call out the remainder of the labourers. Thus, Langford was faced with a rural alliance with only one thing in mind, the redistribution of his untenanted lands.

The murder of Sir Arthur Vicars and the burning of Kilmorna were attributed to him being a spy, but might there have been other ulterior motives? Vicar's valet, Michael Murphy, said in his BMH witness statement that Vicars was 'a thorough gentleman who mixed freely with the tenants on the estate which comprised 650 acres'.[53] Murphy most likely meant that Vicars retained untenanted lands that he let on the eleven-month system to graziers, a contentious arrangement when there was such a hunger for land. Contemporaries had a strong sense of this. In April 1921, the month that Kilmorna was burned, the County Inspector reporting on several attacks on Big Houses in Kerry concluded: 'I think the greed of land is at the root of this class of crime.'[54] And the following month: 'There appears to be a determination to burn out all the old gentlemen's country houses. This is a Bolshevist scheme within Sinn Féin. The idea is to keep the old families from returning after "peace" and to grab their demesne lands.'[55] In 1937, an eleven-year-old schoolboy, Thomas Flavin, wrote down his elderly neighbour's version of what had happened at Kilmorna for the school's folklore project; Michael Keane recalled that Vicars 'was put up against a tree and shot dead' and 'Kilmorna [demesne] was breaking up every day from that on, until at last the land was divided among the uneconomic holders of the neighbouring district.'[56] Vicars may have been killed as an informer but his death ultimately led to the redistribution of his remaining lands.

There were similar cases the length and breadth of Ireland. In her study of Co Louth, Jean Young has also shown that agrarianism was a factor in burnings there.[57] Her detailing of the possible reasons for the destruction of Ravensdale on 18 June 1921 begins with 'the presumed reason' that it was 'to prevent its use as a barracks'.[58] However, as Young explains, this was another house no longer owned by the original aristocratic family, the Earls of Clermont. It had changed hands on several occasions since 1898 and most recently in 1919 when it was bought by Thomas Archer, a Dublin-based timber merchant, for £15,000. Archer was not interested in the house: he had made 'a speculative purchase' given the potential there was to sell hundreds of acres of timber from the demesne.[59] As soon as he had the timber harvested, he put the house and 2,000 acres up for sale in May 1920 and bidding reached just over £22,000 before it was withdrawn. Just over a year later, the unoccupied mansion was burned, supposedly by the local IRA.[60]

But why had it and the demesne been taken off the market? The answer lies in the local agitation for the redistribution of its demesne. In 1924, Archer sold the 2,000 acres, not to the highest bidder, but to the Land Commission for £9,000, which was less than half of what he could have received four years before. Father McAleer, the Catholic parish priest of Lordship, had made it

5.3 Ravensdale Park, Co Louth, burned in June 1921.

clear that 'The local farmers who held miserable small holdings in his parish and in the adjoining parish of Jonesborough wanted an addition to their farms in order to make some sort of living.'[61] The following year, Canon Peter Sheerin, parish priest of Upper Creggan, bought the salvage from Ravensdale for £250, and the building of his new Catholic church at Glassdrummond began in 1927: the granite Ionic columns and entablature of Ravensdale formed the portico of the church, while the bell tower was also reconstructed.[62] At the time of its destruction, Ravensdale Park was no longer a 'landlord' residence: it was owned by timber merchants who were exploiting the post-war demand for woodland (and in the process altering a rural landscape that had remained unchanged for generations). There was no political contamination linked to their ownership, so there had to be an ulterior motive, and that motive was no different than if the house had continued in aristocratic ownership: it was to be found in the local demand for land redistribution.

In neighbouring Monaghan, in March 1921, Gola House, the residence of William Black, was burned by the local IRA. Said to be one of the oldest (c.1703) and finest of Co Monaghan's houses, it was architecturally unusual in that it was a five-bay Palladian design with an attic tower rising from the apex of the roof and single storey-wings. There was a rumour that the military intended to occupy it.[63] This is substantiated in a handwritten IRA report in Monaghan County Museum that simply states: 'Burning of Gola mansion by

5.4 The salvage from Ravensdale Park was later used to build Glassdrummond Roman Catholic Church, a short distance away in Co Armagh. The architectural style of the original house was clearly replicated in the new church.

order of brigade OC' (who at the time was probably Patrick McKenna).[64] The burning had an afterlife. Black's politics had made him unpopular with his Nationalist neighbours. He was a staunch Unionist and vice-president of the North Monaghan Unionist Association during the third Home Rule crisis. His grand-nephew believed that Gola was not burned because of possible occupation by the crown forces but because William 'was a typical target of oppositional violence'.[65] A great-grandson was more forthright: 'It's hard not to think that this [the burning of Gola] was political retribution for their Unionism rather than for their economic advantage over their neighbours.'[66] His mention of 'economic advantage over their neighbours' may also have been instructive. This advantage was historically linked to the confiscation of Catholic lands in

5.5 Gola House, Co Monaghan, one of the area's most impressive and architecturally unusual country houses, burned by the IRA in March 1921, allegedly because the crown forces were about to take it over. Subsequent events also suggested a local agrarian motive.

the county in the seventeenth century, and long held resentments played out after the burning when Black decided to sell his lands.

On 11 September 1921, John Murray, the chairman of the Scotstown Sinn Féin club, brought the proposed sale of the estate to the attention of its members and proposed that 'It should be divided into small farms and sold at a [?reasonable] price so that men in the neighbourhood or men who had sons in jail could have a chance, and that no strangers should be allowed to come in and give an unreasonable price.'[67] Those with sons in jail were republicans; in all probability the dreaded 'strangers' were wealthy Protestants prepared to keep Protestant lands in Protestant hands. (Patrick Duffy in his monumental survey of landownership in Monaghan showed that 'Vacated Protestant farms in the main were consolidated by neighbouring Protestant farmers. Thus, land-ownership did not reflect the upheavals which occurred in the Protestant community.'[68]) For the next twelve months, there was a good deal of local tension and anyone defying Sinn Féin law was intimidated: one man who took part of the Gola demesne for grazing had his cattle driven away, he was assaulted and 'cow dung was forced into his mouth'. In the summer of 1922 Protestant demesne workers were warned to leave the district 'or the coffins will be your lot'.[69]

Eventually, in 1924, by which time William Black had decided to leave Ireland and return to the Umtata region of South Africa, Father Philip Mulligan, the local parish priest, had purchased the demesne for redistribution amongst local farmers.[70] How did this transaction take place? Did the Irish Land Commission officially sanction this land divide? The point needs to be made that the Irish revolution in all its complexities cannot be understood until the records of that state body are made available.

On the night of 25 April 1919, Oakgrove, Co Cork, the ancestral home of Captain John Bowen-Colthurst, was burned. During the Easter Rebellion Bowen-Colthurst had taken the pacifist and women's suffrage-campaigner Francis Sheehy Skeffington as hostage when doing a tour of duty in Rathmines. Sheehy Skeffington witnessed Bowen-Colthurst's murder of a young man named Coade that night and the following morning he and two other prisoners were shot in Portobello barracks. A court-martial followed but the plea was accepted that Bowen-Colthurst had been of unsound mind at the time of the murders. His actions undoubtedly explain the intimidation of his landed family in Cork that began as early as September 1916 when the police reported that both his mother and sister-in-law were being boycotted by Sinn Féiners.[71] During 1919, the intimidation increased and culminated in the burning of Oakgrove in June 1920. A few days later, Drumgowna House, belonging to Bowen-Colthurst's sister, Peggy, and Dripsey House, belonging to his mother, were burned within hours of each other.[72] Donnelly points out that almost exactly a year later, raiders came back and burned what remained of the three houses.[73] Revenge was undoubtedly present; as Donnelly points out Bowen-Colthurst's atrocity was 'seared . . . into the Irish nationalist consciousness'.[74] But the return of the arsonists to finish the destruction of the houses also meant there were people who were determined to ensure that the three houses would not be reinhabited, and for good reason, to ensure the redistribution of the demesne lands.[75] In January 1920, Oakgrove demesne was put on the market with a reserve of £10,000. No one would give the asking price – local nationalist communities were sending out clear messages of solidarity just as they had done during the Land War. It was eventually purchased by the Land Commission for just £4,000.[76]

In summation: what is evident from all these cases is that the burning of Big Houses such as Moydrum or Summerhill or Kilmorna, for whatever loose political or military reason, simultaneously ended centuries of landlord presence in an area and provided access to a sizeable amount of productive agricultural land to be divided amongst locals: in essence, micro social revolutions took place across the country. The inevitability of enquiry leading back to land issues was, as others have found, even more true of the Civil War period.

2. 'This place is just sheer hell'

During the Civil War, the main theatre of political violence was much the same as during the War of Independence, the southern province of Munster. There, forty-nine houses were burned in 1922–23, accounting for just over 31 per cent of the total. Several counties, including Galway, Longford, Westmeath, Offaly, Kildare, Kilkenny, Monaghan, Meath, Cavan, Leitrim, Roscommon and Donegal, 'saw hardly any fighting'.[77] Yet in those counties seventy-three houses were burned, almost 47 per cent of the total, so there must have been factors other than militarism at play. Existing analyses of revolutionary violence across the 1920–23 period have their shortcomings, most especially because they ignore social or agrarian crimes. Thus, there is validity in Gavin Foster's questioning of Peter Hart's 'narrow conception' of revolutionary violence as exclusively IRA violence measured in 'casualties per 10,000 people', because it ignores, as Foster puts it, 'the victims of labour, agrarian, sectarian, and criminal violence whose perpetrators do not appear to have been volunteers'. It fails to capture the much wider picture in which people's everyday lives were disrupted as much by social and agrarian crimes as political crimes.[78] The burning of country houses is a case in point.

J.C. Davies in his seminal paper, 'Towards a Theory of Revolution', put forward the argument that 'Revolutions are most likely to occur when a prolonged period of objective economic and social development is followed by a short period of sharp reversal. People then subjectively fear that ground gained with great effort will be quite lost; their mood becomes revolutionary.'[79] As well as people who do not want to lose what they have gained, there are, of course, many others who strive for a more equitable share of those gains. Davies's theory, summarised as the revolution of rising expectations, was later employed to good effect by James S. Donnelly Jr in his examination of the Land War in Ireland when the economic downturn of the late 1870s, following upon a period of sustained economic growth, gave rise to the Land League, an organisation which the aristocracy regarded as revolutionary in composition and intent.[80] One should not, therefore, overlook the parallels with the post-war era and the fact that the Civil War was fought amidst an economic depression that followed the unprecedented economic boom of 1914–18.

In the aftermath of the war, the British and home markets were flooded with wheat, meat, wool and other agricultural products from the trans-oceanic countries and, as had happened in the late 1870s, the price of agricultural produce dropped dramatically, and the farmer was once again badly hit. According to a report of the Department of Agriculture and Technical Instruction, 1922–23 was a 'a year of anxiety and struggle'.[81] In 1923, an unusually late spring characterised by heavy rains, followed by harsh winds and night frost in April and May and a cold, sunless summer badly affected the harvest.[82] Because of global depression, the agricultural price index (1911–13 = 100) which had stood at 288 in 1920 slumped to 160 in 1924.[83] There was continued rationing, food shortages, growing inflation and the exploitation of market shortages as greedy shopkeepers and merchants breached price regulations. The less well-off faced a daily struggle, which, as we shall see in chapter seven, explains to some extent the widespread looting of demesne vegetable gardens during the Civil War.

Agrarian agitation during the Civil War followed a well-worn historical path, beginning in the western counties, where socioeconomic conditions were so bad that the Irish White Cross set aside £25,000 for the relief of distress there in the spring of 1922.[84] It has been stated that the IRA in the west went predominantly anti-Treaty; according to David Seth Jones, they drew the bulk of their support from the small farmers and agrarian radicals.[85] In May 1922, Colonel Maurice Moore, whose brother owned Moore Hall in Mayo (burned 1 February 1923), wrote to the Minister for Defence: 'The anti-Treaty politicians and IRA, finding themselves in a hopeless minority, have adopted a policy very dangerous to the country and to the present ministry, though it has not been openly avowed. They are now making a bid for support through an agrarian movement.'[86] In what had become a tradition in Irish politics, anti-Treatyite leaders looked to the timeless slogan of 'the land for the people' to popularise their continuation of the struggle, which did have an agrarian agenda that very much focused on the aristocracy and their Big Houses.

On 1 May 1922, the anti-Treatyite Four Courts garrison issued a circular to divisional commandants informing them that the IRA Army Council had sanctioned 'that certain lands and properties in this country shall forthwith [be] seized and controlled . . . on behalf of the army council in trust for the Irish people'. These were to include the demesne lands and mansions of absentee landlords and 'transient landlords' (those who resided in Ireland only for brief periods) and 'whose records show hostility to the National interest'. Notably, landlords who resided permanently were to be left in possession of their mansion houses but only with sufficient land to provide them with adequate means of subsistence. The 'favourable national record of a landlord', whether, for example, he or she provided employment, was also to be considered (as it would be after the passing of the 1923 Land Act). Socialist republicans such as Liam Mellows, who was amongst the Four Courts garrison, and Peadar O'Donnell, who came under Mellows's influence when they were both in Mountjoy gaol, both strongly advocated the confiscation of all the large demesnes and estates and their distribution among the landless and agricultural labourers.[87] In their 1923 propaganda pamphlet, the Irish Claims Compensation Association drew attention to Mellows's teachings when setting out what it regarded as the main reasons for the burning of country houses.[88]

The Anglo-Irish treaty did not deliver a thirty-two county Irish republic but that was not necessarily the most important consideration on the minds of small farmers, the landless and agrarian radicals, including former members of the IRA.[89] O'Donnell was later condemnatory of the fact that: 'All the leadership wanted was a change from British to Irish government; they wanted no change in the basis of society.'[90] Rank and file IRA disappointment was eloquently expressed by a Monaghan Volunteer, Tom Carragher:

> During the period of the Truce, the politicians and respectables took over. It was they who interpreted our dream, the dream we fought for. It was they would decide the terms to which we must agree. In the mind of every soldier was a little republic of his own in which he was the hero. But his

dream was shattered. The process-server that he once made easy talk to was back in business, the same gripper, the same sheriff with the same old laws while the little hero was back at his plough.[91]

The lines between agrarian agitators and the anti-Treaty IRA became blurred. At the beginning of March 1922, a report appeared in the *Tipperary Star* under the heading 'Land for the IRA' in which 'A landless, penniless soldier of Ireland' pleaded:

> Hundreds of us have not a perch of land nor a peep at the prospect of an individual livelihood in the country we fought for. We cannot all become clerks, police, or soldiers. There are many other ranches besides the Clanwilliam areas for distribution. What about the areas around Dundrum and Cappawhite and lands elsewhere in Tipperary?[92]

While in the Mansion House in Dublin politicians debated forsaken principles and fealty to the British crown, in rural Ireland ordinary people waited for the sanctioned transfer of their farms and many more for the redistribution of untenanted and demesne lands. Some became impatient. At the beginning of the truce period, the County Inspector of Tipperary reported: 'The hunger for land is great, those who are landowners want more, while those who have none and who have been gunmen believe that the estates of Loyalists such as Kilboy once cleared will be divided up amongst them.'[93] There was a suggestion here that a confusion of people were involved in the campaign for land redistribution, but also that those who fought in the IRA felt they deserved some material reward. Kilboy was burned a year later. It will probably never be established who was responsible, but the motive was clear enough.

Kilboy was owned by Henry O'Callaghan Prittie (1851–1927), 4th Baron Dunalley. In the 1880s, his north Tipperary estate covered just over 21,000 acres. The bulk of it was sold under the land acts but in 1906 he still retained around 2,500 acres, including a 550-acre demesne, and large tracts of untenanted lands in townlands such as Cooleen (370 acres), Curryquin (320 acres), Lahid (400 acres) and Templederry (215 acres). That area of north Tipperary witnessed large scale IRA violence during the War of Independence, bitter strife during the Civil War and agrarianism throughout both. Kilboy's tale of woe began shortly after the Anglo-Irish truce, at a time when no local markets were being held, food prices were soaring and socioeconomic and political chaos fomented criminality.

On 13 November 1921, the first in a series of raids on the mansion resulted in the theft of silver pots, cuff links, overcoats, a silk muffler valued at almost £137, brass finger bowls, a razor, torches and other household items valued at over £400.[94] These seemed clearly to be thefts of valuables for profit. In the spring and summer of 1922, there was a change in orientation: raiders focused on farm machinery, livestock and timber, they stole a horse and cart, tools from the outbuildings, ploughs, harrows, 40 head of cattle (valued at £800) and 50 sheep (£50), while outside almost 800 trees were either cut down or damaged, and 400 yards of fencing, including stakes and wire netting, were stolen. In total almost £6,000 worth of looting and damage.[95] It could be said that these materials were all stolen because they were all useful to local farmers, but it should also be considered that their theft made Dunalley's ability to farm impossible. If he could not work it, what purpose did his demesne farm serve?

Evidently, Dunalley did not get the intended message, so his assailants went a step further. On 28 May 1922, a volley of shots was fired at him as he was on his way to church.[96] Four more attempts followed, including shots fired at himself and his wife as they stood on the steps of Kilboy itself.[97] Years later, their grandson Henry Cornelius Prittie claimed that he spoke to one of the men involved, who was then working as a porter at Nenagh railway station: 'He told me there was no ill feeling and they had nothing against my grandparents but their orders were to drive them out.'[98] By the summer of 1922, the Dunalleys felt 'so persecuted' that they decided to leave for England.[99] While a certain political hostility existed towards Dunalley, land redistribution issues were more central to the intimidation. On 19 July 1922, Howard Dudley, the family solicitor, reported to Dunalley that the fences on the Kilboy demesne 'were completely down' and that locals had driven their own cattle onto the lands to graze.[100] The estate steward, Samuel Doupe, was visited by nocturnal raiders who threatened to shoot him if he did not leave the locality within the month. He wrote to Dunalley: 'This place is just sheer hell. With the [farm] machinery gone I don't see how we can carry on.'[101] On the night of 2 August, Kilboy was burned. Towards the end of the month, Dunalley, whose income stream had dried up, instructed Dudley to let the meadows at Dolla and Cooleen on

5.6 Kilboy House, Co Tipperary. Subjected to a number of raids and robberies during the War of Independence, the house was burned in August 1922 because of local agrarian tensions.

conacre, but anonymous warning notices were soon posted throughout the area threatening anyone who would take these lands. Dudley told Dunalley it was useless trying to proceed because any prospective purchasers would be targeted by the 'local mountainy men'.[102] One of these, Jim 'the Ginnett' Murphy, is said to have boasted that, in time, 'Dunalley will be thinning turnips for me'.[103]

On 1 May 1923, as a new Land Bill was about to be introduced in the Dáil (chapter nine), Dudley predicted to Dunalley: 'I do not think that the present government have the money to finance Land Purchase on any large scale . . . I don't see where the money is to come from to buy up large tracts of land for division, and even if they attempted this it would be at a very low price.'[104] On 18 May, Dudley again warned Dunalley of the difficulties in letting the lands on conacre: 'Though there are several prospective purchasers who could put down the money they will not be allowed to do so by other more turbulent spirits, particularly the men in the mountain area who will not allow anyone to touch their lands at present.'[105] Moreover, there was now a fear that if the lands were let the new occupiers would hold on to them 'permanently no matter what agreement they sign' and then, as 'tenants', attempt to avail of the new legislation.[106] Dudley suggested selling to 'outside committees' for cash rather than wait for a Land Bill to deal with the untenanted estate; cash, he told the estate agent, was still king.[107] And there was a final consideration, and an important one: Dudley believed that if Dunalley sold the greater portion of his estate voluntarily, 'this would help to ensure his safety and give him a better prospect of living there in peace'. At that stage, Dunalley had made his intentions clear that he was going to rebuild Kilboy.[108]

For the next eighteen months, local political representatives lobbied for the purchase and redistribution of Dunalley's lands. On 30 October 1924, Domhnall O'Muirgheasa TD asked Patrick Hogan in the Dáil whether 'the Land Commission had or propose to acquire the lands at the Dunalley estate, the progress made if any and when they would be in a position to parcel out the lands between uneconomic holders and labourers', to which Hogan replied that 'steps were being taken' and 'when the lands are acquired they will be allotted as expeditiously as possible'.[109] Two months later, the Land Commission offered £16,000 to Dunalley for his untenanted lands, which he accepted.[110] Dunalley managed to hold on to his demesne and to rebuild Kilboy, but the burning of the house had ultimately expedited the sale of his untenanted lands. The available sources do not reveal who burned Kilboy, or whether they had any IRA connections at all. The extent to which this really mattered probably played itself out in a local power struggle with the Irish Land Commission in the years after as the land was being divided; it is a great shame, therefore, that the Land Commission inspectors' reports are not available to illuminate that struggle!

The burning of Lord Lansdowne's Derreen in Kerry had a similar context and outcome. During the Civil War, the new government found it difficult to establish any semblance of authority in that county, where again the IRA went predominantly anti-Treaty.[111] On the Lansdowne estate, in 1922, conditions were described as 'anarchic' as boathouses were burned, poaching became the order of the day, and robberies from Derreen House and the demesne became 'frequent', culminating in the burning of the house on 20 September 1922. This was a particularly high-profile case. Henry Petty-Fitzmaurice, 5th Marquess of Lansdowne, had been Governor-General of Canada, Viceroy of India, Secretary of State for Foreign Affairs, leader of the Unionists in the House of Lords, and by 1922 a senator in the Irish Free State. Until the 1880s, he owned 122,000 acres in Ireland. His reputation as a landlord was tarnished during the Plan of Campaign of the mid-1880s, when landlord–tenant relations on his estates deteriorated badly, accentuated by his removal of thousands of tenants in emigration schemes.[112] He himself fell from grace in British political circles at the end of 1917 when he publicly declared that Britain could not win the war, but he still remained a public figure of some note.[113]

Arguably, the destruction of Derreen could have been to rid the area of a strong colonial presence; this was certainly the way it was presented by the Irish Compensation Claims Bureau in London, who used the burning of Derreen to bolster their propagandist argument: 'The process of destruction which has been applied to Lord Lansdowne's residence is only part of a well organised system which is being applied at the present moment all over Ireland for the murder and expulsion of the Irish gentry, their dependents, and all those who have in the past shown any British sympathy.'[114] Lansdowne's name also appeared on the list of senators' homes to be destroyed in reprisal for the execution of anti-Treatyite prisoners. However, the local rector, Reverend Almoner, made a telling disclosure to the Minister for Home Affairs regarding who he thought was responsible for the burning: 'The offenders were Republicans and Free Staters in about equal proportions and acting on no mandate but their own.'[115] In other words, the destruction had nothing to do with civil war politics. Before he died in 1927, Lansdowne sold his estates to the Irish Land Commission, the primary outcome desired by those who wreaked havoc on the estate in 1922–23.

In early June 1922, Sir John Keane, also a senator in the Irish Free State government, recorded in his diary that he and his wife and two servants were the only people at Cappoquin House, commenting: 'The country is in a state of anarchy and we're preparing for a siege,' and that, for them, 'Times are nerve racking. Every day one or more problems arising out of lawlessness. It may be good for the wits, but it is trying to the nerves.'[116] A few months later, at the beginning of January 1923, as the burning of houses escalated and those of senators were being targeted as reprisals for the execution of anti-Treatyites, Keane wrote: 'As a senator I am warned to be discreet in my movements and I find I look around when crossing from the club to see if anybody is watching me. Similarly, I take careful notice of people who follow me.'[117] On 5 February, two weeks before his house was burned, he observed: 'Daily reports from Ireland of burning houses: ours must go in time.'[118] By

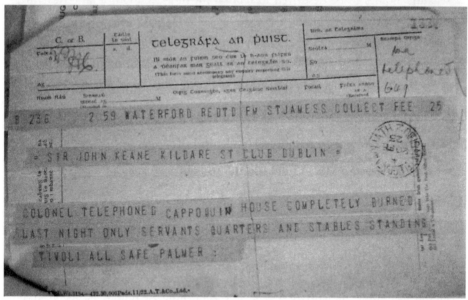

5.7 and 5.8 Cappoquin House, home of Sir John Keane, and the telegram he received informing him of its destruction. Cappoquin epitomised a country house where a variety of factors possibly fed into its destruction. The house was rebuilt a few years later and is still owned by the Keane family.

then, like so many others, he had begun to take precautions by removing valuable contents.[119]

It would be easy to attribute the burning of Cappoquin to the fact that Keane was a senator. But, while it played a role, Glascott Symes's study has shown that it was not all-important. During the Civil War, Keane had feared that 'a bitter class war' was inevitable.[120] At the time, he was chairman of the Waterford branch of the Irish Farmers' Union, which had established a national network in the aftermath of the First World War, its leaders drawn predominantly from the old landlord class, the same men who had led the Irish Landowners' Convention. Simultaneously, the ITGWU formed a branch in Cappoquin. In the agricultural downturn of 1922–23, both organisations came into conflict as the farmers of the Blackwater Valley wanted to reduce wages by up to 30 per cent, while the labourers stood firm. Cappoquin demesne found itself at the centre. In June 1922, Keane's estate employees went on strike. Conditions in the area deteriorated and, while it cannot be certain that his employees were involved, his cattle were driven from the demesne (though later retrieved), and like many other former landlords he was forced to go to Dublin to speak with Patrick Hogan, whom he found 'sympathetic and angry' about the way rural Ireland had deteriorated into social anarchy.[121]

Over the next year, the Blackwater Valley became embroiled in further labour disputes: Keane received threatening letters, the 'Sinn Féin flag' was flying over neighbouring Lismore Castle, which had been commandeered, demands were being made for the redistribution of lands and, on 23 June 1923, 500 men of the Special Infantry Corps, established in March by the Free State government to tackle agrarian crime, were drafted into the county.[122] The labour strike was resolved on the Keane demesne, but it left a bitter taste amongst trade unionists. On 12 August 1923, an article entitled 'Keane's Battered Halo' appeared in *Voice of Labour*, deploring his employees for returning to work at reduced wages and concluded: 'We have less contempt for them than we have for Keane. For his feat in humiliating his men to this degradation, he is now welcome to all the glory that he is due in this world and the next. The end is not yet, Sir John.' As Glascott Symes concludes, Keane's role as a senator is not enough in itself to explain the destruction of Cappoquin by anti-Treatyites; the climate of bitter hostility towards him because he had 'taken a strong line during the farm workers' strike in support of landowners' may have been just as pertinent.[123]

3. 'Give the land back to the rightful owners'

On 1 March 1923, President W.T. Cosgrave addressed the Dáil informing its members that there had been cases 'in which mansions have been destroyed for the very express purpose . . . [of] making it compulsory upon the owner of a demesne or other land to have it distributed amongst certain people', but, he warned, 'We are going to see in such cases, as far as the resources at our disposal permit, that no such distribution of land will take place to persons who have practised the destruction in order to gain their ends. I think it is the duty of the State to do something of that sort.'[124] More broadly speaking, the government had to get a grip on rural Ireland and ease the tensions around land issues. On 1 April 1922, representatives of ninety-five unpurchased Ulster estates had attended a conference in the town hall in Cavan where they resolved that no rents would be paid pending a successful land purchase scheme.[125] That same month, at the far end of the country, the unpurchased tenants in Bantry in Cork held a large meeting where it was agreed to demand 50 to 60 per cent reductions on rents until purchase took place.[126]

Shortly after, the regional movements came together in Dublin to form a national organisation. A representative from Tullamore in Offaly told those gathered that 'The lands had been unjustly acquired by force from their rightful owners by the landlords, and it was for the Republican government, now that the British force was gone, to do what lay in their power to give the land back to the rightful owners.'[127] At that stage, Patrick Hogan estimated that there were only 10 to 15 per cent of estates in Ireland where rents were paid up to date; otherwise some were up to three years in arrears.[128] Moreover, annuitants were not making their annual payments to the Land Commission, in anticipation of independence doing away with them completely. This was a situation that had to be addressed in the interests of future national prosperity and international credibility. When Cosgrave addressed the Dáil in March 1923 the government was in the process of preparing a suite of legislation to achieve stability. The Compensation Ireland (Act) was passed in May (chapter 7) and the Irish Land Act and the Public Safety (Emergency Powers) Act were both passed in August.[129] All three would work in tandem to facilitate the state in restoring law and order, to garner support from the democratic majority and to show the new state's resolve to punish its enemies, past and present (chapter 9).

There are many international parallels to what happened in Ireland as evidenced in Stathis Kalyvas's influential work *The Logic of Violence*, which demonstrates how the privitisation of the politics of civil war, personal conflicts, selective violence, the denunciation of targeted civilians and so on can come to the fore. While considerable work needs to be done on these issues in Ireland, this work has indicated that the burning of Big Houses is as good a place as any to begin. In the final analysis, while a Big House owner may have been a Protestant and a Unionist/Loyalist, a spy or informer, it was their traditional role as landlord that explained the lingering resentment in many localities, especially amongst those who had agrarian as opposed to political agendas, and it is arguable that the former were in the majority.[130] Thus, as we have seen in this chapter, the burning of Big Houses, and more widespread intimidation of their owners, was an effective stratagem to drive the owner away, leaving lands available for redistribution.[131] Hence, when the exiled Herbert Sullivan applied for compensation for the burning of his home, Curramore House (August 1922), his representatives claimed: 'But for the driving of Applicant out of the country and keeping him out, these lands would not have been acquired under the . . . 1923 Act in Ireland.'[132] While countrywide agitation affected farmers as well as Big House owners in 1920–23, the large holdings of the aristocracy were the most prized of all and, as it turned out, not just by the smallholders and landless who demanded land, but also by the Free State government, who saw in compulsory acquisition and redistribution a political expedient to restore social stability in the countryside (chapter 9).

III
'THIS IS WHAT YOUR PAST HERE MEANS TO US'

Destruction, Looting and Compensation

6

'GRASS GROWS WHERE THE SALOONS WERE'
A CASE STUDY OF MITCHELSTOWN CASTLE

Touring the area and taking in the site where once stood Mitchelstown
Castle, scene of the unforgettable garden party of August 1914 described in
Bowen's Court, it becomes searingly clear just how the world of the Anglo-
Irish in this pocket of the country fell asunder from that moment on.

(Sadbh, 'Tracking Elizabeth Bowen', *Irish Times*, 12 June 1999)

1. 'The mills of God grind slowly'

On 13 August 1922, just eight years after the Cork aristocracy and gentry had
gathered there at the outbreak of the Great War, Mitchelstown Castle was
burned by evacuating anti-Treatyite troops.[1] The great conflagration could be
seen for miles around. Alec King-Harman, who was to inherit the ruin, later
considered the preparation that must have been necessary to achieve the end
result: it was 'almost impossible', he reflected, 'to have burnt the whole of that
magnificent building, and the most fiendish ingenuity must have been
displayed to accomplish such an end'.[2] As the fire lit up the night sky around
the town a young boy named Patrick Glavin sat mesmerised on the demesne
wall at Cahir Hill; when he went home and explained to his mother why he
was so late, she simply remarked: 'The mills of God grind slowly, but exceeding
small.'[3]

Built c.1823–25 for the 3rd Earl of Kingston, to the design of James and
George Richard Pain, at an estimated cost of £100,000, Mitchelstown was
reputedly Ireland's largest Gothic Revival castle. Occupying three sides of a
quadrangle – the fourth was a terrace – the principal entrance on the eastern
side was flanked by two 106-foot high square towers, while on the northern
side there were two equally imposing octagonal towers. The castle had at least

6.1 Mitchelstown Castle, home of the Webber/King-Harman family. Burned by retreating anti-Treatyites in August 1922, it was probably the largest house destroyed in Ireland. Its owner later reflected that it was 'almost impossible to have burnt the whole of that magnificent building, and the most fiendish ingenuity must have been displayed to accomplish such an end'.

sixty principal and twenty minor rooms: the magnificent entrance hall opened into a 100-foot-long gallery, there was a dining room capable of seating 100 people, and three libraries.[4] In 1837, Samuel Lewis wrote that 'The whole pile has a character of stately baronial magnificence, and from its great extent and elevation forms a conspicuous feature in the surrounding scenery.'[5]

The architectural extravaganza was built rather foolishly at a time when the Irish economy was in a downward spiral that had begun with the ending of the Napoleonic Wars a decade before. A descendant later recognised that George Kingston's overextended ambition to emulate Windsor Castle had 'ushered in an era of folly and disaster which led finally to the ruin of the great Mitchelstown inheritance of the Kings'.[6] And its baronial magnificence only served as a quintessential symbol of feudalism for later generations of Nationalists; it represented to the tenantry, in this case both rural and urban, the difference between 'us' and 'them' and, in that context, the wry gist of Mrs Glavin's remark was revelatory.

This short chapter presents a case study of Mitchelstown Castle as a microcosm of what happened on so many Irish aristocratic estates in the revolutionary period 1920–23. It provides a bridge between what has been written so far and the discussions to follow on looting and compensation.

2. 'A more final scene than we knew'

In 1922, Mitchelstown Castle was owned by William Downes Webber, second husband and widower of the Countess Kingston, who had died in 1909. In her will, she had stipulated that Webber should 'leave back the remains of the estates to that member of the Kingston family whom he considered best entitled by birth to come into it'.[7] It was her favourite nephew, Alec, that she had in mind.[8] On the evening of 29 June 1922, Webber was hosting a dinner party for a small number of family and friends when, late in the evening, they were disrupted by anti-Treatyite forces who forced their way into the castle and announced that they were commandeering it.[9] Mitchelstown Castle was an ideal fortress to establish temporary headquarters: massive in scale, it could accommodate a large number of men – according to Michael Casey, one of the IRA officers, there may have been up to 600 soldiers based there[10] – and its towers and battlements commanded a sweeping view of the town and surrounding countryside. The anti-Treatyites were led by Patrick 'Pa' Luddy, a 23-year-old farmer's son, whose family had for generations been tenants on the Kingston/Webber estate. Indeed, Luddy claimed in his BMH witness statement that his grandfather had once been 'in charge of a number of farms on the estate' and, according to family lore, he 'was usually consulted by the landlord in connection with such matters as water rights and subdivision in the case of the tenants'.[11] Luddy's memoir has remembrances quite common in IRA witness statements: for instance, he recalled that his father had been 'out' in the 1867 Fenian rebellion, and that he was then involved in the land agitation of the 1880s when 'the men and women of the Mitchelstown district took strong and active steps to ensure that the landlord's men were effectively dealt with'.[12] 'It was,' Luddy said, 'in the atmosphere of the history of those times that I was reared as I listened to the stories of the period being recounted at fireside chats in my home.'[13] His witness statement – no different to any other – may be characterised by questionable recall of historical facts but one does get a sense of what Raymond Gillespie describes as 'the complex evolution of the Irish experience'.[14]

If ancestral anti-landlord grievances fed into the reasons for the burning of Mitchelstown Castle, it is not difficult to explain why. In the 1880s, the

25,000-acre Kingston estate was front and centre in the extended Land War, not just in Cork but in the country as a whole, and this would channel resentment towards the family and by extension towards the Big House.[15] James S. Donnelly has written that before the Land War 'landlord-tenant relations had previously been harmonious' on the estate, evictions were rare and rents were generally moderate.[16] However, the economic downturn of the late 1870s greatly altered the estate dynamic.[17] The refusal of the Countess of Kingston and her agent/husband, William Webber, to grant even a small abatement because of their own enormous debts – including a £236,000 mortgage to the Representative Church Body – led to a threatened rent strike and public tenant demonstrations that, in turn, were met with the serving of eviction warrants that gave rise to riots between tenants and police.[18] Tensions so escalated that by the end of June 1881 there were around 700 soldiers and 300 police encamped on the grounds around Mitchelstown Castle to protect its owners; the improvised military camp only served to highlight what the Big House stood for in the colonial landscape and radicalised attitudes towards it. In the months that followed, levels of violence grew as evictions were resisted and 'grazing grabbers', those who willingly took on evicted farms, were targeted along with bailiffs, process servers and farmers who, despite the strike, paid their rents behind the backs of their neighbours. Some 200 tenants were evicted but the widespread nature of the agitation, the media attention it attracted and most pertinently the need for income forced the Countess Kingston and Webber to relent and 90 per cent were eventually reinstated. According to Donnelly, the tenants had achieved 'a great moral victory that inspired the tenants of other estates to resist their landlords'.[19]

However, the easing of tensions was only temporary. During phase two of the Land War, from the mid-1880s, the National League organised the Mitchelstown tenants to adopt the Plan of Campaign – a blanket refusal to pay rents unless a significant abatement was granted – and this once again shook the Kingston estate to its financial core. The tenants were aware of the Countess's rising burden of debt – by 1887 the interest due to the Representative Church Body was £15,000 in arrears and the mortgagees were 'getting restive'.[20] Plan leaders exhorted the tenants to 'steel your hearts and go to war, in the name of God and with the blessing of the [Roman Catholic] Church'.[21] Tensions escalated, violence reignited, the tenant representatives urged a

unified front to resist eviction. This was the era of Arthur Balfour's chief secre-
taryship, after which he passed into nationalist myth as 'Bloody Balfour' for his
enforcement of the Crimes Act (1887).[22] On 9 September 1887, a demonstration in the town of Mitchelstown resulted in police firing into the crowd,
killing three men – John Casey, John Shinnick, Michael Lonergan – and seriously wounding twenty others.[23] The so-called 'Mitchelstown massacre' had
national repercussions and in local populist opinion the Kingstons/Webbers
were sure to be represented from that point on as usurpers of Irish land. This
was a typical outcome of the Land War era: as R.V. Comerford puts it, the Big
House was from then on 'made into a symbol of oppression and decadence in
order to justify the long land war, and the dominant party politics of the occupants was sufficient pretext to perpetuate the antipathy into the revolutionary
years and beyond'.[24] Mitchelstown Castle typified this.

After years of agitation and diminishing income, the Countess, like the
majority of her peers, was only too willing to sell the entire estate under
the 1903 Land Act, its generous terms too good to ignore. While the bulk of
the proceeds, roughly £300,000, was eaten up by the estate charges, there was
enough left over, thanks to the 12 per cent cash bonus (£36,000), to allow the
Countess and Webber live on in some comfort in the castle. They also retained
the 1,200-acre demesne, which Webber farmed progressively. Almost 900 acres
were under pasture, while a small corner was given over for the Mitchelstown
Golf Club, established in 1908, which brought local elites together from across
the politico-religious divides.[25]

Three years after the passing of the Wyndham Act, an impressive 18-foot-
high monument was erected in the town to commemorate John Mandeville,
agrarian leader, as well as the victims of the Mitchelstown massacre. William
O'Brien, founder of the United Irish League and MP for Cork City, told a
crowd estimated at 20,000: 'Monuments of this sort are not mere monuments
to individuals. They are monuments of undying principles. They are land-
marks in the history of a race.'[26] He encapsulated the polarisation of Irish
politics since the alignment of the Home Rule and land questions with
the issue of national identity, but still a very large crowd 'from all parts of the
district' attended the Countess Kingston's funeral in October 1909.[27] The
garden party organised by her widower in August 1914 was a much less representative affair. Before she ended her memoir, Elizabeth Bowen returned her

mind to the garden party, a pivotal scene in her Big House drama. The Great War, she wrote, would leave '[m]any of those guests, those vehement talkers . . . scattered, houseless, sonless, or themselves dead'. Then would come the War of Independence and the burning down of many of the Big Houses, including Mitchelstown, and so, Bowen concluded: 'The garden party was also a more final scene than we knew, ten years hence, it was all to seem like a dream – and the Castle itself would be a few bleached stumps on the plateau. Today, the terraces are obliterated, and grass grows where the saloons were.'[28] This is the story of what happened.

3. 'At the time there was great bitterness'

Back in 1917, Pa Luddy had joined the reorganised Volunteers, at a time when his brother was serving with the British army on the Western Front. By 1919, he was OC of Mitchelstown Company of the IRA (his rank at the truce was vice OC of Castletownroche Battalion) and his brother, now a returned war veteran, was training officer. He was working at the time with the Mitchelstown Co-Operative Agricultural Society Ltd, which had been formed in June 1919 by a group of local farmers in reaction to the continued exploitation of wartime markets by local seed merchants. In October, following an investment of £100, Webber became the largest shareholder.[29] In the tit-for-tat reprisal warfare that characterised the War of Independence from 1920, co-operatives were often the chosen reprisal targets of the Black and Tans, a calculated way to strike at the heart of a local agricultural community.[30] It became dangerous for them to have any employees who were suspected IRA officers and so, according to Bill Power, for this reason Luddy was sacked.[31] As the war against the RIC intensified in the spring of 1920, Luddy's men raided the Mitchelstown demesne to steal a large pump on wheels, used to spray weed killer, which the IRA hoped could be used to spray paraffin onto the roof of the local RIC barracks.[32] It failed. But no attempt was made on the castle. In truth, it would have been a challenging target given that the military officers based at Kilworth, Fermoy and Buttevant were regular visitors there.[33]

By the spring of 1922, the British army had left Cork, the RIC had been disbanded and the IRA had split over the treaty with most of Luddy's Mitchelstown company going anti-Treaty. Without any protection, the castle was in a more vulnerable position than at any time in its history. On the night Luddy's men commandeered it, they ordered Webber and his family and guests to leave; Webber refused to do so and instead he and his guests spent time lifting carpets and storing paintings, silver and other valuables into two rooms which they then locked.[34] Having allowed them the opportunity, Luddy's men forcibly evicted Webber on 30 June. Two days later, one of the dinner guests, Miss Hare, formerly of Convamore which had been burned in April 1921, was allowed to return to pick up her personal belongings; her story of what she saw was later recounted by Edith Somerville: 'Photograph frames were smashed and the bits of glass . . . used as darts to throw at the valuable big Rembrandt that they [the family] had not been able to get down in time.'[35] If Somerville's telling of the story is authentic, tearing the Rembrandt to shreds with shards of glass now seems like an act of wanton vandalism, which one might deplore as the destruction of an artefact of international heritage significance. But, in the context of the time, how sensitive was the average rank and file IRA volunteer, mainly drawn from the lower ranks of Irish society, and poorly educated, to the cultural value of works of art, Classical statuary and architecture? Moreover, in the context of war, there was nothing unusual in this type of soldier behaviour, regardless of how the victims might perceive it. In comparison, in August 1920 Lady Adair at Glenveagh in Donegal was disgusted by the 'barbarians' and 'philistines' who made up the IRA party who invaded the castle and who 'injured four oil paintings of some value and tore up a group photograph that had Lord Kitchener in it'.[36] To the IRA Kitchener represented an iconic figure of the empire they were fighting. And the oil paintings were just as symbolic of an alien culture as was Lady Adair's Big House. It is questionable what, if anything, the name Rembrandt meant to the Mitchelstown occupiers.

Hardly surprisingly, as soon as the family left Mitchelstown Castle, the locked rooms were broken into, and the contents removed. The carpets were relaid, but not for any enhancement or comfort, for when Miss Hare returned she found them 'indescribably filthy with cigarette ends, mud and spit'. She was shocked by the fact that lavatories 'being considered useless institutions, the walls of the corridors were used instead'.[37] All the books in the library were used as barricades for the windows, while the heavy furniture was used to fortify the doors. Outside, streams of lorries and motor cars crossed the decorative lawns and the recently refurbished tennis courts. Trenches were dug at the front of the castle and barbed wire fences erected. Urinating on the walls was a gesture of disdain, defiance and provocation, and the destruction of the castle's contents and its surrounds just another stage in the despoliation of the coloniser's landscape.

The occupation went on until mid-August 1922 when, as the National Army advanced, and the town of Mitchelstown became caught up in 'the very danger zone of strife', Luddy gave the order to evacuate and torch the castle.[38] When presiding over the subsequent compensation claim, Judge Kenny condemned its destruction as an 'act of vandalism'; he could see no military reason why it should have been destroyed.[39] One former employee believed it was 'an act of hostility to the [Provisional] Government of the State' but it could just as likely have been an act of hostility towards the former regime.[40] The residual hostility inherited from the Land War era, and, indeed, before, has to be considered a factor. For example, in 1910 the *Weekly Freeman's Journal* carried stories of the Earl of Kingston who had commanded the North Cork Militia during the 1798 rebellion. It noted that 'tradition has preserved the history of the flogging and persecution of the Catholic population, and the burning of churches by his bloodhounds in those evil times', and that the militia was 'composed of the scum of society and was quartered at Mitchelstown Castle', thereby highlighting it as a symbol repugnant to Irish Nationalists.[41] A hundred years later the Land War on the estate added another layer and, as R.V. Comerford concludes of the more general case, landlord and Big House became the 'synecdoche for all the historical grievances of the nationalist narrative'.[42] The family were acutely aware of this. When Colonel Anthony King-Harman paid a visit to the ruins of his ancestral home in 1994, he reflected: 'To a certain extent we have always felt that the way things were handled by Webber and his wife contributed to the burning of the castle by the IRA' and concluded: 'The disasters here were inevitable. I think, at the time, there was great bitterness . . . He [Webber] put it in the position where people wanted to burn down the castle.'[43] Back in the 1920s, when compensation was sought from the Irish Grants Committee, the secretary concluded that, if the castle had been rebuilt, 'In all probability having regard to the local animosity against Colonel King-Harman and his family the Castle would have been burnt a second time.'[44] As for the chief perpetrator, Pa Luddy spent his lifetime boasting locally that, by ordering the burning of the castle, 'He was avenging centuries of landlordism and English occupation, as well as erasing what little was left of the Kingston presence in Mitchelstown.'[45]

4. 'Putting stuff behind trees and bushes'

In 2000, historian Bill Power controversially argued another reason for the castle's destruction, that while military strategy was 'The Republican's official line . . . the truth was not so easily confronted by Luddy's generation or, for that matter, their children. The castle had to be burnt to cover up the looting of the priceless paintings, furniture, and silver by the Republicans, their friends, and supporters.'[46] Although generations after the event, this was a painful revisiting of a very sensitive topic in Mitchelstown's history and Power was excoriated locally. One correspondent wrote angrily to the provincial press:

> I see that your historian Mr [Bill] Power is at it again, extolling the virtues of the notorious Kingstons of Mitchelstown. There is no need to write a book on those people because their notoriety has been discussed in every chimney corner over the last 150 years – murderers, cowards, rapists, extortioners, and any other adjectives one could think of . . . I would like to remind Mr Power that the Kingston dynasty have now gone . . . How dare he castigate the republicans of that time who sacrificed their lives so we and he could enjoy the freedom we now have?[47]

As an aside, but a relevant one, back in February 1924, when the courts were deluged with compensation claims for looting, amongst very many other things, the editor of the *Sligo Champion* condemned 'this appalling collapse not only of the national "moral" but of ordinary morality', and predicted that 'future historians will pore lovingly' over the details of such wanton crimes, 'finding in them material for a series of cynical comments on some of our patriotic war-cries, and a mass of curious illustrations as to the working out in practice of principles which we were told contained all that was necessary to our political salvation'.[48] It was a very prescient statement in relation to how aspects of the narrative of the revolutionary period would evolve over the century.[49] In fairness to Bill Power, he used all the relevant primary sources available to him – newspapers, BMH witness statements, compensation files and oral evidence; the criticism of his interpretation was merely a very strong indicator of vestigial local hostility towards the Kingstons. There were still those who preferred to celebrate the Luddy interpretation that he and his comrades were 'avenging centuries of landlordism and English occupation, as well as erasing what little was left of the Kingston presence'. Then again, if that was what the anti-Treatyies had been intent on doing, they might also have considered burning the King's Square in Mitchelstown, which remains one of the finest rows of Georgian buildings in existence in Ireland.

At this remove, it would be very difficult to prove Power's theory that a conspiracy to cover up looting was the primary motive but there is no doubt in this case that there was widespread civilian participation in the looting of the castle (see below). When the compensation hearing began in 1924, the Free State government appointed John Butler to investigate on its behalf. In June, Butler 'heard in Fermoy and Mitchelstown, in the course of conversation with different people, that there had been considerable looting from the Castle, and that the claimants either did not wish to go into the matter or were afraid to do so'.[50] Later, he went through the ruins and concluded: 'There was no salvage, but from my investigation I am perfectly sure there was considerable looting.'[51] This was corroborated by several eye witnesses: Miss Needham, for instance, who had been in the castle when the IRA evicted the Webbers, recalled 'looting about the Castle, and putting stuff behind trees and bushes'.[52]

No inventory of the contents of Mitchelstown was produced during the compensation case nor is it certain that one even existed. Unanswerables, therefore, remain regarding what exactly was destroyed, what had been removed beforehand – sold or stored for safe keeping before 1922 – and what was left to be looted. Arthur Webber testified that he had been allowed into the castle about two weeks before the fire: 'The furniture was all over the place, but he could not swear to anything being missing.'[53] He later surmised the heavy furniture had, therefore, been burned. Most of it could not physically have been removed and at any rate would have been of little practical value to anyone in or around Mitchelstown, given that most of it had been constructed on site specifically to suit the castle's Gothic interiors. However, what is illuminating is that all the basement furniture – used for the servants' quarters – was looted including tables, chairs and beds (and linen), all of which were more practical and more useful to local households. Butler noted: 'The fire does not seem to have reached the basement, yet none of the contents are to be seen, and all the fine mantelpieces seem to have been forcibly wrenched from the walls and carted away.'[54] James O'Neill, a local plasterer, also witnessed men and women dragging furniture from the basement which was 'stored around the ground for the time' before it could be safely removed.[55]

The most valuable contents were the paintings, the family silver and personal jewellery. Robert Douglas King-Harman in his memoir claimed that the most important painting, an impression of the royal palace in Berlin, presented to the family in 1834 by Frederick William IV, last king of Prussia, was 'like all the others at Mitchelstown . . . destroyed in the fire in 1922', and concluded, 'All that remains of Mitchelstown Castle are a few books from the library, a few pieces of family silver, and a few odds and ends like seals and knick-knacks.' He also lamented the loss of the family archive, especially the manuscripts of Edward, Lord Kingsborough, relating to his work on the *Antiquities of Mexico*.[56] Butler maintained that the silver was looted before the fire, including a magnificent chandelier with over 64 pounds of silver, and a silver tea urn on a stand weighing 7.5 pounds. He was bemused by the fact that the Gardai had been unable to trace the looted goods: 'I cannot understand why there was no salvage in the case of the silver, the silver could not have been burned away,' he reported.[57] Moreover, two local jewellers, Thomas Hartigan and Thomas Morrisey, later gave evidence of having been offered unspecified silver artefacts by locals. On 14 January 1990, 78-year-old Fr. Edward J. Kilbride, who was 10 years old at the time of the burning, told Bill Power that he remembered 'several objects were thrown over our back gate possibly by way of restoring them to their owners – which we did', and these included 'a silver teapot and broken epergne, as well as a muffin dish – very Victorian'.[58]

The *Hampshire Telegraph* also carried a report relating to a local woman, Mrs Florence Williams of Cosham, who was staying in the castle at the time, and whose jewellery box 'was taken out of the cellar in the Castle and afterwards found broken open in a wood, and the contents missing'. Judge Kenny awarded Mrs Williams £608 in compensation, which possibly verifies her claim.[59] According to Power, a local solicitor who he did not identify, 'with an appreciation of the finer things in life', removed many of the valuable paintings 'for his personal pleasure and advantage'.[60] In 1957, Sir Cecil Stafford-King-Harman received a letter from D.F. O'Shaughnessy with an address at Kilfinane in Limerick informing him that over forty paintings had been sold at Sotheby's for almost £101,000 and that one of the anti-Treatyite garrison had told him they had come from Mitchelstown castle.[61] Unless more evidence turns up, such claims cannot be substantiated, but neither should they be sceptically dismissed.

5. 'A delight in wrecking whatever had escaped'

William Webber made a very substantial claim for compensation amounting to £148,000 under the Damage to Property (Compensation) Act 1923 (chapter 8), including £18,000 for contents.[62] It cannot be said that Webber was hopeful of rebuilding, nor that he had any great desire to do so. He was elderly and his health was failing but he was also pragmatic enough to realise 'It is impossible that it, the Castle, can ever be used again as a Family Residence.'[63] Webber died on 23 February 1924 before the compensation case was heard. His successor, Alec King-Harman, subsequently endured years of delay and frustration; on several occasions the state solicitor and the state valuer applied for adjournments, leading him to conclude: 'It seemed plain to me that the State intended to postpone the hearing of my case until they had exhausted my patience.'[64] King-Harman later articulated his frustrations to the Irish Grants Committee:

> The reported decisions given in compensation cases seemed to follow no general rule, but to depend entirely upon the whim of the Circuit Judge; and when what appeared to be a just decision was given the State invariably appealed. No Loyalist could have any confidence in the Courts, as they were then being constituted, and I felt that I had better accept almost anything that was offered rather than let my case hang on indefinitely, and perhaps get little or nothing in the end.[65]

It was unrealistic to expect that the Free State government would be in a position, or sympathetic enough, to award such an enormous sum to any single individual owner. There was also the problem, as Robert King-Harman put it, 'that Alec was not the owner of the castle at the time of its destruction' and this had 'a serious and damaging effect on his efforts to get adequate compensation, so that Anna's [Countess Kingston] will was finally the cause of great financial injury to the family she had intended to benefit'.[66] The best King-Harman and his legal representatives could hope for was an out-of-court settlement. Thus, his solicitor Anthony Farrell came to an arrangement with the Ministry of Finance that, subject to the approval of the county court judge, King-Harman would accept a greatly reduced figure of £27,500, of which £25,000 would have to be used towards rebuilding a house on the original site.[67] King-Harman later argued that he 'only accepted the offer in the same way as a starving man will accept half a loaf rather than get no bread'.[68]

The Minister for Finance made it clear to King-Harman that the state felt 'it was absurd to build such a vast house in these days' and that if he did not accept the offer of £27,500 with a £25,000 reconstruction condition attached, he would only get £7,500 with no condition attached.[69] Alec was frustrated enough to later complain that 'The methods of the Government are not much better than those of card sharpers.'[70] These were very different times to when his ancestors might have expected such levels of compensation to be paid at the expense of local ratepayers under compensation acts administered by the British government. The Free State government was operating under massive financial restrictions and the aristocracy were only a small percentage of all the total claimants seeking compensation.

On 25 April 1926, the agreed award of £27,500 was sanctioned, though modified in that Webber was allowed to use the money to build houses in Dublin instead of reinstating a house on the original site.[71] About a year after the burning, King-Harman advertised salvage from the ruined structure, valued by Hill architects in Cork at £50,000, but there was no local interest.[72] This was hardly accidental; no doubt there was an understanding amongst the local population, whether orchestrated or not, that they were not going to pay for the Big House. In 1928, Alec King-Harman described what happened in the intervening years:

It was soon made clear to me that local feeling was still distinctly against the owner of the place; constant acts of annoyance continued for a year or two after Mr Webber's death; indeed, I can still hardly call the place my own, for it is even now subject to perpetual trespass and damage. Some local people seemed to take a delight in wrecking whatever had escaped the attentions of the Republicans and Free State troops.[73]

In the 1930s, King-Harman was approached by Dom Marius O'Phelan, the Abbot of the Cistercian Monastery at Mount Mellaray in Co Waterford, who secured the magnificent cut limestone blocks to build a new abbey. Bill Power claims that over a five-year period 'two consignments were loaded into steam lorries and taken to the site' about 28 miles east in the Knockmealdown Mountains.[74] Three carved stones from the castle went elsewhere, to an ancestral Kingston house in Newcastle, Co Longford, where another stone with the following inscription was placed above them: 'These armorial bearings were brought from Mitchelstown Castle after it had been wantonly burnt on the 13th August 1922. They represent the arms of successive owners of Mitchelstown; Fitzgibbon the White Knight, Fenton and King, Earls of Kingston.'[75]

Finally, in the 1930s, under the Fianna Fáil government, the remainder of the demesne was compulsorily purchased by the Land Commission. Some of it was sold to Mitchelstown Co-Op, which, under the management of Eamon Roche, a staunch Republican, built factories on the castle site, which Power contends was 'an achievement of great political symbolism to his old revolutionary colleagues in Mitchelstown and elsewhere'.[76] Some years later, the demesne walls were lowered for 'safety reasons', and large gaps began to appear in them as sites were sold to build bungalows. To the north-east the wall was also broken to accommodate an extension to the local golf course that had originally been built on land donated by William Webber. The demesne trees were felled, including some magnificent and exotic species, and 'The fish-pond became the site of the town sewerage works and the boat lake an effluent lagoon.'[77]

The remainder of the demesne was redistributed for the relief of local congestion. According to Power: 'In many cases, the Land Commission's disposal of the demesne was used to reward local freedom fighters of the War of Independence.'[78] This was in line with what had become official government policy under the 1933 Land Act.[79] One of those who secured a farm was Pa Luddy.[80] As in so many other cases, the burning of Mitchelstown Castle did not merely result in the disappearance of an aristocratic presence that had been there for hundreds of years, it was seen to have benefited the local community in different ways, primarily through the expansion of the local co-operative and the redistribution of lands. But what difference might the existence of Ireland's largest neo-Gothic castle now make to Irish tourism and the local economy, if Kilkenny Castle is a benchmark?

7

'THERE WERE HENS ROOSTING ON VALUABLE OIL PAINTINGS'

DESTRUCTION AND LOOTING, 1920–23

They are closely knit bands, often little differing from bandits, under local leaders whose names have gained a reputation much like that of some robber thief of the story books. It is often hard to tell where the political outlaw ends and the looter begins.

(*Tuam Herald*, 2 February 1923)

In their pursuit of rural occupations, they [the aristocracy] afforded much employment, and conduced in no small degree by their patronage to increase the prosperity of the towns in their vicinity, and their loss, if they should decide to leave the country permanently, would be widely felt.[1]

(*Irish Times*, 5 November 1921)

1. 'The fiery torch that flew the country'

If a common narrative of an arson attack on an Irish country house can be revealed, and it would be wise to remember that common narratives hide very many anomalies, it is along the lines that a gang of (armed) men – estimated numbers varied greatly from single digits up to 300 – arrived at a typically isolated country house usually in the early hours of the morning.[2] Attacks were rarely spontaneous: an attack on an occupied house, in particular, had to be planned to ensure minimum resistance – during the War of Independence, armed forces were still patrolling the countryside, however sporadically, and officers were frequently being entertained in the Big House. The raiders usually came to the front door – perhaps a deliberate statement that they were no longer subservient or deferential – and they banged loudly, demanding entrance. If that was refused, and it seems to have been seldom the case, the

179

raiders were well prepared and equipped; those who came to Moydrum Castle, as we have seen, were armed with hammers and sledges 'borrowed' from a neighbouring forge. Having announced why they were there, raiders piled the heavy furniture into the middle of rooms on the ground floor, or sometimes demanded servants to do so, and then saturated the stacks and the wooden/carpeted floors with paraffin and set it all alight. As in the case of Tubberdaly in Co Offaly, if this was not effective, they used home-made bombs, or, at Ballybay House in Monaghan, locally and widely grown flax was used like dried straw to ignite the fire.[3] Windows were broken, holes were bored in the ceiling and slates ripped off the roof to ensure the wind fanned the flames.[4] Raiders waited until they were sure destruction was a foregone conclusion and until such time as they departed no neighbour or estate employee who might have witnessed the orange glow of early flames dared come to the scene. As the newspaper report on the burning of Kilbrittain in Co Cork in May 1920 pointed out: 'No one seems to have attempted to save the fine building. That was, of course, because no one dared so to act. The men may have remained until they were satisfied the Castle would ultimately become a ruin, and any interference would have led to bloodshed.'[5]

The available sources are generally very restrained in what they reveal about the mayhem and chaos during the destruction of a Big House; seldom do they adequately describe the undoubted fear and terror of owners and occupants, or the nervousness and excitement of raiders, or the despair and jubilation depending on whether victim or perpetrator. A fictionist might imagine much more vividly what the historian can rarely describe factually.[6] Lady Fingall's memoirs fall somewhere in between. On the night of 23 April 1923, when neighbouring Lismullin House in Meath was burned by the IRA, its owner Sir John Dillon got a letter to the Fingalls at Killeen warning them that their house was next. Lady Fingall later recalled the 'preparation, lest the fiery torch that flew the country . . . should reach us'.[7] She gathered her jewellery, put on her fur coat and sat with her husband in front of the study fire and waited and wondered would they see or hear a car approach, would the raiders come to Fingall's study door as their tenants had always done (was she suggesting that the arsonists were likely to come from that community?), how would Killeen burn, would the servants be got out in time (hardly a very comforting thought for them). Her husband dozed, she stayed awake all night, but the raiders

7.1 Lismullin, Co Meath, home of Sir John Dillon, burned by
anti-Treatyites in April 1923. Its demesne was later redistributed in
part to IRA veterans celebrated by the local press as 'the breed of men,
who fought and wrought and bled for Ireland'.

never came.[8] At Monksgrange in Co Wexford, Adela Orpen's apprehensions
during the Civil War were not confined to one night; she recorded in her
journal:

> Oh these terrible long nights. These endless hours when one is waiting to be
> burnt. I feel so cold, it is as if the heart's blood had ceased to have any
> warmth. It beats hard, so that breath comes fast but no other sign of warmth.
> I suppose this is the effect of terror. We have lived under it so long now, and
> each night the grim thing draws nearer. So when the dogs barked I was sure
> the raiders had come. Small wonder if I couldn't sleep till four o'clock, when
> the dogs had long been quiet and our home was still standing.[9]

Yet, during the Civil War Adela and the other women in Monksgrange behaved
stoically during several raids by the anti-Treatyites. On 10 November 1922,
her daughter Lilian recorded one incident in her diary:

> I watched the scene, a curious one for a civilized country. The stable lantern
> in the middle of the floor lit up the white blankets as they lay in a heap.

One man sat on a chair under the better sack with his rifle between his knees, the other, a very tall young man, was standing beside him looking down at the proceedings, while the third was filling the two sacks as hard as he could with our blankets & overcoats while Dad made suggestions as to the best method of getting everything in.[10]

The same stoicism could be attributed to Lady Castlemaine on the night of the burning of Moydrum Castle; IRA leader Thomas Costello later remembered her being 'very dignified under the circumstances and never winced. She thanked me for my co-operation in saving her treasures and assured me that she quite understood.'[11] But then again Costello's description of her stoicism also reflected the way he wanted his behaviour to be understood.

There were owners for whom the experience was much more traumatic. When the aged Colonel Spaight's residence near Skibbereen was burned in early April 1921, it was reported that he and his wife were brought into the library and forced to witness the wanton destruction of valuable works of art, and the breaking up of a valuable bookcase. Mrs Spaight was then taken on to the front lawn to watch looted furniture from the house being loaded onto carts, before she and her husband 'were marched through the steward's house, being prodded in the back with rifles as they walked'. From the steward's house, they were then forced to watch their house burning.[12] All of this suggests that a particular form of deliberate punishment was meted out to the elderly couple, and the background to the burning may explain this. Spaight was a retired British army officer who owned the RIC barracks in nearby Leap that had housed a reinforcement of Black and Tans from the autumn of 1920. Shortly after their arrival, the Black and Tans came under attack from the local IRA, and they responded with reprisal attacks on the Roman Catholic parochial hall and local farmers' houses. The barracks were burned by the IRA and it was subsequently reported in the newspapers that Spaight had claimed £3,000 for it in compensation. James S. Donnelly reasonably concludes: 'The submission of such a claim to a court no longer recognised by republicans was itself contrary to Volunteer dictates, and the very provision of the barracks meant that the Spaights were linked in the minds of local republicans with the introduction of the Black and Tans into that corner of the county.'[13] One of the IRA leaders is said to have told Lucy Spaight that they were burning the house because 'she was responsible for bringing the Black and Tans into the district'.[14]

In a similar incident, in July 1921, when raiders came to Ballyrankin House near Enniscorthy in Wexford, they locked W.G. Skrine and his wife into one of the rooms, allowing the servants to leave – a deliberate separation of those who the raiders thought were deserving of punishment from those perceived to be innocent – while they prepared the house for destruction.[15] When they were released, the Skrines, who lost everything including their wardrobes, had to walk four miles in their night attire to Newtownbarry.[16] On 26 December 1921, during the truce period, a group of men broke into Moystown House in King's County where Mary Waller-Sawyer lived alone. According to her correspondence with the Minister for Home Affairs, 'The men got hold of me – a woman and alone – in the hall. They knocked me down, pulled out handfuls of my hair, kicked me about the body, struck me on the face, and repeatedly expressed their intention to have my life.'[17] The local IRA arrested six named men, all of whom were later released on bail. Waller-Sawyer wrote angrily to the Minister: 'As a member of the Provisional Government it is your duty to protect the people of this land from outrage.'[18] Some of the servants in Sopwell Hall in Tipperary were subjected to a similar ordeal when it was raided in August 1922. Two Protestant servants were physically assaulted by the raiders, while a Catholic servant went unmolested, again suggestive of deliberate and discriminate separation. The servants were able to identify their attackers, three of whom were subsequently sentenced to ten years penal servitude. The *Irish Times* vehemently denounced the crime: 'acts as vile as had ever been committed by the Huns in Belgium, with the difference that the crimes . . . were committed by native Irish upon their compatriots.'[19] Mrs Charles Guinness of Clermont Park in Dundalk never recovered from her ordeal, and in 1927, four years after the burning, she was diagnosed as suffering from 'cardiac angina and extreme nervousness', which medical experts contended was a direct consequence of the trauma experienced 'by the trouble she had to undergo in 1923'.[20]

But reports of such cruel behaviour do not seem to be as common as might be expected in a time of revolution, and historians have now come to accept that 'Ireland's wars were not as lethal as they might have been.'[21] Certainly not in comparison to the horrendous crimes perpetrated against other aristocracies during twentieth-century revolutions. Some Irish aristocrats even claimed they were treated most civilly by raiders: for instance, in January 1923, the Earl of Mayo said the anti-Treatyites who burned Palmerston House 'behaved courteously' and granted him the time to remove his more valuable paintings.[22] Sir John Dillon of Lismullin received an apology from those he referred to as 'courteous arsonists', who also helped him remove pictures and plate.[23] Louisa Bagwell of Marlfield reported the raiders 'offered no personal violence' in any way and allowed family to remove personal belongings.[24]

Compare this to the Russian aristocratic experience of Countess Kleinmichel, for example, whose Petrograd palace was overrun in the February 1917 revolution. She was locked into two rooms along with her servants, while soldiers sang their revolutionary songs and used paintings of the Romanovs along the grand staircase for rifle practice, before they murdered all three of her husband's brothers, one of whom was a 25-year-old Huzzar: 'First the soldiers ripped out one of his eyes and forced him to watch as they killed several of his fellow officers; next they took out the other eye, broke his hands, his feet, and then tortured him for two hours by lifting him up on their bayonets and beating him with their rifle butts until he finally expired.'[25] Scholten's study of the Romanian aristocracy, who 'In the first half of the twentieth century . . . felt strongly attracted by English [aristocratic] culture' emphasises just how lightly those in Ireland escaped. From the 1940s, first the Nazis and then the Communists burned the Romanian aristocracy's houses, expropriated their lands, looted their treasures and deliberately destroyed their libraries and family archives.

These events also happened in Ireland, but in Romania aristocrats were brutally tortured – the unfortunate Baron Jozsef Huszar, for example, 'had a glass ampoule pushed into his urethra, which was then smashed with a hammer, and boiling oil was poured over his wounds'.[26] In Hungary in 1951, over 100 nobles and hundreds of other untitled landowners were rounded up and sent to concentration camps in Hortobagy where they were 'forced to perform hard labour and sleep in stables and barracks, surrounded by barbed wire.'[27] The Irish Big House community did not suffer such terrorisation; they certainly were not rounded up and sent to concentration camps. The IRA never adopted the tactics of the Russian Cheka and the IRA leadership had no equivalent of Cheka leader Yakov Peters, whose intent it was to destroy and crush the aristocracy and other enemies of the working classes 'by the heavy hammer of the revolutionary proletariat'.[28] In 1918, the Russian aristocrat Vladimir Golitsyn asked: 'Who is to blame that the Russian people, the peasant and the proletarian, proved to be barbarians? Who, if not all of us?'[29] In contrast, it might be argued that British government reforms for Ireland in the nineteenth and early twentieth centuries were enough to provide the aristocracy with some form of dispensation. In 1920–23, and after, they were merely made irrelevant.

2. 'A sad picture of the terrible power of fire'

Once the fire was started, trying to quench a raging inferno was inevitably futile: estate firefighting services were useless and fire brigades were too far away and too slow in arriving to be of much assistance. For instance, by the time the police and fire brigade from Trim arrived at Summerhill House in Meath, 'The fire had gained such a hold that there were no hopes of saving the building.' The police fired rifle bullets into a large tank of water on the top of the house but the water made no impact on the flames, and nothing could be done to prevent the house being 'reduced to a mass of blackened ruins'.[30] Similarly, in the days after Castlemary in Cork was set alight in September 1920, 'There were still [flames] licking parts of the building, the walls of which now stand out a skeleton black mass, the very reverse of what the house was in its beautiful completeness.'[31] When Castleshane in Monaghan began to burn on Saturday 14 February 1920, the steward, George Morgan, attempted to quench the dining room blaze with a hose but he was quickly defeated by the intense heat and billowing smoke. By the time help arrived, the roof had collapsed.[32]

A mansion of the magnitude of Castleshane could burn for days and become an attraction of great curiosity and this had further consequences. On Sunday 15 February 1920, crowds of townspeople from Monaghan walked out to witness Castleshane burning: the local newspaper reported that 'The beautiful lawns around the house were sadly tramped and mutilated by the feet of men and wheels of carts brought to bring the salvaged furniture to a place of safety.'[33] The death of Castleshane was vividly captured in a local newspaper report:

> In the afternoon of Sunday, the remains of Castleshane House presented a sad picture of the terrible power of fire. What had once been a stately and

7.2 Castleshane, Co Monaghan, was one of the very first houses to be burned in February 1920. There remains some uncertainty as to whether it was accidental or to prevent its occupation by the crown forces.

beautiful building was in a few short hours reduced to a few blackened and smoking walls. The interior . . . was a glowing mass of material of all kinds. The twisted remains of a bedstead could be seen protruding from a mass of brick, and the remains of many other household fittings were in evidence. On all the interior walls the fireplaces could be seen, and this was the only thing to show where the rooms had been.[34]

The following day the employees raked through the debris, occasionally finding a piece of family silver, 'no longer of any value except as crude metal – the beautiful workmanship . . . being destroyed'.[35] As the IRA increasingly focused on inhabited houses, it was inevitable there would be such significant collateral damage to their interior embellishments and collections: at Castle Bernard there was the loss of a magnificent collection of paintings, furniture, silver plate and a wonderful library. When Mary Gaussen, Lord Bandon's niece, visited the ruins she found: 'The ruin is absolute and all one can do is to

7.3 Mary Gaussen, Lord Bandon's niece, amidst the ruins of
Castle Bernard burned in June 1921 as part of Cork IRA's counter-reprisal
campaign. IRA leader, Tom Barry, later recalled that it 'blazed half a day
before it crumbled in ruins'.

wander across the mass of debris in those precious rooms'.[36] In February 1923,
the steward at Moore Hall wrote to Colonel Maurice Moore: 'There is absolutely nothing left but the walls, not a vestige of glass, timber or even plaster
from the ground floor up, such wholesale destruction in a few hours is difficult
to understand.'[37]

Before the fire was started, family members and servants were usually
offered around fifteen to thirty minutes to remove what valuables they could.
Then began the pandemonium of trying to decide what to take: the valuable
silver plate or the family portraits, paintings or Chippendale chairs. Lady

7.4 Lord Listowel's house, Convamore, Co Cork, burned by the IRA during the War of Independence. Its owner was told by the local leader: 'You being an aggressively anti-Irish person, and your residence being in the battalion area of enemy reprisals, I have hereby ordered that same be destroyed as part of our counter reprisals.'

Fingall's emotive claim – 'Often it was valueless things that were stacked on the lawn, to be examined when the cold light of day broke on the blackened walls and ashes, while the Romneys and the Chippendale furniture and Waterford glass, or old Irish silver had perished'[38] – needs to be treated with a degree of caution in relation to the value of what was lost but it probably fairly reflects the bric-a-brac nature of what was salvaged. And not all raiders were accommodating. Lord Listowel's niece was told the family had half an hour to remove personal valuables and foodstuffs from Convamore, but they were not allowed to remove any other contents.

When Ardamine House in Gorey was attacked in early July 1921, the raiders allowed the caretaker and his wife to remove their personal belongings but they refused them permission to remove anything belonging to the owner, A.W. Mordaunt-Richards, and so 'The accumulation of about a century was destroyed utterly.'[39] Similarly, when Hazelwood House in Quin, Co Clare, was burned in early July 1921, Gore Hickman was allowed to remove only 'the clothes on his back'.[40]

In almost 300 burnings, great treasures were undoubtedly lost (aside from the magnificent decorative plasterwork; Adam, Bossi, Carrera fireplaces; architecturally important staircases; and other historically significant interior artistic features). On 29 June 1921, Stradone House in Cavan, the late-Georgian mansion home of T.J. Burrowes, was burned to a 'charred shell', and the paintings reported lost included two attributed to Jacob Ruysdael, valued at £750 and £1,000, one by Peter Lely valued at £500 and two by Godfrey Kneller valued at £150 each.[41] At Desart Court, several family portraits were lost, including one three-quarter length of Colonel W. Cuffe by Zoffany, one of the 2nd Earl and another of his wife by Hugh Thompson and one of Agmandesham Cuffe by Kneller.[42] In January 1922, Springfield Castle the home of Lord Muskerry – 'a studious and a most industrious bibliophile' – was burned with the loss of all the family portraits and the 6,000 volumes in the library.[43]

When Ballina Castle, the Mayo seat of the Earl of Arran, was burned in September 1922, 'some 350 pictures were destroyed'.[44] The Earl of Mayo reported he saved three Sir Joshua Reynolds, two Titians and 'most of my hunting clothes' (rather interesting the value he placed on the latter) but without an inventory there is no way of knowing what exactly was lost in Palmerston House: a headline in the local newspaper merely reported the loss of 'Priceless Treasures', and noted the fact that Mayo was 'one of the greatest living authorities on old English and French furniture. He is president of the Irish Arts and Crafts Society and organised more than one notable exhibition in Dublin when superb collections of Chippendale and Sheraton and Louis XIV and Louis XV furniture were exhibited. His own specimens were of almost priceless description.'[45] Kilkenny Castle was not burned but its interiors were greatly damaged during a Civil War siege when the National Army attempted to oust anti-Treatyites who had commandeered the castle on 2 May 1922.[46] Incessant machine gun fire ripped through the castle windows; after the siege ended the family went round 'sadly noting in room after room the favourite bits of furniture, pictures, china, tapestries, which were shattered and damaged, some beyond repair'.[47] And in the picture gallery, Lord Ossory found that many of the pictures 'had been riddled by bullets'.[48] There is no mention of what was there at the time but the gallery had in the past housed portraits and landscapes attributed to Van Dyck, Holbein, Kneller, Murillo, Rubens, Lawrence and Reynolds.[49] In fairness to Ossory, he was more disturbed by the sight of 'three or four bodies, contorted in all the hideous agonies of death' than the material damage.[50]

It will never be possible to establish all that was destroyed in the houses burned, or if attributions were authentic, not least because owners such as the Earl of Mayo had been so poor at keeping inventories. H.D. Conner KC, who represented Lord Bandon at his compensation trial, admitted that 'There was no detailed inventory showing what were the contents of the mansion.' All they had to go on was their memory and that of their 'confidential servant' who 'was intimate with every room'.[51] The same applied to Lady Wallscourt of Ardfry, whose solicitors informed the Irish Grants Committee: 'There was not at any time any list of them [valuables] in existence', so they had to generalise that they included her 'wedding presents, furs, laces, fans and wearing apparel'.[52] Referring to Bessborough in Kilkenny, M.J. Crotty, solicitor on behalf of the Board of Works, stated: 'I found that in some cases that inventories of goods destroyed have been prepared with very little care and sometimes copied from old inventories containing goods that had been removed long before the fire.'[53]

The absence of an inventory for James Mackay Wilson's Currygrane meant the chief state solicitor was advised that 'The necessary particulars can only be obtained by verbal enquiries and it would appear that the information can best be obtained from the claimant.'[54] Moreover, the same case file strongly suggests the shenanigans that went on in relation to valuables looted, valuables returned and even phantom valuables that never existed in the first place: the state solicitor found out that clothes and other chattels claimed for by Wilson had been shipped to England before the burning. Plate, silver and various other valuables that had been looted on 3–5 September 1922 were recovered by the local Garda Siochána in June 1924, stored in the premises of West Jewellers on Grafton Street, but when the claim came to be settled there was a discrepancy between the list handed over by the Gardai and what was found in West's, and no one was able to explain where the missing items had gone.

In November 1921, the *Irish Times* was correct to point out that many lost contents were heirlooms 'of value only to the family which treasured them'.[55] Sir Thomas Esmonde's house, Ballynastragh in Co Wexford, burned in March 1923, fairly typified this. Esmonde was unusual, in the Parnell mould of a landlord Nationalist who had been an Irish Parliamentary MP for North Wexford from 1900 to 1918, and he was also the first chairman of Wexford

7.5 Sir Thomas Esmonde's home, Ballynastragh, Co Wexford.

County Council in 1899. Initially, he was somewhat philosophical about the burning: 'The only reason for such an act is that I am a senator of the Free State, and, of course, I am in no worse a position than anybody else.'[56] As time went by, he became more aggrieved at what he had lost. He was particularly affected by the loss of the library: 'After my burning,' he confided in a friend, 'I lost heart and gave up books altogether, so much so that I refused to accept books from several literary friends who wanted to give me their publications as I had no place to keep them.'[57] He also began to feel resentful that his house should have been burned in light of the contribution he had made to Irish political life as a Nationalist, and that as an agriculturalist – a tillage farmer – he had given all the local employment he could.[58] His sense of injustice was fed by correspondence from friends, relatives, acquaintances, representatives of public bodies and members of the various churches. 'Wanton' was by far the most common adjective used by them to describe the destruction. Paula Hornstein, for example, wrote to Esmonde: 'Can it possibly be that a whole life of devotion to your country, so many sacrifices, are rewarded with the blackest ingratitude … We live in a very sad time, hatred, revenge ruling everywhere.'[59]

Similarly, Howard Dudley wrote to Lord Dunalley following the destruction of Kilboy: 'The whole business is too sad for words and we are all profoundly grieved that your beautiful residence has been destroyed and that you have lost so much that is valuable and that no money could compensate you.'[60] In other words, Kilboy was more than bricks and mortar, or a repository of fine and decorative arts: it contained generations of family heirlooms, personal mementos, memorials to loved ones that were irreplaceable. Thus, when houses were destroyed it was not always the valuable art collections that first sprung to mind: when Lady Dartrey sympathised with Sybil Lucas-Scudamore after the destruction of Castleshane, her first query was about 'the picture', reference to a portrait of Sybil and her late husband painted by Jane Inglis. Sybil's son, Jack, was also greatly saddened by its loss, and he was also 'sick about the library going' and wondered had the gramophone 'pipped it' and had the records been melted?[61] He had concerns about a more contemporary material culture, while his young sister, Gill, summed up not just her feelings about the loss of the family home, but the feelings of a whole generation who were wearied of war and revolution: 'I can't believe it. . . . it seems everything we love goes . . . Is everything we love gone forever? I did so love Castleshane, I don't seem to think we have any real "home" anymore.'[62] Not only had Gill lost everything that was familiar to her, she was also threatened with losing her link between the historical past and the future, something that was extremely important to the aristocracy (as testified to by the existence of works such as *Burke's Peerage, Baronetage & Knightage*), and this common experience amongst her peers partially explains the sense of deracination one so often finds in Anglo-Irish literature of the period.

The burning of Castleshane also resulted in the destruction of an important Great Famine archive (1845–51), made up of the correspondence between Robert Peel, when Chief Secretary of Ireland, and Edward Lucas, his Under Secretary, covering the period 1841–46, during part of which Lucas was chairman of the Famine Relief Commission of Ireland. Similarly, Durrow Abbey in King's County [Offaly] lost a particularly impressive library with many rare manuscripts.[63] At Kilboy, 'A great quantity of historical manuscripts . . . many letters written by George Ponsonby . . . hundreds of letters and interesting documents relating to the period of the Commonwealth, including roll calls of many of Cromwell's regiments . . . filling twenty-two deed boxes' were lost.[64] In conflagrations across the country these losses meant not just the destruction of a family's history, but that of a whole community, and, indeed, represented an incalculable loss to the history of the nation.[65]

3. 'Tutankhamun's tomb'

Looting is a universal phenomenon of war and civil commotion; it can be driven by a wide variety of motivations, not least the despoliation of enemy culture. Big House looting in 1920–23 could be justified as another means of plundering the coloniser's landscape, even a form of retribution for ancestral wrongs; after all, since the Land War era nationalist rhetoric had taught Irish people that landlords had preyed on them for hundreds of years. Moreover, it could also be practised as a form of retribution for the burning and looting carried out by the Black and Tans and Auxiliaries. In February 1921, David Lloyd George in a letter to the Irish Chief Secretary, Hamar Greenwood, condemned the activity of the crown forces, as he knew there were likely to be repercussions:

I am not at all satisfied of the state of discipline in the Royal Irish Constabulary and its auxiliary force. Accounts reach me from too many and too authoritative quarters to leave any doubt in my mind that the charges of drunkenness, looting and other acts of indiscipline are in too many cases substantially true . . . [This is] causing grave uneasiness in the public mind . . . It is vital that the violence and indiscipline which undoubtedly characterises certain units in the Royal Irish Constabulary should be terminated in the most prompt and drastic manner. It is weakening seriously the hands of the executive . . . Public opinion, which is already unhappy, will swing round and withdraw its support from the policy which is now being pursued by the Government in Ireland. There is no doubt that indiscipline, looting and drunkenness in the Royal Irish Constabulary is alienating great numbers of well-disposed people in Ireland and throwing them into the arms of Sinn Fein.[66]

Stathis Kalyvas has argued that civil war predisposes ordinary people to new levels of criminality, they become immune to violence and crime, and neither plays on their moral conscience.[67] It was an argument as old as Thucydides (c.460 BC–c.400 BC), who argued that civil war encouraged the privatisation of war, or Edmund Burke, the eighteenth-century philosopher, who considered that 'Civil wars strike deepest of all into the manners of the people. They vitiate their politics; they corrupt their morals; they pervert even the natural taste and relish of equity and justice.'[68] And whether Minister for Home Affairs Kevin O'Higgins was familiar or not with Thucydides or Burke, he, too, in March 1923, drew similar conclusions about the correlation between civil war in Ireland and the impact it was having on the moral fibre of ordinary people. He wryly told the Dáil: 'There were persons . . . who would fret for a week if a hen happened to lay away from home. Yet they would cheerfully burn and plunder their neighbours' houses.'[69] The following month, he reiterated that 'People who possibly considered themselves respectable had no hesitation in looting wholesale.'[70] And Big Houses were frequently the targets. Take, for example, two servants at Moydrum Castle – Michael Grady, the butler, and Patrick Delaney, a footman – who shortly after it was burned in July 1921 were both charged and found guilty of the larceny of a fur coat, dress suits, a bicycle and other goods to the value of £360 from Lord Castlemaine. When passing sentence, the judge could only conclude that this was 'a bad case. These two men, holding positions of trust, had taken advantage of a catastrophe to benefit themselves.'[71] But they may very well have got away with much more than they were accused of, and if they did not someone else did, perhaps some of the IRA volunteers who helped Lady Castlemaine collect her valuables, because on 20 April 2018 at Christie's Exceptional Sale in New York six items from a rare Irish silver collection – an octagonal casket, a pincushion, a pair of covered boxes, a clothes brush and a hair brush – came up for auction with estimates between $60,000 and $90,000 (€48,746 to €73,119).[72] It had been bought by Richard Cushing Paine of Boston in the 1930s, and it was rumoured that the set originally belonged to Lord Castlemaine and that it may have been looted during the burning of Moydrum.[73]

The Moydrum servants were captured, tried and convicted under the British administrative system, but different circumstances prevailed after the Truce when the countryside was denuded of forces of law and order and country house looters seem to have worked with impunity. In late August 1922, four

7.6 Desart Court, Co Kilkenny, garden front, c.1900. Lord Desart was awarded £19,000 in compensation for its burning, of which £12,000 was conditional on it being rebuilt. Newly designed by Richard Orpen, Desart's niece lived there for several years 'until the anti-English feeling in the neighbourhood made that impossible'. It was demolished in 1957.

men were charged at a special hearing at Nenagh 'with the alleged larceny of property belonging to Lord Dunalley'. Before its burning, Kilboy had been raided several times and silver plate and jewellery was targeted; these were valuable items that could generously reward criminal endeavour.[74] Despite the fact that the defendants were caught on Dunalley's property 'with horses and carts, with the looted goods in them' they were admitted to bail.[75] At the very same time, Thomas O'Connell was given ten years penal servitude for looting a train at Nenagh, in the same district as Kilboy, the two crimes less than a month apart. O'Connell would have been better off looting a country house.

Similarly, in March 1923 the Garda inspector investigating the burning of Desart Court in Kilkenny identified four suspects he found on the demesne, local men, who 'were there for the purpose of removing hidden stuff' (he believed that while the furniture was burned, smaller valuables such as clocks, silver ring stands, china and pictures were all looted). He also could identify five others who had hijacked and burned a van and lorry at Cuffesgrange carrying away artefacts saved from the house.[76] But he was in no hurry to prosecute any of these men, which, as we shall see below in the case of the Garda sergeant in Silvermines, was not unusual.

Kalyvas argues that one of the more 'powerful attractions' provided by war is access to 'looted luxury items'.[77] But luxury is, of course, relative to degrees of poverty. When Roslevan was burned in Clare in July 1922, Lord Inchiquin, brother of the owner, offered his personal reflection on the motive and consequences:

> On Saturday night Roslevan was burnt to the ground, only the walls left standing. All furniture, linen, blankets, nic-nacs etc. were destroyed and now everybody in Ennis is looting the place. Women with perambulators collecting odds and ends, all the potatoes and vegetables are being taken out of the garden. We got the carriages away and I have sent five carts to get whatever is left such as electric light engine, corn bins, water barrels, horses, mowing machines, if there are now any of them left, which I doubt. I . . . think it was the work of a lot of Free-booters and robbers who looted the place and then burnt it to hide traces of their work.[78]

Bill Power, as previously noted, came up with a similar motive for the burning of Mitchelstown Castle, and without proof one way or the other should not be discounted. But the theft of potatoes and vegetables from the garden spoke of another dimension to looting: the Civil War coincided with an economic downturn that caused great hardship to very many families, so the poor and destitute who were going hungry saw an opportunity too good to be missed. As a colleague once quipped to this author, it was unlikely local IRA leaders were about to open a fruit and vegetable stall to make a commercial profit, and therefore this type of looting was driven by subsistence.[79] In fact, the more general case stated seems to be that the ordinary people looted what might be termed 'practical luxuries': a plough, in other words, was more useful to a small farmer than a silver epergne. Thus, in March 1923, Mr Justice Devitt described the looting at Glenfarne, Co Leitrim: 'From far and near – from Fermanagh, Cavan and Leitrim – the people came with carts and carried away from Glenfarne everything that was portable – the timber, the rails, the whole interior of the house so that only the four walls and the roof were left, and the roof went eventually.' Devitt found no evidence of this looting being 'the concerted action of people banded together in an unlawful or seditious association' and concluded that it 'was done by people of the neighbouring counties with the object of enriching themselves'.[80] Certainly, they were enriching their lives. On 6 August 1922, Samuel Doupe wrote to Lord Dunalley: 'The inner yard next to the Mansion House was destroyed and the outer farmyard was looted of all agricultural machinery and implements, in fact everything of value.'[81] The looters took what was necessary to farming but often unaffordable to smallholders: ploughs, shares, harrows; and from the stables they took saddles, harnesses and bridles. (It has already been suggested that this might have been in the best traditions of Luddism: if his farm implements were stolen, Dunalley could not farm, and this would force him to sell his untenanted lands.)

Similarly, when Leap Castle in Offaly was attacked on successive nights, 30–31 July 1922, 'endless crowds with donkey and horse carts' were seen 'coming and going looting all worth taking'. Michael Walsh, a former employee, later recalled that 'in front of the house [were stacked] armchairs, tables, bedclothes, shirts, books an' anythin an' everythin. You'd think there was going to be an auction.'[82] There was no mention of silver plate and paintings; anything on the lawn was practical and useful. When Castlesaunderson in Cavan was abandoned, it became: 'a sort of Tom Tiddler's ground for the countryside. Baths, fireplaces, water pipes, doors, windows, and fittings of all descriptions vanished like magic; even the lead from the roof was stripped off and stolen.'[83] At Ravensdale House in Dundalk, the steward received several warnings threatening him with death if he dared interfere with locals who removed all the woodwork in the stables, and the lead on the roof of the burned house and outbuildings, while 'stairs had been cut away with saws, floors had been pulled up, and grates and presses had been torn from the walls'.[84] In August 1922, Lord Ashtown reported clothes and numerous breakfast, dinner, tea and dessert services missing from Woodlawn, his Galway home. It did not matter whether these were Minton or Wedgwood: not only would they look well on a kitchen dresser, they were also of practical use.[85]

Outside on demesnes, ornamental gardens were also plundered. A typical small farmer might know every native flower, tree, vegetable and weed, but he probably never saw an exotic plant before he tramped onto a derelict demesne, and so ornamental plants and shrubs were coveted. In August 1922, the *Irish Times* reported that:

> In the history of looting there has been nothing more scandalous than that which has taken place at Brookfield House, Tullamore, which was recently burned by the irregulars. Everything that could be seized in the ruined building, which was a very fine well-furnished residence, is being taken. The garden at the rear of the premises has come in for particular attention. It was one of the noted fruit and flower gardens in the Midlands. Rare plants have been torn from their roots, and carried away, so have gooseberry bushes, fruit trees, and the well-kept beds have been destroyed. The looters have spared nothing and the place has been completely devastated.[86]

At Warrenscourt, between July 1921 and May 1923, specimen shrubs and plants, 'two large plantations of hybrid rhododendrons' (not a wise choice) and a wide variety of glasshouse plants were all stolen (while the steward also reported that the stones from the demesne wall were carted away 'by neighbours' to build cattle sheds). The estate manager knew these people: he could identify Joe McSweeney from Coachford, who took four loads of shrubs from the front lawn, while three members of the Leahy family 'came and calmly tied up their horse in the yard while they dug up a whole load of valuable shrubs'.[87]

Timber was scarce and valuable after the war, so demesne woods were also pillaged after houses were burned. Sometimes, this was for firewood as the depression began to impact on the working classes. In March 1921, a year after Castleshane was burned, an old retainer informed Sybil Lucas-Scudamore, then resident in Wales, that people were 'making a total hand of the woods' with 'three out of the one house in it at a time carrying them [trees] out the road and wheeling them home in a barrow, and others even pulling up evergreen shrubs by the root to set'.[88] There were also more large-scale operations that must have had some commercial intent. In October 1922, 140 ash, elm, oak, sycamore and beech trees were cut down and carted away after Macroom Castle was burned.[89] At Mount Uniacke, between December 1922 and

February 1923, 54 beech trees, 23 ash and 10 oak were cut down and removed.[90] These operations did not happen overnight, and the fact that they were carried out undisturbed merely reflected the disinterest of the authorities in preventing them.

It is little wonder that on 2 February 1923 the editor of the *Tuam Herald*, commenting on those involved in widespread looting concluded, 'It is often hard to tell where the political outlaw ends and the looter begins.'[91] The reports on the destruction and looting of Lord Lansdowne's Kerry property, Derreen, were indicative of this social, rather than political, dimension.[92] When Winston Churchill was lobbied by Lansdowne to intervene in the looting of his property, Churchill wrote to W.T. Cosgrave on 22 September 1922: 'It seems to me from the account to have been an incident of squalid private pillage without even a perverted political motive behind it.'[93] Between 1 and 5 September, the house 'was constantly raided by a large number of men who brought carts and other vehicles and removed the furniture and effects'.[94] As was fairly typical, 'all the beds, bedding and linen . . . and also some of the smaller furniture' were stolen, but more of the contents, the larger furnishings, for example, were maliciously smashed, being the type of contents that were of no practical value in small homes. For weeks the pillaging was relentless: towards the end of September, Lansdowne's agent reported that, 'All the windows, doors, floorings etc. have been taken, motor garage gone . . . all outbuildings either removed or burnt, greenhouses smashed up, laundry pulled down and removed . . . In fact, there is nothing left of Derreen or its surroundings.'[95] In June 1923 Eamon Ó Frighil of the Department of Defence informed the Commissioner of the Garda Síochána that 'farmers and other householders throughout Kenmare and neighbouring unions have built outoffices, and sheds etc. with timber stolen from woods belonging to the Marquis of Lansdowne . . . There is scarcely a house in Gurtamullane that has not had new sheds built near them.'[96] According to Lansdowne's agent, William Rochfort, the looting of the demesne woodland and gardens resulted in 'the disfigurement of the scenery which has been described by visitors as recalling that of the shell-swept areas of France and Belgium.'[97]

Cosgrave did not reply to Churchill's correspondence for a month, until 23 October, when he wrote: 'We of the Irish Government have been shocked and greatly saddened by it. It is one of the symptoms of the demoralisation which has already seized the whole social fabric when we took over the administration of government.'[98] It seems Cosgrave had deliberately waited until the government had established military courts earlier that month to try people for offences including 'looting, arson, destruction, seizure, unlawful possession or removal of or damage to any public or private property'.[99] But the widespread pillaging did not end. In March 1923, Kevin O'Higgins, Minister for Defence, told his Dáil colleagues that the National Army had searched houses which they found crammed with loot and resembling 'Tutankhamun's tomb . . . There were hens roosting on valuable oil paintings, there were silver candlesticks and valuable *prieu dieux* plundered out of the house of a neighbour that had been burned.'[100] The middle class politicians such as Cosgrave, O'Higgins, and Hogan had come to view looting in the same way they viewed land grabbing: it was a despicable lower class crime that did not augur well for the credibility of the new Irish Free State and could be damaging to its international credit rating. Cosgrave specifically referenced working class homes where 'costly candlesticks, trouser presses, gilt mirrors and articles of that kind were found'.[101] The Garda Commissioner, Eoin O'Duffy, could hardly have composed any more synonyms in his 'state of the country reports' to describe the 'hooligan element', 'rowdy class', scoundrels, brigands, roughs, marauders and so on who were responsible for everyday crime.[102] But, as Gavin Foster has rightly concluded: 'These criminality discourses and the outraged moral tone in which they were conveyed reflected a deeper anxiety inside the government camp that wider "anti-social forces" were at play in the Civil War and threatened not only the survival of the state but the very social order itself.'[103] It was why the Dáil had also been determined to put down landgrabbing.

But looting was not the sole preserve of the lower classes. Bill Power's claim that a local solicitor 'with an appreciation of the finer things in life' removed many of the valuable paintings for his personal advantage from Mitchelstown Castle has already been referenced.[104] There is anecdotal evidence of IRA members looting artworks and other treasures and selling them to antique dealers along the Dublin Quays and these, in turn, being purchased by professionals and merchants, strangely incurious about their provenance but arguably complicit in looting as the indirect receivers of stolen goods. More substantive evidence is difficult to find, but in a 1999 Mealy's and Christie's auction catalogue advertising the sale of the James Murnaghan Collection it was pointed out that 'Collecting in the years following 1916 was serendipity. As the large Anglo-Irish houses were dispersed, stock in dealers' shops along the [Dublin] quays, *en route* from the Four Courts, bourgeoned, giving collectors ample opportunity to expand their own collections.'[105] Justice James Murnaghan had managed to amass a collection of 1,200 paintings in his Fitzwilliam Street home, including Old Masters bought on the Dublin quays in the 1920s, that had once been hung in Big Houses, and in her preface to the catalogue his niece admitted that he did not concern himself with provenance.[106] Conceivably, there is a hidden history yet to be unveiled of how local respectables – auctioneers, solicitors, bank managers, men of property – sometimes connived to take advantage of the revolutionary period for personal advantage through the sale of Big Houses, their contents and lands, or acquiring them cheaply as private residences for themselves, as was the case with Lough Bawn in Monaghan, bought by Charles Laverty, a Castleblayney solicitor and the last Home Ruler to have contested a seat in south Monaghan in 1910.

But one of the great imponderables is whether paintings, silver, family plate, Georgian delft and other valuable objects adorned farmhouses and Irish cottages for generations, no one aware of their provenance and true value. Did owners ever retrieve all their valuable contents put into storage for safe keeping in local banks and national institutions such as the National Gallery and Museum? In March 2019, former Bank of Ireland official Jim Connolly revealed to the *Irish Times* that he had seen 'huge paintings' and other artefacts 'housed in pallets, travel chests, suitcases and trunks'.[107] Following Connolly's evidence to the Joint Committee on Rural and Community Development on 6 March 2019, Deputy Éamon Ó Cuív claimed that opening the vaults 'would show us some . . . beautiful items that have been hidden away. There is probably a Caravaggio, a Rubens or something else there.' Whether he was right remains to be seen.

It is true that loot from country houses very often ended up locally. For instance, Bryan Cooper later claimed that when the National Army evacuated his Markree home: 'Nearly all the furniture left behind was to disappear, some to a neighbouring military camp, some to cottages in Co Sligo.'[108] After Durrow Abbey was burned, 'Some of the furniture from the house that had escaped the flames' was later identified in the houses of former tenants.[109] The night that Woodstock was burned, 'The contents of the library were moved out, and carted away', and 'stray fragments of domestic life ended up scattered on the lawns outside, to be picked up by those people who gathered from miles around'. One of the IRA involved in that burning, Paddy White, later admitted to taking a tablecloth – 'an exquisite example of Irish linen, with its hand-scalloped edges and embroidered flowers and shamrocks' – which his son still retained in his Dublin home in 1999.[110] When Lord Dunalley's claim for compensation was dismissed by the county court judge in May 1924, his solicitors wrote to him: 'We were unable to prove that the things were taken by the Irregulars and as a matter of fact I believe they were not taken by these people for the whole place was plundered principally by the mountainy people [of Silvermines] after the burning.'[111] In October 1924, the Garda sergeant in Silvermines told Dunalley that some of the contents of Kilboy were prominent in farmers' houses in Upperchurch but Dunalley's solicitor advised him not to undertake the task of identifying them personally: 'It would be putting you in a most invidious position and would, I think, cause great ill feeling, which has now happily died down.'[112]

On 3 August 1923, in their determined attempt to combat looting and general lawlessness, and to restore law and order, the government passed the Public Safety (Emergency Powers) (no. 2) Act.[113] It promised imprisonment to every person brought before a district judge for the possession of stolen or unlawfully obtained goods. Where stolen property was recovered, it was to be returned to the rightful owner. Significantly, this act worked in tandem with the 1923 Land Act, passed a week later, which threatened to punish those enemies of the state who continued to involve themselves in agrarian crime, most particularly land grabbing (see chapter 9).

4. 'Cautious faces, emptied cabinets, bare walls'

It should be noted that many Irish country house owners, anticipating attack, put valuable contents into safe storage in bank vaults, galleries and museums, or sent them off to safe havens in England. In March 1921, Ardtully Castle in Kerry was completely gutted by fire, but the castle had been vacated a few days before by the Constable family and most of the furniture removed. Castleffogarty in Tipperary – 'at one time famous for its large picture gallery, which housed a collection valued at many thousands of pounds'[114] – was burned in April 1922 but the paintings had been removed to London in 1920.[115] Elizabeth Bowen claimed her father had the good sense to remove the family portraits and other valuables 'for a sojourn in a cottage at the end of the woods' so that when the IRA arrived they were met by 'cautious faces, emptied cabinets, bare walls'.[116] Lady Gregory wrote in August 1922 that in Galway: 'Furniture vans engaged for nine months ahead are taking goods from the country to England.'[117] And even when destroyed, the loss of Irish furniture was not terribly regretted. In the early 1920s, it was neither valuable nor popular with dealers: in 1921, R.W. Symonds, the influential English furniture historian, dismissed its 'heavy appearance, superfluity of carved ornament, and absence of elegant and graceful lines that make its present-day appreciation and value considerably less than that of contemporary English furniture.'[118] In a like vein, the judge in the Mitchelstown Castle compensation trial dismissed the value of the furniture destroyed: 'A good deal of it was built or constructed specially for the Castle, and would be of little use in modern times.'[119] The loss of Irish furniture was regretted only when a market for it was manufactured towards the end of the twentieth century.[120]

Furthermore, the impact of the Troubles should not be overstated in relation to the loss of the most valuable of the original collections. Denuding Big Houses of their contents had begun forty years previously with the passing of the Settled Land Act (Ireland) in 1882. Until then the Big House owner, essentially a tenant for life, had the responsibility of handing down estate, house and heirlooms intact to the next generation. From the late 1870s, the greatly changed economic, social and political climates in Ireland (chapter one) resulted in diminishing landlord rental income and increased indebtedness. The Settled Land Act was basically a trade-off against the government introducing fair rents under the 1881 Land Act. It relaxed the law of settlement, allowing owners to sell heirlooms (and outlying estates) to meet their financial obligations. From then on, financially constrained owners came to regard their collections as liquid assets that could be sold to support their lifestyles, or simply keep a roof on their houses. From the mid-1880s, the sale of paintings and the family silver would help to pay newly introduced death and succession duties, and a generation or so later escalating income and super tax.

In many respects, revolutionary activity was a sideshow to dispersals as families continued to struggle with the unsustainability of their houses. In 1919, years

7.7 Kilruddery, Co Wicklow, home of the Earls of Meath. During the inter-war period, the house was closed, shuttered and the furniture covered in dust sheets as Reginald Brabazon, 13th Earl of Meath, claimed he could not afford to live there. Partly demolished in the 1950s, it is still owned by the Brabazon family and is a popular wedding venue and location for films and TV series.

before the damage of the Civil War siege, the Ormondes of Kilkenny Castle were faced with death duties and legal expenses of almost £166,000 that made their long-term continuance in residence impossible. The economic downturn of the 1920s then decimated their share portfolio with the result that they were eventually forced to vacate the castle in 1935 and auction off its entire contents.[121] Thus, it was events either side of the revolutionary period, and primarily economic in nature, that ended the Ormonde's residency of almost 800 years. In September 1921, the Earl of Meath closed Kilruddery in Wicklow because of increased taxation and unaffordability: 'My father was always a poor man,' he told his estate employees, 'his income was never more than from £1,500 to £2,000 a year' – most of those listening would have been on around £60 per year – and 'he never knew anything about the present heavy taxation of 6s[hillings] in the pound income tax and super tax.' That year Meath's tax bill was almost £4,500 accounting for 43 per cent of the estate charges. He was no longer prepared, he said, to draw on his invested income to supplement the upkeep of Kilruddery.[122] He closed the house for years. The havoc wreaked by taxation in Ireland merely reflected what was happening across Britain. In August 1921, the editor of the *Irish Times* opined:

The burden of taxation is crushing the life out of rural England. During the last two years many great landowners have been forced to sell their historic mansions and estates . . . The charges on land, the demands of the income tax collector, and the prospect of heavy death duties . . . [make] a closing down of the larger country houses almost inevitable.[123]

In Ireland, revolution and its consequences undoubtedly expedited the sale or abandonment of Big Houses; between June 1921 and May 1922, almost sixty houses, their contents and demesne lands were advertised for sale in the *Irish Times* alone.[124] In December 1921, as treaty negotiations were ongoing, Battersby & Co set out their programme of forthcoming sales, which included Bert House in Kildare, a 'commodious mansion with 198 acres'; Bellamont Forest in Cavan with 800 acres, 'a fine old Georgian mansion with every accommodation for a gentleman's family'; Hazelwood in Sligo with 2,800 acres and a shooting estate of 8,250 acres.[125] The dates during which these sales took place might suggest owners wanted to get out of Ireland and that they went in search of refuge elsewhere in the empire. But even without revolution and its political consequences, the precarious financial position of the aristocracy would have led to Big House sales and abandonment, as was the case across Britain. Financial difficulties were every bit as damaging as cans of paraffin carried by the IRA. This was because the Irish landed elites's post-1903 invested wealth had become more susceptible to the vagaries of the stock market during the turbulent post-war years. Their investments were decimated as markets failed to readjust, inflation and deflation negatively impacted fixed incomes and the world's financial system headed towards eventual collapse in 1929–30.[126] This was doubly compounded by the compulsory acquisition of their demesne and untenanted lands under the 1923 Land Act (chapter 9).

And this was similarly reflected in the sale of their collections: in the early 1920s, the aristocracy was selling as much as was being destroyed, and they were selling for reasons of indebtedness rather than revolution. The Duke of Leinster's estate was brought down by family misfortune, poor capital management and an heir's profligacy rather than the Troubles.[127] Just over a week after the 6th Duke's death in February 1922, the secretary to Edouard Jonas, art expert to the French government, wrote to enquire 'whether the estate of the late Duke of Leinster includes any valuable pictures or works of art of which you might wish

205

7.8 Lord Dunalley and his family on the steps of Kilboy, 1933, on the occasion marking the coming of age of Hon. Desmond Prittie, at centre front. The house had been rebuilt a few years before.

to dispose', such as Old Masters, Gothic tapestry, Oriental China and French eighteenth-century furniture.[128] There is no record of a reply, but evidently the vultures were beginning to circle the carcasses of declining Irish country houses. Following the bankruptcies of the 7th Duke, the contents of Carton were sold off in several high-profile sales between 1925 and the late 1940s.[129] And the Leinsters were certainly not alone in this respect. In 1920, over 200 works of art were sold from Killua Castle in Westmeath.[130] In the years leading up to 1920, Bennett and Sons sold huge quantities of Irish plate and paintings attributed (often dubiously) to artists such as Gainsborough, Rembrandt, Van Dyck, Verner, Kneller and Breughel, as well as Chippendale and Sheraton furniture, and rare books from the collections of families such as the Moncks at Charleville in Wicklow and their neighbours the Wicklows at Shelton Abbey, Lord Courtown in Wexford and J.R. Garstin at Braganstown in Louth. Courtown, Garstin and Wicklow all had to meet legacy or death duties.[131]

During the inter-war years American plutocrats exploited the impoverished aristocracies of Europe, creating a market that was impossible to ignore.[132] In one auction alone in New York in 1921, hundreds of pieces of Irish silver from Big Houses were sold, the property of Lord Ashbrook of Castle Durrow in Queen's County, Lady Ardilaun of St Anne's in Dublin, the Earl of Mayo in Palmerstown (notably *before* the house was burned), Lord Fermoy of Rockbarton Castle in Limerick and Lady Coote of Ballyfin in Queen's County, amongst many others.[133] And dispersals would continue long into the future. Therefore, the 1920–23 period merely acted as a catalyst in an ongoing process of social and economic decline that had contributed to the sale of Big Houses and the dispersal of contents that went all the way back to the early 1880s.

8

'SERMONS IN STONES'
COMPENSATING COUNTRY HOUSE OWNERS

The story of the compensation paid to the southern Irish Loyalists for the losses they suffered, and the atrocities committed against them for the crime of loyalty to England does not make pretty reading.

(R.D. King-Harman, *The Kings, Earls of Kingston: An Account of the Family and Their Estates in Ireland between the Reigns of the Two Queen Elizabeths*, London, 1959, p. 264)

The whole business is too sad for words and we are all profoundly grieved that your beautiful residence [Kilboy] has been destroyed and that you have lost so much that is valuable and that no money could compensate you.

(Howard Dudley to Lord Dunalley, 12 August 1922, NLI, MS 29810 (17))

1. 'Sermons in stones'

On 23 February 1924, a report appeared in the provincial *Sligo Champion* under the heading 'Sermons in Stones' – presumably inspired by Duke Senior's speech in Shakespeare's *As You Like It* – in which the writer deplored the pillaging of country houses and demesnes, reports of which he pointed out 'stuffed' every contemporaneous provincial newspaper. In sarcastic tones, it was noted that such crimes had become so ubiquitous they no longer merited reporting in the national press, 'except where the depradations have been on a heroic scale'.[1] In particular, the writer referred to a recent compensation claim heard in the courts for the looting of Ravensdale Park in Co Louth (described in chapter 5), which led the writer to conclude: 'This is not a description of a Russian Soviet in action, or a raid by Turkish partisans upon their Christian neighbours. It is simply an incident from a recent chapter of Irish history, some details of which are being made known to the world through the proceedings in the Compensation Courts.'[2] The comparison of the fate of the Irish aristocracy to their Russian counterparts whom the Bolsheviks had stripped of their estates, wealth, status and dignity, and to the horrendous 1922 experience of tens of thousands of Orthodox Christians in the city of Smyrna at the hands of an avenging Turkish army was grossly overstated, but the report successfully highlighted the ongoing difficulties that Irish country house owners faced in search of compensation for the loss of their homes and contents in the courts. In the long term, Big House owners could argue they were not adequately compensated, but so too could all other sections of rural and urban society.[3]

2. 'No risk of riot or civil commotion was covered'

Big House owners were obviously a minority amongst the many thousands of compensation claimants who lost their homes, their businesses, their farms or even ricks of hay, who had money, goods and personal effects stolen, or in the worst-case scenarios had been shot and maimed, or whose husbands, wives, sons or daughters had been murdered. However, as might be expected, given the scale of the physical destruction, the aristocracy's individual claims for their Big Houses were amongst the highest made. While what follows focuses specifically on the latter, it is well to remember the landed elite also experienced and claimed for malicious damage to gate lodges, hunting lodges, outbuildings, police stations (which they built and leased to the RIC), demesne churches, livestock and losses accruing from the occupation of their lands and subsequent diminution of profits, the theft of timber from their demesnes, and the list could go on. Sometimes, there were so many attacks and raids on individuals and their properties it was impossible to keep track. For example, in November 1922 Lord Dunalley's solicitor informed him: 'I think we are making every possible claim on your behalf, but you have no idea how difficult it is to get the necessary information about the various damages done from time to time at Kilboy.' He followed up in May 1923: 'We have such a multitude of decrees and claims that it is very hard to keep track of them all.'[4]

Owners such as Dunalley were unable to claim on their insurance policies, in his case from the Northern Assurance Company, because they were not

8.1 Castleboro in Co Wexford was described as 'one of the finest dwelling houses in Ireland'. The Irish Grants Committee was far from sympathetic to Lady Gordon Cary, who inherited the burned ruin, and refused her any compensation.

covered against riot and civil commotion.[5] Like Kilboy, Mount Uniacke in Cork was insured against fire for £5,950 but 'no risk of riot or civil commotion was covered'.[6] Richard Power O'Shee had Gardenmorris insured for £5,000 with Commercial Union Insurance against accidental loss or damage by fire but not against civil commotion. In fact, it seems also to have been the case that houses and contents were hopelessly under-insured (if at all). After Ardamine House in Gorey, Co Wexford, was burned on 9 July 1921, the insurance was reported to have been 'totally inadequate'. The legal representatives of Castleboro in the same county said the house was insured for £26,700 (whilst claiming rebuilding costs of treble that figure): 'As no insurer for fire premeditates a fire which would cause complete destruction, this is an intimation of the value which the owner put on the residence.'[7] In 1902, Lord Castletown's policy with Hand in Hand Fire and Life Insurance Society placed a value of only £4,000 on Doneraile Park in Cork and a paltry £2,000 on contents, including paintings, prints, drawings, sculptures, articles of vertu and all other household furniture.[8]

Without (adequate) insurance cover, owners could resort to claiming compensation through the courts, as would have been typical in the past in relation to malicious and criminal injuries. Claims during the early period of the War of Independence therefore came under the terms of the 1898 Local Government (Ireland) Act, and then the Criminal Injuries (Ireland) Acts of 1919 and 1920, the latter two acts introduced to deal with the unprecedented national crisis of property damage.[9] Under the 1898 Act, application for compensation was made against the council of the county in which the damage occurred. Each year, the council had to levy a rate to raise the money to meet its annual expenditure, which included claims for malicious injuries and damage to property. The 1919 Act modified this to spread the growing burden: compensation could now be levied against either the council of the county in which the house was located or spread across neighbouring counties. Increased claims led to further modification of the legislation in 1920. If the county councils made representation to the Lord Lieutenant that the amount of compensation could not be raised by means of the rates in one year 'without imposing an excessive burden on the ratepayers', he could direct that the amount be paid in instalments over a maximum five-year period. Critical in all of this was that, under these acts, the financial burden fell on the ratepayers. When Macroom Castle in Cork was burned, Thomas Healy, state solicitor, put it bluntly that it was the ratepayers who 'have greatly suffered by the burning of this castle and the buildings round it'.[10] Traditionally, the ratepayers resented any increase in taxation resultant from criminal activity. By the time the 1920 Act was passed on 23 December (the same day that the Government of Ireland Act ratified the establishment of Northern Ireland), there were further hindrances at local government level: the composition of county councils and most other local government bodies in the Free State was dominated by Sinn Féin. Following the January and May elections of that year, Sinn Féin won control of 28 out of 33 county councils (on the island of Ireland), 182 out of 206 rural district councils and 72 out of 127 urban district councils.[11]

It was unrealistic to consider that Sinn Féin-dominated councils would levy burdensome rates on the county at large to compensate country house owners (and others); nor, of course, were they willing to work with or within the British administrative structures. Thus, in June 1921, Sir Hamar Greenwood, the last chief secretary for Ireland (1920–22), informed the House of Commons that damages claimed came to almost £5.4 million but county councils were ignoring awards made by the county court judges, and refusing to budget for them in their rate assessments, so no money was being raised and compensation was not being paid. In June 1920, Monaghan County Council, for instance, voted to ignore all compensation claims.[12] Clonmel Rural District Council ignored Lord Ashtown's claim for £25,000 for the destruction of his hunting lodge in Waterford.[13] In September 1920, Loughrea District Council ignored a claim for £3,000 compensation for the burning of Tallyho House.[14] By October 1921, during the truce period, the *Irish Times* lamented: 'Whether these awards are being paid to the claimants is not clear, since in the areas upon which the amounts have been assessed there appear to be difficulties in the way of collection.'[15] In November 1921, it was estimated that £1.6 million was leviable off Co Cork alone, where the highest number of Big Houses had been destroyed. The only money available to meet the claims was from the Local Taxation Account to local authorities but this amounted to only £1.65 million for the whole of Ireland.

As claims for 'the loss of persons' received first consideration, it meant that Big House owners who were awarded significant sums by (arguably) sympathetic county court judges working under the British administrative system were not paid their awards. For example, in October 1920 Violet Tynte claimed £26,400 for the burning of Saundersgrove. The judge awarded £26,100 to be levied off the county of Wicklow.[16] It was never raised. In Westmeath in October 1921, Lord Castlemaine was awarded £101,360 for the burning of Moydrum. Frederick Denning, his counsel, claimed Castlemaine 'would sooner live in Ireland than any other country' and wanted to rebuild the castle. Westmeath County Council, as had become the norm, did not contest the case and the judge awarded just over £101,000.[17] It was later reduced by the Compensation (Ireland) Commission (see below) to just over £66,000 and Moydrum was never rebuilt.[18] Lord Listowel claimed £150,000 for the burning of Convamore and was awarded £56,300 for the house, £21,324 for the furniture, £7,500 for pictures and £120 for the transit of some articles to London, a total of around £85,000.[19] Again, this does not seem to have been paid.

As far as Big House owners were concerned, the early appeal mechanisms were no more satisfactory. In February 1921 Baroness Massy of Ardfinan House in Cahir took a case in the Kings Bench Division Dublin against the county councils of neighbouring Limerick and Clare to secure the £29,000 awarded her in October 1920 for the burning of The Hermitage at Castleconnell. Her solicitor had written to both county councils in January but had 'received evasive replies'.[20] He asked that the rates due to the councils be used to pay the award and Justice Moore granted the order.[21] But granting the order and receiving payment were two different matters. In October 1922 Lord Shaw of Dunfermline, who was to chair the Compensation (Ireland) Commission, pointed out that: 'County councils who, in ordinary circumstances, would have stood defendants in the issue of claims for malicious damage to property, were declining to defend the cases. The reasons for that may have been partly financial and partly owing to the state of the country.'[22] The councils were in an invidious position. The majority gave their allegiance to Dáil Éireann in defiance of the Local Government Board, which in retaliation threatened to cut off their annual grants so that by the end of 1920 county councils' finances were in crisis.[23] This was compounded by the ratepayers generally taking advantage of the political and social chaos to avoid paying any rates at all, just as unpurchased tenants were refusing to pay rents to their landlords and annuitants were refusing to pay annuities to the Irish Land Commission.

3. 'I do not think we should mention the point officially'

The compensation issue was not on the treaty talks agenda. But the day before the treaty was signed the Irish Chief Secretary, Hamar Greenwood, admitted in the Commons: 'Those who have lost their property only are not likely to receive much consideration.' Even if they did, he argued, 'There is little prospect that those who have suffered in this way are likely to re-invest their money where so little security to life and property is to be found.'[24] By that stage, many owners who had been burned out had already migrated permanently to England with no intention of returning. The inheritor of Summerhill, Colonel Rowley, sought advice from his relatives about the prospect of rebuilding; his cousin Douglas Rowley wrote to him from the Riviera: 'Much as I should like to see the old house rebuilt, one must remember that even if this was done you could not put back the old things that formed part of it.'[25]

Nevertheless, both sides recognised that the compensation question had to be tackled and on 24 January 1922, in London, it was formally recognised in the working arrangements set out for implementing the treaty agreed by ministers of both the British and Irish governments. According to clause 3, 'fair compensation' was to be paid: 'in respect of injuries which are the subject of compensation under the enactments relating to criminal injuries, including losses sustained through the destruction of property by order of the military authorities under martial law'.[26] Each side was to pay the losses it had inflicted between 21 January 1919 and 11 July 1921, the period of the War of Independence. Unpaid and undefended decrees were suspended because it was felt that too many claims had been inflated and so it was back to the drawing board for those who had come through the county court process. Clause 5 provided for the setting up of a commission to hear claims and determine awards for malicious damage to property to be comprised of three members (one appointed by each government and an agreed chairman), which became known as the Compensation (Ireland) Commission. In March 1922, Lord Shaw of Dunfermline, Scottish Liberal peer and judge, was appointed chairman; James Dowdall, a member of the Incorporated Chamber of Commerce and Shipping, formerly a member of the Cork Harbour Board, and who served on the Commission of Inquiry into the Industrial Resources of Ireland, was the Irish nominee; while C.J. Howell Thomas, Deputy Chief Valuer to the Board of Inland Revenue, was the British nominee.[27] The Compensation (Ireland) Commission sat in Ireland under the presidency of Shaw and subsequently Sir Alexander Wood-Renton until 1925 (when the Irish Free State government assumed all liability in respect of malicious damage done to property after 21 January 1919, and was provided with £900,000 by the British government in assistance).[28]

The Shaw Commission diminished awards previously made after both governments came to realise the potential scale involved. One Irish official noted in July 1922 that 'A general revision of independent decrees would seem to be in the interest of the two governments, as the fall in prices which has occurred since the decrees were granted would be a reason for fixing revised awards at lower levels.'[29] A few months later, in October, two senior civil servants shared an opinion; A.P. Waterfield wrote to Joseph Brennan: 'It is of course essential that the Commission should in no case go beyond the amount of the existing decree . . . I do not think we should mention the point officially.'[30] For instance, in the case of Herbert Sullivan, his preliminary claim for the destruction of Curramore House was £18,000 and this was reduced to £8,300 (the original had been prepared by Sullivan's less than independent valuers[31]).

The Shaw Commission began its operations in May 1922 and made it clear that the compensation which they recommended was to be 'in full substitution of all rights' under previous proceedings.[32] Kiltannon House in Clare, burned on 3 September 1920, was one of the first to come before the Commission in Green Street Courthouse in May 1922. Gerald Fitzgibbon KC appeared for the applicant and Timothy Healy KC appeared for the Provisional Government. Fitzgibbon outlined that the original claim amounted to just over £47,000, including £18,000 for rebuilding, £6,600 for contents and almost £2,000 for silver plate and pictures. In October, a month after the burning, the county court judge had made a decree for the full £47,000.[33] The process now was much more thorough because the state contested and questioned the original valuations and decrees. There was considerable time spent hearing the evidence of various engineers, architects and builders as to what material would be required, whether such materials were available in the post-war economy, what of the ruins could be recycled, in other words what walls were sturdy enough to be retained. Valuators and auctioneers were queried about the estimated prices of pictures. When Bennett Valuators were asked at the Kiltannon House hearing about the original value they had placed on the paintings, their representative admitted: 'He did not see the pictures for which he had estimated – the judge at the hearing fixed the prices estimated.' Nor did he know the names of the artists.[34] When Healy asked its owner, William Molony, if he would be prepared 'to have annexed a condition to rebuild', Molony replied, 'Not at present'. Healy wondered, therefore, how he could justify asking for rebuilding costs if he was not prepared to live in the area. Molony quickly had a change of mind and told the chairman he wanted to return to Ireland as 'There is plenty of fishing and shooting, and the place is very picturesque.'[35] It was hardly a convincing reason. Molony was awarded £30,000.[36]

In September 1921, Lord Langford had claimed just over £102,500 for Summerhill in Meath: the house was 389,000 cubic feet, the cost of rebuilding at 3s 6d per foot would amount to £72,500, and £30,000 for the contents. Edward Swayne KC and Theodore Kingsmill Moore appeared on Langford's behalf at the county court hearing. Meath County Council was not represented. Judge Fleming of the county court said: 'There was a great difficulty in fixing compensation in a case such as this, where only one side was heard' and

8.2 Kiltannon House in Co Clare, burned in 1920, and now in a ruinous state. Amongst the many treasures and family heirlooms lost was a marble inlaid table given to the family by King Louis XIV of France.

awarded £65,000 for the house and £11,000 for the contents, to be levied off the county.[37] This sum was never paid. In April 1923, the Shaw Commission reviewed the award and reduced it dramatically to £16,775, at least £12,000 of which had to be spent on the building of a new house on the demesne or else used towards the rebuilding of the old house. If no building was carried out the award was to be further diminished to a mere £2,000.[38] An appeal was lodged in August 1923 and the award for the house was raised to £27,500 with no obligation to rebuild. £16,500 was added for contents bringing the total up to £44,500, which was still £32,500 less than Judge Fleming's original award, and £59,000 less than the original claim submitted.[39]

Delays in settling claims were a grave source of concern. As early as July 1922 Mark Sturgis, Assistant Under-Secretary for Irish Services (1922–24) and a former senior civil servant in Dublin Castle, had written to the Provisional Government that 'The inevitable delay in starting to dispose of claims on this agreed system has naturally caused apprehension and sometimes hardship among those whose claims await settlement.'[40] In September, Sir Samuel Hoare, Conservative MP, visited Dublin and was 'shocked by how slowly the

Commission was working'.[41] Throughout 1922, the Irish government was criticised for the delays in processing cases, and there were accusations that appeals were a deliberate ploy to ensure that judges of their own nomination – 'who might be regarded as antagonistic to the claims of Loyalists' – were sure to diminish awards, if not disqualify them.[42] It seems to have been a fair enough point, but could anything else have been expected in a post-colonial scenario? In Clare, Judge Bodkin achieved notoriety in the eyes of Loyalists for reducing awards by at least 50 per cent and refusing to accept any recommendation for compensation for loss by looting or larceny.[43] By April 1923, the landlord-sympathetic *Morning Post* was bemoaning the fact that the working of the Commission was 'unsatisfactory' and that Loyalists were being coerced into accepting very reduced amounts 'through the fear of suffering a total loss unless they agreed with their adversary quickly'.[44]

Country house owners were similarly complaining and arguing hardship. By 1923, Captain Cook Collis of Castlecooke in Cork had received nothing of the compensation awarded to him over two years before and wrote: 'I have to leave the country forthwith. Until I get some of the £26,716 awarded to me, I have nothing to live on . . . merely because I am and ever have been loyal is the only cause of my appalling state.'[45] In 1920, R.C. Williams had been awarded £16,000 for the burning of Coolcower, also in Cork, but over two years later had received nothing. He was by then 'in urgent need of cash' and feared that if he did not get at least an advance he would lose his herd of Angus cattle (of which he claimed he was the largest breeder in the Free State) and therefore his livelihood.[46] In 1924, M.J. Crotty, on behalf of the Earl of Desart, complained that 'The premises at Desart Court are deteriorating by being exposed to the weather and every day that passes before they are put into repair will increase the ultimate cost of the repair.'[47] In March 1924, Louisa Uniacke of Mount Uniacke in Cork wrote to the Minister for Finance: 'I would be greatly obliged if you could let me know when our claim for compensation will be heard as this uncertainty is very trying, and my husband and his two sisters are nearly 80 years of age and it is very hard to keep things paid, and keep a house of any sort without something coming in.'[48]

The Shaw Commission certainly did not give priority to the aristocracy, a privilege they might have been extended in the past, and in fairness most of the delays were simply down to the levels of applications and the lack of manpower to adjudicate on them. In October 1922, Lord Shaw estimated that the total number of claims would be in the region of 30,000 and that £20 million would be needed to meet them. It was impossible to find that scale of funding. In March 1926, the Commission finished its work, by which time it had dealt with a total of 40,700 claims for £19.1 million and had made awards in 17,800 cases paying £7.04 million.[49] It may have fallen far short but, in fairness to the Commission, it was still a remarkable achievement for the length of time it had operated.

4. 'These exceptional claims'

In the interim there were, of course, more ominous developments. The Civil War compounded the compensation problem. On 7 July 1922, Winston Churchill announced in the Commons that a new set of considerations had now come into play because 'the damage done in the post-truce period is evidently going to be very extensive'.[50] Three weeks later, Mark Sturgis asked the Free State government what measures were being adopted 'to meet these exceptional claims' because 'His Majesty's Government cannot divest them-selves of a duty to see that such claims are met equitably and as promptly as inevitable difficulties allow.'[51] Senior politicians within the British administration argued that it was incumbent upon their government to ensure Irish Loyalists were not deserted. In October, the Conservative Prime Minister, Andrew Bonar Law, promised that 'It certainly will be the business and the duty of this Government by constant communication with the Government of the Free State to see that these claims for compensation are fairly, honourably and justly considered.'[52] In November, Lord Birkenhead, the Lord Chancellor and signatory to the Anglo-Irish treaty, commenting on the 'destruction and savagery' of the Civil War, urged that 'The ultimate position' of Britain 'by whatever quasi-legal terms you may attempt to describe it, must be that of a guarantor to a liability which was incurred by pursuance of Imperial inter-ests'.[53] The only way the British Government could interfere at this stage was to provide a contribution to the fund, which, as we shall see presently, they did. However, it was not until May 1923 that the Irish Free State Government introduced the Damage to Property (Compensation) Act while it was also debating a Land Bill.[54] The coincidence was significant (chapter 9).

Under the terms of the new act, injuries committed after 11 July 1921, the beginning of the Anglo-Irish truce, on which a decree had been made prior to the passing of the act, were to be reopened and reheard on the application of the applicant or the Minister for Finance. The funding of the act fell once more upon the county councils; the sum required to be paid by the county at large was to be assessed and raised in much the same manner as under the earlier Criminal Injuries Acts. Again, this was ominous for Big House owners. It had to be proved that those who burned or stole had been 'engaged in or purporting to act or who might reasonably be presumed to have been acting in the name or on behalf of any combination or conspiracy' for the overthrow of the Free State Government. The right to compensation was limited to damage done to the house during its burning and did not extend to consequential damage or the loss of 'articles of personal ornament'. There was an obvious reluctance, driven by economic necessity but also historical grievance, to compensate the aristocracy for the loss of luxury goods. For example, Lord Inchiquin had two cars stolen, one a 24-horsepower 8-cylinder De Dion-Bouton and the other a 12-horsepower 4-cylinder Talbot 'with a specially made body to carry eight people, with a permanent hood and side curtains'. The De Dion was recovered 'wrecked'; the Talbot never seen again. Not for the first time, Lord Inchiquin wrote to W.T. Cosgrave, President of the Executive Council, who forwarded the correspondence to Ernest Blythe, Minister for Finance, who, in turn, replied to Inchiquin: 'I have again considered the case of your cars and I have nothing further to add to my previous letter.'[55] In other words, no compensation would be forthcoming.

Lord Dunalley had a similar experience. He claimed £75,500 and received £17,400 for the destruction of Kilboy, and £9,500 for contents. He claimed a further £18,400 for the outbuildings and received £5,100.[56] Dunalley was still unhappy that his wife received only £20 in compensation for her claim of £220 for stolen jewellery. Dudley explained: 'I point out to you that all jewellery looted are expressly excluded and with reference to all other articles taken the applicant must be in a position to state that the parties who took them represented themselves as belonging to the IRA.' The theft of the jewellery took place in November 1921 and in his original claim Dunalley stated that 'Five or six men entered Kilboy by the kitchen door having imprisoned maids by locking them in a larder and then ransacked the house and looted the articles mentioned.' He did not say it was the IRA, thus the greatly diminished award.[57] Dudley advised:

> To enable us to succeed we have to prove that they were not common ordinary robbers or burglars, but in determining this question the judge takes into account the manner and appearance of the raiders, how they were dressed, whether in uniform or in leggings, trench coat, bandoliers, rifles etc. and also whether they appear to be acting under orders from a leader, so that often a chance piece of evidence or a chance remark just turns the scale.[58]

Dunalley was determined to proceed but, just as Dudley had predicted, the case was dismissed by the county court judge in May 1924. Dudley wrote to Dunalley: 'We were unable to prove that the things were taken by the Irregulars and as a matter of fact I believe they were not taken by these people for the whole place was plundered principally by the "mountainy" people [locals around the Silvermines area] after the burning.'[59]

Furthermore, when assessing the amount of compensation, judges had to take into consideration 'the steps taken or which might reasonably have been taken by the owner of the property, his servants or agents' to protect the house from any anticipated injury, or to resist, prevent or defeat the committal of the injury'. Firstly, as we know, many Big Houses were vacant when burned and rarely, even where the family or staff were resident, was any type of resistance forthcoming. Almost certainly that would have been tantamount to a much worse fate for the occupants. Thus, in April 1923, an article in the ultra-Unionist *Morning Post* made the point: 'Take the case of the Loyalist owner having to leave the country to save his life. He may be deprived altogether of compensation by the judge for failing to take steps to protect the property from an injury he could anticipate.'[60] The biased *Post* denounced the 1923 Compensation Bill as, 'an extraordinary and barefaced travesty of justice' intended to deprive Loyalists 'who have suffered loss of the compensation to which they are entitled'.[61]

Clause 10 was also contentious. It stipulated that compensation would be payable only upon fulfilment of conditions which the court might impose requiring the building to be wholly or partially reinstated. Full reinstatement required the erection of a house on the original site, essentially a rebuild. Partial reinstatement meant the erection of a new house in a place approved by the court. Aristocrats were critical of these restrictions. Lord Dunalley was advised by his solicitors that the first question he was likely to be asked was whether he intended to rebuild:

> Well and good – you will certainly be awarded a very large sum with the reconstruction and rebuilding clauses attached, which means that the money will never be paid into your own hands to do what you like with, but will only be paid to the actual building contractor on the architect's certificate from time to time as the work proceeds. None of this money will be free to do what you like with . . . Every penny of this will be tied up for building and reconstruction and will be of no earthly use to you except for those special purposes . . . If you don't build, you don't get the money.[62]

Dunalley was clearly displeased because Dudley had to further advise him:

> You must put the old [compensation] procedure . . . entirely out of your head. In the old days . . . the amount awarded as compensation was . . . based on restoration with no condition as to rebuilding or reconstruction attached, so that a man who had suffered a loss could put the amount rewarded in his pocket and do what he liked with it. That is all a thing of the past now.[63]

Full reinstatement was not palatable to those who did not want to return to Ireland; early in 1923, the Duke of Devonshire wrote to Timothy Healy: 'There are owners of property who feel that they cannot with safety return to Ireland or in view of the destruction of homes to which they were attached, do not wish to return.'[64] During the debate on the Bill, Cosgrave showed his own awareness that 'There are some who feel that it would not be safe to return to the insecurity in which the loss has been occasioned.'[65] But the government was determined that compensation money would not leave Ireland to be invested elsewhere, as had happened under the 1903 Land Act. It was argued in the Department of Finance that, in light of the 'general housing shortage', the attachment of a reinstatement condition was 'desirable in every case in which an award was made in respect of a building'; if owners did not want to rebuild the Big House, they could do something useful for the state by building houses for sale elsewhere, as was the case with the Mitchelstown Castle compensation award (chapter 6).[66] Cork County Council demanded that any compensation to be paid Lady Ardilaun for the burning of Macroom Castle 'should be expended in the erection of dwelling houses suitable to the requirement of the neighbourhood of Macroom'.[67] This case was still dragging on in the early 1930s.

While the British Government did not interfere directly, a Commission of Enquiry under Lord Dunedin was set up to review a sample of twenty-five cases concerning those deemed to have received inequitable compensation or who had suffered inordinate delays in relation to payment. The Dunedin Commission concluded that the 1923 Compensation Act had breached the original terms of agreement between the two governments. Dunedin heavily criticised the act for abolishing compensation for consequential loss, for making 'market value' the criterion instead of real value, with the result that the compensation awards made were a fraction of what they would have been under the earlier legislation. Niamh Brennan has concluded that all of Dunedin's criticisms 'seemed to point one way: to the cold indifference of the Free State government to the fate of a significant proportion of its population which faced persecution, largely from a people which up to recently it had declared to be the enemy of the state.'[68]

Evidence of this can easily be found in Dáil rhetoric which followed the familiar path of demanding some form of retribution from the aristocracy for historical wrongs and rectifying social inequality. Labour TD William Davin referred to the aristocracy as 'the remnants of England's loyal garrison in this country', who were different from 'the Irish people', less deserving of financial assistance than the estate workers who lost their jobs because of the destruction of a house.[69] It was understandable that a Labour TD would take this stance, but annotations to W.T. Cosgrave's draft speech on the Compensation Bill were no less revelatory: 'Practically every claim for financial accommodation to economic interest is accompanied by a statement [from Loyalists] that the government can find millions to compensate a class which never benefited the nation and drew its revenues from rents and lands etc. etc.'[70] It might reasonably be argued that the Free State government, through its diminished awards, was deliberately punishing the old colonial elite, doing little to entice them to remain in Ireland. However, the Dunedin review also presented a long list of the broken pledges made to Irish Loyalists from 1922 by British politicians including Churchill and Birkenhead.[71] And, very pertinent to this study, Dunedin also acknowledged that 'The problem of the Big House is not confined to Ireland. For many years past the accommodation in such houses has, as a rule, been only very partially used; they are extremely expensive to maintain: and it may fairly be said that in most cases the owners would prefer to have a house half the size or less.' The Dunedin report concluded that it was not, therefore, unreasonable that the Free State government 'being compelled to study economy, should protect themselves against having to pay the replacement value of such houses'.[72]

Even aristocrats themselves understood that Big Houses were 'white elephants', no longer viable or sustainable in a rapidly changing society; in April 1923, Lord Glenavy told the Senate: 'Nobody was anxious to have a building reinstated in its old form. It had grown out of their needs and they wanted a different style of architecture.'[73] Sir John Keane agreed; after Cosgrave addressed the Senate on the Compensation Bill in March 1923, Keane said that the rebuilding clause was understandable: 'The economic welfare of the country must be preserved.' He believed that, for many of his peers, 'Financial conditions alone would make it impossible for them to resume the character of their past life.'[74] The point has already been made that even without revolution, hundreds of great houses would have been (and were) abandoned across Ireland from the 1920s, a trend that was equally evident across Britain as their owners could no longer afford their upkeep.[75]

A register of claims under the 1923 Compensation Act survives recording the claims of individual Big House owners throughout the country and the final awards granted along with any conditions attached.[76] From this register a random sample of fifty Big Houses was chosen. In total the owners made claims for £1,908,605. They were awarded £493,428, or around 26 per cent. Twenty-six (52 per cent) of these Big Houses were rebuilt. Cecilia Burrows, owner of Milestown in Louth, had claimed £17,400 of which she was awarded £11,750 (£8,500 subject to reinstatement). Milestown was rebuilt in 1925 using the old walls. Sir Bryan Mahon claimed £60,000 for Mullaboden in late February 1922, and in November 1924 was awarded £10,900 with a partial reinstatement condition for the rebuilding of a less extravagant house.[77] In Galway, Colonel Bernard was awarded £33,500 and rebuilt a downsized two-storeyed Castle Hackett.[78] In the same county, William Persse claimed £33,500 for Roxborough and was awarded £17,000. He did not rebuild. Lady Augusta Gregory, who had been born and reared there, visited the ruins in 1924: 'The house – the ruin – is very sad, just the walls standing, blackened, and all the long yards silent . . . I am afraid the house will never be built up, all silent that had been so full of life and stir in my childhood, and never deserted until now.'[79]

In December 1925, Lord Mayo's case was heard at Naas district court before Judge Doyle. The counsel for the applicant told the court that Mayo intended 'the restoration of the house worthy of the occupants, and not more extravagant or better than the one which had been destroyed'.[80] In his judgement, Doyle praised Mayo: 'By this patriotic action the applicant has relieved the State from a very large sum of money.'[81] Mayo was awarded £52,000 and Palmerstown was rebuilt. Glascott Symes makes the significant point that 90 per cent of the senators' houses were rebuilt, including Palmerstown, Ballynastragh, Desart Court, Marlfield, Mullaboden and Cappoquin, because the aristocrats 'who had accepted nomination to the Senate had already made a firm commitment to remain and adapt to the new order in Ireland'.[82] However, as the following case study of Sir Thomas Esmonde will illustrate, they were not given any special consideration.

5. 'I do not feel in any way beholden to the Government of the Free State'

Ballynastragh in Co Wexford had been the ancestral home of the Esmonde family for over three hundred years. Like so many great houses it had undergone several phases of remodelling and modification. In the second half of the eighteenth century, Sir Thomas Esmonde, 8th Baronet, enlarged and modernised the original house to a three-storey over basement construct with seven bays, a three-bay breakfront and a colonnaded portico, while his son, also Thomas, carried out further embellishment between 1803 and 1825, castellating it as was the early-nineteenth century fashion. In 1837, Samuel Lewis described the house as: 'A handsome modernised mansion, with a light

Grecian portico. The grounds are tastefully laid out and embellished with a fine sheet of water and rich woods.'[83]

A rare surviving inventory from 1910 shows that Ballynastragh was rich in contents and collections. The many paintings included attributions to Albert Cuyp (*War Vessels and Other Shipping at Rotterdam*); Breughel (*St Catherine Amidst a Wreath of Flowers*); Lenfranco (*St Jerome*); and two attributed to Caravaggio (*Evangelist Pointing to the Scriptures* and *John the Baptist*).[84] According to a newspaper account of 1925, the silver collection dating from the seventeenth to nineteenth centuries was 'famed throughout the country' and had been exhibited in Dublin in 1872.[85] Sir Thomas had travelled the world as a collector as was shown in the vast array of curios: ornaments from New Zealand; shells and beads from the South Sea Islands; ivory and ebony from Asia; Etruscan, Mexican and Greek pottery. Ballynastragh was further adorned by pieces of historical and antiquarian interest: a Flemish buffet taken from a wreck of the Spanish Armada; a monk's refectory table reputedly used by Oliver Cromwell in St John's Abbey in Enniscorthy in 1649; a mahogany high-backed chair belonging to Henry Grattan, the Irish politician and patriot. The archival collection was of huge importance, containing family correspondence with Grattan, Charles J. Fox, Daniel O'Connell, William Smith O'Brien, John Mitchel, W.E. Gladstone, Charles Stewart Parnell and various popes. In 1910, the total contents were valued at £17,238 including: furnishings (including carpets, bedding, fixtures and fittings) at £6,721; paintings at £3,164; the silver at £2,258; family plate at £359; engravings, pastels and water colours at £574; and the library at £691.[86]

Given his nationalist credentials – including Irish Parliamentary Party MP for South Dublin (1885–92), West Kerry (1892–1900) and North Wexford (1900–18) – it was no surprise that Sir Thomas, 11th Baronet, was nominated to the Seanad in 1922. On 9 March 1923, the anti-Treatyites burned Ballynastragh as a reprisal for executions. Sir Thomas was in London at the time and the only occupants were his brother, Laurence and five servants. They were given ten minutes to evacuate the house. Laurence received permission to remove the gold chalice and vestments from the chapel. Otherwise, only five Chippendale chairs, six Queen Anne chairs, Henry Grattan's chair and one mahogany Jacobean chair were rescued, valued in total at £775.[87] There were subsequent reports of looting, and of locals making off with quantities of silver, Old Sheffield and electroplate and farm implements from the outbuildings.[88] However, while thirty-two paintings were reported destroyed, Sir Thomas had taken the precaution of removing some of the more valuable ones from the house before he left for London, including paintings that went into storage in the National Gallery of Ireland.[89]

From the outset, it was Sir Thomas's intention to rebuild Ballynastragh. In June 1923, he wrote to Lord Eversley: 'I have only the one country after all and there is a place in it where the happiest and the best and holiest of my memories are centred. If I can rebuild I certainly will, but these things take time.'[90] His words were to prove prophetic. Esmonde made a claim for £77,500 under the 1923 Compensation Act. His case was not heard until February 1925, by which time he had become increasingly disillusioned. During the hearing, the solicitor representing Gorey District Council claimed that, while the burning of Ballynastragh was 'wanton and outrageous', the claim was 'somewhat excessive'.[91] John Costello SC (future Taoiseach 1948–51, 1954–57), representing the Minister for Finance, argued that the old walls could be used for rebuilding and that £21,000 would be sufficient compensation.[92] Judge Doyle was, however, less convinced and decreed that 'it would be a far too dangerous risk' to require Esmonde to rebuild on the old walls and awarded £55,100, based on full reinstatement. Sir Thomas was advised by Myles Higgins, his solicitor: 'I think in the present times the amount sufficient to replace not all, but middling things, is sometimes best.'[93]

In March, the government used its right to appeal the county court judge's award. A clipping from the *Irish Independent*, which Sir Thomas kept in his personal papers, mirrored his own frustrations: in it, the editor, while warning that the government had to guard against exorbitant claims, argued there were no excuses for the 'vexatious delays in payment, the repeated appeals against obviously reasonable awards, the petty haggling of officials and the want of courtesy displayed by ignoring complaints'.[94] In May 1925, Esmonde wrote to W.T. Cosgrave that he had not yet found 'a suitable house' and that 'the increasing discomfort ... of the nomad existence I am forced to live is my reason for writing this letter'.[95] He was even having issues with the National Gallery: in January 1924 the director, Philip Hanson, had informed him that he could no longer guarantee the safety of his paintings. A despondent Esmonde replied: 'My trouble is that I have nowhere to house them, and I see no prospect of being able to house them for some time to come as my compensation case has not yet been heard.'[96]

The appeal was eventually held in July 1924 in the High Court in Dublin and the award was reduced by Justice Sullivan to £44,800, or by around 25 per cent: £31,700 for the house, £10,000 for the furniture, £900 for personal effects and £2,200 for the contents of the library. Thus, Esmonde was awarded less than 60 per cent of what he had originally claimed. His disillusionment was clear in a letter to Cosgrave on 27 July 1925 that is worth quoting at length as it was surely indicative of the plight and frustration of many other Big House owners:

The proceedings in my compensation case are now ended. I think it right to tell you that I do not feel in any way beholden to the Government of the Free State for the result. From the outset of this very unpleasant business, I have been treated as a criminal on his trial. If I had destroyed somebody else's home and property I would not have been used as harshly . . .

The award in the matter of my library and family papers I regard as an outrage. I am granted in compensation about what I spent out of my own pocket in improving the library in my time while the historical manuscripts which I regard – and any student of history would regard – as priceless are deemed to be worthless. [He argued he should have received at least £6,000]

As to the £30,000 awarded for rebuilding . . . what everybody knows is that I got none of the nominal £30,000 and that to obtain whatever this £30,000 may represent I shall have to spend many thousands of my own in addition. In my own time I spent at least £100,000 on the estate.

I have helped so far as I could in the formation and in the proceedings of the Senate: though from the outset I was aware that neither my help nor my co-operation were desired . . .

You must excuse me if after the treatment I have received from the officers of your government I do not continue to support it with enthusiasm. I shall reconsider my purpose of rebuilding as well as remaining in a country where such things are possible.[97]

Here then was an aristocrat who had accepted nomination to the Senate, who considered himself very much in the mould of an Irish patriot, but who was bitterly aggrieved by the lack of sympathy from the government. In the end, his affection for Ballynastragh won out and Esmonde rebuilt a more modest mansion which was completed in 1937 to the design of Dermot St. John Gogarty.[98]

6. 'Only a little justice for the rich'

Inadequate compensation or delays in payment, as well as the rise in the number of loyalist emigrees who made their way to Britain in the early 1920s, gave rise to the establishment of the Irish Distress Committee (May 1922), reconstituted as the Irish Grants Committee (IGC) on 23 March 1923 with the backing of the British government. On 11 November 1925, Lord Danesfort outlined why he thought it was necessary:

> The Free State has wholly failed to carry out its undertakings. They passed in 1923 an act . . . which fundamentally, to the great detriment of the Loyalists, altered the principles on which compensation was provided by the British Criminal Injuries Acts, repealed all the British statutes relating to this subject, cancelled all awards already made and . . . deprived British subjects of their vested rights to compensation.[99]

The IGC was tasked to pay advances against decrees or 'well-founded claims of compensation'.[100] It first met on 8 October 1926 to deal with cases of 'special hardship' that occurred from 11 July 1921 to 12 May 1923, from the Anglo-Irish truce to the end of the Civil War. In December 1927, a limit of £400,000 expenditure was placed on the committee. The first £250 of a payment recommended by the IGC would be paid in full, 50 per cent from £250 up to £1,000 and 30 per cent from £1,000 to £50,000.[101]

As Niamh Brennan points out, 'It was the importance of the link between loyalty and injury that was emphasised by the committee.'[102] Question 5 on the IGC claim form asked: 'Do you claim that the loss or injury described was occasioned in respect of or on account of your allegiance to the Government of the United Kingdom?' The point has earlier been made that, from the historian's perspective, it was an unfortunate leading question that distorted the facts behind many burnings. But from the perspective of those aristocrats who had accepted nomination to the Free State Senate, it also had consequences. Both Sir John Keane and John Bagwell were refused awards because the IGC told them that 'a role in independent Ireland was incompatible with their allegiance to Britain'. Keane was informed: 'The destruction in your case may be attributable to a motive other than the record of the public services to which you refer', thereby denying his twenty years' service in the British army from the Boer War to the end of the First World War.[103] Bagwell's modest claim for the loss of his wife's jewellery was rejected on the grounds that 'His action in allowing himself to be nominated was the act of a Loyalist determined to support the new Government placed in power on the withdrawal of the British Government from Ireland.'[104]

In other cases, the IGC found that Boskell Hall in Limerick was burned 'in the course of a conflict between the Irish Regular and Irregular Forces', and ruled that the 'claimant cannot say that this injury was directed against him on account of his support of the British government prior to the Truce'.[105] Under question 5, Lord De Freyne cited as evidence of his loyalism that several of his brothers had served in the Great War. The committee was not impressed: 'He is now only 43 and not apparently incapacitated. He might have served himself.'[106]

In 1923, the representatives of the deceased Lord Carew sold three holdings on the Castleboro demesne totalling around 1,300 acres for around £9,000. They argued that in peacetime they could have received £17,800; the estate representatives submitted that: 'The impossibility of the owners occupying the estate and to the conditions existing in Ireland and to the loss of the residence applicant had to sell the lands . . . at a gross undervalue and under conditions amounting to a forced sale.'[107] They sought to make up the difference through the IGC but it had little sympathy and ruled: 'The lands were, in fact, sold at the prevailing market value for land of this description, and it is well known owing to the operations of the Irish Land Act of 1923, and the general economic depreciation of the Irish Free State, that the price of land fell considerably between 1921 and 1926.' Furthermore, they saw it as a voluntary sale by an absentee who 'No doubt, thought it best to realise the asset which she [Lord Carew's heir] had inherited during the disturbances.'[108] No compensation for loss was paid.

Levels of hardship suffered since the destruction of their houses was another determining factor in receiving IGC support. Robert King-Harman, inheritor

8.3 The impressive glasshouses at Castleboro, Co Wexford, c.1910.

of Mitchelstown Castle, later complained that 'The committee were to take account of the degree of hardship suffered in all cases, which, as interpreted, meant that a well-to-do man was not to get as much compensation for a proved loss as a man who had lost everything.' He felt it was 'justice for the poor, but only a little justice for the rich'.[109] The case of Castleboro in Co Wexford is illuminating in this respect.

Castleboro was a 'palatial house' built in the Classical style and described as 'one of the finest dwelling houses in Ireland'.[110] The ground floor contained the great hall, south and north drawing rooms, dining room, library and study. On the first floor, there were two galleries which surrounded a magnificent library that extended through two storeys. There were ten family bedrooms and five dressing rooms. On the second floor there were six further bedrooms and four dressing rooms. And in the basement, thirty-five apartments including rooms for all the servants, a hall, kitchens and a variety of utility rooms. The yard complex had three coach houses, numerous stables, two dairies, a gardener's house with five rooms, a steward's house with nine rooms, living quarters for at least eight men, a whole range of outbuildings including forges, slaughterhouse, hothouses, hay barns, piggeries and so on. There were 5 acres of walled gardens, 30 acres of front lawn, 33 acres of back lawn, 64 acres of plantation to screen the house, 32 acres along the main avenue, 9 acres of fishponds, 500 acres of outer plantations and miles of private avenues interspersed with 5 gate lodges.

It was estimated that the house was 597,000 cubic feet which at a cost of 4 shillings and 6 pence per foot would cost £134,528 to rebuild, minus £73,990

8.4 The ruins of Castleboro, Co Wexford, its once magnificent gardens and designed landscape no longer evident.

for the surviving walls. In Ireland, the compensation case was heard on 3 May 1924 by the county court judge and a mere £15,000 was awarded for the mansion. An appeal was lodged by the state and at the hearing in March 1925 it was further reduced to £13,000. Lord Carew died the following month and was succeeded by his sister-in-law, Lady Gordon Cary.[111] The IGC heard that Lady Gordon lived with her second husband in Monmouth, and concluded she 'would appear to be a person of considerable means'. As it could not be determined that they suffered any 'special hardship within the meaning of the committee's terms of reference', the case was dismissed.[112] Castleboro remains a spectacularly haunting ruin on the Irish landscape.

7. 'The feeling that one had a base, that one really belonged somewhere'

The rebuilding of a Big House in the mid-1920s must have represented an interesting short period in a local community's history, but very little is known about this aspect. What, for example, were the feelings of those who burned a house when they saw it rise phoenix-like from the ashes? Local tradesmen – in the case of Cappoquin, a local mason, Edward Brady, and a carpenter, James Hackett – were sufficiently skilled to oversee building projects, as had been the case in the eighteenth century, and employment was surely welcomed in an otherwise depressed economic climate. A new generation of architects – professional and amateur – were provided with exciting opportunities to replicate, and modify, the architectural grandeur of the Georgian era. For instance, Richard Orpen, brother of William the renowned artist, was the architect in charge of the rebuilding of Cappoquin; he introduced several architectural changes from the original house: the main entrance was changed from the south to the north front; the parapet balustrade was extended around the whole roof; the original pitched roof was replaced by a flat concrete one designed by Delap and Waller engineers.[113] Sir John Keane instructed the project team to purchase as much as possible from the local co-operative, but the contracts for the highly skilled decorous interior work all went to London firms, including the contract for the fibrous plaster decoration and embellished joinery in the door architraves and window shutters, which went to G. Jackson and Sons of London. Perhaps indicative of the difficult times being faced by country house owners throughout Ireland was a response to an advertisement Keane placed in the *Irish Times* looking for antique doors: Walter Bond of Newtown Bond in Longford offered to take out the doors in his own house and sell them to Keane.[114]

Another of the great Georgian houses rebuilt was Kilboy in Co Tipperary. Lord Dunalley received only about 23 per cent of his original claim and a reinstatement clause was added to the award.[115] A diminished award obviously meant rebuilding on a reduced scale; Dunalley was advised that 'If the cellars were sealed up altogether and the top storey taken off', it would allow him 'sufficient space for a smaller staff of servants but with sufficient accommodation for a fair-sized ordinary house fitted up with modern requirements such as central heating, electric light etc.'[116] This was the plan adhered to.[117] Desmond Prittie, later 6th Baron Dunalley, was not, however, impressed by the new design and later complained that his parents 'had not included some very necessary conveniences. There was no strong room, no box room, no larder, no dairy.'[118] But Terence, his younger brother, born in 1913, who had lived a peripatetic life with his parents and Desmond since the burning of Kilboy, was much more relieved:

> For the first time in about seven years Desmond and I had rooms of our own, a place for our books and other belongings, a feeling of security. And Kilboy was a wonderful home. There was a lake where one could fish or

bathe. There were acres of garden and woodland in which there was much to do . . . There was good rough shooting all around us.[119]

The real joy was 'the feeling that one had a base, that one really belonged somewhere', no more hotels, relatives' lodgings, suitcases, no more being an imposition. But the rebuilding of Kilboy soon reflected the fact that Big Houses were no longer sustainable. The family financial situation deteriorated rapidly in the late 1920s and 1930s; Henry Cornelius, 5th Baron, continued to serve in the Rifle Brigade but the income was not sufficient to maintain Kilboy.[120] His wife did not understand the concept to 'economise'; her grandson recalled: 'Dismissing any of the staff was a sin against her feudal instinct. Standards of eating, drinking and hospitality had to be maintained. My grandmother took to darning the carpets herself, while still employing a lady's maid.'[121] When Henry died in 1948, the debts were insurmountable for his heir and so Kilboy was demolished and a bungalow built in its place.[122] However, at the beginning of the twenty-first century, Kilboy was spectacularly rebuilt a second time by Mr and Mrs Shane Ryan; the aim was to replicate the architectural structure of the original house, the end result was the creation of what *Country Life* described as 'The Greatest New House in Europe'.[123]

There were considerably more owners who did not rebuild either because their awards were inadequate to allow them to do so or because they were reluctant to come back to live in Ireland. George Moore put in a claim of £25,000 for Moore Hall but was awarded only one third of that sum.[124] He knew he would possibly have received a better settlement if he had agreed to rebuild but he told a friend: 'Since the burning of my house, I don't think I shall ever be able to set foot in Ireland again.'[125] The house has remained an impressive ruin ever since. In 1925, Colonel Charles Warden made his feelings known about rebuilding Derryquin (burned in 1922), after he and his mother were forced to flee to England:

I bought Derryquin [and 25,000 acres in 1879] to live in, and to end my days in, and I expended thirty years of labour on it, but after my experiences there in 1922, it would be impossible for me to have any further pleasure in living there, and therefore, I do not care to rebuild Derryquin Castle.[126]

He applied for compensation under the 1923 Act. At a meeting in London between an architect for the Free State government and Warden, a sum of £62,000 was agreed for compensation on a restoration basis. In October 1927, the award was diminished in the Kerry circuit court to £25,000 plus £2,000 for the electric light and refrigeration plants. The following month, the government appealed and the £2,000 was struck out and £25,000 awarded on a partial restoration condition. Warden's spokesperson had argued: 'The sole reason against reconstructing Derryquin Castle was the continuance of the criminal acts and conditions which rendered it impossible for applicant to reside on his property . . .'[127] In the end Warden entered into an agreement to sell his decree for £20,000 to Dublin Corporation payable in 5 per cent compensation stock to build houses there.[128] Twenty-six houses were subsequently erected on Griffith Avenue in Clontarf, and Warden was entitled to the lease on up to four of them. Neither did the equally disillusioned J.M. Wilson, who claimed £59,000 but was awarded only £12,000, rebuild Currygrane in Longford. Instead, he built several villas in south Co Dublin.

Similarly, Alec King-Harman used the £27,500 compensation money for Mitchelstown Castle to build seventeen houses in the Dublin suburb of Clontarf.[129] In this way, historic landscapes were altered (in a way yet to be fully elucidated): in one place the great house and demesne that for generations had dominated the local rural landscape disappeared, while Dublin suburbs expanded because of the building conditions attached to the compensation awards. In this respect, the Irish government had been astute, refusing to allow compensation awards to leave the country at a time when there was a housing crisis, though it could be argued that the building of villas in the leafy suburbs of Clontarf or Dun Laoghaire (formerly Kingstown) only benefited another emerging elite.

8. 'We should have a smaller comfortable house for two people growing old'

Long before it was burned, a massive edifice such as Mitchelstown had outlived its original purpose and affordability and large parts of it were already in an advanced state of deterioration, locked off from use as the family retrenched to a small area for comfort and affordability. Some families were possibly better off by the fact that their houses were burned.[130] Mount Uniacke 'was not in a good state of repair at the time of its destruction', the feeling was that Mrs Uniacke did well to get £5,000 in compensation to build a more modest version.[131] Sir Horace Plunkett's Kilteragh was not a country house as in the definition used here, but his comments following its burning were interesting: 'It is all very sad, but a small cottage will do me for the rest of my days.'[132] As Lady Fingall awaited the raiders, she contemplated the advantages of having Killeen Castle burned:

> We should have a smaller comfortable house for two people growing old, and their children and their friends. I thought of my struggles to heat Killeen, and how all the roaring wood and turf fires could only warm corners of the great rooms. We should have a lower house, well-fitting windows, no draughts or ghosts, and the bathrooms that I had always dreamed of, with plenty of hot water.[133]

After the burning of Castleshane, Sybil Lucas-Scudamore was advised by her agent to sell the entire demesne because 'The possibility of rebuilding any class of house that would be in keeping with the demesne is entirely out of the question.' The practicalities were simple enough: 'Demesnes are being split up and sold all over the country, and I am just working the sale of a very large demesne in Galway, where the family will never be able to reside again, though the house was not burned down, but it would take the majority of the income to keep it up in firing, lighting, servants etc.'[134] It was an opinion that would have resonance for those families who struggled to maintain their houses in Ireland long after revolution had finished with them.[135]

In February 1923, Lord Oranmore returned to his ancestral home, Castle MacGarrett, to arrange the transport of his furniture and family portraits to England. He summed up how many of his peers felt: 'We must try to save what we can out of the wreck, but I don't think it will ever be possible to go back and live at home. Even if the Free State functions, it is certain that they will curtail all our demesnes and what is the good of a big house with a couple of hundred acres in the West of Ireland? Better have it in Kent.'[136] It was to prove a prophetic diagnosis: over time, the 1923 Land Act (and its successors) would target the 'couple of hundred acres', and not just in the west, denuding Big Houses of what defined them, and ultimately sustained them, and completing the revolution that had begun in 1879.

IV
'THE LAST REMNANT OF IRISH LANDLORDISM'
Conclusion

9

THE END OF REVOLUTION?

It is but fair to ourselves and to the nation that they [landlords] should get the treatment proposed by the Minister. Perhaps it is fitting that they should have held out until a National Parliament would dispose of the last remnant of Irish landlordism. This Oireachtas will put an end to a system that was the curse of this country, and I hope we will hear no more of it in that shape.

(William Sears TD (Mayo, Cumann na nGaedheal),
Dáil Debates, vol. 3, 28 May 1923, 1152–53)

Damage to cultural property belonging to any people whatsoever means damage to the cultural heritage of all mankind, since each people makes its contribution to the culture of the world.

(Hague Convention for the Protection of Cultural
Property in the Event of Armed Conflict (1954);
quoted in Bevan, *The Destruction of Memory*, p. 23)

1. 'There are numerous demesnes with Big Houses on them'

The aim of this book has been to provide an additional dimension to the scholarly understanding of the Irish revolution by examining how the tumultuous events of the period 1914–23 impacted on the Irish landed elite, most particularly the aristocracy, the class which most experienced revolutionary change, certainly in the more extended period from 1879 to 1923 and beyond, and yet which has been largely neglected in the historiography. The 'beyond' is important because the story of the aristocracy illustrates how the social ambitions of revolutionaries eventually played out in the longer term.

In this study, the landlord experience has been examined through the prism of the Big House. One of the central arguments has been that the British Land Acts passed for Ireland (1870–1909) failed to address rural inequalities which meant that land questions remained vibrant and came to the fore once more during the First World War when the former landed elite were at their most vulnerable. Of course, their continued loyalism to Britain during the War of Independence left them in an invidious political position, but so also their retention of extensive tracts of demesne and untenanted lands post-1903 left them in an equally precarious social position. This work has therefore argued that the burning of almost 300 Big Houses in 1920–23 was as symptomatic of the continued land question as it was of the aristocracy's continued loyalism. When a burning was linked to an agrarian motive rather than a political one, the chances of it being recalled in a local community were diminished. This is not unusual in the global context of revolution and the destruction of architecture associated with the perceived enemy. As Robert Bevan has written:

> If the touchstones of identity are no longer there to be touched, memories fragment and dislocate – their hostile destruction is an amnesia forced upon the group as a group and on its individual constituent members. Out of sight can become, literally, out of mind both for those whose patrimony has been destroyed and for the destroyers.[1]

In the Irish context, to recall a house being burned for agrarian reasons as opposed to political was at odds with the nationalist narrative. In her study of the burning of Ballydugan House, Ann O'Riordan describes how the local community fell into conspiratorial silence when in 2014–15 she asked questions about the motivation. The hunger for land was not the version of events that was palatable to locals who preferred to remember that it was not even the IRA but the Black and Tans who burned the house (if that was the case it would have made Ballydugan unique).[2] In line with Timothy Mawe, O'Riordan argues that 'Nobody was willing to stick their head above the parapet to challenge a version that was best left alone.'[3] Historians are sometimes guilty of the same.

It is arguable that post-1922 the credibility of Irish independence depended upon the decolonialisation of the new state. In this respect, the final dismantling of the aristocracy's physical landscape began with the passing of the 1923 Land Act. When it was being debated at the Bill stage in Dáil Éireann, it was clear that a residue of grievance relating to colonial land confiscations and plantations, which had long set political and social agendas in Ireland, continued to exist. One TD was delighted to tell his parliamentary colleagues: 'I believe that implicit in this event alone is the undoing of the conquest of Ireland. For the conquest of Ireland was the conquest of the land of Ireland, held by Irish tenure, from the people of Ireland by foreigners who held by foreign tenure from a foreign king.'[4] There were TDs who called for the 'expropriation' of aristocratic lands, and reference to 'descendants of Cromwellian planters', and calls for retribution for Famine 'hardships', 'sufferings' and 'penalties'. It was clear from the rhetoric of many TDs that all existing demesnes and untenanted estates were obvious targets. John Lyons (Longford-Westmeath, Labour) pointed out that 'There are thousands of acres in the hands of a few people, and the least we can expect from our own Government is that these lands will be taken over. A large part of this land is in the hands of the descendants of Cromwell's settlers and should be taken over and given to the descendants of those to whom it formerly belonged.'[5] William Sears (Mayo, Cumann na nGaedheal) got to the crux of what the act would mean: 'There are numerous demesnes with Big Houses on them. I hope the Minister is not going to be too tender about dealing with these demesnes. They have been for 500 years in the possession of these landlord families. I think that is long enough for them to have them, and it is time for the people to get them now.'[6]

This type of rhetoric had been inherited from the Land War, as had the doctrine of confiscation and redistribution, and both strongly hinted at the rural grievances that underpinned the burning of so many houses. This was by no means unique to Ireland; after all, the backdrop to modern revolutions in agrarian societies, where people have risen in revolt against alien or oppressive regimes, has frequently been land redistribution. 'The land for the people', a catch-cry for revolutionaries in nineteenth-century Ireland, has more recently been echoed as far away in distance and time as Iran in 1960–80 and Indonesia in the early twenty-first century.[7] More contemporary with the Irish revolution, the decree on land adopted by the Russian Congress on 8 November 1917 laid the foundation for the confiscation of landlords' estates and the nationalisation of all lands. Within months, 75 per cent of Russian estates were appropriated. Between 1917 and 1923, revolutionaries in Hungary and Bulgaria demanded land redistribution. In Spain, in 1919, estate owners abandoned their country houses because of a revolt of landless labourers. In Italy, conditions of the landless who had served in the war were exacerbated by the broken promises of the ruling classes who had pledged land redistribution as a reward for service.[8] In Mexico, between 1910 and 1920, village peasants and revolutionaries continuously negotiated land redistribution.[9]

The latter revolution seems to have had some influence on the mindset of Kevin O'Higgins, Minister for Home Affairs, who, in his much-quoted remark, described his contemporaries as the 'most conservative-minded revolutionaries that ever put through a successful revolution'.[10] Sometime around

9.1 Kevin O'Higgins (1892–1927), Minister for Home Affairs, and close friend and political ally of Patrick Hogan. Shot and killed by the IRA on 10 July 1927 when on his way to Mass.

9.2 Patrick Hogan (1831–1936), Minister for Agriculture (1922–24) and architect of the 1923 Land Act. Killed in a car accident in 1936.

1923, O'Higgins wrote a piece called 'Mexican Politics' which, as the title clearly indicated, emphasised that he wanted no peasant revolt as had happened under Emiliano Zapata (1879–1919), leader of the peasant revolt in Morelos and founder of the agrarian *Zapatismo* movement.[11] During the Civil War, O'Higgins and Patrick Hogan, Minister for Agriculture, both tellingly from strong farming and middle-class professional backgrounds, worked together to put an end to agrarian activism and any threat of a social revolution through repression and legislation, something of the traditional coercion and conciliation tactics that had been familiar in rural Ireland in the nineteenth century.[12]

They were chief amongst those in the Cumann na nGaedheal government who realised they had to be astute in their financial engineering in order to advance social policy in a country with very limited financial or material resources of its own.[13] They moved towards an economic liberalism rather than the revolutionary socialist model that had emerged in Russia and which had influenced Sinn Féin's pre-independence *Democratic Programme* of 1919.[14] As Roy Foster has argued, they were amongst a clique who, in the construction of the new state, 'resolutely ignored even the vague social and economic desiderata once outlined for Pearse's visionary republic'.[15] Thus, in December 1922, Hogan, in pursuit of international credit rating, called upon the Irish Government to deal resolutely with land agitation emphasising that:

> If we miss this chance of getting English credit on easy terms because the tenant and the landless men refuse to see anything like reason, it will be an incalculable loss . . . It will alienate from us all conservative support in Ireland, and this will probably have serious reactions on the financial settlement which we must make this year with England.[16]

The Irish government needed to raise £30 million that Hogan estimated it would cost to complete land purchase and implement other land reform, especially redistribution.[17] It had to look to Britain and, as the British cabinets of Andrew Bonar Law (October 1922–May 1923) and Stanley Baldwin (May 1923–January 1924) were still predominantly patrician with the likes of Salisbury, Curzon, Devonshire, Derby, Cecil and Peel in positions of influence, it had to tread carefully in relation to land policy. Secret negotiations held in February 1923 between Hogan, Cosgrave and members of the British cabinet resulted in the latter agreeing to provide the cash and stock to guarantee the 1923 Land Act and, in return, the Irish government undertook to collect each year the full amount of annuities (annual interest repayments from purchasing farmers) and to hand them over to the British Treasury.[18] With the funding in place, an attempt could now be made to return the countryside to law and order. On 28 May 1923, O'Higgins, speaking on the Land Bill, told the Dáil of his intentions:

> Within the last year, under cover of activities against the Government, men have gone out in an entirely selfish, wilful, and criminal spirit to seize land by the strong hand, or by the hand which they thought was strong . . . [I will urge] on the Minister for Agriculture from my department, that the people who go out in that spirit, who go out in defiance of the law and in defiance of the Parliament to press their claims by their own violence and their own illegalities be placed definitely outside the benefits of this Bill.[19]

The speech deliberately emphasised that those found guilty of offences would be barred from land redistribution schemes, in the knowledge, or at least the hope, that such a threat would help halt agrarianism and any residual support for the anti-Treatyite cause, especially in the west, that emanated from its land policy. That same month O'Higgins also saw through the Dáil a Public Safety Act that was intended to put an end to pervasive criminality; it gave the government wide-ranging powers to seize trespassing cattle, and to restore stolen goods and property, including lands, to their rightful owners. On 14 June 1923, O'Higgins again told the Dáil that land grabbers would be those most severely dealt with:

> They cannot have law and violence. They cannot have an act and their own plunder and, in so far as I can secure it, I will see that they do not have it . . . and by the time this Bill reaches its closing stages, I hope to be able to assure the Dáil that there is not in any county, over which we have for the time being responsibility and jurisdiction, one acre of land in the possession of any person but the legal owner.[20]

The politics of land redistribution were now being used to threaten potential enemies of the state.

The 1923 Land Act had two main objectives, the first of which was the completion of land purchase. By 1923, there were around 114,000 farms comprising roughly 3,125,000 acres still to be transferred.[21] On 10 April 1923, matters had come to a head at the Land Purchase and Arrears Conference in Dublin, where landlord and tenant representatives met to discuss the current state of the land question. Afterwards, Hogan reported to his cabinet colleagues, emphasising the mood of a significant proportion of the electorate:

> They [the tenant representatives] informed the landlords in all moods and tenses that a great change had come; that they were now in a small minority, and an unpopular minority; that they could take the land from them for nothing if they wished; that the people meant to have the land cheaply, and that if the present government did not meet the wishes of the people in this respect, they would put in a government the next time who would.[22]

Hogan then informed W.T. Cosgrave that the tenant representatives wanted a Bill 'on terms which would amount to confiscation'. But that could not happen, given the settlement reached with the British government less than two months before and so Hogan told the Dáil: 'No matter how obnoxious a landlord may be personally his legal position as vendor confers on him certain rights which cannot be ignored without running the risk of such diminution of the credit of the nation.'[23] Thus, the aristocracy's lands were not expropriated, as revolutionaries might have demanded, but neither were they paid for in cash, so the aristocracy were denied the generous terms available under the 1903 Land Act. They did not publicly challenge this; their legal representative, Harry Franks, had informed Hogan at the land conference that they were 'prepared to take what they can get now, providing it is anything approaching fair play, rather than take their chance of what they can get from the next parliament'.[24] In the Senate, instead of barking loudly, the aristocratic interest acquiesced, with the exception of Sir John Keane, who 'opposed the basic principle of the bill and . . . fought Hogan doggedly on almost every issue', but to little avail, largely because his numerous amendments were not supported by his more lethargic aristocratic colleagues.[25]

Amongst the largest of the tenanted estates were the Lansdowne estate in Kerry (47,818 acres); Coote estate in Co Laois (24,460); Wrixon-Becher in Cork (16,338); Courtown in Wexford (12,706); and Windham in Monaghan (10,940).[26] Already the houses on the Derreen and Courtown estates had been burned (as well as Lady Windham's land agent's house) and within a decade Ballyfin, Castle Hyde and Dartrey would be sold and/or demolished, their lands transferred to the tenant occupiers. Either fate emphasised the role of land in the Irish revolution and that a Big House without its land bank was inevitably unsustainable.

The second aim of the act was the redistribution of land for the relief of congestion. Politically, the smallholders and the landless were not as influential as the strong farmers, but they were the very classes that had provided significant support to the rank and file of the revolutionary movement. Promises of redistribution made them compliant, at least in the short term. They welcomed the fact that the reconstituted Irish Land Commission was provided with powers to compulsorily acquire the lands of those represented as the traditional enemies of Ireland.[27] At the same time, the targeting of demesnes for acquisition took the focus away from the larger middle-class farmers who had experienced their fair share of agrarianism in 1917–23. A policy to relieve congestion was not the same as one supportive of a revolution of the proletariat: as far as both Hogan

9.3 Ballyfin, Co Laois, sold by the Coote family in the 1920s to the Patrician Brothers for use as a secondary school. The photo taken c.1901 shows the then owner, Sir Algernon Coote, standing outside his classical mansion. In the early 21st century, Ballyfin was magnificently restored by Fred and Kay Krehbiel.

and O'Higgins were concerned the support of middle Ireland was crucial to future stability, and as far as the large farmers were concerned the 1923 Land Act, working in tandem with the Public Safety Act, provided comfort and security and so they very quickly came to support the institutions of the new state, even though they had shown no strong commitment to the Republic or the War of Independence. By using the democratic legislative process, the government could not be compared to the Bolshevists in Russia. Much the same approach had been adopted a long time before in New York during the American Revolution of the 1770s, where Howard Pashman found that redistribution of property 'drove the change from popular uprising to stable legal systems . . . because it offered both material relief and revenge against Britain's supporters at a time when society demanded these actions'.[28]

In the decade after the passing of the 1923 Land Act, the Irish Land Commission compulsorily acquired and redistributed at least 178 demesnes and untenanted estates.[29] Significantly, amongst the first demesnes targeted for acquisition were those belonging to houses burned in 1920–23, including those of Lord Castlemaine, Lord Langford, Chichester Constable and Sybil Lucas-Scudamore. None of these owners had any intention of returning to Ireland. The example of Castleshane epitomises the fact that once the house and the owner were taken out of the equation, local conditions changed dramatically though not always immediately. After Sybil Lucas-Scudamore left for England, the management of the estate was taken over by George Morgan, the steward. He was soon reporting how difficult matters were in a depressed economy. In August 1920, farming was disrupted by 'the most awful weather nothing but rain and very cold, nothing seems to grow . . . potatoes are blighted very bad all round'. Until then pigs were doing well selling at £12 a hundred-weight but at the beginning of August, just as the second lot of pigs that year were ready for market, the bottom fell out of the market.[30]

To compound matters, with the landlord presence removed, farmers who had taken Lucas-Scudamore lands on conacre became reluctant to pay their rents. The family solicitor advised the issuing of writs, but Morgan believed this would only lead to a boycott.[31] By March 1921, the demesne was being pillaged.[32] Less than a month after the Treaty had been signed, T.F. Crozier, the estate agent, strongly advised Sybil that the entire demesne should be sold because a Land Bill was imminent: 'I should not be a bit surprised that there might be compulsory powers to acquire land situated such as Castleshane is now, namely the owners living in England, and the mansion house burned.'[33] At the end of 1921, during the truce period, Morgan reported an attempt to destroy the surviving wing of the castle.[34] There were obviously those who were now intent on ensuring that the Lucas-Scudamores never returned.[35]

Sybil eventually took Crozier's advice and sold off the untenanted lands in 1922 but she retained the demesne. For almost a decade she held out, for what reason is not clear, perhaps some romantic notion that her son Jack might want to return to Ireland. However, local smallholders exerted pressure on the Land Commission to have the demesne redistributed, and in 1931 M.T. Henchey was sent to carry out a survey of the demesne.[36] It was on the eve of a general election and to win local votes Cumann na nGaedheal were anxious to expedite land redistribution because the rising Fianna Fáil party in their election manifesto had committed to do so if returned to office. The following year the demesne was compulsorily acquired for £3,715 payable in 4.5 per cent land bonds, ending the Lucas-Scudamore association with Monaghan.

9.4 Woodlawn, Co Galway, formerly the home of Lord Ashtown, described as 'one of the creepiest places in Ireland'.

Under the 1923 and subsequent land acts, the revolution that had been begun in 1879 against the 'alien usurpers' of Irish lands was eventually completed 100 years later; by 1973, virtually all the untenanted lands recorded in the 1906 Return had been eliminated.[37] As demesnes were compulsorily acquired, the Land Commission inherited emptied country houses. In 1944 when Deputy Oliver Flanagan asked the Minister for Lands if he would 'arrange to hand over mansions and large houses of divided lands to organisations such as *An Oige* [Irish youth council], Irish Tourist Board, Youth Training Body etc. instead of permitting them to fall into decay, or be demolished, as often happens', he received from Fianna Fáil's Seán Moylan the following rather unsympathetic reply:

Residences on lands acquired by the Land Commission for division which are not suitable for disposal to allottees may be demolished in order to provide material for building smaller houses for allottees or may be sold by public auction, at which it is open for such bodies as the Deputy mentions to bid for them.[38]

Because records are not accessible, it is impossible to determine how many houses from 1923 onwards were acquired by the Irish Land Commission.

However, Emer Crooke, using Department of Lands records has identified thirty-six houses acquired by the Land Commission for the period 1954–58 alone, and it should be noted that this was long after land acquisition had begun to slow down.[39] On 5 August 1958, the secretary of the Department of Lands explained to his superiors that 'in acquiring land the Land Commission acquire a number of mansions and large houses in good repair which are unsuitable for their uses' and that 'with comparatively little adaptation save the erection of new buildings for institutional use for agricultural education, homes, hospitals, residential schools, etc., or as country-type houses to stimulate tourism'.[40] Some houses with minimal 'accommodation land' were sold to religious orders and converted to schools, convents and monasteries or used by the state as training facilities: Ballyfin, Garbally, Kylemore Abbey, Johnstown Castle and Ballyhaise for instance. But the more general case was that Big Houses, especially those of an aristocratic nature, 'proved unsaleable and had to be demolished'.[41]

At least nine of the houses listed in the ownership of the Land Commission in 1958 were demolished at this time, including Dalystown in Galway ('Considered to be suitable only for demolition and is therefore unlikely to be available for sale') and Shanbally Castle in Tipperary, which was still in very good condition ('stone built, slated roof, 20 principal bed and dressing rooms, bathrooms and ample servant accommodation').[42] Built c.1806, Shanbally was considered John Nash's 'most important and largest Irish castle'.[43] The Land Commission's intention was to try to sell it and 173 adjoining acres, but no bidders could be found. Despite local opposition – the local TD, for example, told the Minister for Lands, Erskine Childers, that this was seen to be 'a national calamity in the eyes of the people of South Tipperary and adjoining counties' – the mansion was demolished.[44] According to N.K. Robinson, The Knight of Glin and D.J. Griffin: 'Its destruction was one of Ireland's great architectural losses this century.'[45] In 1988, the same authors catalogued around 600 Big Houses demolished or abandoned to ruin (including some burned in 1920–23) and theirs was by no means a complete inventory. These included such architecturally imposing structures as Castle Morres in Kilkenny (demolished following a demolition sale in 1940), Courtown in Wexford (demolished mid-1940s), Dunsandle in Galway and Mote Park in Roscommon, both demolished in 1958.

9.5 Moydrum Castle in ruins, c.2020. A similar image was famously used by
U2 on the cover of their album *The Unforgettable Fire*.

Thus, the Land Commission completed the process begun by political and
social revolutionaries in 1920–23. Houses no longer had to be burned; they
could instead be financially strangled by being denuded of whatever lands they
had retained (exceptions will be discussed below).[46] Lord Ashtown had struggled through the revolutionary period at Woodlawn in Galway but, as L.P
Curtis Jr has shown, under the 1923 Act he was forced to sell virtually all his
tenanted and untenanted land, almost 21,700 acres for £136,000 in 4 per cent
land bonds.[47] It ultimately ended the family's presence in the area, so that by
2012, Woodlawn was described as 'a vast crumbling mansion in Co Galway
. . . so scary in its ruinous state that even the team who produced *The Blair
Witch Project* thought it was one of the creepiest places in Ireland'.[48]

Similarly, in 1927, the Land Commission compulsorily acquired the
Ballinahinch demesne of around 1,100 acres – 'splendid grazing tillage
and meadow lands' – paying Mrs Gore £8,000 in 4.5 per cent bonds. The
Commission treated the Big House as 'valueless', allowing her only £90 for the
outbuildings, including a greenhouse that had been built for £2,000. Even

9.6 Castleshane in ruins. Having been burned in 1920, it was later commandeered by anti-Treatyites and used by local people as a dance venue. Its demesne was eventually acquired by the Irish Land Commission in the 1930s and planted with firs.

before the boom of the war years, £15 per acre would have been a modest price for good quality land and would have yielded Mrs Gore £16,500 in cash. The Land Commission demolished the mansion 'to use stones for cottages'.[49]

Under the Cumann na nGaedheal government of 1923–32 several extensive demesnes managed to evade acquisition. There may have been some who did so because of sheer luck, or possibly even political connections, but most did so because of safeguards in the 1923 Land Act. For example, in 1926 the Land Commission inspected the 2,000-acre demesne and untenanted lands in the possession of Lady Howard Bury of Charleville Forest in Tullamore with a view to compulsory acquisition, but on finding that thirty-eight local families were dependent upon employment provided by the demesne decided not to proceed.[50] The following year, Patrick Hogan told the Dáil that the Land Commission was not going to acquire the substantial Franks estate in Cork because of the progressive manner in which the land was farmed and because it gave employment to 'a substantial number' of labourers.[51] In 1927, the Commission did not proceed against George Mansfield, who had a 600-acre demesne at Caragh in Kildare, because 'this man tills considerably and gives a lot of employment'.[52] In other words, the government was prepared to balance the loss of employment against acquisition.

Under the 1923 Act, the breeding of thoroughbred animals or the existence of historical woodland also exempted a demesne from acquisition. Some TDs quickly became cynical about the rather sudden establishment of stud farms on demesnes at Ballinlough, Killeen and Slane Castle in Co Meath alone.[53] When Martin Roddy told the Dáil in 1927 that the Gill estate in Offaly was not to be divided, William Davin enquired sarcastically: 'Is this another of the many stud farms supposed to be allowed in this particular area?'[54] The breeding of Kerry Blues and the existence of historic woodlands meant that the owners of Carton House – by 1923 it had passed out of the ownership of the Duke of Leinster to Sir Henry Mallaby-Deeley – were allowed to retain in excess of 1,200 acres. The same applied to the Earl of Dunraven at Adare, who held on to 1,160 acres in Limerick; Lord Rossmore, who retained 1,430 acres in Monaghan; Lord De Vesci, who kept over 1,000 acres in Laois; and Lord Rathdonnell, around 1,290 acres in Carlow.[55] All of these houses survived with the exception of Rossmore Park, a very large Tudor Revival house built in 1827 to the design of William Vitruvius Morrison, which was invaded by dry rot in the 1940s and demolished in the mid-1970s. Carton and Adare evolved to fulfil very different functions by the end of the twentieth century as exclusive country house hotels with golf courses; only the retention of their demesnes allowed for this transition.

Finally, the objective of the 1923 Land Act is brought into further relief by contrasting the situation with Northern Ireland where, as Olwen Purdue points out, the 1925 Land Act provided them with much more favourable terms on the sale of their tenanted estates than the Hogan Act and 'allowed landowners to retain their untenanted land for their own use [which] was of major importance as it enabled some of them to farm on a sufficiently large scale to generate a good income or utilise their remaining natural resources in other ways'.[56] Granted, supplementary incomes were more often necessary but at least their lands were not targeted for compulsory acquisition and redistribution. The northern aristocracy were, it seems, more adept at connecting with the commercial world of Belfast than the southern aristocracy were in moving from the old world of landed income to the investment world of the City. Very importantly for them, they remained part of the United Kingdom and so 'rather than being a small, provincial and declining clique they had a strong sense of being an integral part of a larger, active and vibrant social group' because of their attachment to the empire, and their sense of identity guaranteed they had less reason to migrate from the island than their southern counterparts.[57]

2. 'These men and their dependents are entitled to anything we can do for them'

There are remaining loose ends to be tidied up in this book. For example, were members of the IRA eventually rewarded with lands under the government redistribution schemes post-1923? The answer is yes, but how many and to what extent is impossible to determine because of the inaccessibility of the Land Commission records to the research public. Other evidence is, however, worth considering. Before the Civil War broke out in earnest, the first debate on providing land for the IRA took place in the Dáil on 1 March 1922. David Kent (Cork, Sinn Féin, later Coalition Republic) introduced a motion:

> That it be decreed [by Dáil Éireann] that all lands which were in the occupation of enemy forces in Ireland and which have now been evacuated, except those that may be retained as necessary training grounds for the IRA, be divided up into economic holdings and distributed among landless men; and that preference be given to those men, or dependents of those men, who have been active members of the IRA prior to the Truce, July 1921 . . . These men and their dependents are entitled to anything we can do for them. These men came out not for any pecuniary gain, but for love of country. And the first duty of a nation should be to the soldiers who fought for them.[58]

Kent's proposal was never implemented, essentially because of the outbreak of the Civil War.

When Patrick Hogan formulated the terms of the 1923 Land Act and set out the hierarchy of allottees to whom land was to be given, there was no mention of the IRA but that is hardly surprising given that the anti-Treatyites had been held responsible for much of the land agitation that accompanied the Civil War. However, there were certainly officers of the National Army who were given farms. A document drawn up by the Old IRA Association of County Meath in the 1930s listed 'Free State army pensioners and gratuitants (who took up arms against the Republican troops) and who are resident in County Meath and environs', at least ten of whom had received land in Meath, including Seán Boylan, the most prominent IRA leader in Meath during the

War of Independence and later a Free State army officer, who had given the order to burn Summerhill. He received fifty acres from a 'grateful' Land Commission.[59]

The issue of land for the rank and file remained a vibrant one. In January 1923, the government's reluctance to reward IRA veterans for their efforts prompted General Liam Tobin and some others to establish the organisation that became the Old IRA. The intention was to bring to the government's attention the widespread grievances of men who felt that they had not been compensated for their sacrifices during the War of Independence. For instance, in the Dáil in December 1925 John Nolan (Limerick, Cumann na nGaedheal) contended that:

> There is one class who seems to be nobody's children and they are the ex-army men of the old Volunteers. I think if any class of people are entitled to consideration as regards land, they have first claim, because the Act of 1923 would not have been in existence at all, and we would not be here, were it not for them. They seem to have been forgotten in every department, and I hope when the minister sends his inspectors out that he will give them directions to have these men given special consideration.[60]

After being voted into power in 1932, Fianna Fáil provided impetus with a Land Act the following year. Richard Dunphy has argued the pivotal role that the IRA played in the rise of Fianna Fáil from the mid-1920s: the most important source of recruitment of supporters to the party, he writes, was 'the large pool of disillusioned republicans who had not been politically active at all since the end of the Civil War; many of them may not even have voted in 1923'.[61] Fianna Fáil organisers toured the country, contacting local former IRA commanders who more often than not were highly regarded in their local communities 'as heroic or charismatic figureheads' because of 'their (real or legendary) exploits during the War of Independence and Civil War'.[62] After Fianna Fáil entered the Dáil for the first time in 1927, giving the party political legitimacy, established Old IRA associations simply evolved into local Fianna Fáil *cumainn* [units] offering support to the party.[63] Very soon a *cumann* existed in nearly every parish in the country and their lobbying at local and national levels became crucial in securing farms and allotments for their members, not just Old IRA. In the lead up to the 1932 general election, one of Fianna Fáil's central planks was to expedite land division, which greatly appealed to the small farmer electorate.[64] In office, they quickly developed their own land act.

As David Seth Jones reveals, the loopholes of the 1923 Act that allowed the aristocracy to retain their demesnes were 'a matter of urgent concern' to De Valera.[65] In 1926, he had told the Fianna Fáil *Ard Fheis* [conference] that it was the party's aim 'to complete land purchase, break up the large grazing ranches, and distribute them as economic farms amongst young men and agricultural labourers, such as those compelled at present to emigrate'.[66] Thus, under the 1933 Land Act, the Land Commission was given more radical powers: it could now acquire the demesne lands, parklands and home farms previously exempted; an abandoned Big House could no longer be used as proof of residency, so absentees were particularly targeted; lands not used 'in the same manner as an ordinary farmer in accordance with proper methods of husbandry' ruled out those who had claimed exemption status as stud farmers.[67]

Reforms introduced by the temporary Minister for Lands, Frank Aiken, increased the opportunity for allocating land to landless men, including IRA veterans. It became commonplace for Fianna Fáil politicians to promise members of the Old IRA that they would be rewarded with land for past sacrifices. In 1935, Dr Con Ward (Monaghan, first Fianna Fáil parliamentary secretary to the Minister for Local Government) told a rally in Monaghan: 'He would see that those who fought for their country had first claim in the division of land in the county, and they would also have first preference in the division of large ranches in Meath and Roscommon.'[68] In 1933, a resolution passed by the Tipperary Old IRA bolsters the argument made in chapter five that if men fought for patriotic reasons they also fought in the hope of bettering their economic futures:

> Governments in the past have proved themselves notoriously ungrateful and convinently [*sic*] forgetful of the men who made them and as our only hope of compensation is through the medium of land, we mean to see it, as far as in our power lies that a reoccurence [*sic*] of this treatment is not meted out to those who gave the best years of their lives to make this country a land without footing or shelter for slaves.[69]

Six months previously, on 2 October 1932, a conference of the South Tipperary Old IRA, held in Thurles, passed a series of resolutions proposing inter alia that the 1923 Land Act should be abolished; that the ranches of Tipperary should be distributed immediately amongst local uneconomic holders and landless men with 'first preference [to] be given to Republican soldiers'.[70] In 1935, Sam Waddell, one of the chief land commissioners, issued his staff with instructions that: 'Pre-Truce IRA men who have been awarded small pensions for national service under *Saorstat* Pensions Acts are not affected if eligible for land and capable of working it.'[71] That same year, the editor of the *Meath Chronicle* was delighted to announce:

> We are able to give the names of some of the allottees on the Deerpark and at Dunmoe and for those of us who lived in and had a fair share of our being in the resurgent years from 1916 to 1922 and 1923, it is pleasant to see amongst them brave men and brave families that took their full share of the perils of that glorious if dangerous epoch . . . families that sheltered the soldiers of the Republic when the hounds of England were at their heels. . . . Too long were many of these men forgotten and the Land Minister can rest assured that there are few indeed who begrudge the restoration of the land to the men, and to the breed of men, who fought and wrought and bled for Ireland.[72]

This was part of the Dillon demesne of Lismullin House, which had been burned in April 1923.

One must remember that this work has focused primarily on lands attached to Big Houses that were burned; it has not dealt with the hundreds of other estates where agrarianism was a feature of the 1920s, where lands were taken over by locals and it was then up to the Land Commission to sort out the muddle. That is an even more ambitious study for someone else in the future. The final case study in this work looks at a Big House – Tubberdaly in King's County – burned because of agrarianism, but where there was very likely also IRA involvement, and where the muddle was not sorted until the 1930s. It elucidates the impact of the national on the local during the 1914–23 period and by going beyond 1923 it underlines the necessity to look past the end of the Civil War to fully understand the Irish revolution in all its complexity.[73]

3. 'The campaign was originated with a view to terrorizing Mr Nesbitt'

In April 1920, an article in the *Irish Times* presented the revolutionary movement in Ireland as tripartite arguing that it began as a labour movement during the war; it developed into a political movement for independence after 1919; and by the spring of 1920 it had also taken on an agrarian character, 'not directed against high rents or against grazing ranches as such but seems to be animated by a general desire for the expropriation of land'.[74] This judgement was particularly relevant to the Tubberdaly estate.

In 1886, at the height of the Plan of Campaign, Edward John Beaumont-Nesbitt, the eldest son of a Suffolk Church of England rector, inherited an 8,000-acre estate from his cousin Catherine Downing Nesbitt of Leixlip House in Kildare.[75] The bulk of the estate was in King's County, so he came to reside at Tubberdaly, a rather plain and austere Georgian house built near the site of a ruinous medieval castle that added little but antiquity to the aesthetics of the landscape. Beaumont-Nesbitt quickly became respected amongst the King's County aristocracy, becoming high sheriff of the county in 1892 (he would later become the last Lord Lieutenant of the county, 1918–22). As a progressive farmer, he also became internationally renowned as a breeder of Aberdeen Angus cattle, winning many prestigious prizes including the Queen Victoria Cup for best herd in 1905.[76] His diversified estate enterprise included a demesne sawmill that provided a great deal of local employment.[77] Like most of his peers, he sold the bulk of his estate under the Wyndham Land Act but retained around 1,200 acres of demesne and untenanted lands. Up to the First World War the Tubberdaly estate was a hive of industry, and, in typically aristocratic fashion, a major centre of leisure activity that ranged from organised sports days for the employees and their families held on the front lawn of Tubberdaly to annual shooting parties – 'a major social event in the county' – for the aristocracy and gentry.[78]

Beaumont-Nesbitt was well regarded as a landlord but at the same time there were local tensions coincident with the rise of the land and national movements from the 1880s. On New Year's Eve 1898, on the eve of the first county council elections in Ireland, a letter appeared in the nationalist *Leinster Leader* from the anonymous 'Ratepayer':

9.7 Tubberdaly, King's County, home of E.J. Beaumont-Nesbitt, burned as a result of local agrarian issues and the demand to have its demesne and untenanted lands redistributed. It was not rebuilt; Beaumont-Nesbitt argued: 'There is no use trying to fight out my corner . . . if I started to rebuild or build anything new, I should just be robbed.'

Mr Nesbitt is an Englishman who came to this country a few years ago, and during his short stay took such a lively interest in public affairs and had the welfare of the country so much at heart, that when the last Home Rule Bill was before Parliament, he exerted himself so much as to organise a meeting in Edenderry to oppose a measure that would prove disastrous to the country. Mr Nesbitt's entire retinue of Scotch and English servants attended the meeting, and, like their master, signed a petition against Home Rule for a country of whose requirements they knew nothing.[79]

There were several grievances at play in this letter: firstly, Beaumont-Nesbitt was presented as an Englishman, an outsider, a new generation 'planter' who did not understand or care about Ireland. 'Ratepayer' portrayed him as a staunch Unionist. That was true: he played a high-profile role in the Irish Unionist Alliance at local and national levels. But the charge that he may have been discriminatory towards Catholics in terms of his employment policy was more complex. As was the case with most landlords of the era, his house and estate management staff shared his religion and were taken in from outside the area, but those employed on the estate farm and mill were local Catholics, mainly from Rhode and the surrounding areas.[80] The creation of myths that bred hostility, especially those that had roots in the 1880s, had long-term consequences.

The First World War brought great change for the family. Typical of an aristocratic second son, Wilfrid (b.1894) had been educated for colonial service, in his case for the Navy at Osborne and Dartmouth. However, he left the navy in 1912 (the reason has not been ascertained) and went to Trinity College, Cambridge. He left as soon as the war broke out and joined his brother, Frederick, in the Grenadier Guards and in 1915 he was promoted to the rank of captain. In the summer of 1916, he was wounded at the Somme. Meanwhile, back home in King's County, with Home Rule on the statute books, and southern unionist opposition and organisation on the decline, it looked for a while as if there might be some local rapprochement between opposing parties. In March 1915, Beaumont-Nesbitt and the Nationalist chairman of the county council convened a meeting in Tullamore 'for the purpose of impressing upon the young people of the County the urgent duty which is cast upon them of joining the army in defence of their King and Country, in the present terrible crisis of the fortunes of the Empire'.[81] Any optimism was misplaced. In the family memory, the fallout from the Easter Rising of 1916 had a damaging effect on their local standing: Beaumont-Nesbitt's eldest son, Frederick, later recorded in his memoirs: 'I do not recall a single incident during my boyhood when hostility was shown either to myself or a member of my family, at least not until the outbreak of Easter week 1916.'[82]

While, as we have already seen, the 1916 Rising became an iconic nationalist site of memory for those wanting to commemorate the beginning of the Irish fight for independence, for Frederick and the wider Anglo-Irish aristocracy it signalled the beginning of the Troubles. Just over a year later, Wilfrid was killed at Fontaine on 27 November 1917.[83] It was a blow from which his parents struggled to recover.[84] His mother died the following year aged just forty-nine and from then on Edward spent considerable time away from Tubberdaly, leaving the management of the estate to stewards. Perhaps this was a mistake that many aristocrats made during the Great War, based on a decision very often dictated by their concentration on the war effort but also by emotional strain: through absence they lost their local influence and whatever popularity they may have had was forgotten.

The rise of Sinn Féin, its success at the 1918 General Election, the establish-ment of Dáil Éireann and the rise of Labour changed the deferential landscape in King's County. In local politics, attitudes hardened towards Beaumont-Nesbitt. In June 1919, at the statutory meeting of the Edenderry Rural District Council, he was nominated for the position of vice-chairman, which he had held up to then, but an objection was made 'on the grounds that Mr Nesbitt was a member of a recent deputation to the Government asking for more coercion and more militarism against the Irish people'.[85] His nomination was withdrawn.

At the same time, the labourers on Tubberdaly's demesne farm and sawmill went on strike for four months for higher wages and better working condi-tions.[86] It was a growing trend in midland counties such as Offaly and neigh-bouring Kildare.[87] When it was eventually resolved, three of the ringleaders were dismissed by Beaumont-Nesbitt: Christopher Jones, a carpenter, John Connor, a labourer, and Matthew Geraghty, the sawyer. For some years, Jones, who Beaumont-Nesbitt described as 'a jolly bad carpenter', had lived in one of the estate cottages rented from a tenant farmer who held around thirty-five acres. When the farmer emigrated, Beaumont-Nesbitt bought the tenant interest, grazed it, but allowed Jones and his family to stay on in the cottage.[88] According to the 1911 census Jones, then aged forty-one, was married with four sons and a daughter (the eldest Christopher Jr, then aged thirteen, and his sister, Mary, aged twelve, will feature later). Beaumont-Nesbitt initiated proceedings to have him ejected from his home but in January 1920 his peti-tion for ejection was rejected by the court.[89] Three months later, Christopher Jr joined the IRA; his pension application form shows he was a member of the 1st Offaly Brigade, 3rd Battalion, D Company between 1 April 1920 and 30 September 1923, for which he successfully received a pension under the Military Service Pensions Act, 1949, and a Service Medal (1917–1921) without Bar.[90] His sister, Mary, was a captain in the 3rd Battalion of the Offaly Cumann na mBan.[91] According to one of her pension application referees, Colonel Liam Egan: 'She was a member of the Jones family of Tubberdaly, all of whom rendered constant and unselfish service to the National Cause.'[92] How signifi-cant was this when their father came into conflict with his former employer?

For sure, Jones became more aggressive as revolution took hold. Beaumont-Nesbitt later told his sister that 'When the bad times came he [Jones] put stock on my land, turned mine off, and later on when I was letting the grazing, he threatened to shoot anyone who disturbed him' and later complained that 'He has given me all the trouble he can ever since he was unemployed, and I look upon him as the ringleader of most of the attempts to damage my property.'[93] If newspaper reports can be relied upon, this was a time of rising criminality in the county as a whole. At the summer assizes in King's County in 1920, where Beaumont-Nesbitt was chairman of the Grand Jury, one of the visiting magistrates pointed to the fact that, on the list of 100 crimes, 'only four persons are amenable to the law, there being absolute immunity for the remaining 96. Well, that means that the criminals have a free hand to do as they like. As far as I can see the state of the county is very sad.'[94] The breakdown in the British judicial system may in part explain the fact that it was not until May 1921 that Beaumont-Nesbitt got a decree for possession of his estate cottage but, as he put it, 'owing to the state of the country', he was unable to enforce it.

As Beaumont-Nesbitt said in his letter, there were numerous attempts on his property. On 11 July 1921, the morning on which the Anglo-Irish truce was called, his Scottish estate steward, Lewis Fraser, was attacked by a gang of men who came to his home. He made good his escape, but his house was burned down. The following month he was replaced by Henry McMullan. Full of bravado, McMullan called all the employees together and told them that 'If Jones was allowed to so graze the lands, it would lead to others doing the same, and eventually Mr Nesbitt might be forced to give up the lands with the result that they would be out of employment.' He asked the men to help him drive Jones's cattle off the demesne. Most complied, but there was a cohort of around seven who did not. That night a group of armed men called at McMullan's house, dragged him out and threatened to shoot him.[95] Jones was not in the gang, but McMullan would later claim that he instigated it and that the men who threatened to shoot him said 'Jones had no place else to put his cattle.'[96] It is not beyond the realms of possibility that comrades of Christopher Jr became involved in this intimidation. Young Jones was interned at the time, having been lifted in May 1921, but in his pension application, Christopher Jr included under an earlier date of April 1920 that he had 'fired into Tubberdaly steward's house at [?] Frazer who luckily escaped then', perhaps suggesting some crossover in activity.[97]

The culmination of the intimidation was the burning of Tubberdaly on 15 April 1923, coming towards the end of the Civil War. At about 2 a.m. on that

9.8 Lewis Fraser, the steward at Tubberdaly, who was driven away by agitators.

Sunday morning, a party of armed men called on McMullan – whose house was about 300 yards from Jones's home – and ordered him to hand over the key of Tubberdaly.[98] Like all Big House burnings it was a monumental task; in this case when the flames did not take as quickly as the raiders might have liked, they used 'incendiary bombs'. The newspaper reports simply stated that 'The place was filled with valuable furniture, including three pianos, while the library was packed with rare and costly volumes, all of which went to the flames.'[99] When the job was finished, the raiders were said to have 'cheered and fired shots'.[100] The papers were also quick to point out the repercussions: one noted, for example, that 'a large number of employees are thrown out of work', and that it would be the ratepayers who ultimately would pay the price.[101] The nationalist *Leinster Leader* was sympathetic towards Beaumont-Nesbitt:

He is very popular in the district in which he has resided for many years.
. . . He worked very hard in the effort to ameliorate the conditions of

people around him, took the deepest interest in their work and doings, and aided the District Council very materially in their administration by his energy, initiative, and help. He supported schemes for erection of labourers' cottages, a great many of which were built in his district, gave wide employment at good wages, proved to be a kind landlord and generally tried in every possible way to act up to the best traditions of his class.[102]

This was in the best tradition of an obituary, in this case for a Big House and a way of life. Two months later, whatever had been salvaged from the ruins, as well as various modes of transport – motor car, trap, carriage – were sold by public auction.[103] And in the following September 'the entire famous herd' of Beaumont-Nesbitt's Aberdeen Angus was sold at the Royal Dublin Show (and his other farm stock and farm implements in a separate auction at Tubberdaly House), the same day that Sir John Dillon's Lismullin herd was also sold.[104] Farming on both estates had become the victim of the destruction of the Big House.

One of the central arguments of this book is that it is challenging to ascribe any single motive to the burning of a country house. Tubberdaly is no exception. Beaumont-Nesbitt himself claimed there was a political dimension. When filling in his compensation appeal form for the Irish Grants Committee, he wrote: 'I was Lord Lieutenant of the county and well-known as a Unionist, and the policy of the Republican party in the Free State at the time was to select Unionists for reprisals when they destroyed property. I am satisfied that it was the primary cause . . .' However, that was in answer to the question, was the burning 'occasioned in respect or on account of your allegiance to the Government of the UK?'[105] As detailed in a previous chapter, that was a prerequisite for compensation in the first place. Beaumont-Nesbitt knew he was being disingenuous in his claim.

Local historian Philip McConway has suggested that the burning of Tubberdaly should be linked to the execution of two anti-Treatyites, Joseph Byrne and Patrick Geraghty, on 27 January 1923, under the Public Safety Act of November 1922.[106] Chapter four has shown it was certainly true that the anti-Treatyites burned Big Houses in reprisal for the execution of their comrades, including Greenhills in Offaly, where it was reported: 'The leader announced they were republicans who had come to burn the house as a reprisal for the execution of Patrick Geraghty.' In 1943, when Christopher Jones Jr applied for a military service medal, he included in his list of commanding officers 'Patrick Geraghty (executed)'.[107] Jones Jr had been arrested in October 1922 and spent consecutive terms in military prisons at Templemore (Co Tipperary), and Newbridge and the Curragh (Co Kildare) until February 1924.[108] When he later filled in his pension form he claimed to have fired shots 'when Tubberdaly House – an enemy link – was destroyed by the IRA'.[109] He could not have been there, but he does identify the house as 'an enemy link', which would suggest some loose politico-military basis. Moreover, on his sister's active service record are listed the 'Destruction of Ballyburly and Greenhill Houses' and the 'Destruction of Tubberdaly House'.[110] And Patrick Cox witnessed that she had acted as lookout for the IRA when they burned Fraser's house at Tubberdaly.[111] All of this points to some republican involvement but the burning of Tubberdaly took place almost two months after the executions of Byrne and Geraghty, and while reprisal may have played a role, further investigation suggests other ulterior motives were more important.[112] It does not mean that the IRA were not involved but rather that members had simultaneous agendas.

While Mary Jones's role in the burning of country houses and the attack on Fraser were later represented as acts of patriotic endeavour, contemporaries had a different view of it. On 2 July 1923, Eamonn Coogan, the Garda Deputy Commissioner, wrote a comprehensive report to O'Higgins's Department of Home Affairs: 'The trouble is not strictly labour . . . The campaign was originated with a view to terrorizing Mr Nesbitt and his employees and ultimately to succeed by such methods to have the ranch [meaning demesne farm] divided up and distributed.'[113] As studies by Gemma Clark and Gavin Foster have shown, the Civil War changed the landscape of everyday violence, including a rise in agrarian crime, a rise that, as we have seen in chapter 5, greatly disturbed Patrick Hogan and Kevin O'Higgins.[114] Related to this was the escalation in country house burnings, and their wider geographical dispersal.[115] In Offaly, as it was renamed by 1922, Ciarán Reilly has found that 'land-related issues played a predominant role'.[116] Reilly references a meeting of Tullamore Rural District Council in April 1923, held about a week after Tubberdaly was burned, where Councillor Dunne boasted (mistakenly) that Offaly led the way in Big House burnings and put it down to the fact that 'it had been the most planted part of the country', thereby associating such actions with the undoing of the Tudor colonisation scheme of the sixteenth century. However, the editor of the

Midland Tribune rebuked Dunne: 'The burnings in Offaly is not a matter to boast of,' he wrote, 'land hunger and not the Gaelic state or republic was the motive of a good many of them.'[117]

Local land issues, entwined with labour disputes, therefore provided the main motive for the burning of Tubberdaly. The burning took place after three years of local agrarian unrest during a period of intense civil unrest which provided the opportunity to burn the house to ensure that Beaumont-Nesbitt would never return. Jones Snr and his followers, including the Geraghtys, had been occupying demesne buildings and lands. Two successive stewards had been intimidated, threatened with murder and eventually driven away from Tubberdaly. Beaumont-Nesbitt had no home to return to, even if he wanted, though he remained relatively unperturbed. He told the Irish Grants Committee in 1926: 'I am in quite comfortable circumstances and have a sufficient income not to have been more than inconvenienced by what has occurred.'[118] It is legitimate to argue, therefore, that Christopher Jones Snr, his followers, and even his own children, decided to take advantage of the times.

After the burning, sometime in May 1923 Beaumont-Nesbitt wrote to the Irish government telling them of his situation; this was while the new Land Bill was being prepared. At that very time, Kevin O'Higgins made public his contempt for the men who had 'gone out in an entirely selfish, wilful and criminal spirit to seize land by the strong hand'.[119] He promised to 'bring to bear on the Minister for Agriculture, and whatever influence I can bring to bear upon the Executive Council . . . to seeing that such people do not benefit by this Act'.[120] In early July, Patrick Hogan met with Beaumont-Nesbitt in Dublin.[121] In preparation for the meeting, an inspector of the Land Settlement Department had reported to Hogan on the importance of Beaumont-Nesbitt's Aberdeen Angus herd and advised that he 'should get ample protection for this herd and his splendid yards etc.'[122] He further pointed out that Beaumont-Nesbitt's yearly wage bill was at least £1,400, so he was a major employer that the locality could ill afford to lose.[123] He suggested the arrest of Jones and four others.[124] Almost concurrently, on 10 July, Beaumont-Nesbitt received a letter from Jones:

> Sir, This is the fourth letter I wrote you. Got no reply about the farm. I have my case entered this two years. I expect you have a letter from IRA

Headquarters. I am going to cut the meadows. I have no other means. I'll pay you for grass and clear you of all debts. I am willing to buy the farm honestly as no one else will be allowed to do so.[125]

It deserves a little unpacking: Jones presumably had made application to Beaumont-Nesbitt to buy the farm he was occupying (that went with the cottage). Beaumont-Nesbitt could have sold it to him, as he had purchased the tenant right from the previous farmer who had emigrated to America. But he was not prepared to facilitate Jones, a fact he made clear in his letter to Mrs Savage-Armstrong:

> There are several of my old labourers whom I want to help as much as I can, and if I do sell I think that I can arrange that these get helped first, and thereby I can put a spoke in the wheels of some that I do not want to help. I am quite philosophic about it all, I've had my innings and am out now, and if I can help any decent men to get a living out of the wreck, that is all I care about.[126]

Jones was willing to act in a reasonable manner, as he saw it, by paying for the cut meadow. As in the Land League days, he anticipated that no outsider would bid on the farm, and he could claim, with some authority, that he had the local anti-Treatyite IRA behind him. When several of Christopher Jr's former officers submitted a statement to support his pension claim, they finished off:

> The said Christopher Jones endured prolonged hardships on and off the run, and in internment camps, his home was a rendezvous for many prominent IRA men and members of the ASN. He and his family harboured and maintained, and scouted for, escorted and conducted to safety, wanted IRA men during the Black and Tans and 1922–23 struggles. He deserves the maximum consideration and support of the Pension Board.[127]

On 13 July 1923, Hogan wrote to O'Higgins: 'Mr Nesbitt is a very useful man, a first class farmer and employs a very large number of labourers, and he has done a lot for livestock in this country. It is a case that should be dealt with very firmly and I think it would be well to get a report from the Committee of Order as to the present condition.'[128] The letter suggested Cumann na nGaedheal's empathy for the large farming class which was to be much derided by their political opponents in the years ahead. Hogan followed the communication up on 14 July with a note to O'Higgins: 'Jones is the principal cause of the trouble down there and he should be arrested at once. Could you have that arranged?'[129] It was just over two weeks before the 1923 Land Act was passed on 3 August. O'Higgins had to stand by his Dáil speech of 28 May.[130] Jones was arrested and on 24 July he was charged at Tullamore with being 'in illegal possession of a farm of land, the property of Mr Nesbitt'. McMullan testified that on the night he had been attacked the armed but unmasked men had told him 'Jones had no place else to put his cattle'.[131] Jones, who denied any complicity, was remanded in custody to Tullamore Districts Court Sessions on 3 August.[132] According to Garda William Hickey of Rhode, Jones said to him: 'Ye are no Irishmen to come and arrest me. I wrote to Mr Nesbitt on three or four occasions offering him a price for the land, but he never replied to any of my letters. I could get no employment and I had to find some means of living.'[133] The last sentence is worth consideration: land grabbing should not necessarily be associated with greed, sometimes it was driven by necessity. Jones had probably not been employed since he was dismissed by Beaumont-Nesbitt.

The date of the remand hearing was significant. It was two days after the government enacted the Public Safety (Emergency Powers) Act on 1 August 1923. The act was directed against all enemies of the Free State government who 'have created a spirit of rebellion'. Amongst the crimes punishable by arrest, imprisonment and whipping were 'wrongful entry on and retention of possession of land without colour or pretence of title or authority'.[134] When Jones came back before the Tullamore court, he was charged with 'unlawfully and by force entering the lands of Tubberdaly . . . and retaining the land by force and excluding Mr Nesbitt by force and threats from the use of the lands from Sept[ember] 1922, to the present time'.[135] However, Jones, who had no legal representation, was released on bail to be returned for trial at a later date. The reason was set out by a frustrated Deputy Commissioner Coogan, who pointed out that, because Jones's offence took place before 3 August, 'he could not be made amenable under the Public Safety Act'.[136] To Coogan, Jones was 'a thoroughly lawless scoundrel, and his family being connected with the

Irregulars, he would get a certain amount of assistance from that section of the people in the locality'.[137]

The adjourned case came before the Tullamore Quarter Sessions in June 1924. This time Jones was represented by a solicitor, and on advice he pleaded guilty 'of trespassing on the lands'. His solicitor pleaded 'mitigating circumstances'. His client, he argued, 'like a good many other people at the time, foolishly thought he could get a bit of land, he put his cows on Mr Nesbitt's farm. He had since given up possession.'[138] On undertaking that he would not again interfere, Jones was discharged under the Probation of Offenders Act under his own recognisance of £50.[139] It was an astute move, for Section 1 of the Act provided as follows:

> Where any person is charged before a court of summary jurisdiction with an offence punishable by such court, and the court thinks that the charge is proved, but is of opinion that, having regard to the character, antecedents, age, health or mental condition of the person charged, or the trivial nature of the offence, or to the extenuating circumstances under which the offence was committed, it is inexpedient to inflict any punishment or any other than a nominal punishment, or that it is expedient to release the offender on probation, the court may, without proceeding to conviction, make an order . . . discharging the offended conditionally on his entering into a recognizance . . . to be of good behaviour . . .[140]

Jones was introduced to the court as a 'small farmer': he may have given up his career as carpenter but he was not prepared to give up possession of the land he had grabbed and that was more information than the judge required. Jones returned to his estate cottage on the Tubberdaly demesne and to the land he had grabbed, that the local authorities were now turning a blind eye to. In 1925, Beaumont-Nesbitt wrote to his sisters that Jones, 'with a good many' of the former labourers, 'decided that if any dividing up takes place no one is to come in until they are satisfied'.[141]

Under the Damage to Property (Compensation) Act, Beaumont-Nesbitt, then in residence in Penton Lodge in Hampshire, claimed £24,574 for the destruction of Tubberdaly (with separate claims for other properties bringing the total up to around £35,000). He received less than one third. Like many other burned-out country house owners, he was not prepared to accept a 'rein-statement clause' that would have forced him to rebuild on the original site, even though he would have received considerably more. He was resigned to all of this, accepted that 'there is no use trying to fight out my corner' and that 'if I started to rebuild or build anything new, I should just be robbed'.[142] He may have been misinformed that the Irish people were asking 'when [will] the English come back?' but was more accurate in his assessment that 'The so-called Free State is broke, and that for generations there will be poverty and want far greater than ever occurred in the remembrance of anyone now living.'[143] He never returned to Ireland. In 1925, the Land Commission purchased the demesne and paid Beaumont-Nesbitt £8,138, £2,038 in cash and £6,100 in 5 per cent compensation stock (which he sold for £5,777).[144] Many years later, when his grandson Brian visited the ruins of Tubberdaly in 1991, he felt 'a mixture of anger against the blackguards who burned it, nostalgia for something I never knew – and regret that the site had been invaded by so many buildings including the power station [at Rhode] and all those electricity pylons'.[145] Whether he knew it or not, salvage from Tubberdaly and other burned houses in Offaly had been used to build the power station: old Ireland had literally helped give rise to the new.[146] When around the same time, this author spoke with a descendent of one of 'the blackguards' still resident on the demesne, he had a very different remembrance: 'We burned the bastards out!' he gleefully told me.

For almost ten years, the Cumann na nGaedheal government failed to deal with the redistribution of the Tubberdaly demesne. By late 1931, the writing was on the wall for the government; the country was fed up with austerity, and rural Ireland was frustrated with the delays in land redistribution so much promised in 1917–23. Fianna Fáil was on the rise and expediting land redistribution was at the core of its rural policies. Revealingly, it was not until October 1931 that a meeting was held in Rhode to form a branch of Cumann na nGaedheal, a case perhaps of locking the stable door after the horse had bolted. One participant lamented the 'very strange' and 'long promised distribution of the lands of Tubberdaly' and that 'Since the place was put in the hands of the Land Commission there was a decided change for the worse.'[147] It was more stagnation than change and John O'Connor only felt comfortable in hinting at it: 'Some strange things had happened which were not for the good of the people of the district.'[148] These may never be revealed but undoubtedly were due to the local influence of those who had 'decided that if any dividing up takes place no one is to come in until they are satisfied'. At that Cumann na nGaedheal meeting, there was no mention of Joneses or Geraghtys who had continued to reside on the demesne, all staunch Fianna Fáil supporters. Jones's sister, Mary (whose married name was now Swords), told the IRA pensions board that her brother, Christopher Jr, 'has been an ardent worker for F[ianna] F[áil] all down the years'.[149]

Three months after Fianna Fáil came to power, in May 1932, the new Minister for Lands and Fisheries, P.J. Ruttledge, replied to an answer in the Dáil that a scheme for the redistribution of the Tubberdaly demesne would be 'put into operation at an early date'.[150] Ruttledge was an IRA veteran of the War of Independence who was elected as Sinn Féin TD for Mayo in 1921 and later wounded in the Civil War. During the Civil War, he had worked on behalf of the IRA Executive in drawing up a programme which included 'the question of the demesnes and ranches and had adopted a scheme for their confiscation and distribution'.[151] What he postulated in 1923 was carried through under the first Fianna Fáil government's land legislation a decade later, and IRA veterans were given priority in local land division schemes.[152]

In June 1923, the newly elected Fianna Fáil representatives for Offaly – Patrick Boland and P.J. Gorry – met with a 'large deputation' including the 'uneconomic holders of Rhode' to hear an 'important development in connection with the proposed distribution of the lands of Tubberdaly'.[153] (Years later, P.J. Gorry was one of those who supported Christopher Jones Jr's IRA pension application.[154]) The meeting was chaired by Patrick Cox, Jones's former IRA officer. John O'Connor said those present 'did not deplore the going of such as he [Beaumont-Nesbitt] from Ireland, but they did deplore the fact that nothing had been done to substitute the livelihood got from him'.[155] The irony of the comment was lost on himself, but those who had lost their livelihood included Jones.

The following year, Fianna Fáil introduced its own Land Act and changed the hierarchy of allottees, giving preference to discharged labourers, uneconomic holders in the immediate vicinity of the estate being divided and landless men 'of a deserving class'. Preference in all categories was to be given to IRA veterans.[156] Both Joneses, father and son, came under the heading of 'discharged labourers' (at least technically) and IRA veterans. In 1936, when

Christopher Jones Jr was making his IRA pension application, the review board received an enquiry from the Irish Land Commission to say that he had applied for land and to confirm whether he had given 'first class meritorious IRA service during the Pre-Truce period', to which the board replied in the affirmative. Jones Jr got an additional divide to what his father already held, and the other labourers, including James Geraghty, were at last officially installed in their demesne farms and houses, Geraghty in the one that formerly belonged to Fraser. In the end, local power brokers might be said to have outmanoeuvred Hogan and O'Higgins. When Christopher Jr died in June 1964, his obituary in the *Irish Press* stated that his funeral took place with full military honours. He was a War of Independence hero. His other story and that of his father and the Tubberdaly labourers was not given the same airing.

4. 'His lordship was a good man'

Finally, if there were roughly 1,500 Big Houses occupied in Ireland in 1906, the burning of 20 per cent of them represents a modest rate of destruction.[157] This begs the question as to why many more were not destroyed. While this would make for an interesting book in its own right, some preliminary points may be offered.

After the burning of Lismullin in Meath in April 1923 the editor of the nationalist *Leinster Leader* complained that: 'The burning of this beautiful building seems inexplicable as the owner [Sir John Dillon] has not been identified with any political organisation, merely confining himself to his principal occupation as a large farmer and breeder of pedigree stock.'[158] And the *Meath Chronicle* praised Sir John for 'attending to his home and his demesne, where he gave a great deal of employment. His permanent staff exceeded thirty, and his weekly wages bill amounted to a very considerable sum indeed. He was justly regarded as an excellent employer, paying the highest standard wage.'[159]

The importance of the Big House to the local economy is often overlooked, because traditionally it was more often associated with oppression rather than progression. While there were those who burned Big Houses for material gain, equally there were others to whom the burning of the local Big House made no economic sense, and, indeed, the loss of the Big House to the local economy from 1903 onwards deserves closer examination. This was particularly true in

9.9 Kilboy House in Co Tipperary, 2021. Originally the home of
Lord Dunalley, the house was burned in 1922, rebuilt in the late 1920s,
demolished by the family in the 1950s and rebuilt once more in magnificent
style by Mr and Mrs Shane Ryan in 2013.

relation to the loss of employment. For instance, after the burning of Lord
Dunalley's Tipperary mansion and his temporary migration to London, the
Irish Times lamented that 'Thirty men have been thrown out of work owing to
the destruction of Kilboy.'[160]

Local lore has it that when a group of anti-Treatyites came to torch Carton
House in 1922, they were shown a portrait of Lord Edward FitzGerald (1763–
98), son of the 1st Duke of Leinster, but more crucially a leader of the United
Irishmen in 1798. The raiders are said to have been so impressed with his
Republican credentials that they departed. The story was apocryphal; the
more likely reason for not burning Carton was less romantic, and significantly
more practical. Despite the sale of the estate under the 1903 Land Act, house
and demesne continued to be one of the largest employers in north Kildare
and a major contributor to the local economy. In June 1922, when it was
learned that Carton had been lost by the FitzGeralds as the result of a gamble
and that it was to be taken over by Sir Henry Mallaby-Deeley, there was local

consternation.[161] This was assuaged to some degree by Mallaby-Deeley's assertions that 'I am bearing the whole expenses of the estate, and my agreement with the Duke is that everything should be carried on exactly as it has been in the past.'[162] He had also been informed by the Leinster estate agent Charles Hamilton that 'Carton has been run in the past with the view of giving as much employment as possible to the people in Maynooth.'[163] The *Leinster Leader*, picking up on Mallaby-Deeley's comments, pointed out:

> Any severance of the FitzGerald family with the management of the Leinster property will be greatly regretted in Kildare, where despite the fact that the land has been largely sold to tenants they still retain large interests in the ground rents and many buildings and homes in practically all the towns being held from them. Very extensive employment is given on the demesnes, tillage being intensive and a splendid class of livestock bred. Being a resident family, a very deep interest was taken in the welfare of the employees, who are comfortably housed and well treated. In addition, the Leinster estate trustees always subscribed generously to any object that tended to benefit Kildare and its people.[164]

In 2021, while circumstances have greatly changed, Carton remains one of the largest employers in north Kildare.

During the Civil War, as burnings escalated, some employees made their concerns known to the Free State government. In November 1922, the workers on the Bessborough estate in Kilkenny wrote to W.T. Cosgrave reporting several raids on the house and pointing out that 500 people were dependent upon wages from the estate and expressing their fear that they would lose their jobs if Bessborough should be destroyed.[165] A few months previously, in May 1922, the Marquess of Sligo had written to the Minister for Local Government complaining that the Town Workers Association – dominated by republicans, or so he claimed – were demanding the breakup of his 1,500-acre demesne. Sligo described himself as 'a serious farmer' and argued that, if the demesne was acquired, he would have to close Westport House and leave. He finished with a warning: 'I need hardly point out, that if I am driven away, my departure will entail much financial loss to Westport. No one has ever given so much employment, and it is not likely anyone ever will.'[166] The family remained resident for almost a century more and Westport House played a pivotal role in the development of the town's tourism potential.

At the height of Big House raids in Meath, Sir Nugent Everard of Randalstown, described as 'a very popular landowner' and one who showed 'keen interest . . . in the Irish industries movement', had his home protected by the National Army.[167] In 1929, M.R. Heffernan TD (Tipperary, Farmers' Party) argued in the Dáil for the continuation of this: 'Serious consideration', he argued, 'should be given to the fact whether more useful work could not be done by leaving the land in the hands of a man who is giving considerable employment on those lands than by placing a number of agricultural workers without capital on the same land.'[168] In the mid-1920s, the McCalmont family at Mount Juliet in Kilkenny continued to run a 1,000-acre farm giving employment to at least fifty families in the area.[169] The same was true of other huge demesne farms at Adare in Limerick (1,160 acres), Rossmore Park in Monaghan (1,430 acres) and Rathvinden in Carlow (1,290 acres).[170] This was one of the reasons why working demesnes were protected under the 1923 Land Act: it was not to allow the house privileged privacy, but rather to protect the employment of stewards, bailiffs, herdsmen, gardeners, agricultural labourers and tradesmen, as well as to protect modernising agricultural practice.

During the Civil War, some community representatives made successful representations to the government for the protection of the local Big House. In January 1923, Father Brett of Kilmaine in Mayo wrote to William Sears, his local TD, asking that protection be given to Lord Iveagh's Ashford Castle at Cong.[171] It has survived to become one of Ireland's most exclusive hotels. In December 1922, T.M. Healy, formerly one of the Irish Parliamentary Party's most prominent MPs and by then Governor General of Ireland, wrote to Richard Mulcahy, Minister of Defence, looking for protection for Glin Castle in Limerick: 'I hear that the Knight of Glin . . . is being very badly treated', Healy wrote. 'He is paralysed and unable to protect himself, and he does not know who to blame and to whom to appeal for protection. If it is in your power to afford him a little protection, I should feel obliged.' Mulcahy wrote to the officer in command at Limerick to 'make arrangements to have the Knight of Glin seen, with a view to assuring him of whatever protection from molestation he may require'.[172] During the Truce period, the Knight had endeared himself to local Nationalists by allowing numerous Gaelic Athletic

9.10 Thomastown House in Co Roscommon during its demolition, 1958, following acquisition of its remaining lands by the Irish Land Commission.

Association matches to be played on the demesne; a report on one game in October 1921 stated that it was played 'within touch of the castle' while the IRA 'held a gate collection and maintained order'.[173] Glin Castle has remained in the family ownership.

The Carton story was apocryphal, but similar versions are to be found elsewhere. Lyons House, also in Kildare, was the home of Valentine Lawless, 2nd Baron Cloncurry (1773–1853), imprisoned for three years in the Tower of London for his involvement with the United Irishmen in 1798.[174] The story goes that when the anti-Treatyites came to burn it, they were shown a bust of Cloncurry; according to Sir Shane Leslie (who loved a good story): 'The Republicans solemnly saluted the figure in turn and left the house in peace and under protection.'[175] Perhaps its salvation lay in the fact that in April 1922 Lord Cloncurry made a donation of £10 to the Free State election fund. The acknowledgement from its secretary K. Dorrian was instructive: 'In accordance with your wish your name will not appear on any published list.'[176]

Lady Daisy Fingall claimed of Castletown House, Ireland's most impressive Palladian mansion:

> Just before the petrol was thrown, a motorcycle came up the long avenue in a great hurry. And a breathless young man, with some mysterious authority, rode into the group of burners, to say that on no account was the house to be touched that had been built with Irish money by William Conolly, who was Speaker of the Irish House of Commons two hundred years or so earlier.[177]

Again, there is no reliable substantiating evidence, but these stories are all, individually and collectively, revelatory in relation to local attitudes to Big Houses. It was suggested by Lord Dunsany's biographer that his ancestral home was left untouched because one of the family's gate keepers 'was an ardent Sinn Féiner . . . [who] could dissuade anyone who thought of bothering the castle'.[178] Mark Bence-Jones related anecdotes of Lord Dunraven employing a Republican gillie during the revolutionary period who kept Adare safe and Sir Ralph Coote at Ballyfin, who 'was sensible enough to put in a caretaker who was an ardent Sinn Féin supporter and had been imprisoned by the British at the Curragh Camp.'[179] Philip Bull found a more authentic example in Myles Fenlon, 'an employee and able carpenter' at Monksgrange House in Wexford, who by the time of the Civil War was also a member of the 2nd Battalion of the North Wexford IRA (anti-Treatyite). The anti-Treatyites may have raided Monksgrange on several occasions, but the house was not burned. Adela Orpen later pointed out that Fenlon's presence was important, but she perceptively noted 'the house was the source of his livelihood'.[180] Marie Coleman has similarly suggested just how detrimental the loss of a Big House could be to a local community: in the years after Currygrane in Co Longford was burned there was a 72 per cent decrease in the local Church of Ireland population (from fifty-four to fifteen), most of whom were probably domestic and farm servants, gamekeepers and gardeners who had been made redundant.[181]

According to family lore, Glaslough in Monaghan was spared because of the family's benevolence during the Famine but, and not necessarily meaning to detract from that, it was also the case that Glaslough was unusual in a twenty-six county setting in that it was located in a strongly Protestant village and was guarded by well-armed former members of the Ulster Volunteer Force

9.11 Glin Castle, Co Limerick, an example of a house protected from destruction by political sympathy. In December 1922, Timothy Healy, Governor General of Ireland wrote to Richard Mulcahy, Minister of Defence, 'I hear that the Knight of Glin . . . is being very badly treated . . . If it is in your power to afford him a little protection, I should feel obliged.' The house remains in the ownership of the FitzGerald family in 2021.

and dead-shot gamekeepers such as James Vogan, who had instructed the local company of the UVF in the use of arms in 1913–14.

Fred Madden of neighbouring Hilton Park in Clones gave an interview to the *Irish Times* in April 2016: 'The house wasn't a plantation house,' he said, 'It was purchased and built by ancestors and so it was spared during the Troubles.' But Fred also added, which was even more pertinent, that during the revolutionary period Major J.C.W. Madden, one of Monaghan's most ardent Unionists, 'trained every man on the estate in rifle practice to defend the house in event of attack'.[182] Olwen Purdue has shown that well-armed estate workforces played an important role in the protection of country houses in the partitioned area of Ulster that became Northern Ireland.[183] In the wider context, Andy Bielenberg has argued that: 'In the border counties generally, Protestants made greater efforts than elsewhere to put in place armed opposition to the IRA, which gave the ethno-religious conflict there a somewhat different dynamic.'[184] Further south, families

9.12 James Vogan and fellow gamekeepers at Glaslough House, 1920s.
Loyal (and armed) retainers such as these probably helped to safeguard
Castle Leslie during the Troubles.

or employees, as we have seen, were in a much more isolated and vulnerable
position and much less disposed to trying to physically oppose Big House raiders,
although, as we have also seen, they could defy the IRA in a variety of other ways
such as supplying information to the crown forces. As Brian Hughes' study illustrates, they were certainly not alone in this respect.[185]

During the revolutionary period, not everyone was willing to take up arms,
or to grab land, and not everyone condoned the burning of Big Houses. If
newspapers reflect public opinion, then obviously many people did not
subscribe to the idea that the destruction of country houses was patriotic or
socially advantageous. Following a spate of burnings in Galway in June 1921,
the *Tuam Herald* bemoaned:

Thus it goes on. One by one our fine old country houses are being ruth-
lessly destroyed. First Tyrone House, the finest in Ireland architecturally,
next Ower, an old Burke mansion, now comes Marble Hill, another Burke

house of some imposing beauty and family association . . . the destruction of houses is a social crime on whatever side it takes place.[186]

Five months later, in November, under the headline 'The Torch of War', the *Irish Times*, as might be expected, lamented the loss of 'landowners . . . men of education, distinction, and high ideals . . . indispensable to the welfare and progress of the community at large', and concluded:

> But the present spectacle of the countryside . . . studded as it is, with blackened ruins of once stately mansions, cannot have any but the most depressing effect, not only on those immediately concerned, but on all who have the welfare of the country at heart, and who pride themselves in our national institutions, beauty spots, and splendid buildings.[187]

Some ruins are spectacular enough to this day, creating powerful visual impact, such as Tyrone House in Galway, a reminder of what Hannah Arendt tells us: 'The reality and reliability of the human world rests primarily on the fact that we are surrounded by things more permanent than the activity by which they were produced.'[188] Castleshane remains a haunting but gradually disappearing ruin on the Monaghan landscape. Moydrum's ruins came to prominence in the early 1980s when Anton Corbijn's photograph was controversially used on the front cover of U2's album *The Unforgettable Fire*. In Burton Constable in Yorkshire, there is a 1920s photograph of the ruins of the Chichester Constable Roscommon home with the simple but telling pencil inscription: 'Runnamoat House. Burned July 2nd 1922 by Irish'. Summerhill became one of the country's crumbling spectacles. Years after its destruction, Mark Bence-Jones described it thus:

> Even in its ruinous state, Summerhill was one of the wonders of Ireland; in fact, like Vanbrugh's Seaton Delaval, it gained added drama from being a burnt-out shell. The calcining of the central feature of the garden front looked like more fantastic rustication; the stonework of the side arches was more beautiful than ever mottled with red lichen; and as the entrance front came into sight, one first became aware that it was a ruin by noticing daylight showing through the front door.[189]

9.13 Hilton Park, Co Monaghan, home of the Madden family, untouched during the 1920–23 period. A descendant wrote of Major J.C.W. Madden, who lived there at the time, that he 'trained every man on the estate in rifle practice to defend the house in event of attack'.

Ruins are not just the physical reminders of the imposing structure that once was, but they also symbolise the fall of the people who gave them meaning. Over time, the physical disappearance of the Big House very often led to the eradication of the memory of the house and those who occupied it.[190] Where ruins remained, they became icons of revolutionary mythology in Ireland, for both sides: as trophies for those who boasted for years of their role in their destruction, or symbols for those who lamented Big Houses as victims of the Troubles. The poet laureate John Betjeman (1906–84), who lived in Ireland from 1941 to 1943, thought it romantic to immortalise 'the distant house and its weedy walled garden and reed-choked lake' as 'the shell of an Adam-style mansion burnt down in "the Troubles"'.[191] In the 1930s, Sir Shane Leslie likewise pronounced that 'The Anglo-Irish families were largely burnt out' and repeated for emphasis: 'Others were burnt out in the later Troubles.'[192] In many respects, associating ruins with revolution was a historical convenience for the aristocracy; it would have been altogether less gallant to consider the more nuanced socioeconomic factors. For those who wanted to remember the War of Independence as a glorious episode in Irish history, the social dimension that gave rise to so many house burnings was best forgotten. (The process firstly of destruction and then forgetting also endangered both the ability and the resources to remember those millions of ordinary Irish men and women who inhabited aristocratic estates, whether their lives were comfortable or deplorable.) And, as happens in post-colonial societies, nationalist Ireland tried very hard to forget its colonial past. Such forgetting may be seen as part of the healing process, but it can also endanger the memory of what brings us to the present.[193] Thus, in the century after the beginning of the long revolution in 1879, the narrative of the revolutionary experience of the Big House became as fragmentary as country house ruins.

This book does not claim to have provided all the answers to the very many complex questions around the revolutionary experience of the Big House, but, then again, its aim was always to open a debate rather than definitively close one. It is hoped that, above all, this book has illuminated the experiences of the

9.14 Tyrone House, Co Galway, burned by the IRA in 1920 because of rumours that it was about to be taken over by the IRA. At the time it was unoccupied except by a caretaker and 'rather dilapidated'. The ruins have become an iconic symbol of the fall of the Irish Big House.

former landed elite by repositioning their story in revolutionary and independent Ireland, showing that their experiences were entwined with everything that happened in Irish life, politics and society from 1879 to 1923, and did not stand apart in isolation. It has been emphasised that the Big House experience clearly shows that the convolutions and repercussions of the revolutionary period can be more fully understood and gauged by projecting backwards to the Land War era (at least) and looking far beyond 1923. That was also a pivotal year because of the introduction of land and compensation legislation that simultaneously promised and threatened but ultimately delivered enough in terms of land redistribution to dampen any large-scale social revolution.

Imperative in the process of elucidation has been the use of local case studies which can so often reveal the totality of the past; as Raymond Gillespie has argued, local case studies 'involve the dissection of the local experience in the complex and contested social worlds of which it is part as people strive to preserve and enhance their positions within their local societies'.[194] The revolutionary experience of the Big House provides ample testimony to this.

Still, there is much that remains to be done. There is, for example, a need to more the Irish aristocracy's revolutionary experience in a wider global context, to examine why the levels of violence directed against the former landed and colonial elite in Ireland were so restrained as opposed to the experiences of their peers in other jurisdictions around the world at different times (which calls to mind E.P. Thompson's remark that, in a time of social chaos, 'It is the restraint, rather than the disorder, which is remarkable.'[195]). Finally there is also a need to analyse and develop in more detail why the call for 'the land for the people' was as universal as it was parochial.

ENDNOTES

1 'The Irish Landlords Have Become the Victims of a Revolution': Before The Great War

1. Shane Leslie, *The Irish Tangle for English Readers* (London, n.d. [1946]), p. 146; the landed class's revolutionary experience in the six counties of Northern Ireland has been comprehensively covered by Olwen Purdue in her seminal, *The Big House in the North of Ireland: Land, Power and Social Elites* (Dublin, 2009).
2. Elizabeth Bowen, *Bowen's Court* (London, 1942), p. 338.
3. Quoted in Peter Somerville-Large, *The Irish Country House: A Social History* (London, 1995), p. 342.
4. Terence Dooley, *The Decline of the Big House in Ireland* (Dublin, 2001); Purdue, *The Big House in the North of Ireland*.
5. https://www.chg.gov.ie/about/special-initiatives/commemorations/decade-of-centenaries/ [Accessed 20 Oct. 2020].
6. K.T. Hoppen, *Elections, Politics and Society, 1832–1885* (Oxford, 1984), pp. 147–48.
7. David Cannadine's, *The Decline and Fall of the British Aristocracy* (London and New Haven, 1990), pp. 16–17.
8. The definition of aristocracy used here borrows heavily from Cannadine's, *The Decline and Fall of the British Aristocracy*, pp. 8–15.
9. W.E. Vaughan, *Landlords and Tenants in Mid-Victorian Ireland* (Oxford, 1994), p. 218.
10. L.P. Curtis Jr, 'Incumbered Wealth: Landed Indebtedness in Post-Famine Ireland', *The American Historical Review* (Apr. 1980), 85:2, pp. 332–67.
11. S.J. Connolly, *Contested Island: Ireland 1460–1630* (Oxford, 2007); Jane Ohlmeyer, *Making Ireland English: The Irish Aristocracy in the Seventeenth Century* (New Haven, 2012).
12. See Colm Lennon, *Sixteenth-Century Ireland: The Incomplete Conquest* (Dublin, 1994).
13. Toby Barnard, *A New Anatomy of Ireland* (New Haven and London, 2003); S. J. Connolly, *Divided Kingdom: Ireland 1630–1800* (Oxford, 2008); L.M. Cullen, *The Emergence of Modern Ireland* (London, 1981); David Dickson, *Old World Colony: Cork and South Munster 1630–1830* (Cork, 2005); Raymond Gillespie, *The Transformation of the Irish Economy, 1550–1700* (Dundalk, Economic and Social History Society of Ireland, 1991); see also T.C. Barnard, 'Further reading' in Barnard, *The Kingdom of Ireland, 1641–1760* (Basingstoke, 2004).
14. There were notable exceptions as shown in Emma Lyons, *Morristown-Lattin, County Kildare, 1630–1800: The Estate and its Tenants* (Dublin, 2020).
15. Rolf Loeber et al. (eds.), *Art and Architecture of Ireland* (Dublin, London, New Haven, 2014), p. 329.
16. Mark Bence-Jones, *A Guide to Irish Country Houses* (London, 1988 revd. edn), pp. xi–xxiv; on smaller houses, Maurice Craig, *Classic Irish Houses of the Middle Size* (London and New York, 1976); Terence Dooley and Christopher Ridgway (eds.), *Country House Collections: Their Lives and Afterlives* (Dublin, 2021).
17. Fergus Campbell, *The Irish Establishment 1879–1914* (Oxford, 2009), p. 19.

18. See Christine Casey, *Making Magnificence: Architects, Stuccatori and the Eighteenth-Century Interior* (New Haven and London, 2017).

19. *Catalogue of Paintings Sold by Trustees of Carton, 4 December 1902* (PRONI, Leinster papers, D3078/10/6/2); Alison FitzGerald, 'Desiring to "Look Sprucish": Objects in Context at Carton', in Patrick Cosgrave et al. (eds), *Aspects of Irish Aristocratic Life: Essays on the FitzGeralds and Carton House* (Dublin, 2014), pp. 118–27.

20. Shane Leslie memoirs (NLI, Leslie papers, MS 22,885); Elizabeth Bowen, 'The Big House', in Hermione Lee, *The Mulberry Tree: Writings of Elizabeth Bowen* (London, 1986), p. 29.

21. Terence Dooley, *The Decline and Fall of the Dukes of Leinster: Love, War, Debt and Madness* (Dublin, 2014), p. 67.

22. R.F. Foster, *Modern Ireland, 1600–1972* (London, 1988), p. 377; Virginia Crossman, *Local Government in Nineteenth-Century Ireland* (Belfast, 1994); W.L. Feingold, 'Land League Power: The Tralee Poor Law Election of 1881', in Samuel Clark and James S. Donnelly Jr (eds.), *Irish Peasants: Violence and Critical Unrest 1780–1914* (Manchester, 1983), pp. 285–310.

23. Annie Tindley, *Lord Dufferin, Ireland and the British Empire, c.1820–1900: Rule by the Best?* (Abingdon, 2021), pp. 7–8; also, Olwen Purdue, *The Big House in the North of Ireland*, p. 233.

24. Tindley, *Dufferin*, p. 28.

25. He has been the subject of numerous biographies, see for example: R.F. Foster, *Charles Stewart Parnell, the Man and his Family* (London, 1976); F.S.L. Lyons, *Charles Stewart Parnell* (London and New York, 1977); Paul Bew, 'Parnell', *ODNB*.

26. R.F. Foster, *Vivid Faces: The Revolutionary Generation in Ireland 1890–1923* (London, 2014), p. xvii.

27. Foster, *Vivid Faces*, p. xvi; for 'pre-revolution studies', see Senia Paseta, *Before the Revolution: Nationalism, Social Change and Ireland's Catholic Elite 1879–1922* (Cork, 1999); Patrick Maume, *The Long Gestation: Irish Nationalist Life 1891–1918* (Dublin, 1999).

28. Lord Dufferin to Brinsley Sheridan, 25 Feb. 1881; quoted in Tindley, *Lord Dufferin*, p. 42.

29. Tom Garvin, *Nationalist Revolutionaries in Ireland 1858–1928* (Oxford, 1987); Alvin Jackson, *Ireland 1798–1998: Politics and War* (London, 1988); Paul Bew, *Land and the National Question in Ireland, 1858–82* (Dublin, 1979); Samuel Clark, *Social Origins of the Irish Land War* (Princeton, 1979); James S. Donnelly Jr, *The Land and People of Nineteenth-Century Cork* (London, 1975).

30. Dooley, *Decline of the Big House*, pp. 94–107; Purdue, *The Big House in the North of Ireland*, pp. 31–63.

31. Terence Dooley, 'The Land Question in Ireland, 1870–1923', Tom Bartlett (ed.), *Cambridge History of Ireland, vol. iv, 1880–The Present* (Cambridge, 2018), pp. 117–44.

32. Michael MacDonagh, 'Are the Irish Landlords as Black as They are Painted?', *Fortnightly Review*, 73:438 (June, 1903), p. 1030; Patrick Lavelle, *The Irish Landlord Since the Revolution* (Dublin, 1870), p. 259; Michael Davitt, *The Fall of Feudalism in Ireland* (New York, 1904), p. xvii. See also, Philip Bull, 'Land and Politics, 1879–1903', in D.G. Boyce (ed.), *The Revolution in Ireland, 1879–1923* (Dublin, 1988), p. 27.

33. R.V. Comerford, 'Foreword', Terence Dooley and Christopher Ridgway (eds.) *The Irish Country House: its Past, Present and Future* (Dublin, 2011), p. 11.

34. Bowen, *Bowen's Court*, pp. 25–27.

35. *Connaught Telegraph*, 30 Aug. 1879; see also Louis Paul-Dubois, *Contemporary Ireland* (Dublin, 1908), p. 289.

36. Tom Barry, *Guerilla Days in Ireland* (Dublin, 1991), p. 216.

37. R.V. Comerford, 'The Land War and the Politics of Distress, 1877–82', in W.E. Vaughan (ed.), *A New History of Ireland. Vol 6: Ireland under the Union, pt. 2, 1870–1921* (Oxford, 1996), pp. 26–52; Cannadine, *Decline and Fall of the British Aristocracy*, pp. 63–66; Dooley, *Decline of the Big House*, pp. 79–108; Purdue, *The Big House in the North of Ireland*, pp. 1–12; Tindley, *Dufferin*, p. 29.

38. Cannadine, *Decline and Fall of the British Aristocracy*, p. 169.

39. W.L. Feingold, 'The Tenants' Movement to Capture the Irish Poor Law Boards, 1877–1886', *Albion* vii (1975), pp. 222–24.
40. Quoted in Cannadine's, *The Decline and Fall of the British Aristocracy*, p. 65; Campbell, *The Irish Establishment*, pp. 36–40; Eugenio Biagini, *Liberty, Retrenchment and Reform: Popular Liberalism in the Age of Gladstone, 1860–1880* (Cambridge, 1992), pp. 50–58.
41. Tindley, *Dufferin*, p. 29.
42. Curtis Jr, 'Encumbered Wealth', pp. 332–67; Dooley, *Decline of the Big House*, pp. 79–111; Purdue, *The Big House in the North of Ireland*, pp. 31–63.
43. Shane Leslie, *Doomsland* (London, 1923), pp. 361–62.
44. Dooley, *Dukes of Leinster*, pp. 70–71.
45. J.R. Mahon to G.C. Mahon, 25 Apr. 1887 (NLI, Mahon papers, MS 22,231).
46. Dooley, *Decline of the Big House*, p. 107.
47. *Report of the Royal Commission on the Land Law (Ireland) Act, 1881, and the Purchase of Land (Ireland) Act, 1885* (Earl Cowper, chairman): *Minutes of Evidence and Appendices* [C4969], HC 1887, xxvi, p. 473.
48. Ibid., p. 647.
49. Maura Cronin, *Agrarian Protest in Ireland 1750–1960* (Dundalk, 2012), p. 48.
50. Patrick Cosgrove, 'The Wyndham Land Act 1903: The Final Solution to the Irish Land Question?' (PhD thesis, NUI Maynooth, 2008), pp. 171, 183, 196, 198; Dooley, *Decline of the Big House*, p. 114.
51. Maurice FitzGerald [Kildare] to Evelyn de Vesci, 5 Apr. 1906 (Somerset Record Office, De Vesci papers, DD/DRU/90).
52. Somerville-Large, *The Irish Country House*, p. 352.
53. L.P. Curtis, Jr, 'The Last Gasp of Southern Unionism: Lord Ashtown of Woodlawn', *Éire-Ireland*, 40:3&4 (Fall/Winter, 2005), p. 175; idem., 'Ireland in 1914' in Vaughan (ed.), *A New History of Ireland*, p. 275.
54. Leslie, *The Irish Tangle*, p. 146.
55. Quoted in Somerville-Large, *The Irish Country House*, p. 347.
56. Seymour Leslie, *Of Glaslough in the Kingdom of Oriel* (privately published), p. 34; in the wider context Bielenberg contends that 'the revolution in land ownership partially contributed to the relatively higher and rising levels of emigration among Protestants from the beginning of the twentieth century, more especially after the Wyndham Land Act of 1903, which dramatically accelerated land reform and the departure of the gentry and their Protestant retainers'; A. Bielenberg, 'Exodus: The Emigration of Southern Irish Protestants during the Irish War of Independence and the Civil War', *Past and Present*, no. 218 (2013), p. 204.
57. Quoted in Robert O'Byrne, *The Last Knight: A Tribute to Desmond FitzGerald, 29th Knight of Glin* (Dublin, 2013), pp. 98–99.
58. Cynthia O'Connor, 'The Dispersal of the Country House Collections of Ireland', *Bulletin of the Irish Georgian Society*, vol. xxxv, 1992–93, pp. 38–51.
59. *Return of Untenanted Lands in Rural Districts, Distinguishing Demesnes on Which There is a Mansion, Showing . . .*, HC, 1906, c.177.
60. *The Nationalist*, 3 Oct. 1903.
61. Mario Corrigan, 'Carton House through the Pages of the *Kildare Observer*, 1880–1935', http://www.kildare.ie/library/ehistory/2012/02/carton_house_through_the_pages.asp [15 Mar. 2012].
62. *Kildare Observer*, 7 Mar. 1908.
63. Ibid.
64. *Carlow Sentinel*, 7 Mar. 1908.
65. Quoted in William O'Brien, *An Olive Branch in Ireland and its History* (London, 1910), p. 478.
66. Tony McCarthy, 'From Landlord to Rentier: The Wyndham Land Act 1903 and its Economic Consequences for Irish Landlords 1903–1933' (NUI Maynooth, PhD thesis, 2017), p. 157.
67. Quoted in Cosgrave, 'The Wyndham Land Act', p. 217.
68. Alvin Jackson, *Colonel Edward Saunderson: Land and Loyalty in Victorian Ireland* (Oxford, 1995), p. 208.

69. Vaughan, *Landlords and Tenants*, p. 221.
70. Ibid., pp. 222–23.
71. Earl of Dunraven, *The Crisis in Ireland: Account of the Present Condition of Ireland and Suggestions Toward Reform* (Dublin, 1905), p. 21; also Earl of Dunraven, *The Outlook in Ireland* (Dublin, 1907), pp. 53–54.
72. Horace Plunkett, *Noblesse Oblige: An Irish Rendering* (Dublin, 1908), p. 26.
73. Purdue, *The Big House in the North of Ireland*, pp. 100–01.
74. *Seanad Debates*, vol. 3, 10 July 1924, 793.
75. Vaughan, *Landlords and Tenants*, p. 227.
76. *Royal Commission on Congestion in Ireland*, [Cd 4007], HC 1908, xliii, p. 177.
77. Emmet O'Connor, 'Agrarian Unrest and the Labour Movement in County Waterford 1917–1923', *Saothar*, vi (1980), p. 47.
78. Glascott Symes, *Sir John Keane and Cappoquin House in Time of War and Revolution* (Dublin, 2016).
79. McCarthy, 'From Landlord to Rentier', p. 237
80. See David Seth Jones, *Graziers, Land Reform, and Political Conflict in Ireland* (Washington DC, 1995).
81. Bull, 'Land and Politics, 1879–1903', p. 28.
82. Cronin, *Agrarian Protest in Ireland*, p. 48; for a useful local study, see Patrick Cosgrove, *The Ranch War in Riverstown, Co. Sligo, 1908* (Dublin, 2012).
83. Quoted in Cosgrove, 'The Wyndham Land Act', p. 203.
84. Patrick J. Sammon, *In the Land Commission: A Memoir 1933–1978* (Dublin, 1997), pp. 264–78.
85. Dooley, *Decline of the Big House*, pp. 171–207; idem., 'The Burning of Irish Country Houses During the War of Independence', John Crowley et al. (eds.), *Atlas of the Irish Revolution* (Cork, 2017), pp. 447–53.
86. Ciarán J. Reilly, 'The Burning of Country Houses in Co. Offaly, 1920–23', in Terence Dooley and Christopher Ridgway (eds.), *The Irish Country House: Its Past, Present and Future* (Dublin, 2011), pp. 110–33; James S. Donnelly, Jr, 'Big House Burnings in County Cork During the Irish Revolution, 1920–21', *Éire-Ireland*, 47:3&4 (Fall/Winter 2012), pp. 141–97; Gemma Clark, *Everyday Violence in the Irish Civil War* (Cambridge, 2014); Ann O'Riordan, *East Galway Agrarian Agitation and the Burning of Ballydugan House, 1922* (Dublin, 2015); Glascott Symes, *Sir John Keane and Cappoquin House in Time of War and Revolution* (Dublin, 2016); Jean Young, 'Changing Times: The Big House in County Louth, 1912–1923'; Donal Hall and Martin Maguire (eds.), *County Louth and the Irish Revolution 1912–1923* (Newbridge, 2017), pp. 146–74.
87. Just some examples of books that take different chronological spans: Joost Augusteijn (ed.), *The Irish Revolution, 1913–1923* (London, 2002); Marie Coleman, *County Longford and the Irish Revolution 1910–1923* (Dublin, 2002); Francis Costello, *The Irish Revolution and its Aftermath 1916–1923* (Dublin, 2003); Diarmaid Ferriter, *A Nation and not a Rabble: The Irish Revolution 1913–1923* (London, 2015); Ronan Fanning, *Fatal Path: British Government and Irish Revolution 1910–1922* (London, 2013). The *Irish Revolution* county series edited by Mary Ann Lyons and Dáithí Ó Corráin uses 1912–23. David Fitzpatrick used 1913–1921 in his seminal *Politics and Irish Life: Provincial Experience of War and Revolution 1913–1921* (Dublin, 1977), while Peter Hart used 1916–23 in his *The IRA and Its Enemies: Violence and Community in Cork 1916–1923* (Oxford, 1998).
88. Fitzpatrick, *Politics and Irish Life*, p. 66.
89. Ibid., p. 253.
90. Ibid., pp. 61, 62.
91. Peter Hart, 'Defining the Irish Revolution', in Joost Augusteijn (ed.), *The Irish Revolution 1913–1923* (Basingstoke, 2002), p. 27.
92. https://www.independent.ie/irish-news/top-irish-economist-patrick-lynch-dies-26251868.html; Lawrence William White, 'Lynch, Patrick (Paddy)', *Dictionary of Irish Biography* (ed.) James McGuire, James Quinn (Cambridge, 2009) (http://dib.cambridge.org/viewRead-Page.do?articleId=a4954).

93. Patrick Lynch, 'The Revolution That Never Was', in T. Desmond Williams (ed.), *The Irish Struggle 1916–1926* (London, 1966), p. 41.
94. Ibid.
95. Bill Kissane, *Explaining Irish Democracy* (Dublin, 2002), p. 77; Tony Varley, 'On the Road to Extinction: Agrarian Parties in Twentieth-Century Ireland', *Irish Political Studies*, 25:4 (2010), pp. 581–601.
96. Fergus Campbell, 'The Last Land War? Kevin O Shiel's Memoir of the Irish Revolution (1916–21)', *Archivium Hibernicum*, vol. 57 (2003), pp. 155–200, quotation on p. 170; see also Eda Sagarra, *Kevin O'Shiel: Tyrone Nationalist and Irish State-Builder* (Sallins, 2013).
97. *Irish Times*, 22 Nov. 1966.
98. L.P. Edwards, 'Review, Brian O'Neill, *The War for the Land in Ireland* (London, 1933)', in *American Journal of Sociology*, vol. 40, no. 3 (1934), pp. 397–98.
99. Fearghal McGarry, 'O'Donnell, Peadar', in James McGuire and James Quinn (eds), *Dictionary of Irish Biography* (Cambridge, 2012). (http://dib.cambridge.org/viewRead Page.do?articleId=a6700) (28 Mar. 2020).
100. On Ireland and the 'red scare', see Enda Delaney, 'Anti-Communism in Mid-Twentieth-Century Ireland', *The English History Review*, vol. 126, no. 521 (Aug. 2011), pp. 878–903; on Gralton's deportation, see Ferriter, *A Nation and Not a Rabble*, p. 231.
101. Peadar O'Donnell, 'Introduction', in O'Neill, *The War for the Land in Ireland*, pp. 14–15; see chapter 9 for more on this.
102. David Gahan, 'The Land Annuities Agitation in Ireland 1926–32' (NUI Maynooth, PhD thesis, 2017).
103. Charles Townshend, *Political Violence in Ireland: Government and Resistance since 1848* (Oxford, 1983), , p. 339.
104. Paul Bew, 'Sinn Féin, Agrarian Radicalism, and the War of Independence 1919–21', in D.G. Boyce (ed.), *The Revolution in Ireland* (London, 1988), p. 220.
105. Ibid., p. 223.
106. Campbell, *Land and Revolution*, p. 303.
107. Ibid., p. 304.
108. Ibid.
109. https://languages.oup.com/google-dictionary-en/; Terence Dooley, 'Land and Politics in Independent Ireland, 1923–48: The Case for Reappraisal', *Irish Historical Studies*, vol. 34, no. 134 (Nov. 2004), pp. 175–77.
110. Fergus Campbell, 'Author's Response' to Patrick Cosgrove, 'Reviews in History: Fergus Campbell, *Land and Revolution: Nationalist Politics in the West of Ireland 1891–1921* (Oxford, 2005) at https://reviews.history.ac.uk/review/734.
111. O'Riordan, *East Galway Agrarian Agitation* ; see also chapter 5.
112. Patrick Cosgrove went on to complete a thesis entitled 'The Wyndham Land Act 1903: The Final Solution to the Irish Land Question?' (PhD thesis, NUI Maynooth, 2008). See also Terence Dooley and Tony McCarthy, 'The 1923 Land Act: Some New Perspectives', in Mel Farrell et al. (eds.), *A Formative Decade: Ireland in the 1920s* (Sallins, 2015), pp. 132–56.
113. Bew, 'Sinn Féin and Agrarian Radicalism', p. 222.
114. [George O'Callaghan Westropp] *Notes on the Defence of Irish Country Houses* (1912), p. 1. I would like to express my gratitude to Brian Fitzelle for making a copy in his possession available to me.
115. Ibid.
116. Ibid.

2 'The Un-Martialled Loyalists of the South': The Great War, Part I

1. Tindley, *Lord Dufferin*, p. 167.
2. See Patrick Buckland, *Irish Unionism I: The Anglo-Irish and the New Ireland 1885–1922* (Dublin, 1972).

3. Irish Unionist Alliance, *Great Demonstration in Dublin* (Dublin, 1911), p. 2.
4. Earl of Midleton, *Records and Reactions, 1856–1939* (New York, 1939), pp. 226–27.
5. Patrick J. Buckland, 'The Southern Irish Unionists, the Irish Question, and British Politics 1906–14', *Irish Historical Studies*, vol. 15, no. 59 (Mar. 1967), pp. 228–55.
6. Purdue, *The Big House in the North of Ireland*, p. 179.
7. Ibid.
8. Quoted in A.T.Q. Stewart, *The Ulster Crisis* (London, 1967), p. 72.
9. Leslie, *The Irish Tangle*, pp. 24–25.
10. *Belfast Newsletter*, 22 Sept. 1913.
11. Raymond Gillespie, *The Borderlands: Essays on the History of the Ulster–Leinster Border* (Belfast, 1989).
12. Ibid., 6 July 1912.
13. Inspector General Confidential Monthly Report [IGCMR], June 1914 (Britain in Ireland series, TNA, CO 904).
14. Gerald Madden to Jack Madden, 25 June 1915 (PRONI, Madden papers, D3465/J/37/48).
15. Donal Hall, 'The Bellingham Family of Castlebellingham, Co. Louth, 1914–24', in Dooley and Ridgway, *The Country House and the Great War*, p. 100.
16. *Irish Independent*, 17 June 1914; quoted in ibid., p. 100.
17. *Dundalk Democrat*, 30 June 1914.
18. County Inspector Confidential Monthly Report [CICMR], Cavan, Mar. 1912 (TNA, CO 904).
19. CICMR, Cavan, June 1913.
20. Ibid., Mar. 1914.
21. CICMR, Donegal, Mar. 1914.
22. CICMR, Monaghan, Jan. 1914.
23. IGCMR, June 1914.
24. CICMR Monaghan, May 1914.
25. *Dundalk Democrat*, 2 May 1914.
26. Ibid.
27. Ibid., 18 July 1914.
28. CICMR, Monaghan, June 1914.
29. *Belfast Newsletter*, 16 Apr. 1914.
30. CICMR, Donegal, June 1914.
31. Ibid.
32. Buckland, 'The Southern Irish Unionists', p. 234.
33. Quoted in Butler, John, 'Lord Oranmore's Journal', *Irish Historical Studies*, vol. 29, no. 116 (November 1995), pp 553-59.
34. Ibid.
35. W.J. Reader, *At Duty's Call: A Study in Obsolete Patriotism* (Manchester, 1988), p. 104.
36. Plunkett, Elizabeth, Countess of Fingall, *Seventy Years Young: Memories of Elizabeth, Countess of Fingall* (London, 1937),p. 358.
37. For a fuller description of the castle and its history see chapter 6; also R.D. King-Harman, *The Kings, Earls of Kingston: An Account of the Family and Their Estates in Ireland between the Reigns of the Two Queen Elizabeths* (Cambridge, 1959); Bill Power, *White Knights, Dark Earls: The Rise and Fall of an Anglo-Irish Dynasty* (Cork, 2000).
38. Daily columns of the *Irish Times* May–August 1914 act as a guide.
39. Bowen, *Bowen's Court,* pp. 435–36.
40. Ian d'Alton, 'Lay Spring Flowers on Our Boy's Grave': Norman Leslie's Short War', Dooley and Ridgway, *The Country House and the Great War*, p. 83.
41. Ian d'Alton, 'Loyal to What? Identity and Motivation in the Southern Irish Protestant Involvement in Two World Wars', Brian Hughes and Conor Morrissey (eds.), *Southern Irish Loyalism 1912–1949* (Liverpool, 2020), p. 120.
42. Nicholas Perry, 'The Irish Landed Class and the British Army, 1850–1950', *War in History*, 18:3, 2011, p. 307; P.E. Razzell, 'Social Origins of Officers in the Indian and British Home Army', *British Journal of Sociology*, xiv (1963), pp. 248–60.

43. Perry, 'The Irish Landed Class and the British Army' p. 317; his eldest son was the future Major General Hugh Montgomery (1870–1955), whose younger brother was later Field Marshal Sir Archibald Montgomery-Massingberd (1871–1947).
44. Gerald Gliddon, *The Aristocracy and the Great War* (Norwich, 2002), p. xix.
45. Hubert Gough, *Soldiering On* (London, 1954), p. 1.
46. Desmond FitzGerald open letter, 17 Nov. 1914 (private possession).
47. Irish Unionist Alliance, *Irish Southern Loyalists, the War and After* (Dublin, 1918), p. 1.
48. https://api.parliament.uk/historic-hansard/commons/1914/aug/03/statement-by-sir-edward-grey#S5CV0065P0_19140803_HOC_71
49. https://www.rte.ie/centuryireland/index.php/articles/redmond-urges-irish-volunteers-to-join-the-british-army
50. Paul Bew, 'Redmond, John Edward (1856–1918)', *ODNB* https://doi.org/10.1093/ref:odnb/35702
51. Quoted in *Irish Times*, 8 Aug. 1914.
52. Ibid., 12 Aug. 1914.
53. Ibid., 7 Aug. 1914.
54. Ibid., 7, 10 Aug. 1914.
55. Ibid., 10 Aug. 1914.
56. Ibid., 16 Aug. 1914.
57. Ibid., 7 Aug. 1914.
58. G. Taafe to Editor, 6 Aug. 1914; *Irish Times*, 7 Aug. 1914.
59. W.H. Mahon to Editor; *Irish Times*, 15 Aug. 1914.
60. Lady Inchiquin to Baron Inchiquin, 19 Sept. 1914 (NLI, Inchiquin papers, MS 45,504/8).
61. Alvin Jackson, *Home Rule: An Irish History* (London, 2003), p. 146; Thomas P. Dooley, *Irishmen or English Soldiers?* (Liverpool, 1995), pp. 191–92.
62. Jackson, *Home Rule*, p. 146.
63. Quoted in Keith Jeffery, *Ireland and the Great War* (Cambridge, 2000), p. 56.
64. *Irish Times*, 4 Aug. 1914.
65. Lord Erne's manifesto to the Orangemen of Ireland, 9 Sept. 1914; quoted in *Irish Times*, 19 Sept. 1914.
66. *Irish Times*, 19 Sept. 1914.
67. On Co Clare, see Fitzpatrick, *Politics and Irish Life*, pp. 53–55.
68. Patrick Buckland, *Irish Unionism I*, p. 30; Dooley, *The Decline of the Big House*, p. 112; d'Alton, 'Norman Leslie's Short War', p. 77.
69. Peter Martin, '*Dulce et Decorum*': Irish Nobles and the Great War, 1914–19', in Adrian Gregory and Senia Paseta, *Ireland and the Great War: 'A War to Unite us All?'* (Manchester, 2002), p. 30; see also Mark Amory, *A Biography of Lord Dunsany* (London, 1972), p. 26.
70. Arthur Maxwell, Baron Farnham, to Aileen, 31 Dec. 1916 (NLI, Farnham papers, MS 18,616).
71. T.R. Henn, *Five Arches: A Sketch for an Autobiography* (Gerrard's Cross, 1980), p. 64.
72. *Irish Times*, 26 Aug. 1914; see Jean Young, 'Changing Times: The Big House in County Louth, 1912–1923', in Hall and Maguire (eds.), *County Louth and the Irish Revolution*, pp. 146–74.
73. A point with which Ian d'Alton agrees; d'Alton, 'Loyal to What', p. 117.
74. Ibid., p. 118.
75. Quoted in Shane Leslie memoirs (NLI, Leslie papers, MS 22,885).
76. d'Alton, 'Loyal to what?', p. 123.
77. Norman Leslie to John Leslie, [?] Aug. 1914 (private possession).
78. Charles Monck to J.E. McDermott, 8 Oct. 1914 (NLI, Monck papers, MS 28,867).
79. Ibid.
80. J.E. McDermott to Charles Monck, 19 Oct. 1914; ibid.
81. Patrick Buckland, *Irish Unionism I*, p. 32.
82. Fragment of Norman Leslie's diary, 9–17 October 1914 (private possession).
83. Sir John Keane to Eleanor, Apr.1915 (private possession).
84. RG [Dick] Hely-Hutchinson to his mother, 3 Oct. 1914 (Fingal County Archives, 1/6/8).

85. RG [Dick] Hely-Hutchinson to Cissy, 6 Oct. 1914 (Fingal County Archives, 1/6/2).

86. See Kevin Myers' essay on Robert Gregory of Coole Park in Kevin Myers, *Ireland's Great War* (Dublin, 2016), p. 195.

87. Dick Hely-Hutchinson to his father, 11 Dec. 1914 (Fingal County Archives, 1/6/13).

88. Dick Hely-Hutchinson to his parents, 7 Mar. 1915 (Fingal County Archives, 1/6/14).

89. Ibid.; see also Colm McQuinn, 'The Hely-Hutchinson Brothers of Seafield and the Great War: Two Sons, One Inheritance', in Dooley and Ridgway, *The Country House and the Great War*, pp. 147–57.

90. Sir John Keane to Eleanor, Mar. 1915 (private possession).

91. Dick Hely-Hutchinson to Cissy, 9 Mar. 1915 (Fingal County Archives, 1/6/3).

92. Ibid., 8 Aug. 1916 (Fingal County Archives, 1/6/5).

93. *Harper's Journal*, 21 Nov. 1914, p. 484.

94. Ibid.

95. Quoted in Symes, *Sir John Keane*, p. 26.

96. Dick Hely-Hutchinson to Cissy, 30 Mar. 1915 (Fingal County Archives, 1/6/4).

97. Open letter written by Desmond FitzGerald, 17 Nov. 1914 (private possession).

98. Edward, Prince of Wales, to Lady Cynthia Graham, 3 Mar. 1916 (private possession).

99. Capt Edward Woulfe Flanagan to Johnny Woulfe Flanagan, 11 Sept. 1914 (private possession).

100. Ibid., 2 Aug. 1916 (private possession).

101. Ibid.

102. Ibid.

103. Quoted in Martin, '*Dulce et Decorum*', pp. 42–43.

104. Lord Castletown, *Ego* (London, 1923), p. 222.

105. Ibid.

106. *Irish Times*, 1 Dec. 1914; Niamh Gallagher, *Ireland and the Great War: A Social and Political History* (London and New York, 2020), p. 31; Eileen Reilly, 'Women and Voluntary War Work' in Gregory and Paseta (eds.), *Ireland and the Great War*, pp. 49–72; Catriona Clear, 'Fewer Ladies: More Omen', in John Horne (ed.), *Our War: Ireland and the Great War* (Dublin, 2008), pp. 157–80; Buckland, *Irish Unionism I*, pp. 29–35.

107. Donal Hall, 'The Bellingham Family of Castlebellingham, Co Louth, 1914–24' in Dooley and Ridgway (eds.), *The Country House and the Great War*, pp. 100–12.

108. T.S. Henry Prittie, 6th Baron Dunalley, 'History of the Prittie family in Ireland 1649–1981' (unpublished, private possession), p. 21.

109. Castletown, *Ego*, p. 221.

110. Circular from Marquess of Sligo, 15 June 1916 (NLI, Clonbrock papers, MS 35,776).

111. Maeve O'Riordan, *Women of the Country House in Ireland* (Liverpool, 2018); Fionnuala Walsh, *Irish Women and the Great War* (Cambridge, 2020), pp. 22–24.

112. Reilly, 'Women and Voluntary War Work', pp. 50–51; Jessica Gerard, *Country House Life: Family and Servants, 1815–1914* (Oxford, 1994), pp. 63–64.

113. *Freeman's Journal*, 21 Oct. 1915; *Kildare Observer*, 13 Feb. 1915.

114. *The Times*, 23 Feb. 1932.

115. 'List of articles sent by Co Galway, 14 Aug.–18 Nov. 1918' (NLI, Clonbrock papers, MS 35,797 (5)).

116. 'Some War Work in County Galway, 1914–1919' (NLI, Clonbrock papers, MS 35,796 (6)); see also *Irish Times*, 3 Dec. 1914; Fionnuala Walsh, ' "The Future Welfare of the Empire Will Depend More Largely on our Women and Girls": Southern Loyalist Women and the British War Effort in Ireland, 1914–1922', in Brian Hughes and Conor Morrissey, *Southern Irish Loyalism, 1912–1949* (Liverpool, 2020), pp. 141–44.

117. Martin, '*Dulce et Decorum*', p. 34.

118. Quoted in ibid., p. 35.

119. Brett Irwin, 'Lady Londonderry and the Great War: Women, Work and the Western Front' in Dooley and Ridgway, *The Country House and the Great War*, p. 139.

120. Ibid., p. 138.

121. *Kildare Observer*, 3 Mar. 1916.

122. *Irish Times*, 23 Nov. 1914.
123. Ibid., 20 Nov. 1914.
124. Ronan Foley, 'Augusta Bellingham and the Mount Stuart Hospital: Temporary Therapeutic Transformations', Dooley and Ridgway (eds.), *The Country House and the Great War*, pp. 87–99.
125. Ibid., p. 90; see also Edward Bujak, *English Landed Society in the Great War: Defending the Realm* (London, 2019).
126. *Irish Times*, 5 Dec. 1914.
127. R.S. Churchill, *Lord Derby, 'King of Lancashire'* (London, 1959), p. 184.
128. Quoted in Pamela Horn, *Country House Society: The Private Lives of England's Upper Class after the First World War* (Stroud, 2015), p. 18.
129. *Irish Times*, 30 Aug. 1914.
130. Ibid., 4 Sept. 1914.
131. Ibid., 5 Sept. 1914.
132. Martin, '*Dulce et Decorum*', p. 33.
133. Mark Bence-Jones, *Twilight of the Ascendancy* (London, 1987), p. 166.
134. Frank O'Connor, Co Westmeath (BMH, WS 1,309), p. 21.
135. Quoted in Martin, '*Dulce et Decorum*', p. 34.
136. J. Ormsby Lawder, Leitrim (TNA, CO 762/13/12).
137. Quoted in Patrick Buckland, *Irish Unionism 1885–1923: A Documentary History* (Belfast, 1973), p. 55.
138. Fitzpatrick, 'Ireland and the Great War', p. 231; for a discussion on the problems of recruitment figures, see d'Alton, 'Loyal to What?', pp. 118–19; Gallagher, *Ireland and the Great War*, p. 143.
139. Quoted in Martin, '*Dulce et Decorum*', p. 33.
140. See chapter 3.
141. *Return Showing to the Latest Year Available, for Ireland as a Whole, the Annual Average Prices for Each Year from 1881 . . .* HC 1921, xli. 93.
142. Ibid.
143. Ibid.
144. *Agricultural Statistics for Ireland with Detailed Report for the Year 1917* [Cmd 1316], HC 1921, lxi.135, p. xiii.
145. Kevin O'Shiel (BMH, WS 1770), p. 942; for his biography see, Eda Sagarra, *Kevin O'Shiel: Tyrone Nationalist and Irish State-Builder* (Sallins, 2013).
146. Martin, '*Dulce et Decorum*', p. 31.
147. CICMR, Donegal, Nov. 1914, Mar. 1915.
148. [Newspaper clipping] William Hutcheson Poe to the editor of [?], 19 Aug 1914, (NLI, Clonbrock papers, MS 35,782 (10)).
149. Alvin Jackson, 'Carson', *ODNB*.
150. Michael Laffan, 'Redmond', *DIB*.
151. Quoted in William Redmond, *Trench Pictures from France* (Belfast, 2007), p. 44.
152. See, however, Buckland, *Irish Unionism I*, pp. 51–82.
153. Butler, 'Lord Oranmore's Journal', pp. 564–65.
154. Letitia Overend to Minnie Overend, 30 Apr. 1916 (OMARC, Airfield papers, PP/AIR/261).
155. 'Diary of Rebellion, May 1916', Charles Hamilton (NLI, Hamilton papers, MS 49,155 (41)).
156. War Diary of Captain Anketell Moutray, 28 Mar. 1916–24 Dec. 1918 (PRONI, Moutray papers, D2023/7/2/30).
157. Rev Richard Butler to 15th Viscount Gormanston, 2 July 1916 (NLI, Gormanston papers, MS 44,425/8).
158. Letter from Jenico Preston, 15th Viscount to Ismay Crichton-Stuart, 8 May 1916 ((NLI, Gormanston papers, MS 44,426/7–8).
159. Letter from William Upton Tyrell to Elizabeth Tyrell, 30 April 1916 (OMARC, Ballindoolin papers).

160. Hall, 'The Bellingham Family of Castlebellingham', p. 106.
161. Diary of Vera Bellingham (private possession).
162. Ibid.
163. Sir John Leslie to Shane Leslie, 27 Oct. 1916 (PRONI, Leslie papers, MIC 606/3).
164. Letter from Jenico Preston, 15th Viscount, to Eileen Butler [his future wife], May 1916 (NLI, Gormanston papers, MS 44,427); a similar report on Markievicz's surrender appeared in *Irish Times*, 2 May 1916.
165. Peter Martin, 'Unionism: The Irish Nobility and Revolution, 1919–23', in Joost Augusteijn (ed.), *The Irish Revolution, 1913–1923* (London, 2002), p. 154.
166. Ibid., pp. 154–55.
167. Bence-Jones, *Twilight*, pp. 188, 193.
168. Carla King, 'Barton, Robert Childers (1881–1975)', *ODNB*, https://doi.org/10.1093/ref:odnb/52523
169. Memoir of Frederick Beaumont-Nesbitt of Tubberdaly, King's County (copy in author's possession).

3 'All the Gentry Have Suffered': The Great War, Part II

1. Patrick Maume, 'Cooper, Bryan Ricco', *DIB* https://dib.cambridge.org/viewFullScreen.do?filename=a2014
2. *Burke's Landed Gentry of Ireland* (London, 1958), p. xviii; see also idem., *Twilight of the Ascendancy* (London, 1987), p. 187; for a similar conclusion, see Somerville-Large, *The Irish Country House* (London, 1995), p. 252.
3. Edward Bujak, *English Landed Society in the Great War: Defending the Realm* (London, 2019), p. 26.
4. I am very grateful to Dr Fidelma Byrne and other researchers who worked on compiling these statistics; see also d'Alton, 'Loyal to what?', p. 122; Perry, 'Irish Landed Class', p. 328. In an earlier case study by this author of 100 landed families, 79 were represented in the army or navy by a father, son, grandson or son-in-law during the war and just under 25 per cent were killed; Dooley, *Decline of the Big House*, pp. 122–27.
5. Martin, '*Dulce et Decorum*', p. 40.
6. Cannadine, *Decline and Fall of the British Aristocracy*, p. 83.
7. Desmond FitzGerald to Aunt Dolly, 16 Nov. 1914 (private possession).
8. Gliddon, *The Aristocracy and the Great War*, p. 461.
9. Ibid., p. xvii.
10. Purdue, *The Big House in the North of Ireland*, p. 218.
11. Their story is told in Fidelma Byrne, '"Not Another Son": The Impact of the Great War on Two Irish Families', in Dooley and Ridgway, *The Country House and the Great War*, pp. 53–61.
12. Duc de Stacpoole, *Irish and Other Memories* (London, 1922), p. 192.
13. Quoted in Lennox Robinson, *Bryan Cooper* (London, 1931), p. 80; statistics taken from d'Alton, 'Loyal to What?', p. 121.
14. Lt Col W.A. Robinson to Lady Ashtown [c.16 Nov. 1916], quoted in 'Lieutenant The Rt. Hon. Frederick Sydney Trench (1894–1916)' (MS copy kindly provided to me by Roderick Trench, Lord Ashtown).
15. Quoted in ibid.
16. See Joanna Bourke, 'Shell-Shock, Psychiatry and the Irish Soldier during the First World War', in Gregory and Paseta, *Ireland and the Great War*, pp. 156–68.
17. Quoted in Byrne, '"Not Another Son"', p. 60.
18. Lady Cynthia Asquith, Diaries, 1915-18 (London, 1968) p. 92; Anita Leslie, *Edwardians in Love* (London, 1972), p. 265.
19. Quoted in Leslie, *Edwardians in Love*, p. 264.
20. Quoted in ibid., p. 271.
21. Fingall, *Seventy Years Young*, p. 386.
22. Quoted in d'Alton, 'Norman Leslie's Short War', p. 86.

23. Anita Leslie, *The Gilt and the Gingerbread: An Autobiography* (London, 1931), p. 11.
24. On this aspect of the American Civil War, see Drew Gilpin, *This Republic of Suffering: Death and the American Civil War* (New York, 2008).
25. Ann Morrow, *Picnic in a Foreign Land: The Eccentric Lives of the Anglo-Irish* (London, 1989), p. 19.
26. Quoted in Richard Davenport-Hines, *Ettie: The Intimate Life and Dauntless Spirit of Lady Desborough* (London, 2008), p. 232.
27. Jane Leonard, 'Getting Them at Last: The IRA and Ex-Servicemen', in David Fitzpatrick (ed.), *Revolution? Ireland 1917–23* (Dublin, 1990), pp. 118–29; Hart, *The IRA and its Enemies*, pp. 293–315; for alternative views see Hall, 'The Bellingham family of Castlebellingham', pp. 104–05; Paul Taylor, *Heroes or Traitors: Experiences of Southern Irish Soldiers Returning from the Great War, 1919–39* (Liverpool, 2015).
28. His youngest brother was killed in 1918 and another lost a leg: https://www.greatwarforum.org/topic/219664-lieutenant-sir-richard-william-levinge-10th-bart-1st-life-guards/
29. Bence-Jones, *Twilight of the Ascendancy*, p. 168.
30. Dunne, 'Westmeath Aristocracy', p. 267.
31. Ibid., pp. 332–33.
32. *Irish Times*, 15 Aug. 1923.
33. Minutes of Kildare County Council, 29 May 1916; quoted in Thomas Nelson, 'Lord Frederick FitzGerald, 1857–1924' in Cosgrove et al. (eds.), *Aspects of Irish Aristocratic Life*, pp. 206–07.
34. Joseph Doran to Lord Frederick FitzGerald, n.d. [May 2016] (private possession).
35. Hall, 'The Bellingham family of Castlebellingham', pp. 104–05.
36. Ibid., p. 109.
37. Gallagher, *Ireland and the Great War*, pp. 177–83.
38. Quoted in Fergal Browne, 'The Death of the Pallastown Heir: Lt Robert Heard, Pallastown Guards', in Dooley and Ridgway (eds.) *The Country House and the Great War*, p. 22.
39. Ibid., p. 24.
40. Ibid., p. 27.
41. Ibid., p. 28.
42. *New York Times*, 12 Oct. 1913.
43. Cannadine, *Decline and Fall of the British Aristocracy*, p. 48.
44. Ibid., p. 97; Purdue, *The Big House in the North of Ireland*, p. 111.
45. Byrne, '"Not Another Son"', p. 57.
46. For the similar case of the Dufferins in Ulster, see Purdue, *The Big House in the North of Ireland*, p. 218.
47. Dooley, *Decline of the Big House*, p. 125; see also Emer Crooke, *'White Elephants': The Country House and the State in Independent Ireland, 1922–73* (Dublin, 2018).
48. Seymour Leslie, *The Jerome Connexion* (London, 1964), p. 49.
49. Ibid.
50. Ibid., p. 58.
51. Leslie, *The Gilt and the Gingerbread*, p. 11.
52. Buckland, *Irish Unionism I*, p. 35; C.F.G. Masterman, *England after War: A Study* (London, 1922), pp. 27–32.
53. Quoted in IUA, *Irish Southern Loyalists, the War and After* (1918), p. 1.
54. Fitzpatrick, *Politics and Irish Life*, p. 55.
55. IUA, *Irish Southern Loyalists*, pp, 1–2.
56. Quoted in Buckland, *Irish Unionism I*, p. 36.
57. Ibid.
58. Ibid., pp. 83ff; Alvin Jackson, *Home Rule: An Irish History 1800–2000* (London, 2003).
59. Sir Henry Bellingham to Shane Leslie, n.d. (NLI, Leslie papers, MS 22,852).
60. *Northern Standard*, 17 June 1916.
61. *Ulster Unionist Yearbook, 1917* (PRONI, D972/17).
62. 'Report of Major Saunderson', n.d. (PRONI, J.M. Wilson papers, D989/A/8/7/1).
63. Journal entry, 30 July 1916; Butler, 'Lord Oranmore's Journal', p. 568.

64. On the conference, see Buckland, *Irish Unionism I*, pp. 83–128.
65. Journal entry, 21 July 1917 in Butler, 'Lord Oranmore's Journal', p. 570.
66. Ibid., 20 Apr. 1918, p. 575.
67. Lord Midleton to Lord Courtown, 18 July 1918 (NLI, Midleton papers, MS 49,708/2).
68. Quoted in *Northern Standard*, 13 Mar. 1920.
69. *Anglo-Celt*, 17 Apr. 1920.
70. Quoted in Cherry, 'Adaptive coexistence', p. 300.
71. Quoted in ibid.
72. Lord Farnham to Hugh Montgomery, 13 Apr. 1920; quoted in Buckland, *Documentary History*, p. 419.
73. Saunderson, *The Saundersons*, p. 73.
74. Quoted in Cherry, 'Adaptive Coexistence', pp. 301–02.
75. Young, 'The Big House in County Louth', p. 152.
76. Diary of Vera Bellingham, Dunany House, Co Louth, 1916–19 (in private possession). My thanks to Jean Young for this reference.
77. Quoted in Fitzpatrick, *Politics and Irish Life*, p. 55.
78. http://www.turtlebunbury.com/history/history_family/hist_family_clements.html
79. J.M. Winter, 'Britain's "Lost Generation" of the First World War', *Population Studies*, vol. 31, no. 3 (Nov. 1977), p. 465.
80. Earl of Dunraven [Windham Thomas Wyndham-Quin], *Past Times and Pastimes* (London, 1922), vol. 1. pp. 196, 198.
81. Butler, 'Lord Oranmore's Journal', p. 582.
82. Bowen, 'The Big House', p. 29.
83. Dick Hely-Hutchinson to his mother, 2 Dec. 1914 (Fingal County Archives, 1/6/9).
84. J.B. Drought, *A Sportsman Looks at Éire* (London, n.d. [1949]), p. 10.
85. Quoted in Fitzpatrick, *Politics and Irish Life*, p. 79.
86. Lord Castletown, *Ego: Random Records of Sport, Service and Travel in Many Lands* (London, 1923), pp. 67–68.
87. Ibid., p. 68.
88. Fingall, *Seventy Years Young*, p. 169.
89. Dooley, *Decline of the Big House*, pp. 262–63; for the experience of the Earl of Fingall, see Fingall, *Seventy Years Young*, pp. 117, 186.
90. Quoted in Bujak, *English Landed Society in the Great War*, p. 83.
91. L.P. Curtis found that in 1881 practically every hunt in Ireland had been disrupted at some stage; L.P. Curtis Jr, 'Stopping the Hunt: An Aspect of the Irish Land War', in C.H.E. Philpin (ed.), *Nationalism and Popular Protest in Ireland* (Cambridge, 1987), pp. 349–402.
92. CICMR, Co Kildare, Jan. 1919.
93. William Murphy, 'Sport in a Time of Revolution: Sinn Féin and the Hunt in Ireland', *Éire-Ireland*, 48: 1–2 (2013), p. 113.
94. Ibid., pp. 120–21; *Irish Field*, 8 Mar. 1919.
95. IGCMR, Jan. 1919.
96. Buckland, *Irish Unionism I*, p. 203.
97. Quoted in Murphy, 'Sport in a Time of Revolution', p. 132.
98. P. Brady to *Meath Chronicle*, 15 Feb. 1919, in ibid.
99. *Tuam Herald*, 8 Feb. 1918.
100. *Leinster Leader*, 1 Mar. 1919.
101. Harris was probably referring to the notorious Clongorey evictions of 1883–92; *Leinster Leader*, 1 Mar. 1919; M.B. Ryan, 'The Clongorey Evictions' (MA thesis, NUI Maynooth, 1999).
102. Fergus D'Arcy, *Horses, Lords and Racing Men: The Kildare Turf Club 1790–1990* (Kildare, 1991); Dooley, *Decline of the Big House*, pp. 264–67; in relation to Kildare, see *Leinster Leader*, 17 June 1922.
103. M.A.G. Ó Tuathaigh, 'The Land Question, Politics and Irish Society, 1922–1960', in P.J. Drudy (ed.), *Ireland: Land, Politics and People* (Cambridge, 1982), pp. 167–89; Paul

Bew, 'Sinn Féin, Agrarian Radicalism and the War of Independence 1919–1921', in D.G. Boyce (ed.), *The Revolution in Ireland, 1879–1923* (Basingstoke, 1988), pp. 217–34.

104. *Report of the Proceedings of the Irish Convention* [Cmd 9019], HC 1918, x, 697.
105. See chapter 5.
106. IGCMR, Jan. 1918.
107. *Report of the Estates Commissioners for the Year from 1 April 1919 to 31 March 1920 and for the Period from 1 November 1903 to 31 March 1920*, Cmd 1150, HC 1921, xiv.661, p. ix.
108. Ibid., p. xiv.
109. Labhras MacFhionnghail [Laurence Ginnell], *The Land Question* (Dublin, n.d. [1917]), p. 4.
110. For an excellent case study see Leigh Ann Coffey, *The Planters of Luggacurran: The Experiences of a Protestant Community in Queen's County, 1879–1927* (Dublin, 2006).
111. *Agricultural Statistics for Ireland with Detailed Report for the Year 1917* [Cmd 1316], HC 1921, lxi.135, p. 14.
112. F.S.L. Lyons, *Ireland Since the Famine* (London, 1971), p. 603.
113. Ibid., p. 519.
114. *Twenty-Seventh Report of the Congested District Board for Ireland for the Period from 1 Apr. 1918 to 31 Mar. 1919*, Cmd 759, HC 1920, pp. 19–20.
115. IGCMR, Sept. 1916.
116. Dáil Éireann, 'A Brief Survey of the Work Done by the Agricultural Department from April 1919 to August 1921', p. 9.
117. Ibid., p. 196; Enda McKay, 'The Housing of the Rural Labourer, 1883–1916', *Saothar*, vol. 17 (1992), pp. 27–38; also D.G. Bradley, *Farm Labourers: Irish Struggle, 1900–1976* (Belfast, 1988).
118. *St Stephen's Review*, 31 July 1886.
119. Quoted in Cosgrave, 'The Wyndham Land Act', p. 230.
120. IGCMR, Mar. 1916.
121. Ibid., July 1916.
122. CICMR, Co Donegal, Sept. 1918.
123. Butler, 'Lord Oranmore's Journal', p. 578.
124. CICMR, Cavan, Mar. 1919.
125. W.H. Mahon of Castlegar Diary, 1922 (NLI, Mahon papers, MS 19,991).
126. Ibid., 16 Apr. 1920.
127. Pauric J. Dempsey, Shaun Boylan, 'Ginnell, Laurence', in James McGuire and James Quinn (ed), *DIB* (Cambridge, 2009). (http://dib.cambridge.org/viewReadPage.do?articleId=a3488) [Accessed 25 May 2021].
128. MacFhionnghail, *The Land Question*, pp. 4–5.
129. Ibid., p. 15.
130. Ibid., p. 7.
131. IGCMR, Feb. 1918.
132. Ibid.
133. Thomas Lavin, BMH witness statement, WS 1001, pp. 2–3.
134. P.J. McElligott, BMH witness statement, WS 1013, p. 6.
135. Andrew O'Donohoe, BMH witness statement, WS 1326, pp. 13–14.
136. IGCMR, Nov. 1918.
137. CICMR, Galway East Riding, Feb. 1918.
138. *Irish Times*, 4 June 1918.
139. Ibid.
140. *Irish Land (Provision for Soldiers and Sailors) Act* 1919 [9 & 10 Geo. V, ch. 82] (23 Dec. 1919); for a more complete study see Edward Tynan, 'War Veterans, Land Distribution and Revolution in Ireland, 1919–23' (PhD thesis, NUI Maynooth, 2012).
141. Peter Hart, *The IRA and Its Enemies*, pp. 171–73.
142. Terence Dooley, *'The Land for the People': The Land Question in Independent Ireland* (Dublin, 2004), pp. 35–37.
143. Barry, *Guerilla Days in Ireland*, p. 117; L.P. Curtis, Jr, 'The Last Gasp of Southern Unionism: Lord Ashtown of Woodlawn', *Éire-Ireland*, 40: 3&4 (Fall/Winter, 2005), p. 180.

144. Quoted in Michael Hopkinson, *Green Against Green: The Irish Civil War* (Dublin, 1988, p. 45.

145. Joseph Barratt, BMH, WS 1324, p. 2.

146. Ernie O'Malley, *On Another Man's Wound* (Dublin, 1979 edn [1st edn London, 1936]), p. 85.

147. Ibid. p. 96.

148. Townshend, *Political Violence in Ireland*, p. 339; Bew, 'Sinn Féin, Agrarian Radicalism and the War of Independence', in Boyce (ed.), *The Revolution in Ireland*, pp. 217–34; Dooley, *'The Land for the People'*, pp. 16–20, 26–56.

4 'Castles, Mansions and Residences Were Sent Up in Flames'

1. *Westminster Gazette*, 23 Jan. 1909.

2. R.B. MacDowell, *Crisis and Decline: The Fate of the Southern Unionists* (Dublin, 1997), p. vii; on the loyalist experience in New York during the American Revolution see Howard Pashman, *Building a Revolutionary State: The Legal Transformation of New York, 1776–1783* (Chicago, 2018).

3. Cannadine, *The Decline and Fall of the British Aristocracy*, p. 487.

4. *Evening Herald*, 31 Jan. 1918.

5. Major Blennerhassett, Ballyseedy, Co Kerry, TNA CO 762/55/18.

6. Don Johnson, 'Post-Famine Landlords of the Flurry Valley', *Journal of the County Louth Archaeological and Historical Society*, vol. 27, no. 3 (2011), p. 419.

7. CICMR, Roscommon, Sept. 1919.

8. Michael Reilly, Galway, BMH, WS 1358, p. 4.

9. *Irish Times*, 9 Jan. 1920.

10. Ibid., 20 Feb. 1920.

11. Ibid., 8 Sept. 1920.

12. Arthur Mitchell, *Revolutionary Government in Ireland: Dáil Éireann 1919–22* (Dublin, 1995), pp. 128–29.

13. Thomas Costello, BMH, WS 1296, p. 6.

14. Lennox Robinson, Tom Robinson, Nora Dorman, *Three Homes* (London, 1938), p. 242.

15. Quoted in Dunraven, *Past Times and Pastimes,* Vol. 2, p. 202.

16. R.E. Longfield to Hugh de Fellenberg Montgomery, 16 Mar. 1920; quoted in Patrick Buckland, *Irish Unionism 1885–1923: A Documentary History* (Belfast, 1973), p. 381.

17. J. Ormsby Lawder, Leitrim, TNA, CO 762/13/12.

18. Barry, *Guerilla Days in Ireland*, p. 6.

19. Liam Deasy, *Towards Ireland Free: The West Cork Brigade in the War of Independence* (Cork, 1973), p. 2.

20. Dan Breen, *My Fight for Irish Freedom* (Dublin, 1981 edn [1st edn 1924]), p. 9.

21. Ibid., p. 100.

22. Ibid., pp. 21–22; for wider context on defying the IRA at this time, see Brian Hughes, *Defying the IRA: Intimidation, Coercion and Communities During the Irish Revolution* (Liverpool, 2017).

23. Thomas Ryan, BMH, WS 0783, p. 106.

24. *Tipperary Star*, 2 July 1921.

25. My thanks to Aidan Gilsenan for providing this information.

26. IGCMR, Jan., July 1920.

27. Quoted in James S. Donnelly Jr, *The Great Irish Potato Famine* (Stroud, 2001), p. 141.

28. Quoted in Oliver McDonagh, 'Irish Emigration to the United States of America and the British Colonies during the Famine', in R.D. Edwards, T.D. Williams (eds.), *The Great Famine: Studies in Irish History 1845–52* (Dublin, 1956), p. 474.

29. *Freeman's Journal*, 25 Apr. 1849; *Tipperary Vindicator*, 11 Apr. 1849.

30. Pashman, *Building a Revolutionary State*, p. 79.

31. Barry, *Guerilla Days*, p. 116.

32. Ibid., p. 214.
33. Ibid., p. 116.
34. Ibid., p. 117.
35. Quotes taken from Ciarán J. Reilly, 'The Burning of Country Houses in Co Offaly, 1920–23', in Dooley and Ridgway (eds.), *The Irish Country House*, p. 126.
36. Ibid., p. 146.
37. *Irish Times*, 31 May 1920.
38. Ibid., 22 May 1920.
39. Bence-Jones, *Twilight of the Ascendancy*, p. 195.
40. Donnelly, Jr, 'Big House Burnings in Cork', pp. 150–51.
41. *Nenagh Guardian*, 25 June 1921.
42. *Irish Times*, 7, 11, 14 May 1920.
43. CICMR, Galway ER, June 1921.
44. *Irish Times*, 25, 27 May, 17 June 1920, 9 Feb. 1921.
45. *The Georgian Society Records of Eighteenth-Century Domestic Architecture and Decoration in Ireland* (Dublin, 1913), p. 55.
46. Ibid., p. 57; https://theirishaesthete.com/tag/summerhill/
47. C.R. Cockerell quoted in https://theirishaesthete.com/tag/summerhill/
48. *The Georgian Society Records*, p. 57.
49. Quoted in https://theirishaesthete.com/tag/summerhill/
50. Fingall, *Seventy Years Young*, p. 435.
51. Quoted in Oliver Coogan, *Politics and War in Meath, 1913–23* (Dublin, 1983), pp. 150–51.
52. Seamus Finn, BMH, WS 1060, pp. 19–20.
53. Seán Boylan, BMH, WS 1715, p. 33.
54. *Irish Times*, 7 Feb. 1920.
55. Ibid.
56. Ibid.
57. Quoted in https://theirishaesthete.com/tag/summerhill/
58. Marquess of Sligo to Chief Secretary, 31 Mar. 1919 (NLI, Westport papers, MS 41,099/16).
59. Lydican Castle Galway, TNA CO762/112/3; Greated also admitted that the burning was 'partly due to agrarian trouble owing to the fact that the RIC had left and no police formed to replace them'.
60. Donnelly, Jr, 'Big House Burnings in Cork', p. 145.
61. *Irish Times*, 6 Apr. 1921.
62. *Limerick Chronicle*, 30 Sept. 1920.
63. Matthew Finucane, BMH, WS, 975, p. 4.
64. P.J. McElligott, BMH, WS 1013, p. 14.
65. Ibid. [including supplementary statement] p.15, p. 1 of supplementary statement.
66. Michael Murphy, BMH, WS 1081, p. 2.
67. Donnelly, Jr, 'Big House Burnings in Cork', p. 159.
68. As recounted in ibid., pp. 159–60.
69. Quoted in ibid., p. 160.
70. Cannadine, *The Decline and Fall of the British Aristocracy*, p. 487.
71. Peter Hart, 'The Geography of Revolution in Ireland 1917–23', *Past & Present*, 155, May 1997, pp. 142–76.
72. Erhardt Rumpf and A.C. Hepburn, *Nationalism and Socialism in Twentieth-Century Ireland* (Liverpool, 1977), pp. 39–40.
73. These figures have been adjusted from those presented in *Decline of the Big House* to take into account all the additional houses found since then to have been burned. The full list of Big Houses burned between 1920 and 1923 can be found at https://www.maynoothuniversity.ie/centre-study-historic-irish-houses-and-estates.
74. Donnelly, 'Big House Burnings', p. 145.
75. IGCMR, May 1921.
76. CICMR, Cork East, May 1921.
77. Ibid., June 1921.

78. Ibid., Tipperary, June 1921.
79. Donnelly, Jr, 'Big House Burnings in Cork', pp. 163–64.
80. Barry, *Guerilla Days*, pp. 214, 218.
81. *Irish Times*, 30 June, 8 July 1921.
82. Ibid., 29 Oct. 1921.
83. Quoted in Donnelly, Jr, 'Big House Burnings in Cork', p. 166.
84. Eugene Dunne, 'The Experiences of the Aristocracy in County Westmeath during the Period 1879 to 1923' (PhD thesis, NUIM, 2016), pp. 15, 20.
85. *Return of Untenanted Lands*, p. 183.
86. IGCMR, June 1921; CICMR, June 1921.
87. *Westmeath Guardian*, 24 June 1921; *The Times*, 21 June 1921.
88. *Irish Times*, 23 June 1921.
89. Quoted in *Westmeath Guardian*, 1 July 1921.
90. *Irish Independent*, 22 June 1921; *Westmeath Examiner*, 9 July 1921; Dunne, 'Westmeath aristocracy', p. 307.
91. *Westmeath Examiner*, 9 July 1921.
92. Bence-Jones, *Twilight of the Ascendancy*, pp. 195, 199.
93. Thomas Costello, BMH, WS 1296.
94. Henry O'Brien, BMH, WS 1308.
95. Frank O'Connor, BMH, WS 1309.
96. Dunne, 'Westmeath aristocracy', p. 247.
97. Thomas Costello, BMH, WS 1296; Henry O'Brien, BMH, WS 1308; Frank O'Connor, BMH, WS 1309; *Westmeath Examiner*, 9 July 1921.
98. Frank O'Connor, BMH, WS 1309, p. 21.
99. Ibid.
100. Richard Coplen, 'Moydrum Castle', *Westmeath Independent*, 14 Jan. 2006.
101. Thomas Costello, BMH, WS 1296, p. 21.
102. *Irish Times*, 9 Sept. 1920.
103. *Westmeath Examiner*, 9 July 1921.
104. Frank O'Connor, BMH, WS 1309, p. 21; Henry O'Brien, BMH, WS 1308, p. 16.
105. Henry O'Brien, BMH, WS 1308, pp. 16–17.
106. J.W. Garvey to F.H. Crawford, 21 Aug. 1921, quoted in Buckland, *Unionism: A Documentary History*, p. 383.
107. Olwen Purdue, '"Ascendancy's . . . Last Jamboree": Big House Society in Northern Ireland, 1921–69', in Dooley and Ridgway, *The Irish Country House*, p. 135.
108. Robinson (ed.), *Lady Gregory's Journals*, pp. 13–14.
109. Martin, 'Unionism: The Irish Nobility', p. 73.
110. Gemma Clark, *Everyday Violence in the Irish Civil War* (Cambridge, 2014) p. 74.
111. Diary of Lady Alice Howard, 31 Dec. 1921 (NLI, Diaries of Lady Alice Howard, MS 3,625).
112. Butler, 'Lord Oranmore's Journal, 1913–27', p. 588.
113. Quoted in *Irish Times*, 6 Mar. 1922.
114. Bowen, *Bowen's Court*, pp. 10–11.
115. de Stacpoole, *Irish and Other Memories*, p. v.
116. Lord Midleton [John Broderick], *Records and Reactions, 1856–1939* (London, 1939), p. 263; Martin, 'Unionism: The Irish Nobility', pp. 161–62; Buckland, *Irish Unionism I*, p. 246.
117. Midleton, *Records and Reactions*, p. 264.
118. Quoted in Martin, 'Unionism: The Irish Nobility', p. 162.
119. *Irish Times*, 16 Jan. 1920, 15 Apr. 1921.
120. Ibid., 11 Aug. 1920.
121. Quoted in Symes, *Sir John Keane*, p. 35.
122. John Garvey to Major C.K. O'Hara, 10 Nov. 1922 (NLI, O'Hara papers, MS 36440/7).
123. J.W. Garvey to F.H. Crawford, 21 Aug. 1921; quoted in Buckland, *Unionism: A Documentary History*, p. 384.

124. John Garvey to Major C.K. O'Hara, 24 Feb. 1923; ibid.
125. Anonymous letter sent to John Garvey [1924]; ibid.
126. Mel Farrell, *Party Politics in a New Democracy: The Irish Free State, 1922–1938* (London, 2017), p. 77.
127. Terence Dooley, 'IRA Activity in County Kildare During the War of Independence', in William Nolan and Thomas McGrath (eds), *Kildare: History and Society* (Dublin, 2006), pp. 625–56
128. Seamus Cullen, 'Loyalists in a Garrison County: Kildare, 1912–1923', in Hughes and Morrissey (eds.), *Southern Irish Loyalism*, p. 265.
129. Irish Claims Compensation Association, *The Campaign of Fire: A Record of Some Mansions and Houses Destroyed* (London, 1924), p. 2.
130. Quoted in Hopkinson, *Green against Green,* p. 90; see also Lord Castletown, *Ego* (London, 1923), p. 220.
131. Quoted in Hopkinson, *Green against Green*, p. 92.
132. 'Notes by Ernie O'Malley . . . on interviews with officers from the 1ˢᵗ Midland Division' 31 Aug. 1922; quoted in C.K.H. O'Malley and Anne Dolan (eds.), *No Surrender Here! The Civil War Papers of Ernie O'Malley* (Dublin, 2007), p. 141 and fn336, p. 593).
133. Marie Coleman, 'Protestant Depopulation in County Longford during the Irish Revolution, 1911–1926', *English Historical Review*, cxxxv, no. 575 (Aug. 2020), pp. 967–68.
134. Eoin O'Duffy to Minister for Home Affairs, 15 Nov. 1922 (NAI, Dept. Justice files, H5/538).
135. Breen, *My Fight for Irish Freedom*, p. 178.
136. William Tenison to [?], n.d.; my thanks to William Tenison, Lough Bawn, for sharing this with me.
137. Report on drilling in Carlow, 8 Sept. 1921 (CO 904, Breaches of the Truce Reports).
138. DI to CI Co Carlow, 2 Oct. 1921; ibid.
139. CI report on 'IRA Rebel Camp at Harristown House, Kildare', n.d.; ibid.
140. IGCMR, Sept. 1921.
141. D.H. Doyne malicious injury claim, n.d. (NLI, Doyne papers, MS 29,770/238).
142. Henry Bourke Jourdan, Thornhill, Co Mayo, TNA, CO 762/62/16.
143. *Irish Times,* 17 July 1922.
144. Macroom Castle compensation file, NAI, FIN/COMP/2/4/1/.
145. See chapter 6.
146. Hopkinson, *Green against Green,* p. 221.
147. Clark, *Everyday Violence in the Irish Civil War*, pp. 54–97.
148. *Irish Times,* 9 Jan. 1923.
149. Col. Loftus Bryan, Upton, Wexford, TNA, CO 762/61/6.
150. Breen T. Murphy, 'The Government's Execution Policy During the Irish Civil War 1922–1923' (PhD thesis, Maynooth University, 2010), p. 16; Gavin Foster, *The Irish Civil War and Society: Politics, Class and Conflict* (London, 2015), pp. 155–56.
151. Ibid., p. 3.
152. In total, over a six-month period, eighty-one men were executed by the Provisional (January–December 1922)/Free State governments; ibid., p. 17.
153. 'Operation Order No. 16: Senators', in O'Malley and Dolan (eds.), *No Surrender Here!,* pp. 533–34.
154. Quoted in *Weekly Telegraph,* 10 Feb. 1923.
155. Mark Bence-Jones, *Burke's Guide to Country Houses. Volume I, Ireland* (London, 1978), p. 230; www.dia.ie; https://theirishaesthete.com/2018/11/14/built-by-his-friends-and-countrymen/
156. Quoted in Brian McCabe, 'Palmerstown and its Owners', http://kildarelocalhistory.ie/articles/palmerstown-and-its-owners/
157. *Leinster Leader,* 12 Dec. 1925.
158. Ibid.
159. *Kildare Observer*, 3 Feb. 1923; also *Leinster Leader*, 3 Feb. 1923.

160. Ibid., 24 Feb. 1923.
161. Ibid.
162. Ibid.
163. *Irish Times*, 10 Jan. 1923.
164. Clark, *Everyday Violence in the Irish Civil War*, p. 79.
165. Ibid., 2 March 1923; *Leinster Leader*, 3 Feb. 1923.
166. Clark, *Everyday Violence in the Irish Civil War*, p. 42.
167. Power, *White Knights*, p. 226.
168. Macroom Castle, NAI FIN/COMP/2/4/1.
169. Clark, *Everyday Violence in the Irish Civil War*, p. 202; Stathis Kalyvas, *The Logic of Violence in Civil War* (Cambridge, 2012), pp. 55–61.
170. Donnelly, 'Big House Burnings in Cork, pp. 142, 195.
171. *Irish Times*, 31 Jan. 1923.
172. Terence Dooley, *The Irish Revolution, 1912–23: Monaghan* (Dublin, 2017), pp. 111–22.
173. Hughes, *Defying the IRA*, p. 206; Coleman, 'Protestant Depopulation in Longford', p. 970.
174. Clark, *Everyday Violence in the Irish Civil War*, p. 198.
175. Ibid., pp. 126–27; Coffey, *The Planters of Luggacurran*, p. 9; see also Michael Farry, *The Aftermath of Revolution: Sligo 1921–23* (Dublin, 2000).
176. Toler Garvey to Geoffrey Parsons, 22 July 1922 (Birr Castle Archive [BCA], T/31); my thanks to Ciarán Reilly and Lisa Shortall for sharing these sources.
177. Garvey letter book (49–50), 5 Dec. 1922 (BCA, Q/360).
178. Ibid., 7, 12, 15, 30 Dec. 1922, 28 Feb. 1923 (BCA, Q/360).
179. Ibid., 5 June 1923.
180. Ibid., 27 June 1923.
181. See Philip McConway, 'Offaly and the Civil War Executions' in *Offaly Heritage*, Vol 5 (2008), pp. 251–74.
182. Garvey letter book (49), 26 Jan. 1923 (BCA, Q/360).
183. Ibid., 26 Jan. 1923.
184. Ibid., 27 Jan. 1923.
185. Ibid., (50), 3 Jan. 1924 (BCA, Q/361).
186. Purdue, *The Big House in the North of Ireland*, p. 146.
187. Quoted in ibid., p. 148.
188. Paul Bew, *Ireland: The Politics of Enmity 1789–2006* (Oxford, 2007), pp. 423–43.
189. Fearghal McGarry, *O'Duffy*, p.100.
190. Bew, *Ireland*, p. 434.
191. The eight houses burned were Crebilly, Garron Tower, Shane's Castle, Antrim Castle, Strangford, Old Court, Glenmona, and Drumnasole.
192. *Irish Times,* 27 May 1922.
193. Purdue, *Big House in the North of Ireland*, p. 147.
194. *Belfast News-Letter*, 24 May 1922.
195. Ibid.
196. *Irish Times*, 22 May 1922.
197. *Ballymena Observer*, 26 May 1922.
198. *Irish Times*, 27 May 1922; Purdue, *The Big Houses in the North of Ireland*, p. 149.
199. Kalyvas, *The Logic of Violence*, p. 380; Clark, *Everyday Violence in the Irish Civil War*, pp. 4–5.
200. *Irish Times*, 21 Apr. 1922.
201. https://www.oireachtas.ie/en/debates/debate/dail/1924-11-18/23/?highlight%5B0%5D=castle&highlight%5B1%5D=fogarty

5 'I Think the Greed of Land is at the Root of this Class of Crime'

1. Clark, *Everyday Violence in the Irish Civil War*, p. 97; Donnelly, 'Big House Burnings in Cork', p. 145.

2. Dooley, *Decline of the Big House*, ch.7.
3. Reilly, 'The Burning of Country Houses in Co Offaly', p. 118.
4. CICMR, Galway ER, Feb. 1920.
5. Kevin O'Shiel, BMH, WS 1770, p. 933.
6. *Irish Times*, 26 Apr. 1920, 22 May 1920.
7. Ibid., 16 Apr. 1920.
8. Quoted in Campbell, *Land and Revolution*, p. 302.
9. *Connaught Tribune*, 28 May 1910; quoted in Ann O'Riordan, *East Galway Agrarian Agitation and the Burning of Ballydugan House, 1922* (Dublin, 2015), p. 26.
10. O'Riordan, *East Galway Agrarian Agitation*, p. 31.
11. Quoted in ibid., p. 42.
12. Ibid., pp. 31, 32.
13. Ibid., pp. 30, 33.
14. Dáil Éireann, 'A Brief Survey of the Work Done by the Agricultural Department from April 1919 to August 1921', p. 9.
15. *Irish Times*, 3 May 1920.
16. Ibid., 15 May 1920.
17. Ibid., 18 May 1920.
18. Ibid., 31 May 1920.
19. Ibid., 12 Apr. 1920.
20. Ibid., 10 May 1920.
21. Ibid., 2 June 1920.
22. *Cork Examiner*, 7 May 1920.
23. R.A. Corr to *Roscommon Journal*, 29 May 1920.
24. Kevin O'Shiel, BMH, WS 1770, p. 934.
25. *Sligo Champion*, 1 July 1901.
26. Quoted in Einion Thomas, 'From Sligo to Wales: The Flight of Sir Charles Phibbs', *History Ireland*, Spring 2004, p.10.
27. Ibid.
28. Ibid.
29. *Dáil Éireann Debates*, vol. 40, 4 Nov. 1931, 800–801.
30. O'Connor, 'Agrarian Unrest', *Saothar*, vi (1980), pp. 54–55; Emmet O'Connor, *Reds and the Green: Ireland, Russia and the Communist Internationals 1919–43* (Dublin, 2004); for a contemporary socialist view see Aodh De Blacam in Foreword to Selina Sigerson, *Sinn Féin and Socialism* (Dublin, n.d.), p. 4; see also the report, 'Agrarian Bolshevism' in *Irish Times*, 29 Apr. 1920.
31. O'Connor, 'Agrarian Unrest', p. 42.
32. Butler, 'Lord Oranmore's Journal', p. 580.
33. Newspapers clippings, untitled and undated (Lucas-Scudamore papers, private possession).
34. Bew, 'Sinn Féin and Agrarian Radicalism', p. 229.
35. Boyce, 'Introduction', p. 18; see also Laffan, *The Resurrection of Ireland*, p. 258; Fearghal McGarry, 'Revolution, 1916–1923', in Thomas Bartlett (ed.), *The Cambridge History of Ireland*, Vol. iv, (Cambridge, 2018), p. 273.
36. [Erskine Childers], *The Constructive Work of Dáil Éireann*, No. 1 (1921), p. 18.
37. Ibid., p. 18; Mary Kotsonouris, *Retreat from Revolution: The Dáil Courts 1920–24* (Dublin, 1994); Arthur Mitchell, *Revolutionary Government in Ireland: Dáil Éireann 1919–22* (Dublin, 1995), pp. 137–46.
38. Bew, 'Sinn Féin and Agrarian Radicalism', p. 234.
39. *Westmeath Independent*, 1 May 1920.
40. Ibid.
41. Thomas Costello, BMH, WS 1296, p. 13.
42. Ibid., p. 5.
43. Dunne, 'Westmeath Aristocracy', pp. 307–08.
44. Thomas Costello, BMH, WS 1296, p. 22.
45. Henry O'Brien, BMH, WS 1308, p. 20.

46. Dunne, 'Westmeath Aristocracy', p. 310.
47. Ibid., pp. 310–11.
48. Ibid., p. 311.
49. Ibid., p. 312.
50. *Dáil Debates*, 30 Jan. 1924, vol. 6, no. 10; https://www.oireachtas.ie/en/debates/debate/dail/1924-01-30/5/?highlight%5B0%5D=moydrum
51. Bew, 'Sinn Féin and Agrarian Radicalism', p. 225.
52. *Meath Chronicle*, 3 Feb. 1923.
53. Michael Murphy, BMH, WS 1081, pp. 2–3.
54. IGCMR, Apr. 1921.
55. CICMR Kerry, May 1921.
56. Michael Keane, 15 Dec. 1937, as told to Thomas Flavin; https://www.duchas.ie/en/cbes/4613712/4611359
57. Jean Young, 'The Big House in Co Louth, 1912–1923', in Donal Hall and Martin Maguire (eds.), *County Louth and the Irish Revolution 1912–1923* (Newbridge, 2017), pp. 157–66.
58. Ibid., p. 155.
59. Ibid., p. 156.
60. Ibid.
61. Johnston, 'Post-Famine Landlords of the Flurry Valley', p. 420.
62. *Dundalk Democrat*, 12 July 1924, 1 Oct. 1932; Johnston, 'Post-Famine Landlords of the Flurry Valley', p. 420.
63. https://www.dia.ie/works/view/61048/building/CO.+MONAGHAN,+GOLA+HOUSE
64. Report on IRA activity 1 April 1920 to 31 March 1921 (Monaghan County Museum, Thomas Brennan papers, uncatalogued); *Dundalk Democrat*, 5 March 1921.
65. Robert Devine email to this author, 8 Feb. 2016.
66. Ibid., 8 Dec. 2015.
67. Notebook Scotstown SF Club: entry for 11 Sept 1921 (Monaghan County Museum, Brennan papers, uncatalogued),
68. Patrick J. Duffy, 'Population and Landholding in County Monaghan' (PhD thesis, UCD, 1976), p. 416.
69. *Weekly Irish Times*, 24 June 1922.
70. *Anglo-Celt*, 2 Feb. 1924; Robert Devine to the author, 8 Feb. 2016.
71. IGCMR, Sept. 1916.
72. *Cork Constitution*, 11 July 1920.
73. Donnelly, Jr, 'Big House Burnings in Cork', p. 147.
74. Ibid., p. 146.
75. *Irish Times*, 5 Nov. 1921.
76. Compensation claim Macroom Castle (NAI, Dept. of Finance Compensation files, 2/4/1/).
77. Clark, *Everyday Violence in the Irish Civil War*, p. 3, drawing on Peter Hart, *The IRA at War, 1916–1923* (Oxford, 2003), p. 41.
78. Foster, *The Irish Civil War*, p. 14.
79. J.C. Davies, 'Towards a Theory of Revolution', *American Sociological Review*, 27 (1962), p. 5.
80. Donnelly, *Land and People of Nineteenth-Century Cork*, pp. 249–50.
81. *Report of Department of Agriculture and Technical Instruction for Ireland 1922–23*, p. 1.
82. Ibid., pp. 2–3.
83. T.K. Daniel, 'Griffith on his Noble Head: The Determinants of Cumann na nGaedheal Economic Policy, 1922–32', *Irish Economic & Social History*, iii (1976), p. 56.
84. Provisional Government, Minutes of Meeting, 5 Apr. 1922 (NAI, G1/2).
85. David Seth Jones, 'Land Reform Legislation and Security of Tenure in Ireland after Independence', *Éire-Ireland*, xxxii–xxxiii (1997–98), p. 117.
86. Maurice Moore to Minister for Defence, 9 May 1923 (Military Archives, A/3126).
87. Marie Coleman, William Murphy, 'Mellows, William Joseph (Liam)', in James McGuire and James Quinn (eds), *Dictionary of Irish Biography*. (Cambridge, 2009). (http://dib.cambridge.org/viewReadPage.do?articleId=a5795)

88. Irish Claims Compensation Association, *The Irish Free State: The Campaign of Fire* (London, 1923), pp. 9–10.
89. Tom Garvin, *1922: The Birth of Irish Democracy* (Dublin, 1996), pp. 44–45; also Henry Patterson, *The Politics of Illusion: Republicanism and Socialism in Modern Ireland* (London, 1989), p. 24.
90. Richard English, *Radicals and the Republic: Socialists Republicanism in the Irish Free State 1925–1937* (Oxford, 1994), p. 31.
91. Witness Statement, Tom Carragher (Monaghan County Museum, Marron papers).
92. *Tipperary Star*, 4 Mar. 1922.
93. CICMR, Tipperary, Aug. 1921 (CO904/116).
94. Inventory of goods stolen from Kilboy, 13 Nov. 1921 (NLI, Dunalley papers, MS 29,810 (17)).
95. Samuel Doupe to Lord Dunalley, 23 Apr. 1922, 10 July 1922, 15 July 1922, ibid.; William Harkness to Lord Dunalley, 12 Aug. 1922, ibid.
96. *Tipperary Star*, 3 June 1922.
97. Teresa Byrne, 'The Burning of Kilboy House, Nenagh, County Tipperary, 2 August 1922' (MA thesis, NUI Maynooth, 2006), p. 26.
98. Prittie, 'History of the Prittie Family in Ireland' (unpublished, private possession), pp. 22–23.
99. *Irish Times*, 15 July, 12 Aug. 1922.
100. Howard Dudley to Lord Dunalley, 19 July 1922 (NLI, Dunalley papers, MS 29,810 (17)).
101. Samuel Doupe to Lord Dunalley, 9 Aug. 1922, ibid.
102. Howard Dudley to Lord Dunalley, 20 Aug. 1922, ibid.
103. Paddy Ryan, 'A Hot August Night 1922', in Silvermines Historical Society, *Mourning the Past: The History, People and Places of Silvermines District* (2020), p. 5.
104. Howard Dudley to Lord Dunalley, 1 May 1923 (NLI, Dunalley papers, MS 29,810).
105. J.H. Dudley to Dunalley, 18 May 1923, ibid.
106. J.H. Dudley to C.H. Maude [agent], 1 May 1923, ibid.
107. Ibid.
108. Ibid.
109. Quoted in Byrne, 'The Burning of Kilboy', pp. 66–67.
110. Irish Land Commission to Lord Dunalley, 27 Dec. 1924 (NLI, Dunalley papers, MS 29,810 (20)).
111. Hopkinson, *Green against Green*, p. 165.
112. Gerard Lyne, *The Lansdowne Estate in Kerry Under W.S. Trench, 1849–72* (Dublin, 2001).
113. Patrick M. Geoghegan, 'Fitzmaurice, Henry Charles Keith Petty 5th Marquess of Lansdowne', in James McGuire and James Quinn (eds), *Dictionary of Irish Biography*, (Cambridge, 2009). (http://dib.cambridge.org/viewReadPage.do?articleId=a3224)
114. *Irish Times*, 3 Oct. 1922.
115. Rev. Almoner to Minister for Home Affairs, 22 Oct. 1923; (NAI, Dept. of Justice files, H5/135).
116. John Keane, diary 1, 6 June 1922; quoted in Symes, *Sir John Keane*, p. 12.
117. Quoted in ibid., p. 37.
118. Quoted in ibid., p. 38.
119. Quoted in ibid., p. 42.
120. Quoted in ibid., p. 33.
121. Ibid., p. 32.
122. *Irish Independent*, 23 June 1923; Anthony Kinsella, 'The Special Infantry Force', *The Irish Sword*, vol. xx, no. 82 (1997), pp. 331–47.
123. Quoted in Symes, *Sir John Keane*, p. 42.
124. *Dáil Debates*, vol. 2, no. 35, 1 Mar. 1923, 1857.
125. *Irish Times*, 18 Apr. 1922.
126. Ibid., 19 Apr. 1922.
127. Ibid.

128. Patrick Hogan to W.T. Cosgrave, 18 Apr. 1923: Memo on Terms of Proposed Land Bill (NAI, Dept. of Taoiseach files, S3192); Memo by Patrick Hogan on 1920 Land Bill, 14 Dec. 1922 (NAI, Dept. of Taoiseach files, S1995).

129. *An Act to Amend the Law Relating to the Occupation and Ownership of Land and for Other Purposes Relating Thereto* [no. 42, 9 Aug. 1923]; *An Act to Provide for the Preservation of Public Safety and the Protection of Person and Property and for Matters Connected Therewith or Arising out of the Present Emergency* [no. 28, 1 Aug. 1923]; *An Act to Alter the Law Relating to Compensation for Criminal Injuries* [no. 15, 12 May 1923].

130. Heather Crawford, *Outside the Glow: Protestantism and Irishness in Independent Ireland* (Dublin, 2010), p. 16.

131. Jones, 'Land Reform Legislation', pp. 116–19.

132. Quoted in Clark, *Everyday Violence in the Irish Civil War*, p. 127.

6 'Grass Grows Where the Saloons Were': A Case Study of Mitchelstown Castle

1. *Irish Examiner*, 29 Apr. 1926; see also Bill Power, *White Knights, Dark Earls: The Rise and Fall of an Anglo-Irish Dynasty* (Cork, 2000).

2. Quoted in King-Harman, *The Kings, Earls of Kingston*, p. 258; there are scraps of detail in the compensation claim file, Mitchelstown Castle (NAI, DIN/COMP/2/4/2191).

3. Quoted in Power, *White Knights*, p. 226.

4. https://archiseek.com/2012/1823-mitchelstown-castle-mitchelstown-co-cork/

5. Samuel Lewis, *A Topographical Dictionary* (London, 1937) https://www.libraryireland.com/topog/M/Mitchelstown-Clongibbons-Cork.php

6. King-Harman, *The Kings, Earls of Kingston*, pp. 81–82.

7. Col W.A. King-Harman of Mitchelstown, Co Cork (TNA, CO 762/29/1).

8. King-Harman, *The Kings*, pp. 246–48.

9. *Londonderry Sentinel*, 8 Aug. 1922.

10. Power, *White Knights*, p. 224.

11. Patrick J. Luddy, BMH, WS 1,151, p. 1.

12. Ibid., pp. 1–3.

13. Ibid., p. 1.

14. Raymond Gillespie, 'Foreword', in O'Riordan, *East Galway Agrarian Agitation*, p. 2.

15. Donnelly, *Land and People of Nineteenth-Century Cork*, pp. 278–82, 335–47.

16. Ibid., p. 278.

17. For a comprehensive description of the Land War era on the estate see Power, *White Knights*, pp. 150ff.

18. King-Harman, *The Kings, Earls of Kingston*, p. 238.

19. Donnelly, *Land and People of Nineteenth-Century Cork*, p. 282.

20. King-Harman, *The Kings, Earls of Kingston*, p. 243.

21. Arthur O'Connor to Kingston tenants in January 1887; quoted in Donnelly, *Land and People of Nineteenth-Century Cork*, p. 342.

22. Andrew Gailey, 'Failure and the Making of the New Ireland', in Boyce (ed.), *The Revolution in Ireland*, p. 54.

23. Donnelly, *Land and People of Nineteenth-Century Cork*, pp. 341–45; Power, *White Knights*, pp. 164–88.

24. R.V. Comerford, Foreword, in Dooley and Ridgway (eds.), *The Irish Country House*, p. 11.

25. Power, *White Knights*, p. 206.

26. Quoted in ibid., p. 188.

27. *Cork Constitution*, 4 Nov. 1909.

28. Bowen, *Bowen's Court*, p. 324; see also, Nora Robertson, *Crowned Harp: Memories of the Last Years of the Crown in Ireland* (Dublin, 1960), p. 88.

29. Power, *White Knights*, p. 217.

30. Proinnsias Breathnach, 'Creamery Attacks', in Crowley et al. (eds.), *Atlas of the Irish Revolution*, pp. 555–57.

31. Power, *White Knights*, p. 218.
32. Patrick J. Luddy, BMH, WS 1151.
33. Bowen, *Bowen's Court*, p. 324.
34. *Irish Times*, 29 Apr. 1926.
35. Quoted in Power, *White Knights*, p. 222.
36. Cornelia Adair to Mr Roberts, 2 Aug. 1920 (on public display, Glenveagh Castle).
37. Power, *White Knights*, p. 222.
38. *Cork Examiner*, 23 Aug. 1922; Hopkinson, *Green against Green*, p. 164.
39. *Irish Times*, 29 Apr. 1926.
40. Ibid.
41. *Weekly Freeman's Journal*, 5 Nov. 1910.
42. Comerford, 'Foreword', p. 11.
43. Quoted in ibid., p. 247.
44. Col W.A. King-Harman (TNA, CO 762/29/1).
45. Power, *White Knights*, p. 225.
46. Ibid., pp. 225–26
47. Quoted in *Irish Times*, June 2000.
48. *Sligo Champion*, 23 Feb. 1924.
49. Dooley, *Decline of the Big House*, pp. 197–207; Clark, *Everyday Violence in the Irish Civil War*, especially pp. 18–53; McDowell, *Crisis & Decline*, pp. 137–62; Niamh Brennan, 'A Political Minefield: Southern Loyalists, the Irish Grants Committee and the British Government, 1922–31', *Irish Historical Studies*, vol. 30, no. 119 (May, 1997), pp. 406–19.
50. Report by J.J. Butler for Board of Works, 10 June 1924, Damage to Property Compensation Act 1923, claim of Arthur Webber, Mitchelstown Castle, Co Cork, Dec. 1925 (NAI, Board of Works files, 2D/62/73, no. 1157/m); quoted in Power, *White Knights*, p. 237 [this file could not be located by this author in the NAI].
51. Ibid.
52. Power, *White Knights*, p. 227.
53. *Irish Examiner*, 29 Apr. 1926.
54. Quoted in Power, *White Knights*, p. 227.
55. *Irish Examiner*, 29 Apr. 1926.
56. Power, *White Knights*, p. 249.
57. Report by J.J. Butler for Board of Works, 10 June 1924.
58. Quoted in Power, *White Knights*, p. 239.
59. *Hampshire Telegraph*, 16 July 1926.
60. Power, *White Knights*, p. 227.
61. Ibid., p. 240.
62. Col W.A. King-Harman (CO, TNA 762/29/1; the compensation process is dealt with in the next chapter.
63. Quoted in King-Harman, *The Kings, Earls of Kingston*, p. 258.
64. Col W.A. King-Harman (TNA, CO 762/29/1.
65. Ibid.
66. King-Harman, *The Kings, Earls of Kingston*, p. 248.
67. Col. W.A. King-Harman (TNA, CO 762/29/1; King-Harman, *The Kings, Earls of Kingston*, p. 81.
68. Col W.A. King-Harman (TNA, CO 762/29/1).
69. Ibid.
70. Quoted in King-Harman, *The Kings, Earls of Kingston*, pp. 265–66.
71. Col W.A. King-Harman (TNA, CO 762/29/1).
72. Ibid.
73. Ibid.
74. Power, *White Knights*, p. 244.
75. Ibid., p. 244.
76. Ibid., p. 246.
77. Ibid.

78. Ibid., p. 245.
79. Dooley, '*The Land for the People*', pp. 99–131.
80. Power, *White Knights*, p. 245.

7 'There Were Hens Roosting on Valuable Oil Paintings': Destruction and Looting, 1920–23

1. *Irish Times*, 5 Nov. 1921.
2. The latter figure according to O'Riordan, *East Galway Agrarian Agitation*, p. 33.
3. *Irish Times*, 3 June 1921.
4. Frank O'Connor, BMH, WS 1309, p. 22.
5. *Cork Constitution*, 27 May 1920.
6. The burnings of 1920 form the backdrop to Elizabeth Bowen's, *The Last September* (London, 1929).
7. Fingall, *Seventy Years Young*, pp. 434–35.
8. Ibid., p. 439.
9. Quoted in Philip Bull, *Monksgrange: Portrait of an Irish House and Family, 1769–1969* (Dublin, 2019), p. 202.
10. Quoted in ibid., p. 206.
11. Thomas Costello, BMH, WS 1296, p. 21.
12. *Cork Constitution*, 6 Apr. 1921.
13. Donnelly, 'Big House Burnings in Cork', pp. 160–61.
14. Ibid., p. 161.
15. *Irish Times*, 9 July 1921.
16. Ibid.
17. Mary Waller-Sawyer to J.E. Duggan, 27 Jan. 1922 (NAI, Dept. of Justice files, H5/35).
18. Ibid.
19. *Irish Times*, 7, 21 Oct. 1922.
20. Clermont Park, Louth, TNA 62/112/3.
21. Ann Dolan, 'Killing in "the Good Old Irish Fashion"? Irish Revolutionary Violence in Context', *Irish Historical Studies*, (2020), 44 (165), p. 24; Fearghal McGarry, 'Revolution, 1916–1923' in Thomas Bartlett (ed.), *The Cambridge History of Ireland, IV: 1880 to the Present* (Cambridge, 2018), p. 258.
22. *Kildare Observer*, 3 Feb. 1923.
23. Clark, *Everyday Violence in the Irish Civil War*, p. 191.
24. Ibid.
25. Smith, *Former People*, pp. 79–80.
26. Jaap Scholten, *Comrade Baron: A Journey Through the Vanishing World of the Transylvanian Aristocracy* (St Helena CA, 2016), pp. 96, 151–52, 231, 248.
27. Ibid., p. 218.
28. Quoted in ibid., p. 5.
29. Quoted in Smith, *Former People*, p. 165.
30. *Irish Times*, 7 Feb. 1920.
31. *Cork Constitution*, 21 Sept. 1920.
32. *Northern Standard*, 21 Feb. 1920.
33. Ibid.
34. Ibid.
35. Ibid.
36. Quoted in Bence-Jones, *Twilight of the Ascendancy*, p. 211.
37. Quoted in Hone, *The Moores of Moore Hall*, p. 264.
38. Fingall, *Seventy Years Young*, p. 414.
39. *Irish Times*, 21 July 1921.
40. Ibid., 7 July 1921.
41. A.F. McEntee, *Memories of a Lifetime in Journalism in Cavan* (Cavan, n.d.), pp. 173–74. My thanks to P.J. Dunne of Cavan for bringing this to my attention.

42. Desart Court (NAI, FIN/COMP/2/10/104).
43. *Irish Times*, 21 Oct. 1921.
44. Ibid., 5 Sept. 1922.
45. *Leinster Leader*, 3 Feb. 1923.
46. Earl of Ossory, 'The Attack on Kilkenny Castle', *Journal of the Butler Society*, vol. I, no. 4 (1972), p. 261.
47. Ibid., p. 273.
48. Ibid., pp. 262–65, 273.
49. K.M. Lanigan, *Kilkenny Castle* (n.d.), p. 15.
50. Earl of Ossory, 'The Attack on Kilkenny Castle', p. 273.
51. *Irish Times*, 8 Oct. 1921.
52. Lady Wallscourt, Ardfry, Co Galway (TNA, CO 762/115/12).
53. M.J. Crotty to Secretary of Board of Works, 14 Jan. 1925 (NAI, FIN Comp/210/44).
54. James Mackay Wilson, Currygrane, Co Longford (NAI, OPW/1/18/2/43). My thanks to Dr Marie Coleman for sharing this source with me.
55. *Irish Times*, 12 Nov. 1921.
56. Quoted in *Freeman's Journal*, 12 Mar. 1923.
57. Sir Thomas Esmonde to Lord Eversley, 20 June 1923 (NAI, Esmonde papers, 981/4/8/2).
58. Sir Thomas Esmonde to President W.T. Cosgrave, 8 May 1925 (NAI, Esmonde papers, 981/4/8/5).
59. Paula Hornstein to Sir Thomas Esmonde, 21 May 1923; (NAI, Esmonde papers, 981/4/8/1).
60. Howard Dudley to Lord Dunalley, 12 Aug. 1922 (NLI, Dunalley papers, MS 29,810 (17)).
61. Jack Lucas-Scudmore to Sybil Lucas-Scudamore, 17 Mar. 1920 (private possession).
62. Gill Lucas-Scudamore to Sybil Lucas-Scudamore, n.d. (private possession).
63. *Connaught Tribune*, 5 May 1923.
64. *Irish Times*, 12 Aug. 1922.
65. Robert Bevan, *The Destruction of Memory: Architecture at War* (London, 2006), p. 84.
66. David Lloyd George to Hamar Greenwood, 25 Feb. 1921 (House of Lords Record Office, Lloyd George papers, F/19/3/4); quoted at https://www.theauxiliaries.com/
67. Stathis N. Kalyvas, 'The Ontology of "Political Violence": Action and Identity in Civil Wars', *Perspectives on Politics*, vol. 1, no. 3 (Sept. 2003), p. 475; idem., ' "New" and "Old" Civil Wars: A Valid Distinction', *World Politics*, 54, no.1 (Oct. 2001), p. 106.
68. Thucydides, *History of the Peloponnesian Wars* (Rex Warner trans, London, 1972); F.W. Rafferty (ed.), 'Peace and War: The Maxims and Reflections of Burke'; https://www.ourcivilisation.com/smartboard/shop/burkee/maxims/chap17.htm
69. *Weekly Irish Times*, 17 Mar. 1923.
70. Ibid., 28 Apr. 1923.
71. *Westmeath Guardian*, 8 July, 5 Aug. 1921; *Irish Times*, 4 Aug. 1921.
72. Eleanor Flegg, 'Treasures: Losing the Family Silver', Independent.ie, 13 Apr 2018. https://www.independent.ie/life/home-garden/treasures-losing-the-family-silver-36801180.html [Accessed 13 Apr. 2020].
73. Ibid.
74. S. Douglas to Lord Dunalley, n.d.; J.H. Dudley to Lord Dunalley, 7 August 1922; W. Harkness to Lord Dunalley, 12 August 1922 (NLI, Dunalley papers, MS 29,810 (17)).
75. *Irish Times*, 30 Aug. 1922.
76. Report of Garda A.J.P. Stapleton (NAI, FIN Comp 2/10/104).
77. Kalyvas, *The Logic of Violence*, p. 46.
78. Quoted in Joe Power, *Clare and the Civil War* (Dublin, 2020), p. 88.
79. My thanks to Prof Chris Ridgway for his many insights on this subject.
80. Claim of J. Lee and J.C. Dixon for damage to Glenfarne Hall, Co Leitrim, 8 May 1923 (NAI, OPW files, 2D/62/76).
81. Samuel Doupe to Lord Dunalley, 6 Aug. 1922 (NLI, Dunalley papers, MS 29,810 (17)).
82. Marigold Freeman-Atwood, *Leap: A Place and its People* (London, 2001), pp. 140–41.
83. Henry Saunderson, *The Saundersons of Castlesaunderson* (London, 1936), p. 73.
84. *Sligo Champion*, 23 Feb. 1924; my thanks to Dr Donal Hall for sharing this information with me.

85. Lord Ashtown, Woodlawn, Co Galway, TNA, 762/15/10.
86. *Irish Times*, 18 Aug. 1922.
87. Warrenscourt, Co Cork, TNA, 762/101/2.
88. S. Simpson to Sybil Lucas-Scudamore, 19 Mar. 1921 (private possession).
89. Macroom Castle, Co Cork (NAI, FIN/COMP/ 2/4/1).
90. Mount Uniacke, Co Cork (NAI, FIN/COMP/2/4/127).
91. *Tuam Herald*, 2 Feb. 1923.
92. Derreen, Co Kerry (TNA, CO 762/63/1).
93. Winston Churchill to W.T. Cosgrove, 22 Sept. 1922 (NAI, Dept. of Taoiseach files, S1940).
94. Derreen, Co Kerry (TNA CO 762/63/1).
95. Extracts of Lord Lansdowne's agent's report enclosed in Lord Lansdowne to Winston Churchill, 20 Sept. 1922 (NA, Dept. of Taoiseach files, S1940).
96. Ibid.
97. Derreen, Co Kerry (TNA CO 762/63/1).
98. Copy W.T. Cosgrave to Winston Churchill, 23 Oct. 1922; ibid.
99. Military Courts – General Regulations as to Trials of Civilians, 2 Oct. 1922; http://www.irishstatutebook.ie/eli/1922/sro/905/made/en/print
100. *Dáil Debates*, vol. 3, no. 38, 7 Mar. 1923, https://www.oireachtas.ie/en/debates/debate/dail/1923-03-07/10/; *Weekly Freeman's Journal*, 17 Mar. 1923.
101. *Dáil Debates*, vol. 4, no. 10, 16 July 1923, https://www.oireachtas.ie/en/debates/debate/dail/1923-07-16/9/
102. Foster, *The Irish Civil War*, p. 39.
103. Ibid.
104. Power, *White Knights*, p. 227.
105. Mealy's and Christie's, *The Murnaghan Collection Auction Catalogue* (14 Oct. 1999).
106. Ibid.
107. *Irish Times*, 6 Mar. 2019 [online version].
108. Robinson, *Bryan Cooper*, p. 139.
109. Co Offaly, Durrow Abbey, Dictionary of Irish Architects 1720–1940. http://www.dia.ie/works/view/2899/building; my thanks to Dr Ciaran Reilly for this reference.
110. *Irish Times*, 27 Jan. 1999.
111. J.H. Dudley to Lord Dunalley, 20, 26 Oct. 1925 (NLI, Dunalley papers, MS 29,810).
112. Ibid.
113. *Public Safety (Emergency Powers) (no. 2) Act*, no. 23, 3 Aug. 1923.
114. *Irish Times*, 21 Apr. 1922.
115. Ibid.
116. Bowen, *Bowen's Court*, p. 327.
117. Quoted in Somerville-Large, *The Irish Country House*, p. 356.
118. Quoted in O'Byrne, *The Last Knight*, p. 97.
119. *Irish Examiner*, 29 Apr. 1926.
120. See O'Byrne, *The Last Knight*.
121. Dooley, *Decline of the Big House*, pp. 138–39.
122. *Irish Times*, 13 Sept. 1921.
123. Ibid., 6 Aug. 1921.
124. Ibid., 13 Aug. 1921.
125. Ibid., 24 Dec. 1921.
126. McCarthy, 'From Landlord to Rentier'.
127. Terence Dooley, *The Decline and Fall of the Dukes of Leinster: Love, War, Debt and Madness* (Dublin, 2014).
128. G. Crutchley to Charles Hamilton, 15 Feb. 1922 (Hamilton papers, private possession).
129. Terence Dooley, 'Carton House and its Contents: Collection and Dispersal in Context, 1729–1949', in Terence Dooley and Christopher Ridgway (eds.), *Country House Collections: Their Lives and Afterlives* (Dublin, 2021), pp. 45–80.
130. Annotated copy of *Catalogue of Auction at Killua Castle, 2 June 1920* (National Gallery of Ireland); Dunne, 'Aristocracy in County Westmeath', p. 28.

131. Dooley, *Decline of the Big House*, p. 140.
132. For example, Cynthia Saltzman, *Old Masters, New World: America's Raid on Europe's Great Pictures* (New York, 2009).
133. My thanks to Cora McDonagh for this information.

8 'Sermons in Stones': Compensating Country House Owners

1. *Sligo Champion*, 23 Feb. 1924 (taken from *Irish Statesman*).
2. Ibid.; Clark, *Everyday Violence in the Irish Civil War*, pp. 18–53.
3. Ronan Fanning, *The Irish Department of Finance, 1922–58* (Dublin, 1978), p. 139.
4. Howard Dudley to Lord Dunalley, 8 Nov. 1922, 14 May 1923 (NLI, Dunalley papers, MS 29,810).
5. R. Walker to Lord Dunalley, 20 May 1924; ibid.
6. Mount Uniacke, Co Cork (NAI, Fin/Comp/2/4/127).
7. Castleboro, Co Wexford (TNA CO762/82/3).
8. Insurance policy for Doneraile Park (NLI, Doneraile papers, MS 34,108/3).
9. *An Act for Amending the Law Relating to Local Government in Ireland and for Other Purposes Connected Therewith* (61 and 62 Vict., c. xxxvii (12 August 1898)); *An Act to Amend the Enactments Relative to Compensation for Criminal Injuries in Ireland* (9 and 10 Geo. V, c. lxvi (16 April 1919)); *An Act to Amend the Enactments Relative to Compensation for Criminal Injuries in Ireland* (10 and 11 Geo. V, c. lxvi (23 December 1920)).
10. Macroom Castle, Co Cork (NAI FIN/COMP/2/4/1).
11. Charles Townshend, 'British Policy in Ireland, 1906–1921', in D.G. Boyce (ed.), *The Revolution in Ireland, 1879–1923* (Dublin, 1988), p. 189.
12. *Irish Times*, 10 June 1921; *The Liberator*, 15 June 1920.
13. *The Liberator*, 15 June 1920.
14. *Irish Times*, 29 Sept. 1920.
15. Ibid., 22 Oct. 1921.
16. Ibid., 9 Oct. 1920.
17. *Westmeath Examiner*, 29 Oct. 1921; Dunne, 'Aristocracy in County Westmeath' pp. 309–10.
18. *Irish Independent*, 5 Mar. 1923; Dunne, 'Aristocracy in County Westmeath', p. 309.
19. *Irish Times*, 29 Oct. 1921.
20. *Limerick Leader*, 9 Feb. 1921.
21. Ibid.
22. Compensation (Ireland) Commission: Interim Report no. 3, 21 October 1922 (NAI, Dept. of Finance files, 169/65); *Irish Times*, 14, 22 October 1921.
23. Tom Nelson, *Through Peace and War: Kildare County Council in the Years of Revolution* (Kildare, 2015).
24. *Irish Times*, 5 Dec. 1921.
25. Quoted in Bence-Jones, *Twilight of the Ascendancy*, p. 238.
26. Fanning, *Irish Department of Finance*, p. 139.
27. Criminal Injuries Compensation Commission. HC Deb 08 May 1922 vol. 153 cc1774-6. https://Api.Parliament.Uk/Historic-Hansard/Commons/1922/May/08/Criminal-Injuries-Compensation-Commission
28. *Compensation for Damage to Property in Ireland*, Cmd 2445, 293 (1925).
29. Compensation Commission: Procedure for dealing with cases: minute sheet initialled by 'J.D.' to Mr O'Brien, 25 July 1922 (NA, Dept. of Finance files, 169/40).
30. A.P. Waterfield to Joseph Brennan, 21 Oct. 1922 (NAI, Dept. of Finance files, 169/40).
31. Dunedin Committee, 'Case of Sullivan, Herbert' n.d. (TNA, CO905).
32. Compensation (Ireland) Commission: Interim Report no. 1, 6 December 1925; (NAI, Dept. of Finance files, 169/40).
33. *Irish Times*, 23 May 1922.
34. Ibid.
35. Ibid.
36. Ibid.

37. Ibid., 22 Sept. 1919.
38. Ibid., 22 Sept. 1923.
39. Bence-Jones, *Twilight of the Ascendancy*, pp. 238–39.
40. Mark Sturgis to Secretary Provisional Government, 26 July 1922; quoted in *Compensation for Malicious Injuries in Ireland*, [Cmd 1736], HC 1922, xvii; Marie Coleman, 'Sturgis, Sir Mark Beresford Russell Grant', in McGuire and Quinn (eds), *Dictionary of Irish Biography*.
41. McDowell, *Crisis and Decline*, p. 140.
42. Dunedin Committee, 'Notes on Compensation for Malicious Injury Payable to the Irish Free State government', (TNA, CO905).
43. Ibid.
44. *Morning Post*, 2 Apr. 1923.
45. Quoted in Buckland, *Irish Unionism I*, p. 214.
46. R.C. Williams to Office of Public Works, 3 May 1922 (NAI, Dept. of Finance files, 169/17).
47. Desart Court, Co Kilkenny (NAI FIN/COMP/2/10/104).
48. Mount Uniacke, Co Cork (NAI, FIN/COMP/2/4/127).
49. Compensation (Ireland) Commission: Final Report, March 1926 (NA, Dept. of Finance files, 19/2/6).
50. *Hansard*, 7 July 1922, Col. 1725–26.
51. *Compensation for Malicious Injuries in Ireland: Letter to the Provisional Government*, Cmd 1736, 1922.
52. Bonar Law at Hotel Cecil, 23 Oct. 1922; quoted in Dunedin Committee, 'Compensation Notes in Command Papers: Extracts from Speeches, Pledges, etc' (TNA, CO905).
53. Quoted in Compensation for Southern Irish Loyalists [6 Nov. 1925] (TNA, CO905, DO 50925/25).
54. *Compensation Act 1923*.
55. Dromoland, Co Clare (TNA 762/14/21).
56. Compensation Claims Register (NAI, OPW files 2D/62/60-9).
57. Howard Dudley to Lord Dunalley, 13 Mar. 1924 (NLI, Dunalley papers, MS 29,810 (19)).
58. Howard Dudley to Lord Dunalley, 10 Apr. 1924; ibid.
59. R. Dudley to Lord Dunalley, 27 May 1924; ibid.
60. *Morning Post*, 2 Apr. 1923.
61. Ibid.
62. Howard Dudley to Lord Dunalley, 13 May 1923 (NLI, Dunalley papers, MS 29,810).
63. Ibid.
64. Lord Devonshire to T.M. Healy, 24 Mar.1923 (NAI, Dept. of Taoiseach files, S2158).
65. Draft of Statement by President W.T. Cosgrave, 27 May 1923 (NAI, Dept. of Taoiseach files, S2158).
66. Minutes of conference to discuss Compensation Act, 30 June 1923 (NAI, Dept. of Finance files, FIN 1/2895).
67. Macroom Castle, Co Cork (NAI, FIN/COMP/2/4/1).
68. Brennan, 'A Political Minefield', p. 413.
69. Crooke, *White Elephants*, pp. 6–7.
70. Draft of statement by President W.T. Cosgrave, 26 March 1923 (NAI, Dept. of Taoiseach files, S2188).
71. Ibid.
72. Dunedin Committee, terms of reference, no. 1 (TNA, CO 905).
73. *Irish Times*, 14 Apr. 1923.
74. Ibid., 29 Mar. 1923.
75. Peter Mandler, *The Fall and Rise of the Stately Home* (New Haven and London, 1997).
76. Damage to Property (Compensation) Act, 1923: Register of Claims (NAI, OPW files, 2D/62/60-69).
77. *Kildare Observer*, 3 Mar. 1923, 29 Nov. 1924.
78. *Irish Times*, 13 Sept. 1927.
79. Quoted in O'Riordan, *East Galway Agrarian Agitation,*, p. 39.

80. *Leinster Leader*, 12 Dec. 1925; my gratitude to Mario Corrigan for providing information on this case.
81. Ibid.
82. Symes, *Sir John Keane*, p. 57.
83. David Rowe and Eithne Scallan, *Houses of Wexford* (Whitegate, 2004), not paginated; Bence Jones, *A Guide to Irish Country Houses*, p. 26.
84. Inventory and valuation of furniture at Ballynastragh, Feb. 1910 (NAI, Esmonde papers, 981/42) [hereafter Esmonde Inventory, 1910].
85. *The People*, 28 Feb. 1925.
86. Esmonde Inventory, 1910.
87. List of contents burned at Ballynastragh, Mar. 1923 (NAI, Esmonde papers, 981/4/5).
88. D. Barrett, 'Circular to Dublin Metropolitan Police Criminal Investigation Department', 12 Apr. 1924 (NLI, Esmonde papers, 981/4/8/2).
89. Messrs Miller and Beatty to Sir Thomas Esmonde, 11 Jan. 1923 (NAI, Esmonde papers, 981/4/2/26).
90. Sir Thomas Esmonde to Lord Eversley, 20 June 1923 (NAI, Esmonde papers, 981/4/8/2).
91. Sir T. Esmonde versus Minister for Finance, February 1925; (NAI, Esmonde papers 981/4/9/4).
92. *Echo and South Leinster Adventurer*, 1 August 1925.
93. Myles Higgins to Sir Thomas Esmonde, 13 March 1925 (NAI, Esmonde papers, 981/4/9/1).
94. *Irish Independent*, 9 Dec. 1924.
95. Sir Thomas Esmonde to President W.T. Cosgrave, 8 May 1925 (NAI, Esmonde papers, 981/4/8/5).
96. Sir Thomas Esmonde to Philip Hanson, 28 Jan. 1924 (NAI, Esmonde papers, 981/4/2/26).
97. Sir Thomas Esmonde to President W.T. Cosgrave, 27 July 1925; (NAI, Esmonde papers, 981/4/9/9).
98. Joseph Brennan to Sir Thomas Esmonde, 6 January 1926; ibid.
99. Lord Danesfort to Lord Dunedin, 11 Nov. 1925 (TNA, Dunedin Committee papers, CO 905).
100. Brennan, 'A Political Minefield', p. 407.
101. Ibid., p. 415,
102. Ibid., p. 417; Clark, *Everyday Violence in the Irish Civil War*, pp. 23–27.
103. Cappoquin, Co Waterford (TNA CO762/82/11).
104. Marlfield, Co Tipperary (TNA CO762/95/19).
105. Quoted in Clark, *Everyday Violence in the Irish Civil War*, p. 27.
106. Frenchpark, Co Roscommon (TNA CO 762/146/16).
107. Castleboro, Co Wexford (TNA CO762/82/3).
108. Ibid.
109. King-Harman, *The Kings, Earls of Kingston*, p. 264.
110. Castleboro, Co Wexford (TNA CO762/82/3).
111. Ibid.
112. Ibid.
113. Symes, *Sir John Keane*, p. 50.
114. Ibid., p. 55.
115. S. and R.C. Walker to Lord Dunalley, 15 August 1924 (NLI, Dunalley papers, MS 29,810 (19)).
116. Howard Dudley to Lord Dunalley, 24 April 1924; ibid., MS 29,810 (19).
117. B.E.F. Sheehy (architect) to Dunalley, 14 April 1925; ibid., MS 29,810 (20).
118. Lord Dunalley, *Khaki and Green* (London, 1940), p. 248.
119. Terence Prittie, *Through Irish Eyes* (London, 1977), p. 42.
120. Prittie, 6th Baron Dunalley, 'History of the Prittie family' (unpublished, private possession), pp. 1, 27.
121. Prittie, *Through Irish Eyes*, p. 32.
122. Bence-Jones, *Guide to Irish Country Houses*, p. 164.

123. *Country Life*, 7 Sept. 2016.
124. Joseph Hone, *The Moores of Moore Hall* (London, 1936), p. 266.
125. Ibid., p. 267.
126. Derryquin Castle, Co Kerry (TNA, CO 62/58/1).
127. Ibid.
128. Ibid.
129. Col. W.A. King-Harman (TNA, CO 762/29/1); *Irish Independent*, 14 May 1926.
130. The same was true in Northern Ireland; Purdue, *The Big House in the North of Ireland*, p. 125.
131. Dunedin Committee, 'Case no. 12 Mrs Uniacke' n.d. (TNA, CO905).
132. Quoted in *Weekly Telegraph*, 10 Feb. 1923.
133. Fingall, *Seventy Years Young*, p. 440.
134. T.F. Crozier to Sybil Lucas-Scudamore, June 1921 (private possession).
135. Terence Dooley, *A Future for Irish Historic Houses?* (Dublin, 2003); https://www.irishher itagetrust.ie/wp-content/uploads/2016/08/Historic-House-Survey-T-Dooley-2003-smaller-file-size.pdf
136. Butler, 'Lord Oranmore's Journal', p. 591.

9 The End of Revolution?

1. Bevan, *The Destruction of Memory*, p. 16.
2. Ibid., pp. 51–52.
3. Timothy Mawe, 'A Comparative Survey of the Historical Debates Surrounding Ireland, World War I and the Irish Civil War', *Historical Studies*, 13 (2012); quoted in O'Riordan, *East Galway Agrarian Agitation*, p. 51.
4. *Dáil Debates*, vol. 3, 28 May 1923, 1163.
5. Ibid., 1818.
6. Ibid., vol. 12, 17 June 1925, 1143.
7. Anton Lucas and Carol Warren (eds.), *Land for the People: The State and Agrarian Conflict in Indonesia* (Ohio, 2013); see, for example, Brian DeMare, *Land Wars: The Stories of China's Agrarian Revolution* (Stanford, 2018); E.J. Hooglund, *Land and Revolution in Iran, 1960–1980* (Texas, 2012); Dana Markiewicz, *The Mexican Revolution and the Limits of Agrarian Reform* (1993).
8. Robert Gerwarth, *The Vanquished: Why the First World War Failed to End, 1917–1923* (New York, 2016) pp. 10, 35, 153–59.
9. Helga Baitenmann, 'Popular Participation in State Formation: Land Reform in Revolutionary Mexico', *Journal of Latin American Studies*, vol. 43 no. 1 (Feb. 2011), pp. 1–31.
10. Foster, *The Irish Civil War*, p. 27; John M. Regan, *The Irish Counter-Revolution, 1921–1936: Treatyite Politics and Settlement in Independent Ireland* (Dublin, 1999).
11. Kevin O'Higgins, 'Mexican Politics' (UCD, O'Higgins papers, P197/137); *Free State*, 18 Mar. 1922; Address by Kevin O'Higgins to the Irish Society at Oxford University, 31 Oct. 1924 (UCD, O'Higgins papers, P197/141); Regan, *The Irish Counter-Revolution*, pp. 244–45.
12. See chapter 6; Paul Bew, Ellen Hazelkorn, Henry Patterson, *The Dynamics of Irish Politics* (London, 1989), pp. 22–23; Brian O'Neill, *The War for the Land in Ireland* (London, 1933), p.104; on the land courts and their success, [Erskine Childers], *The Constructive Work of Dáil Éireann: no. 2* (1921), pp. 9–14; J.J. Lee, *Ireland 1912–1985: Politics and Society* (Cambridge, 1989), pp. 113–15; Mary Kotsonouris, *Retreat From Revolution: Dáil Courts, 1920–1924* (Dublin, 1994).
13. *Dáil Debates*, vol 3, 28 May 1923, 1148, 1153–4.
14. Terence Dooley and Tony McCarthy, 'The 1923 Land Act: Some New Perspectives', in Mel Farrell, Jason Knirck and Ciara Meehan (eds.), *A Formative Decade: Ireland in the 1920s* (Dublin, 2015), pp. 132–156; Eunan O'Halpin, 'Politics and the State 1922–32', in J.R. Hill (ed,) *A New History of Ireland Volume VII: Ireland 1921–84* (Oxford, 2010), p.116.
15. R. F. Foster, *Modern Ireland 1600–1972* (London, 1989), p. 525; J.J. Lee, *Ireland 1912–1985: Politics and Society* (Cambridge, 1989), p. 97.

16. Patrick Hogan, 'Seizure of Land', 22 Dec. 1922 (NAI, Dept. of Taoiseach files, S 1943).

17. Dooley and McCarthy, 'The 1923 Land Act', pp. 132–55.

18. Financial Agreements Between the Irish Free State Government and the British Government, 12 Feb. 1923 (NAI, Dept. of Taoiseach files, S3459); Patrick Hogan, Memorandum on 1923 Land Bill Prepared for President W.T. Cosgrave, 18 Apr. 1923 (NAI, Dept. of Taoiseach files, S3192); 'Irish Free State Land Purchase (Loan Guarantee): Memorandum Explaining Financial Resolution', *British Parliamentary Papers* (1924–25), H.C. [Cmd. 2286]. See also, Maurice Moore, *British Plunder and Irish Blunder: The Story of the Land Purchase Annuities* (Dublin, 1927).

19. *Dáil Debates*, vol. 3, 28 May 1923, 1161–62.

20. Ibid., vol. 3, 14 June 1923, 1972.

21. Sammon, *In the Land Commission*, p. 279.

22. Patrick Hogan, Report on the Land Purchase and Arrears Conference of 10–11 Apr. 1923, 17 Apr. 1923 (UCD, Blythe papers, P24/174).

23. *Dáil Debates*, vol. 3, 28 May 1923, 1165.

24. Patrick Hogan to W.T. Cosgrave, 18 Apr. 1923: Memo on Terms of Proposed Land Bill (NAI, Dept. of Taoiseach files, S3192).

25. Sheehan, 'The 1923 Land Act', p. 135.

26. Ibid., pp. 264–77.

27. David Seth Jones, 'Land Reform Legislation and Security of Tenure in Ireland after Independence' in *Éire-Ireland*, vol. 33–34, no. 4 (1997), pp. 116–43; Regan, *The Irish Counter-Revolution*, p. 204.

28. Pashman, *Building a Revolutionary State*, p. 3.

29. Sammon, *In the Land Commission*, pp. 264–79.

30. George Morgan to Sybil Lucas-Scudamore, 6 Sept. 1920 (Lucas-Scudamore papers, private possession).

31. George Morgan to Sybil Lucas-Scudamore, 9 Feb., 21 Feb. 1921; ibid.

32. S. Simpson to Sybil Lucas-Scudamore, 19 Mar. 1921; ibid.

33. Ibid.

34. George Morgan to Sybil Lucas-Scudamore, 3, 30, 31 May 1920; ibid.

35. Crozier to Sybil Lucas-Scudamore, 1 Mar. 1922; ibid.

36. Report of M.T. Henchey, 30 June, I July 1931; ibid.

37. David Seth Jones, *Graziers, Land Reform and Political Conflict in Ireland* (Washington, 1995), p. 219.

38. *Dáil Debates*, vol. 92, 23 Feb. 1944.

39. Crooke, *White Elephants*, pp. 128–34.

40. Memo for Government: 'Preservation of Mansions and Large Houses', 5 Aug. 1958; quoted in Crooke, *White Elephants*, p. 128.

41. Ibid., p. 127.

42. 'Table A: Big Houses in Hands of Land Commission, 5 Aug. 1958'; Crooke, *White Elephants*, pp. 247–51.

43. Knight of Glin, D.J. Griffin, N.K. Robinson, *Vanishing Country Houses of Ireland* (Dublin, 1988), p. 136.

44. *Dáil Debates*, vol. 164, 30 Oct. 1957, 229–30; Sammon, *In the Land Commission*, p. 45.

45. Glin et al., *Vanishing Country Houses*, p. 136.

46. Somerville-Large, *The Irish Country House*, p. 357; Cannadine, *Decline and Fall of the British Aristocracy*, pp. 90–103.

47. L.P. Curtis Jr, 'The Last Gasp of Southern Unionism: Lord Ashtown of Woodlawn', *Éire-Ireland*, vol. 40, 3:4 (2005), pp. 140–88.

48. Frank McDonald, 'The Mansions Left to Fall into Decay', *Irish Times*, 1 Nov. 2012.

49. Ballinahinch, TNA CO762/82/9

50. *Dáil Debates*, vol. 17, 7 Dec. 1926, 466.

51. Ibid., vol. 18, 17 Feb. 1927, 622–3.

52. Ibid., vol. 19, 25 Mar. 1927, 1123–4.

53. Ibid., vol. 19, 25 Mar. 1927, 101

54. Ibid., vol. 21, 4 Nov. 1927, 854.
55. Ibid., vol. 40, 11, 25 Nov. 1931, 1201, 1998.
56. Purdue, *The Big House in the North of Ireland*, pp. 150, 236.
57. Ibid., p. 217.
58. *Minutes of Proceedings of Dáil Éireann*, 1 Mar. 1922, p. 144.
59. Ibid., vol. 28, 7 Mar. 1929.
60. Ibid., vol. 13, 2 Dec. 1925, 1109.
61. Richard Dunphy, *The Making of Fianna Fáil Power in Ireland 1923–1948* (Oxford, 1995), p. 75.
62. Ibid.
63. T. E. Duffy, 'Old Irish Republican Army Organisation: County of Meath and Environs: Report and Schemes with Appendices Presented to President de Valera and his Government for Consideration', May 1933 (UCD, Aiken papers, P104/2887); *Irish Press*, 16, 17, 18 Jan. 1933.
64. Dooley, *'Land for the people'*, pp. 99–130.
65. Jones, *Graziers*, p. 217.
66. Fianna Fáil, *A Brief Outline of the Aims and Programme of Fianna Fáil* (Dublin, n.d.), p. 4.
67. *An Act to Amend Generally the Law, Finance and Practice Relating to Land Purchase . . .*, no. 38/1933 [13 Oct. 1933].
68. *Meath Chronicle*, 19 Jan. 1935.
69. P.J. Davern to Frank Aiken enclosing resolutions passed by United Republican Association of County Tipperary, 2 Apr. 1933 (UCD, Aiken papers, P104/2875).
70. Report of Thurles Conference of IRA, 2 Oct. 1932 (UCD, Twomey papers, P69/54 (37)).
71. Inspectorate notice no. 11/35: signed by S.J. Waddell, Commissioner and Chief Inspector of Irish Land Commission, 4 May 1935 (NAI, Dept. of Taoiseach, S 6490 (A)).
72. *Meath Chronicle*, 16 Mar. 1935.
73. Since I first wrote about this incident, the availability of a whole range of new sources including BMH witness statements and IRA pension files have shed much new light on this episode; Dooley, *Decline of the Big House*, pp. 175–78. I would like to thank Shaun Evans, Tony McCarthy and Annie Tindley, editors of *Land Reform in the British and Irish Isles since 1800* (Edinburgh, 2001) for allowing me to publish this extended extract from my chapter which appears in the same.
74. *Irish Times*, 16 Apr. 1920.
75. Bernard Bourke, *A Geneaological and Heraldic History of the Landed Gentry of Ireland* (London, 1912), p. 505.
76. James MacDonald and James Sinclair, *History of Aberdeen Angus Cattle* (London, 1910), pp. 327–41, 594.
77. *Westmeath Independent*, 21 Apr. 1923.
78. John Noel McEvoy, 'A Study of the United Irish League in the King's County, 1899–1918' (MA thesis, NUI Maynooth, 1992), p. 29; *Leinster Leader*, 5 July 1902.
79. 'Ratepayer' to editor, *Leinster Leader*, 31 Dec. 1898.
80. Dooley, *Decline of the Big House*, pp. 160–65
81. C.J. Kingston to Under-Secretary, Dublin Castle, 16 Mar. 1915; http://www.rte.ie/century-ireland/images/uploads/further-reading/Ed48-KingsCountyRecruitingCombo2.pdf
82. Memoir of Frederick Beaumont-Nesbitt of Tubberdaly, King's County (copy in author's possession).
83. https://www.everyoneremembered.org/profiles/soldier/1751121/
84. Ibid.
85. *Freeman's Journal*, 12 June 1919.
86. Memo by E.J. Beaumont-Nesbitt [hereafter EJB], 'Tubberdaly, near Rhode, King's County', 28 May 1923 (NAI, Dept. of Justice files, 5/822).
87. On Kildare, see Tom Nelson, *Through Peace and War: Kildare County Council in the Years of Revolution 1899–1926* (Kildare, 2015).
88. EJB to Mrs M. Savage-Armstrong, 19 Jan. 1925; quoted in Patrick Buckland, *Irish Unionism, 1885–1923: A Documentary History* (Belfast, 1973), p. 382.

89. *Tullamore and King's County Independent*, 31 Jan. 1920.
90. Christopher Jones, IRA pension application, no. 2907, MSP34REF18628 http://mspcsearch.militaryarchives.ie/detail.aspx; *Irish Examiner*, 14 Nov. 1921.
91. IRA pension claim form, Mary Swords, 9 Feb. 1952, MSP34REF62664; I would like to thank Ciarán Reilly for bringing Mary Swords to my attention.
92. Reference of Col Liam Egan included in ibid.
93. EJB to Mrs Savage-Armstrong, 19 Jan. 1925; Buckland, *Irish Unionism: A Documentary History*, p. 382; Memo by EJB, 'Tubberdaly, near Rhode, King's County', 28 May 1923 (NAI, Dept. of Justice files, 5/822).
94. *Evening Herald*, 1 July 1920.
95. *Freeman's Journal*, 17 Apr. 1923; Eamonn Ó Cúgáin [Eamonn Coogan] to Secretary of Home Affairs, 2 July 1923 (NAI, Dept. of Justice files, 5/822).
96. *Freeman's Journal*, 4 Aug. 1923.
97. Military Archives, Military Services Pension Collection, http://mspcsearch.militaryarchives. ie/detail.aspx; on the dates of his internment see *Sunday Independent*, 13 Nov. 1921; *Offaly Independent*, 4 Nov. 1922.
98. *Offaly Independent*, 11 Aug. 1923.
99. *Westmeath Independent*, 21 Apr. 1923; *Leinster Leader*, 21 Apr. 1923.
100. *Westmeath Independent*, 21 Apr. 1923.
101. *Leinster Leader*, 21 Apr. 1923.
102. Ibid.
103. Ibid., 9 June 1923.
104. *Irish Independent*, 12 Sept. 1923.
105. Tubberdaly, King's County (TNA, Compensation files, CO 762/64/12).
106. Philip McConway, 'The Civil War in Offaly', *Tullamore Tribune*, 2 Jan. 2008.
107. Christopher Jones, application for service medal, no. 2907, MSP34REF18628, http://mspcsearch.militaryarchives.ie/detail.aspx
108. Ibid.; *Westmeath Independent*, 4 Nov. 1922.
109. Ibid.
110. IRA pension claim form, Mary Swords, 9 Feb. 1952, MSP34REF62664.
111. Reference of Patrick Cox included in ibid.
112. Philip McConway, 'The Civil War in Offaly', *Tullamore Tribune*, 2 Jan. 2008; *Leinster Leader*, 3 Feb. 1923.
113. Eamonn Ó Cúgáin to Secretary of Home Affairs, 2 July 1923 (NAI, Dept. of Justice files, 5/822).
114. Clarke, *Everyday Violence in the Irish Civil War*; Gavin Foster, *The Irish Civil War: Politics, Class, and Conflict* (London, 2015).
115. Dooley, *Decline of the Big House*, pp. 187–92.
116. Reilly, 'The Burning of Country Houses in Co Offaly', p. 111.
117. *Midland Tribune*, 5 May 1923.
118. EBN Irish Grants Committee form.
119. *Dáil Debates*, vol. 3, 28 May 1923, 1161.
120. Ibid., vol. 3, 14 June 1923, 1971.
121. John Kelly to Minister of Agriculture, 4 July 1923 (NAI, Dept. of Justice files, 5/888).
122. Ibid.
123. Ibid.
124. Ibid.
125. Copy of letter from Christopher Jones to Sir [EJB], 10 July 1923 (NAI, Dept. of Justice files, 5/888).
126. EJB to Mrs Savage-Armstrong, 19 Jan. 1925; Buckland, *Irish Unionism*, p. 382.
127. Christopher Jones, application for service medal, no. 2907, MSP34REF18628, http://mspcsearch.militaryarchives.ie/detail.aspx
128. Patrick Hogan to Minister of Home Affairs [Kevin O'Higgins], 13 July 1923 (NAI, Dept. of Justice files, 5/888).
129. Ibid.

130. Quoted above on p. 266.
131. *Freeman's Journal*, 4 Aug. 1923.
132. Superintendent Sean Liddy to Commissioner of Civic Guard, 28 July 1923 (NAI, Dept. of Justice files, 5/888).
133. *Offaly Independent*, 11 Aug. 1923.
134. *Public Safety (Emergency Powers) Act*, no. 28, 1 Aug. 1923.
135. *Freeman's Journal*, 4 Aug. 1923; *Offaly Independent*, 11 Aug. 1923.
136. Eamonn Ó Cúgain to Secretary, Minister for Home Affairs, 30 Jan. 1924 (NAI, Dept. of Justice files, 5/888).
137. Ibid.
138. *Drogheda Independent*, 14 June 1924.
139. Ibid.
140. Quoted in W.N. Osborough, 'Dismissal and Discharge Under the Probation of Offenders Act 1907', *Irish Jurist*, vol. 16, no. 1 (Summer 1981), p. 1.
141. EJB to Mrs Savage-Armstrong, 19 Jan. 1925; Buckland, *Irish Unionism*, p. 382.
142. Ibid.
143. Ibid.
144. Application to Irish Grants Committee, 1927 (TNA, Compensation files, CO 762/64/12).
145. Brian Beaumont-Nesbitt to Bobbie Tyrell, 27 Sept. 1991 (private possession).
146. Ibid.; Reilly, 'Burning of Country Houses in Offaly', p. 131.
147. *Offaly Independent*, 10 Oct. 1931.
148. Ibid.
149. Mary Swords to IRA Pension Board, 6 Sept. 1962; MSP34REF62664.
150. *Dáil Debates*, vol 41, no. 15, 19 May 1932.
151. C. Desmond Greaves, *Liam Mellows and the Irish Revolution* (London, 2004), p. 364.
152. Dooley, *'The Land for the People'*, pp. 99–131.
153. *Offaly Independent*, 11 June 1932.
154. P.J. Gorry to Oscar Traynor, Minister for Defence, 3 Nov. 1953, Christopher Jones, application for service medal, no. 2907, MSP34REF18628, http://mspcsearch.militaryarchives.ie/detail.aspx
155. Ibid.
156. *Land Act 1933*, no. 38 of 1933; Dooley, *'Land for the People'*, pp. 99–131.
157. This is taking into consideration that of the total number of 'mansions' returned in 1906 (see chapter one), not all were aristocratic houses, some were glebes, rectories, lodges and so on.
158. *Leinster Leader*, 14 Apr. 1923.
159. *Meath Chronicle*, 14 Apr. 1923.
160. *Irish Times*, 15 July 1922.
161. For the full story, see Dooley, *The Decline and Fall of the Dukes of Leinster*.
162. Quoted in *Leinster Leader*, 17 June 1922.
163. Charles Hamilton to Henry Mallaby-Deeley, 8 Apr. 1924 (Hamilton papers, private possession).
164. *Leinster Leader*, 17 June 1922.
165. Workers of Bessborough Estate, Kilkenny, to President W.T. Cosgrave, 24 Nov. 1923 (Military Archives, A/7432).
166. Report and Complaint by Marquess of Sligo to Secretary to the Minister of Local Government, 6 May 1922 (Military Archives, A/7065).
167. *Meath Chronicle*, 28 Aug. 1920, 10 Feb. 1923.
168. *Dáil Debates*, vol. 29, 19 Apr. 1929, 18.
169. Ibid., vol. 13, 2 Dec. 1925, 1127.
170. Ibid., vol. 40, 11 & 25 Nov. 1931, 1201, 1998.
171. Fr Brett to William Sears, 22 Jan. 1923 (Military Archives, A/7432).
172. T.M. Healy to Richard Mulcahy, 23 Dec. 1922; Mulcahy to GOC Limerick Command, n.d. (Military Archives, A/7432).
173. Quoted in Ciarán Reilly, ' "Ill-gotten acres": The GAA and the Irish Country House', in Terence Dooley and Christopher Ridgway (eds.), *Sport and Leisure in the Irish and British Country House* (Dublin, 2019), p. 224.

174. Karina Holton, *Valentine Lawless, Lord Cloncurry, 1773–1853: From United Irishman to Liberal Politician* (Dublin, 2018).
175. Leslie, *The Irish Tangle*, p. 149.
176. K. Dorrian to Lord Cloncurry, 5 Apr. 1922 (Cloncurry Diary 1922, private possession).
177. Quoted in James Durney, *The Civil War in Kildare* (Cork, 2011), p. 145.
178. Amory, *Biography of Lord Dunsany*, p. 170.
179. Bence-Jones, *Twilight of the Ascendancy*, pp. 12, 37.
180. Bull, *Monksgrange*, p. 205.
181. Coleman, 'Protestant Depopulation in Longford', p. 968.
182. *Irish Times*, 2 Apr. 2016.
183. Quoted in Purdue, *The Big House in the North of Ireland*, p. 148.
184. Bielenberg, 'Exodus', p. 215.
185. Hughes, *Defying the IRA?*.
186. *Tuam Herald*, 25 June 1921.
187. *Irish Times*, 5 Nov. 1921.
188. Quoted in ibid., p. 13.
189. Robert O'Byrne [The Irish Aesthete], 'Summerhill, A Souvenir', https://theirishaesthete.com/tag/summerhill/
190. Robert O'Byrne has done a great deal to resurrect these memories on his award-winning blog, https://theirishaesthete.com/
191. Quoted in Frank Delaney, *Betjeman Country* (London, 1985), p. 83.
192. Leslie, *The Irish Tangle*, pp. 146. 173.
193. See Bevan, *The Destruction of Memory*, p. 25.
194. Raymond Gillespie, 'Foreword' in O'Riordan, *East Galway Agrarian Agitation*, p. 2.
195. E.P. Thompson, 'The Moral Economy of the English Crowd in the Eighteenth Century' in *Past & Present*, no. 50 (Feb. 1971), p. 112.

BIBLIOGRAPHY

1. Manuscript Sources

Fingal County Archives, Swords
Hely-Hutchinson papers

Irish Architectural Archives (IAA)
Files on individual houses

Military Archives, Cathal Brugha Barracks, Dublin
Brigade Activity Reports
Bureau of Military History Witness Statements, 1916–21
Files relating to the Special Infantry Corps
Military Service Pension Collection, 1916–23

Monaghan County Museum
Thomas Brennan papers
Marron papers
Thomas Toal papers

National Archives of Ireland (NAI)
Estate/family collections: Bellew, Blake, Childers, Congreve, Coote, Esmonde, Guinness
    Mahon, King-Harman
Dáil Éireann files (DE 2, 3, 4 and 5)
Dáil Éireann: Land Settlement Commission papers
Minutes of Proceedings of First Dáil Éireann, 1919–21
Dáil Éireann: Private Sessions of Second Dáil: Minutes of Proceedings 18 Aug. 1921–14 Sept.
    1921
Government and Cabinet Files, 1922–51
Department of Agriculture files
Department of the Environment files
Department of Finance files
Department of Home Affairs files
Department of Justice files
Department of An Taoiseach files
Irish Convention 1917–18 Papers
Minutes of Provisional Government, 1922(A, G1/1)
Minutes of the Executive Council, 1923–32(G2/1–8)
Office of Public Works Compensation Files
Board of Works Files
Papers Relating to the Irish Convention, 1917–18 Sinn Féin Standing Committee, Minutes
    5 June 1919–23 Mar. 1922
1901 and 1911 Census, Household Schedule Returns

BIBLIOGRAPHY

National Gallery of Ireland
Auction catalogues for Irish country houses sold c.1912–50

National Library of Ireland (NLI)
Estate/Family Collections:
Ashtown, Bellingham, Bernard, Blake, Bond, Bowen, Bruen, Butler (Castlecrine), Castletown, Clonbrock, Conyngham, Crofton, Dartrey, De Freyne, Doneraile, Doyne, Dunalley, Dunsandle, Dunsany, Farnham, Fitzwilliam, Garstin, Gormanston, Granard, Headfort, Howard (Diaries of Lady Alice), Inchiquin, Leitrim, Leslie, Louth, Mahon (Castlegar), Midleton, Monck, O'Hara, Ormonde, Powerscourt, Pratt, Sligo (Westport), Wicklow.

Office of Public Works (OPW)/Maynooth University Archive and Research Centre, Castletown House
Airfield papers
Ballindoolin papers
Knight of Glin papers

Public Record Office, Northern Ireland (PRONI)
Estate/family collections: Dartrey, Dunraven, Farnham, Howard-Bury, Kenmare, Leinster, Leslie, Lissadell, Madden, Masserreene, Moutray, Rathdonnell, Rossmore, Shirley, Wilson (J.M.), Wyndham (George)
Minute Books of the Executive Committee of the Irish Unionist Alliance
Minute Book of the General Council of the Irish Unionist Alliance
Southern Irish Loyalist Relief Association papers
Ulster Unionist Council yearbook, 1913–20
Ulster Unionist Yearbooks

Somerset Record Office
De Vesci papers

The National Archives (TNA), London
Colonial Office (CO) papers, CO 904 (Dublin Castle records):
    Part I: Anti-government Organisations, 1882–1921
    Part II: Police Reports, Jan. 1892–Dec. 1897
    Part III: Police Reports, Feb. 1898–Dec. 1913
    Part IV: Police Reports, 1914–21
    Part VI: Judicial Proceedings, Enquiries and Miscellaneous Records, 1872–1926
Claims for Compensation Registers (CO 905)
Dunedin Committee Papers (CO 905)
Criminal Injuries: Irish Grants Committee files (CO 762)

Trinity College Dublin (TCD), Manuscripts Department
Estate/family collections: Bond (Faragh), Courtown, Crofton

University College Dublin (UCD), Archives Department
Frank Aiken papers
Ernest Blythe papers
Cumann na nGaedheal/Fine Gael papers
Fianna Fáil papers
Sean MacEntee papers
Seán MacEoin papers
Richard Mulcahy papers
George O'Callaghan Westropp papers
Kevin O'Higgins papers

Ernie O'Malley papers
Kevin O'Shiel papers
Moss Twomey papers

Private Possession
Ashtown paper
Beaumont-Nesbitt papers
Bellingham papers
Cloncurry papers
Enniscoe papers
Hamilton papers
Keane papers
Lucas-Scudamore papers
Prittie [Dunalley] papers
Tenison papers

2. British Parliamentary Papers

Report of the Royal Commission on the Land Law (Ireland) Act, 1881, and the Purchase of Land (Ireland) Act, 1885 (Earl Cowper, chairman)*: Minutes of Evidence and Appendices* [C4969], HC 1887, xxvi

Return Showing to the Latest Year Available, for Ireland as a Whole, the Annual Average Prices for Each Year from 1881 . . . HC 1921, vol. xli. 93

Return of Untenanted Lands in Rural Districts, Distinguishing Demesnes on Which There Is a Mansion, Showing Rural District and Electoral Divisions, Townland, Area in Statute Acres, Poor Law Valuation, Names of Occupiers as in Valuation Lists, HC, 1906, c.177

Agricultural Statistics for Ireland with Detailed Report for the Year 1917 [Cmd 1316], HC 1921, lxi.135, p. xiii

Memo Dated 10 May 1906 Issued by the Estates Commissioners for Guidance of Assistant Inspectors When Making Inquiries with Reference to Applications Received from Persons Seeking Reinstatement as Evicted Tenants or as the Representatives of Evicted Tenants [Cd 3658], HC 1907, vol. lxx.1171

Royal Commission on Congestion in Ireland: Final Report of the Commissioners [Cd 4097], HC 1908, xlii. 729

Agricultural Statistics for Ireland with Detailed Report for the Year 1917 [Cmd 1316], HC 1921, vol. lxi, p. xiv

Report of the Proceedings of the Irish Convention [Cd 9019], HC 1918, vol. x. 697

Report of Estates Commissioners for the Year from 1 April 1919 to 31 March 1920 and for the Period from 1 November 1903 to 31 March 1920 [Cmd 1150], HC 1921, vol. xiv. 661

Report of the Estates Commissioners for the Year from 1 April 1918 to 31 March 1919 [Cmd 577], HC 1919, xix, 965

Agricultural Statistics for Ireland with Detailed Report for the Year 1920 [Cmd 1317], HC 1921, vol. xli. 99

Relief of Irish Refugees: Correspondence Between H.M. Government and the Provisional Government of Ireland Relating to the Liability for the Relief of Irish Refugees [Cmd] 1684, HC 1922, xvii

Compensation for Malicious Injuries: Letter to the Provisional Government of Southern Ireland, [Cmd 1736], H.C. 1922, xvii

Summary of Agreement Between H.M. Government and the Government of the Irish Free State Relating to Compensation for Damage to Property in Ireland [Cmd 2445], HC 1924–5, xxiii

Compensation: Report of the Commission Presided over by Lord Dunedin [Cmd 2748], HC 1926, ix

3. Irish Government Publications

Annual Reports of the Department of Agriculture and Technical Instruction, 1921–31
Annual Reports of the Minister for Agriculture, 1931–65

Census Reports, 1911, 1926

Commission on Agriculture, Final Report of the Commission on Agriculture, 1923–4 (Dublin, 1924)

Committee of Enquiry on Post-Emergency Agricultural Policy: Reports on Agricultural Policy, 1945

Department of Agriculture (G.A. Holmes), Report on the Present State and Methods for Improvement of Irish Grasslands, 1949

Inter-Departmental Committee on Land Structure Reform: Final Report, 1978

Irish Land Commission, Annual Reports, 1923–84

Programme for Economic Expansion, 1958

Report by the Inter-Departmental Committee on the Problem of Small Western Farms, 1962

Third Programme for Economic and Social Development, 1969–72: Laid by the Government Before Each House of the Oireachtas, March 1969

4. Acts Passed by the British Government for Ireland

An Act to Further Amend the Law Relating to the Occupation and Ownership of Land in Ireland and for Other Purposes Relating Thereto [22 Aug. 1881], ch. 49, 44 and 45 Vict.

An Act for Amending the Law Relating to Local Government in Ireland and for Other Purposes Connected Therewith [12 August 1898] 61 and 62 Vict., c. xxxvii

An Act to Amend the Enactments Relative to Compensation for Criminal Injuries in Ireland [16 April 1919] 9 and 10 Geo. V, c. lxvi

An Act to Amend the Enactments Relative to Compensation for Criminal Injuries in Ireland [23 December 1920] 10 and 11 Geo. V, c. lxvi

An Act to Facilitate the Provision of Land for Certain Evicted Tenants in Ireland and for Other Purposes Connected Therewith, and to Make Provision with Respect to the Tenure of Office by the Estates Commissioners [26 Aug. 1907] ch.56, 7 Edw. VII

Irish Land (Provision for Soldiers and Sailors) Act [23 Dec. 1919] ch. 82, 9 and 10 Geo. V

5. Acts Passed by the Irish Government

Enforcement of Law (Occasional Powers) Act, 1923, [1Mar. 1923], no. 4/1923

An Act to Alter the Law Relating to Compensation for Criminal Injuries [12 May 1923], no. 15/1923

Land Law (Commission) Act, 1923: An Act to Amend the Law Relating to the Irish Land Commission and to Dissolve the Congested Districts Board for Ireland and Transfer its Functions to the Irish Land Commission and for Other Purposes Connected Therewith, [24 July 1923], no. 27/1923

An Act to Provide for the Preservation of Public Safety and the Protection of Persons and Property and for Matters Connected Therewith or Arising Out of the Present Emergency [1 Aug. 1923], no. 28/1923

An Act to Make Provision for the Immediate Preservation of the Public Safety [3 Aug. 1923], no. 29/1923

The Land Act 1923: An Act to Amend the Law Relating to the Occupation and Ownership of Land and for Other Purposes Relating Thereto, [9 Aug. 1923], no. 42/1923

Land Act, 1927: An Act to Amend the Law Relating to the Occupation and Ownership of Land and for Other Purposes Relating Thereto, [21 May 1927], no. 19/1927

National Monuments Act, 1930. An Act to Make Provision for the Protection and Preservation of National Monuments and for the Preservation of Archaeological Objects in Saorstát Eireann and to Make Provision for Other Matters Connected with the Matters Aforesaid (26 Feb. 1930)

Land Act, 1933. An Act to Amend Generally the Law, Finance, and Practice Relating to Land Purchase, and in Particular to Make Further and Better Provision for the Execution of the Functions of the Judicial and Lay Commissioners of the Land Commission and to Provide for the Revision of Purchase Annuities and Certain Other Annual Payments and for the Funding of Arrears Thereof, and to Provide for Other Matters Connected with the Matters Aforesaid (13 Oct. 1933)

Irish Land Commission (Dissolution) Act, 1992. An Act to Provide for the Dissolution of the Irish Land Commission, for the Winding Up of the System of Land Purchase, for the Transfer of Certain Functions Exercisable under the Land Purchase Acts, and for Other Connected Matters (11 Nov. 1992)

6. Printed Parliamentary Debates

Dáil Éireann Debates
Seanad Éireann Debates
Hansard

7. Guides and Works of Reference

Bateman, John, *The Great Landowners of Great Britain and Ireland* (London 1883)
Bence-Jones, Mark, *Burke's Guide to Country Houses. Volume I, Ireland* (London, 1978)
Browne, Vincent (ed.), *The Magill Book of Irish Politics* (Dublin, 1981)
Burke's Landed Gentry of Ireland (London, 1958)
Burke's Peerage, Baronetage and Knightage (various edns)
Connolly, S.J. (ed.), *The Oxford Companion to Irish History* (Oxford, 1998)
Corkayne, G.E., *Complete Peerage of England, Scotland, Ireland, Extant, Extinct or Dormant* (Exeter, 1887–98), 8 vols
Craig, Maurice, *Classic Irish Houses of the Middle Size* (London and New York, 1976)
Dictionary of Irish Biography
Dooley, Terence, *The Big Houses and Landed Estates of Ireland: A Research Guide* (Dublin, 2007)
Ford, Percy and Ford, Grace, *A Breviate of Parliamentary Papers, 1917–39* (Oxford, 1951)
Ford, Percy and Ford, Grace, *A Select List of Reports and Inquiries of the Irish Dáil and Senate, 1922–1974* (Shannon, 1974)
The Georgian Society Records of Eighteenth-Century Domestic Architecture and Decoration in Ireland (Dublin, 1913)
Hussey De Burgh, U.H., *The Landowners of Ireland* (Dublin, 1878)
Lewis, Samuel, *A Topographical Dictionary of Ireland* (London, 1937), 2 vols
Loeber, Rolf et al. (eds.), *Art and Architecture of Ireland* (Dublin, London, New Haven, 2014)
Maltby, Arthur and McKenna, Brian, *Irish Official Publications: A Guide to the Republic of Ireland Papers, with a Breviate of Reports, 1922–70* (Oxford, 1980)
Oxford Dictionary of National Biography
Walker, B.M. (ed.), *Parliamentary Election Results in Ireland, 1918–92* (Dublin, 1992)

8. Contemporary Publications and Memoirs

Annesley, Mabel M., *As the Sight Is Bent: An Unfinished Autobiography* (London, 1964)
Barry, Tom, *Guerilla Days in Ireland* (Dublin, 1981 edn [1949])
Bonn, M.J. [translated by T.W. Rolleston], *Modern Ireland and Her Agrarian Problem* (London, 1906)
Bowen, Elizabeth, *Bowen's Court* (London, 1942)
Bowen, Muriel, *Irish Hunting* (Tralee, n.d.)
Breen, Dan, *My Fight for Irish Freedom* (Dublin, 1981 edn [first edn Dublin, 1924])
Briollay, Sylvain, *Ireland in Rebellion* (London, 1922)
Castletown, Lord, *Ego: Random Records of Sport, Service and Travel in Many Lands* (London, 1923)
[Childers, Erskine], *The Constructive Work of Dáil Éireann: I and II* (Dublin, 1921)
Connolly, James, *Labour in Ireland* (Dublin, 1917)
Cooper, Bryan, *The Tenth (Irish) Division in Gallipoli* (London, 1918)
Cosgrave, W.T., *Policy of the Cumann na nGaedheal Party* (Dublin, 1927)
Costello, John A., *Land Purchase Annuities* (Dublin, 1931)
Cumann na nGaedheal, *To the Electorate of the Irish Free State* (Dublin, n.d. [1932])

Davitt, Michael, *The Fall of Feudalism in Ireland* (New York, 1904)

Deasy, Liam, *Towards Ireland Free: The West Cork Brigade in the War of Independence 1917–21* (Cork, 1973).

Desart, Earl of, and Lady Sybil Lubbock, *A Page From the Past* (London, 1936)

De Stacpoole, Duc, *Irish and Other Memories* (London, 1922)

Devoy, John, *The Land of Éire* (New York, 1882)

Drought, J.B., *A Sportsman Looks at Éire* (London, n.d)

Dunalley, Lord, *Khaki and Green* (London, 1940)

Dunraven, Earl of [Windham Thomas Wyndham-Quin], *Past Times and Pastimes* (London, 1922), vol. 1.

Dunraven, Earl of, *The Crisis in Ireland: Account of the Present Condition of Ireland and Suggestions Toward Reform* (Dublin, 1905)

Dunraven, Earl of, *The Outlook in Ireland* (Dublin, 1907)

Fianna Fáil, *A National Policy Outlined by Eamon de Valera Delivered at the Inaugural Meeting of Fianna Fáil at La Scala Theatre, Dublin, May 1926* (Dublin, n.d. [1927])

Fianna Fáil National Executive, *The Land Annuities* (Dublin, 1932)

Gaughan, J.A. (ed.), *Memoirs of Senator Joseph Connolly (1885–1961): A Founder of Modern Ireland* (Dublin, 1996)

Gough, Hubert, *Soldiering On* (London, 1954)

Harrison, Henry, *The Strange Case of the Irish Land Purchase Annuities* (Dublin, 1932)

Henn, T.R., *Five Arches: A Sketch for an Autobiography* (Gerrard's Cross, 1980)

Hone, Joseph, *The Moores of Moore Hall* (London, 1936)

Hughes, Hector, *The Land Acts 1923 to 1927* (Dublin, 1928)

Irish Claims Compensation Association, *The Campaign of Fire: A Record of Some Mansions and Houses Destroyed* (London, 1924)

Irish Unionist Alliance, *Irish Southern Loyalists, the War and After* (Dublin, 1918)

King-Harman, R.D., *The Kings, Earls of Kingston: An Account of the Family and Their Estates in Ireland Between the Reigns of the Two Queen Elizabeths* (Cambridge, 1959)

Lavelle, Patrick, *The Irish Landlord Since the Revolution* (Dublin, 1870)

Leslie, Anita, *The Gilt and the Gingerbread: An Autobiography* (London, 1931)

Leslie, Anita, *Edwardians in Love* (London, 1972)

Leslie, Seymour, *Of Glaslough in the Kingdom of Oriel* (privately published)

Leslie, Shane, *Doomsland* (London, 1923)

Leslie, Shane, *The Irish Tangle for English Readers* (London, n.d.)

Leslie, Shane, *The Film of Memory* (London, 1938)

McCarthy, M.J.F., *Irish Land and Irish Liberty: A Study of the New Lords of the Soil* (London, 1911)

MacFhionghail, Labhras, *The Land Question* (Dublin, n.d. [1917])

McParland, Edward and Nicholas Robinson (eds), *Heritage at Risk: A Digest of An Taisce's Report on the Future of Historic Houses, Gardens and Collections in the Republic of Ireland* (1977)

Masterman, C.F.G., *England after War: A Study* (London, 1922)

Meath, Earl of (ed.), *The Diaries of Mary, Countess of Meath* (London, n.d.)

Midleton [John Broderick], *Records and Reactions, 1856–1939* (London, 1939)

Monahan, H.J., 'Administration of Land Acts' in F.C. King (ed.), *Public Administration in Ireland* (Dublin, n.d. [c.1944]), pp. 130–42

Moore, Maurice, *British Plunder and Irish Blunder or the Story of the Land Purchase Annuities* (Dublin, n.d.)

Morton, H.V., *In Search of Ireland* (London, 1930)

Moynihan, Maurice (ed.), *Speeches and Statements by Eamon de Valera, 1917–73* (Dublin, 1980)

Neale, J.P., *Views of the Seats of Noblemen and Gentlemen in England, Wales and Scotland and Ireland*, vol. iii (London, 1820)

O'Brien, William, *An Olive Branch in Ireland and its History* (London, 1910)

[O'Callaghan Westropp, George] *Notes on the Defence of Irish Country Houses* (1912)

O'Donnell, Peadar, *There Will be Another Day* (Dublin, 1963)

O'Malley, Ernie, *On Another Man's Wound* (Dublin, 1979 edn [1st edn London, 1936])

O'Neill, Brian, *The War for the Land in Ireland* (London, 1933)

O'Shiel, Kevin, 'Some Recent Phases of the Land Question in Ireland', *Manchester Guardian*, 10 May 1926.

O'Shiel, Kevin, 'The Work of the Land Commission' in F.C. King (ed.), Public Administration in Ireland, Vol. II (Dublin, 1949).

O'Shiel, Kevin, and O'Brien, T., *The Land Problem in Ireland and Its Settlement* (Dublin, n.d. [1954?])

O'Shiel, Kevin, 'Memories of My Lifetime', *The Irish Times*, 11–22 Nov. 1966

Ossory, Earl of, 'The Attack on Kilkenny Castle', *Journal of the Butler Society*, Vol. I, no. 4 (1972), pp. 259–74

O'Sullivan, D.J., *The Free State and Its Senate: A Study in Contemporary Politics* (London, 1940)

Paul-Dubois, Louis, *Contemporary Ireland* (Dublin, 1908)

Phillips, A.W., *The Revolution in Ireland, 1906–23* (London, 1923)

Plunkett, Horace, *Ireland in the New Century* (London, 1904)

Plunkett, Horace, *Noblesse Oblige: An Irish Rendering* (Dublin, 1908)

Plunkett, Elizabeth, Countess of Fingall, *Seventy Years Young: Memories of Elizabeth, Countess of Fingall* (London, 1937)

Prittie, Terence, *Through Irish Eyes* (London, 1977)

Redmond, William, *Trench Pictures from France* (Belfast, 2007)

Robinson, Lennox (ed.), *Lady Gregory's Journals* (New York, 1947)

Robinson, Lennox, *Bryan Cooper* (London, 1931)

Robinson, Lennox, Robinson, Tom and Dorman, Nora, *Three Homes* (London, 1938)

Robertson, Nora, *Crowned Harp: Memories of the Last Years of the Crown in Ireland* (Dublin, 1960)

Sammon, P.J., *In the Land Commission: A Memoir 1933–1978* (Dublin, 1997)

Saunderson, Henry, *The Saundersons of Castlesaunderson* (London, 1936)

9. Newspapers and Journals

Anglo-Celt
An Phoblacht
An tOglach
Architect's Journal
Belfast News Letter
Capuchin Annual
Carlow Sentinel
Church of Ireland Gazette
Connaught Leader
Connaught Tribune
Cork Constitution
Cork Examiner
Country Life
Daily Express
Daily Telegraph
Drogheda Independent
Dundalk Democrat
Echo and South Leinster Adventurer
Evening Mail
Farmers' Journal
Freeman's Journal
Galway Express
Hampshire Telegraph
Irish Ancestor
Irish Examiner

Irish Georgian Society Bulletin
Irish Independent
Irish Press
Irish Tatler and Sketch
Irish Times
Iris Oifigiúil
Kildare Observer
Kilkenny People
Limerick Chronicle
Londonderry Sentinel
Mayo News
Meath Chronicle
Morning Post
Nenagh Guardian.
Northern Standard
Notes From Ireland (Irish Unionist Alliance)
Offaly County Chronicle
Offaly Independent
Roscommon Journal
Roscommon Messenger
Sligo Champion
St Stephen's Review
Sunday Independent
The Liberator
The Nationalist
The Times
Tipperary Star
Tuam Herald
Tullamore and King's County Independent
Weekly Irish Times
Weekly Telegraph
Western People
Westmeath Examiner
Westmeath Guardian
Westminster Gazette

10. Select Bibliography of Secondary Works

Allen, Kieran, *Fianna Fáil and Labour* (London, 1997)

Amory, Mark, *Biography of Lord Dunsany* (London, 1972)

Attwood, E.A., 'Agriculture and Economic Growth in Western Ireland', *Journal of the Statistical and Social Enquiry of Ireland* XX, 5(1961–2): 172–95

Augusteijn, Joost, *From Public Defiance to Guerrilla Warfare: The Experience of Ordinary Volunteers in the Irish War of Independence 1916–21* (Dublin, 1996)

Augusteijn, Joost (ed.), *The Irish Revolution, 1913–1923* (London, 2002)

Barnard, Toby, *A New Anatomy of Ireland* (New Haven and London, 2003)

Bence-Jones, Mark, *Twilight of the Ascendancy* (London, 1987)

Bence Jones, Mark, *Life in an Irish Country House* (London, 1996)

Bevan, Robert, *The Destruction of Memory: Architecture at War* (London, 2006)

Bew, Paul, *Land and the National Question in Ireland, 1858–82* (Dublin, 1978)

Bew, Paul, *Conflict and Conciliation in Ireland. 1898–1910: Parnellites and Agrarian Radicals* (Oxford, 1987)

Bew, Paul, *Ireland: The Politics of Enmity 1789–2006* (Oxford, 2007)

Bew, Paul, 'Sinn Féin, Agrarian Radicalism and the War of Independence 1919–1921', in Boyce (ed.), *The Revolution in Ireland, 1879–1923*, pp. 217–34

Bew, Paul, Patterson, Henry and Hazelkorn, Ellen, *The Dynamics of Irish Politics* (London, 1989).

Bew, Paul, and Patterson, Henry, *Sean Lemass and the Making of Modern Ireland, 1945–66* (Dublin, 1982)

Biagini, Eugenio, *Liberty, Retrenchment and Reform: Popular Liberalism in the Age of Gladstone, 1860–1880* (Cambridge, 1992)

Biagini, Eugenio, 'The Protestant Minority in Southern Ireland', *Historical Journal*, lv, no. 4 (Dec. 2012), pp. 1161–84

Bielenberg, Andy, 'Exodus: The Emigration of Southern Irish Protestants during the Irish War of Independence and the Civil War', *Past and Present*, no. 218 (2013), pp. 199–233

Borgonovo, John, *Spies, Informers, and the 'Anti-Sinn Féin Society': The Intelligence War in Cork City* (Dublin, 2007)

Bourke, Joanna, 'Shell-Shock, Psychiatry and the Irish Soldier During the First World War', in Gregory and Paseta (eds.), *Ireland and the Great War*, pp. 156–68

Bowen, Elizabeth, 'The Big House', in Hermione Lee (ed.), *The Mulberry Tree: Writings on Elizabeth Bowen* (London, 1986), pp. 25–30

Bowen, Elizabeth, *The Last September* (London, 1998)

Boyce, D.G. (ed.), *The Revolution in Ireland, 1879–1923* (Dublin and London, 1988)

Bradley, D.G., *Farm Labourers: Irish Struggle, 1900–1976* (Belfast, 1988)

Brandenburg, S.J., 'Progress of Land Transfers in the Irish Free State', *Journal of Land and Public Utility Economics* viii, 3(1932): 275–85

Breathnach, Proinnsias, 'Creamery Attacks', in Crowley et al. (eds.), *Atlas of the Irish Revolution*, pp. 555–7

Brennan, Niamh, 'A Political Minefield: Southern Loyalists, the Irish Grants Committee and the British Government, 1922–31', *Irish Historical Studies*, Vol. 30, no. 119 (May, 1997), pp. 406–19

Brown, Terence, *Ireland: A Social and Cultural History* (London, 1981)

Browne, Fergal, 'The Death of the Pallastown Heir: Lt Robert Heard, Pallastown Guards', in Dooley and Ridgway (eds.), *The Country House and the Great War*, pp. 18–28

Buckland, Patrick, *Irish Unionism I: The Anglo-Irish and the New Ireland 1885–1922* (Dublin, 1972)

Buckland, Patrick, *Irish Unionism 1885–1923: A Documentary History* (Belfast, 1973)

Bujak, Edward, *English Landed Society in the Great War: Defending the Realm* (London, 2019)

Bull, Philip, *Land, Politics and Nationalism: A Study of the Irish Land Question* (Dublin, 1996)

Bull, Philip, *Monksgrange: Portrait of an Irish House and Family, 1769–1969* (Dublin, 2019)

Butler, John, 'Lord Oranmore's Journal', *Irish Historical Studies*, vol. 29, no. 116 (November 1995).

Byrne, Elaine A. 'A Unique Experiment in Idealism: The Irish Senate 1922–28', in Farrell, Knirck and Meehan (eds), *A Formative Decade*, pp. 59–85

Byrne, Fidelma, ' "Not Another Son": The Impact of the Great War on Two Irish Families', in Dooley and Ridgway (eds.), *The Country House and the Great War*, pp. 53–61

Campbell, Fergus, *Land and Revolution: Nationalist Politics in the West of Ireland 1891–1921* (Oxford, 2005)

Campbell, Fergus, *The Irish Establishment 1879–1914* (Oxford, 2009)

Campbell, Fergus, 'The Last Land War? Kevin O Shiel's Memoir of the Irish Revolution (1916–21)', *Archivium Hibernicum*, vol. 57 (2003), pp. 155–200

Cannadine, David, *The Decline and Fall of the British Aristocracy* (New Haven & London, 1990)

Cannadine, David, *Aspects of Aristocracy* (Yale, 1994)

Carew, Mairéad, 'Politics and the Definition of National Monuments: The Big House Problem', *Journal of Irish Archaeology*, xviii (2009), pp. 129–39

Carey, Anne, 'Harold G. Leask: Aspects of His Work as Inspector of National Monuments', *Journal of the Royal Society of Antiquaries of Ireland*, cxxxiii (2003), pp. 24–35

Casey, Christine, *Making Magnificence: Architects, Stuccatori and the Eighteenth-Century Interior* (New Haven and London, 2017)

Chambers, Anne, *At Arm's Length* (2nd edn, Dublin, 2004)

Cherry, Jonathan, 'Adaptive Coexistence? Lord Farnham (1879–1957), Southern Loyalist in Pre- and Post-Independence Ireland', in Hughes and Morrissey (eds.), *Southern Irish Loyalism*

Clark, Gemma, *Everyday Violence in the Irish Civil War* (Cambridge, 2014)

Clark, Samuel, *Social Origins of the Irish Land War* (Princeton, 1979)

Clear, Caitriona, 'Fewer Ladies: More Women', in Horne (ed.), *Our War: Ireland and the Great War* (Dublin, 2008), pp. 157–80

Coffey, Leigh Ann, *The Planters of Luggacurran: The Experiences of a Protestant Community in Queen's County, 1879–1927* (Dublin, 2006)

Coleman, Marie, *County Longford and the Irish Revolution 1910–1923* (Dublin, 2003)

Coleman, Marie, 'The Military Service Pensions Collection', in Crowley et al. (eds.), *Atlas of the Irish Revolution*, pp. 881–5

Coleman, Marie, 'Protestant Depopulation in County Longford during the Irish Revolution, 1911–1926', *English Historical Review*, cxxxv, no. 575 (Aug. 2020), pp. 931–77

Comerford, R.V., *Fenians in Context: Irish Politics and Society 1848–82* (Dublin, 1998 [1st edn 1985])

Comerford, R.V., *Ireland: Inventing the Nation* (London, 2003)

Comerford, R.V., 'The Land War and the Politics of Distress, 1877–82', in W.E. Vaughan (ed.), *A New History of Ireland. Vol. 6: Ireland Under the Union, Part 2, 1870–1921* (Oxford, 1996), pp. 26–52

Commins, Patrick, *The Impact of Re-Distribution in Ireland 1923–1974: The Michael Dillon Memorial Lecture 1993* (Dublin, 1993)

Connolly, S.J., *Contested Island: Ireland 1460–1630* (Oxford, 2007)

Coogan, Oliver, *Politics and War in Meath, 1913–23* (Dublin, 1983)

Cosgrove, Patrick, *The Ranch War in Riverstown, Co. Sligo, 1908* (Dublin, 2012)

Cosgrove, Patrick, Dooley, Terence and Mullaney-Dignam, Karol (eds), *Aspects of Irish Aristocratic Life: Essays on the Fitzgeralds and Carton House* (Dublin 2014)

Council of Europe, *War Damage to the Cultural Heritage in Croatia and Bosnia Herzgovina* (1994)

Crawford, Heather, *Outside the Glow: Protestantism and Irishness in Independent Ireland* (Dublin, 2010)

Cronin, Maura, *Agrarian Protest in Ireland 1750–1960* (Dundalk, 2012)

Cronin, Mike and Regan, J.M. (eds), *Ireland: The Politics of Independence, 1922–49* (Basingstoke, 2000)

Crooke, Emer, *'White Elephants': The Country House and the State in Independent Ireland, 1922–73* (Dublin, 2018)

Crossman, Virginia, *Local Government in Nineteenth-Century Ireland* (Belfast, 1994)

Crotty, Raymond, *Irish Agricultural Production: Its Volume and Structure* (Cork, 1966)

Crowley, John et al. (eds.), *Atlas of the Irish Revolution* (Cork, 2017)

Cullen, Seamus, 'Loyalists in a Garrison County: Kildare, 1912–1923', in Hughes and Morrissey (eds.), *Southern Irish Loyalism*, pp. 245–68

Curtis Jr, L.P., 'Incumbered Wealth: Landed Indebtedness in Post-Famine Ireland', *The American Historical Review* (Apr. 1980), 85:2, pp. 332–67

Curtis Jr, L.P., 'Stopping the Hunt: An Aspect of the Irish Land War', in C.H.E. Philpin (ed.), *Nationalism and Popular Protest in Ireland* (Cambridge, 1987), pp. 349–402

Curtis, Jr, L.P., 'The Last Gasp of Southern Unionism: Lord Ashtown of Woodlawn', *Éire-Ireland*, 40: 3&4 (Fall/Winter, 2005), pp. 140–87

d'Alton, Ian, '"Lay Spring Flowers on Our Boy's Grave": Norman Leslie's Short War', in Dooley and Ridgway (eds.), *The Country House and the Great War*, pp. 76–86

d'Alton, Ian, 'Loyal to What? Identity and Motivation in the Southern Irish Protestant Involvement in Two World Wars', in Hughes and Morrissey (eds.), *Southern Irish Loyalism*, pp. 117–26

Daniel, T.K., 'Griffith on his Noble Head: The Determinants of Cumann na nGaedheal Economic Policy, 1922–32', *Irish Economic and Social History* iii (1976): 55–65

BIBLIOGRAPHY

D'Arcy, Fergus, *Horses, Lords and Racing Men: The Kildare Turf Club 1790–1990* (Kildare, 1991)

Davenport-Hines, Richard, *Ettie: The Intimate Life and Dauntless Spirit of Lady Desborough* (London, 2008)

Davies, J.C., 'Towards a Theory of Revolution', *American Sociological Review,* 27 (1962), pp. 5–19

Delaney, Enda, 'Anti-Communism in Mid-Twentieth-Century Ireland', *The English History Review*, vol. 126, no. 521 (Aug. 2011), pp. 878–903

Denman, Terence, *Ireland's Unknown Soldiers: The 16th (Irish) Division in the Great War* (Dublin, 1992)

Dickson, David, *Old World Colony: Cork and South Munster 1630–1830* (Cork, 2005)

Dolan, Ann, 'Killing in "The Good Old Irish Fashion"? Irish Revolutionary Violence in Context', *Irish Historical Studies*, (2020), 44 (165), pp. 11–24

Donnelly, J.S. Jr, *The Land and People of Nineteenth-Century Cork* (London, 1975).

Donnelly, J.S. Jr, *The Great Irish Potato Famine* (Stroud, 2001)

Donnelly, J.S. Jr, 'Big House Burnings in County Cork during the Irish Revolution, 1920–21', *Éire-Ireland*, xlvii, no. 3&4 (Fall/Winter 2012), pp. 141–97

Dooley, Terence, *The Decline of the Big House in Ireland: A Study of Irish Landed Families, 1860–1960* (Dublin, 2001)

Dooley, Terence, *A Future for Irish Historic Houses: A Study of Fifty Houses* (Dublin, 2003)

Dooley, Terence, *'The Land for the People': The Land Question in Independent Ireland* (Dublin, 2004)

Dooley, Terence, 'National Patrimony and Political Perceptions of the Irish Country House in Post-Independence Ireland', in Terence Dooley (ed.) *Ireland's Polemical Past: Views of Irish History in Honour of R.V. Comerford* (Dublin, 2010), pp. 192–212

Dooley, Terence, *The Decline and Fall of the Dukes of Leinster, 1872–1948: Love, War, Debt and Madness* (Dublin, 2014)

Dooley, Terence, *Monaghan: The Irish Revolution, 1913–23* (Dublin, 2017)

Dooley, Terence, 'Land and Politics in Independent Ireland, 1923–1948: The Case for Reappraisal', *Irish Historical Studies,* xxxiv, no. 134 (Nov. 2004), pp. 175–197

Dooley, Terence and Ridgway, Christopher (eds), *The Irish Country House: Its Past, Present and Future* (Dublin, 2011)

Dooley, Terence and McCarthy, Tony, 'The 1923 Land Act: Some New Perspectives', in Farrell, Knirck and Meehan (eds), *A Formative Decade,* (2015), pp. 132–56

Dooley, Terence and Ridgway, Christopher (eds), *The Country House and the Great War: Irish and British Experiences* (Dublin, 2016)

Dooley, Terence, and Ridgway, Christopher (eds.), *Country House Collections: Their Lives and Afterlives* (Dublin, 2021)

Dooley, Thomas P., *Irishmen or English Soldiers?* (Liverpool, 1995)

Drudy, P.J. (ed.), *Ireland: Land, Politics and People* (Cambridge, 1982)

Dungan, Myles, *They Shall Not Grow Old: Irish Soldiers and the Great War* (Dublin, 1997)

Dunphy, Richard, *The Making of Fianna Fáil Power in Ireland* (Oxford, 1995)

English, Richard, *Radicals and the Republic: Socialist Republicanism in the Irish Free State 1925–1937* (Oxford, 1994)

Fanning, Ronan, *The Irish Department of Finance 1922–58* (Dublin, 1978)

Fanning, Ronan, *Fatal Path: British Government and Irish Revolution 1910–1922* (London, 2013)

Farrell, Mel, *Party Politics in a New Democracy: The Irish Free State, 1922–1938* (London, 2017)

Farrell, Mel, Knirck, Jason and Meehan, Ciara (eds), *A Formative Decade: Ireland in the 1920s* (Sallins, 2015)

Farry, Michael, *Sligo 1914–1921: A Chronicle of Conflict* (Trim, 1992)

Farry, Michael, *The Aftermath of Revolution: Sligo 1921–23* (Dublin, 2000)

Ferriter, Diarmaid, *A Nation and Not a Rabble: The Irish Revolution 1913–1923* (London, 2015)

FitzGerald, Desmond, Griffin, David and Robinson, Nicholas, *Vanishing Country Houses of Ireland* (Dublin, 1988)

BIBLIOGRAPHY

Fitzpatrick, David, *Politics and Irish Life, 1913–21* (Dublin, 1977)

Fitzpatrick, David (ed.), *Ireland and the First World War* (Dublin, 1986)

Fitzpatrick, David, 'The Geography of Irish Nationalism', *Past and Present* 77 (1978): 113–37

Foley, Ronan, 'Augusta Bellingham and the Mount Stuart Hospital: Temporary Therapeutic Transformations', in Dooley and Ridgway (eds.), *The Country House and the Great War*, pp. 87–99

Foster, Gavin, *The Irish Civil War and Society: Politics, Class and Conflict* (London, 2015)

Foster, R.F., *Modern Ireland 1600–1972* (London, 1989 ed)

Foster, R.F., *Vivid Faces: The Revolutionary Generation in Ireland 1890–1923* (London, 2014)

Furlong, Irene, *Irish Tourism, 1880–1980* (Dublin, 2009)

Gallagher, Niamh, *Ireland and the Great War: A Social and Political History* (London and New York, 2020)

Gamboni, Dario, *The Destruction of Art: Iconoclasm and Vandalism Since the French Revolution* (London, 1977)

Garvin, Tom, *Nationalist Revolutionaries in Ireland 1858–1928* (Oxford, 1987)

Garvin, Tom, *1922: The Birth of Irish Democracy* (Dublin, 1996)

Geary, Laurence, *The Plan of Campaign 1886–91* (Cork, 1985)

Genet, Jacqueline, *The Big House in Ireland: Reality and Representation* (Dingle, 1991)

Gerard, Gerrard, *County House Life: Family and Servants, 1815–1914* (Oxford, 1994)

Gerwarth, Robert, *The Vanquished: Why the First World War Failed to End, 1917–1923* (New York, 2016)

Gillespie, Raymond, *The Transformation of the Irish Economy, 1550–1700* (Dundalk, 1991)

Gilpin, *This Republic of Suffering: Death and the American Civil War* (New York, 2008)

Gliddon, Gerald, *The Aristocracy and the Great War* (Norwich, 2002)

Goldstone, J.A. (ed.), *Revolutions: Theoretical, Comparative, and Historical Studies* (Belmont, CA, 2008)

Grant, Aidan, *Derry: The Irish Revolution, 1912–23* (Dublin, 2018)

Greaves, C. Desmond, *Liam Mellows and the Irish Revolution* (London, 2004)

Gregory, Adrian and Paseta, Senia (eds.), *Ireland and the Great War: 'A War to Unite Us All'?* (Manchester, 2002)

Grigg, John, 'Nobility and War: The Unselfish Commitment', *Encounter* (March 1990), pp. 21–7

Guinness, Desmond and Ryan, William, *Irish Houses and Castles* (London, 1971)

Hall, Donal, *Louth: The Irish Revolution, 1912–23* (Dublin, 2019)

Hall, Donal, 'The Bellingham Family of Castlebellingham, Co. Louth, 1914–24', in Dooley and Ridgway (eds.), *The Country House and the Great War*, pp. 100–12

Hanley, Brian, *The IRA, 1926–1936* (Dublin, 2002)

Hannan, D.F. and Commins, Patrick, 'The Significance of Small-scale Landholders in Ireland's Socio-economic Transformation', in J. H. Goldthorpe and C. T. Whelan (eds), *The Development of Industrial Society in Ireland* (Oxford, 1992), pp. 79–104

Hart, Peter, 'The Geography of Revolution in Ireland 1917–1923', *Past and Present* 155 (May 1997), pp. 142–76

Hart, Peter, *The IRA and its Enemies: Violence and Community in Cork, 1916–1923* (Oxford, 1998)

Hart, Peter, 'Defining the Irish Revolution', in Joost Augusteijn (ed.), *The Irish Revolution*, pp. 17–33

Hopkinson, Michael, *Green Against Green: The Irish Civil War* (Dublin, 1988)

Hoppen, K.T., *Elections, Politics and Society, 1832–1885* (Oxford, 1984)

Horn, Pamela, *Country House Society: The Private Lives of England's Upper Class after the First World War* (Stroud, 2015)

Hughes, Brian, *Defying the IRA: Intimidation, Coercion and Communities During the Irish Revolution* (Liverpool, 2017)

Hughes, Brian and Morrissey, Conor (eds.), *Southern Irish Loyalism 1912–1949* (Liverpool 2020)

Irwin, Brett, 'Lady Londonderry and the Great War: Women, Work and the Western Front', in Dooley and Ridgway (eds.), *The Country House and the Great War*, pp. 136–46

BIBLIOGRAPHY

Jackson, Alvin, *Colonel Edward Saunderson: Land and Loyalty in Victorian Ireland* (Oxford, 1995)

Jackson, Alvin, *Ireland, 1798–1998* (Oxford, 1999)

Jackson, Alvin, *Home Rule: An Irish History* (London, 2003)

Jeffery, Keith, *Ireland and the Great War* (Cambridge, 2000)

Jones, David Seth, *Graziers, Land Reform and Political Conflict in Ireland* (Washington, 1995)

Jones, David Seth, 'Land Reform Legislation and Security of Tenure in Ireland After Independence', *Eire-Ireland* xxxii–xxxiii (1997–8): 116–43

Jones, David Seth, 'Divisions Within the Irish Government over Land-Distribution Policy, 1940–70', *Eire-Ireland* xxxvi (Fall/Winter 2001): 83–109

Kalyvas, Stathis, *The Logic of Violence in Civil War* (Cambridge, 2012)

Kelsall, Malcolm, *Literary Representations of the Irish Country House: Civilisation and Savagery Under the Union* (Virginia, 2003)

Kennedy, Liam, *Unhappy the Land: The Most Oppressed People Ever, the Irish?* (Sallins, 2016)

Keogh, Dermot, *Twentieth-Century Ireland: Nation and State* (Dublin, 1994)

Kinsella, Anthony, 'The Special Infantry Force', *The Irish Sword*, vol. xx, no. 82 (1997), pp. 331–47

Kissane, Bill, *Explaining Irish Democracy* (Dublin, 2002)

Kotsonouris, Mary, *Retreat From Revolution: The Dáil Courts 1920–24* (Dublin, 1994)

Laffan, Michael, *The Resurrection of Ireland: The Sinn Féin Party, 1916–1923* (Cambridge, 1999)

Lee, J.J., *Ireland 1912–1985: Politics and Society* (Cambridge, 1989)

Lennon, Colm, *Sixteenth-Century Ireland: The Incomplete Conquest* (Dublin, 1994)

Leonard, Jane, 'Getting Them at Last: The IRA and Ex-Servicemen', in David Fitzpatrick (ed.), *Revolution? Ireland 1917–23* (Dublin, 1990), pp. 118–29

Lynch, Patrick, 'The Social Revolution That Never Was' in Desmond Williams (ed.), *The Irish Struggle, 1916–1926* (London, 1966), pp. 41–54

Lyne, Gerard, *The Lansdowne Estate in Kerry Under W.S. Trench, 1849–72* (Dublin, 2001)

Lyons, F.S.L., *Ireland Since the Famine* (London, 1973 edn)

McCarthy, Patrick, *Waterford: The Irish Revolution 1912–23* (Dublin, 2015)

McCluskey, Fergal, *Tyrone: The Irish Revolution, 1913–23* (Dublin, 2014)

McConway, Philip, 'Offaly and the Civil War Executions', in *Offaly Heritage*, vol. 5 (2008), pp. 251–74

McDonagh, 'Irish Emigration to the United States of America and the British Colonies during the Famine', in R.D. Edwards and T.D. Williams (eds.), *The Great Famine: Studies in Irish History 1845–52* (Dublin, 1956), pp. 319–88

McDowell, R.B., *Crisis and Decline: The Fate of Southern Unionists* (Dublin, 1997)

McGarry, Fearghal, *Eoin O'Duffy: A Self-Made Hero* (Oxford, 2005)

McGarry, Fearghal, 'Revolution, 1916–1923', in Thomas Bartlett (ed.), *The Cambridge History of Ireland*, vol. iv, (Cambridge, 2018), pp. 258–85

McKay, Enda, 'The Housing of the Rural Labourer, 1883–1916', *Saothar*, vol. 17 (1992), pp. 27–38

McQuinn, Colm, 'The Hely-Hutchinson Brothers of Seafield and the Great War: Two Sons, One Inheritance', in Dooley and Ridgway, *The Country House and the Great War*, pp. 147–57

Maguire, Hugh, 'Ireland and the House of Invented Memory', in Mark McCarthy (ed.) *Ireland's Heritages: Critical Perspectives on Memory and Identity* (Hants, 2005), pp. 153–68

Maher, Jim, *The Flying Column in West Kilkenny* (Dublin 1988)

Mandler, Peter, *The Fall and Rise of the Stately Home* (New Haven & London, 1997)

Marsden, Simon, *In Ruins: The Once Great Houses of Ireland* (Boston & London, 1997)

Martin, Peter, '*Dulce et Decorum*: Irish Nobles and the Great War 1914–19', in Gregory and Paseta (eds.), *Ireland and the Great War*, pp. 28–48

Martin, Peter, 'Unionism: The Irish Nobility and Revolution, 1919–23', in Joost Augusteijn (ed.), *The Irish Revolution, 1913–1923*, pp. 151–67

Maume, Patrick, *The Long Gestation: Irish Nationalist Life, 1891–1918* (Dublin, 1999)

Mitchell, Arthur, *Revolutionary Government in Ireland: Dáil Éireann 1919–22* (Dublin, 1995)

Morrow, Ann, *Picnic in a Foreign Land: The Eccentric Lives of the Anglo-Irish* (London, 1989)

Murphy, William, 'Sport in a Time of Revolution: Sinn Féin and the Hunt in Ireland', *Éire-Ireland*, 48: 1–2 (2013), pp. 112–47

Myers, Kevin, *Ireland's Great War* (Dublin, 2016)

Nelson, Thomas, 'Lord Frederick FitzGerald, 1857–1924' in Cosgrove et al. (eds.), *Aspects of Irish Aristocratic Life*, pp. 197–209

Nelson, Thomas, *Through Peace and War: Kildare County Council in the Years of Revolution* (Kildare, 2015)

O'Brien, George, 'Patrick Hogan', *Studies* xxv (Sept. 1936): 353–68

O'Byrne, Robert, *The Last Knight: A Tribute to Desmond FitzGerald, 29th Knight of Glin* (Dublin, 2013)

O'Callaghan, John, *Limerick: The Irish Revolution, 1912–23* (Dublin, 2018)

O'Connor, Emmet, *Syndicalism in Ireland 1917–23* (Cork, 1988)

O'Connor, Emmet, *A Labour History of Ireland 1824–1960* (Dublin, 1992)

O'Connor, Emmet, 'Agrarian Unrest and the Labour Movement in County Waterford, 1917–1923', *Saothar* vi (1980): 40–58

Ó Gráda, Cormac, *Ireland: A New Economic History 1780–1939* (Oxford, 1994)

Ó Gráda, Cormac, *A Rocky Road: The Irish Economy Since the 1920s* (Manchester, 1997)

O'Halpin, Eunan, *Defending Ireland: The Irish State and Its Enemies Since 1922* (Oxford, 1999)

Ohlmeyer, Jane, *Making Ireland English: The Irish Aristocracy in the Seventeenth Century* (New Haven, 2012)

O'Malley, C.K.H., and Dolan, Anne (eds.), *No Surrender Here! The Civil War Papers of Ernie O'Malley* (Dublin, 2007)

O'Riordan, Ann, *East Galway Agrarian Agitation and the Burning of Ballydugan House, 1922* (Dublin, 2015)

O'Riordan, Maeve, *Women of the Country House in Ireland* (Liverpool, 2018)

O'Rourke, Kevin, 'Burn Everything British But Their Coal: The Anglo-Irish Economic War of the 1930s' *Journal of Economic History*, li, no. 2 (June 1991), pp. 357–66

Ó Tuathaigh, M.A.G., 'The Land Question, Politics and Irish Society, 1922–1960', in Drudy (ed.), *Ireland: Land, Politics and People*, pp. 167–89

Pashman, Howard, *Building a Revolutionary State: The Legal Transformation of New York, 1776–1783* (Chicago, 2018)

Patterson, Henry, *The Politics of Illusion: Republicanism and Socialism in Modern Ireland* (London, 1989)

Perry, Nicholas, 'The Irish Landed Class and the British Army, 1850–1950', *War in History*, 18 (3), 2011, pp. 304–32

Pomfret, J.E., *The Struggle for Land in Ireland 1800–1923* (Princeton, NJ, 1930)

Power, Bill, *White Knights, Dark Earls: The Rise and Fall of an Anglo-Irish Dynasty* (Cork, 2000)

Power, Joe, *Clare and the Civil War* (Dublin, 2020)

Purdue, Olwen, *The MacGeough Bonds of the Argory: Challenge and Change on a Small County Armagh Estate, 1880–1* (Dublin, 2005)

Purdue, Olwen, *The Big House in the North of Ireland: Land, Power and Social Elites, 1878–1960* (Dublin, 2009)

Purdue, Olwen, '"Ascendancy's . . . Last Jamboree": Big House Society in Northern Ireland, 1921–69', in Dooley and Ridgway (eds.), *The Irish Country House*, pp. 134–49

Razzell, P.E., 'Social Origins of Officers in the Indian and British Home Army', *British Journal of Sociology*, xiv (1963), pp. 248–60

Reader, W.J., *At Duty's Call: A Study in Obsolete Patriotism* (Manchester, 1988)

Regan, J.M., *The Irish Counter-Revolution, 1921–36: Treatyite Politics and Settlement in Independent Ireland* (Dublin, 1999)

Reilly, Ciarán, 'The Burning of Country Houses in Co. Offaly, 1920–23', in Dooley and Ridgway (eds.), *The Irish Country House*, pp. 110–33

Reilly, Eileen, 'Women and Voluntary War Work' in Gregory and Paseta (eds.), *Ireland and the Great War*, pp. 49–72

Robinson, Lennox, *Bryan Cooper* (London, 1931)

Rumpf, Erhardt and Hepburn, A.C., *Nationalism and Socialism in Twentieth-Century Ireland* (Liverpool, 1977)

Sagarra, Eda, *Kevin O'Shiel: Tyrone Nationalist and Irish State-builder* (Kildare, 2013)

Saltzman, Cynthia, *Old Masters, New World: America's Raid on Europe's Great Pictures* (New York, 2009)

Scholten, Japp, *Comrade Baron: A Journey Through the Vanishing World of the Transylvanian Aristocracy* (St Helena CA, 2016)

Smith, Robert, *Former People: The Last Days of the Russian Aristocracy* (New York, 2012)

Solow, B.L., *The Land Question and the Irish Economy 1870–1903* (Cambridge, Mass., 1971)

Somerville-Large, Peter, *The Irish Country House: A Social History* (London, 1995)

Stewart, A.T.Q., *The Ulster Crisis* (London, 1967)

Symes, Glascott, *Sir John Keane and Cappoquin House in Time of War and Revolution* (Dublin, 2016)

Taylor, Paul, *Heroes or Traitors: Experiences of Southern Irish Soldiers Returning from the Great War, 1919–39* (Liverpool, 2015)

Thomas, Einion, 'From Sligo to Wales: The Flight of Sir Charles Phibbs', *History Ireland*, Spring 2004, pp. 9–10

Thompson, E.P., 'The Moral Economy of the English Crowd in the Eighteenth Century', *Past & Present*, no. 50 (Feb. 1971), pp. 76–136

Tindley, Annie, *Lord Dufferin, Ireland and the British Empire, c.1820–1900: Rule by the Best?* (Abingdon, 2021)

Tobin, Robert, *The Minority Voice: Hubert Butler and Southern Irish Protestantism, 1900–1991* (Oxford, 2012)

Townshend, Charles, *The British Campaign in Ireland: The Development of Political and Military Policies* (Oxford, 1975)

Townshend, Charles, *Political Violence in Ireland: Government and Resistance since 1848* (Oxford, 1983)

Townshend, Charles, *Ireland: The 20th Century* (Oxford, 1999)

Townshend, Charles, *The Republic: The Fight for Irish Independence* (London, 2013)

Urquhart, Diane, ' "The Female of the Species is More Deadlier than the Male"?: The Ulster Women's Unionist Council, 1911–1940', in Janice Holmes and Diane Urquhart (eds.), *Coming Into the Light: The Work, Politics and Religion of Women in Ulster 1840–1940* (Belfast, 1994), pp. 93–123

Varley, Tony, 'On the Road to Extinction: Agrarian Parties in Twentieth-Century Ireland', *Irish Political Studies*, 25:4 (2010), pp. 581–601

Vaughan, W.E., *Landlords and Tenants in Mid-Victorian Ireland* (Oxford, 1994)

Walsh, Fionnuala, *Irish Women and the Great War* (Cambridge, 2020)

Walsh, Fionnuala, ' "The Future Welfare of the Empire will Depend More Largely on our Women and Girls": Southern Loyalist Women and the British War Effort in Ireland, 1914–1922', in Hughes and Morrissey (eds.), *Southern Irish Loyalism*, pp. 137–54

Warren, Allen, 'The Twilight of the Ascendancy and the Big House: A View from the Twenty-First Century', in Dooley and Ridgway (eds) *The Irish Country House*, pp. 244–56

Winter, J.M., 'Britain's "Lost Generation" of the First World War', *Population Studies*, vol. 31, no. 3 (Nov. 1977), pp. 449–66

Young, Jean, 'Changing Times: The Big House in County Louth, 1912–1923', in Donal Hall and Martin Maguire (eds.), *County Louth and the Irish Revolution 1912–1923* (Newbridge, 2017), pp. 146–74

11. Unpublished Theses

Byrne, Teresa, 'The Burning of Kilboy House, Nenagh, County Tipperary, 2 August 1922' (MA thesis, NUI, Maynooth, 2006)

Callan, Patrick, 'Voluntary Recruiting for the British Army in Ireland During the First World War' (PhD thesis, UCD, 1984)

Cosgrove, Patrick John, 'The Wyndham Land Act 1903: The Final Solution to the Irish Land Question?' (PhD thesis, NUI, Maynooth, 2008)

Dunne, Eugene, 'The Experiences of the Aristocracy in County Westmeath During the Period 1879–1923' (PhD thesis, NUI, Maynooth, 2016)

Furlong, Irene, 'State Promotion of Tourism in Independent Ireland 1925–55' (PhD thesis, NUI, Maynooth, 2002)

Gahan, David, 'The Land Annuities Agitation in Ireland 1926–32' (PhD thesis, NUI, Maynooth, 2017)

McCarthy, Tony, 'From Landlord to Rentier: The Wyndham Land Act 1903 and its Economic Consequences for Irish Landlords 1903–1933' (PhD thesis, NUI, Maynooth, 2017)

McEvoy, J.N., 'A Study of the United Irish League in King's County, 1899–1918' (MA thesis, NUI, Maynooth, 1990).

Murphy, Breen, T., 'The Government's Execution Policy During the Irish Civil War 1922–1923' (PhD thesis, NUI, Maynooth, 2010)

Ryan, M.B., 'The Clongorey Evictions' (MA thesis, NUI, Maynooth, 1999)

Sheehan, J.T., 'Land Purchase Policy in Ireland, 1917–23: From the Irish Convention to the 1923 Land Act' (MA thesis, NUI, Maynooth, 1993)

Tynan, Edward, 'War Veterans, and Distribution and Revolution in Ireland, 1919–23' (PhD thesis, NUI, Maynooth, 2012)

12. Internet Sources

Archiseek, *http://archiseek.com*

Irish Georgian Society, *www.igs.ie*

Irish Statute Book, *www.irishstatutebook.ie*

Landed Estates Database, Moore Institute, National University of Ireland, Galway, *www.landedestates.ie*

Legislation.gov.uk, *www.legislation.gov.uk*

RTÉ News, *www.rte.ie/news*

Theirishaesthete.com

INDEX

Note: Italic page numbers refer to illustrations; bold numbers refer to maps